ENGLISH VILLAGERS
OF THE THIRTEENTH CENTURY

ENGLISH VILLAGERS OF
THE THIRTEENTH CENTURY

BY

GEORGE CASPAR HOMANS

PROFESSOR OF SOCIOLOGY, HARVARD UNIVERSITY

The Norton Library

W·W·NORTON & COMPANY·INC·

NEW YORK

CONTENTS

CONTENTS

BOOK IV

FEASTS

MAPS

PREFACE

THE WORK which resulted in the present book was done while the writer was a Junior Fellow in the Society of Fellows, Harvard University. He is grateful to the Senior Fellows for the opportunity given him and for financial assistance in the publication of this book. His warmest thanks are also due to Professors Lawrence J. Henderson, N. S. B. Gras, and Edwin F. Gay, who read and criticized the manuscript in detail, to Professors Crane Brinton, Elton Mayo, Roger B. Merriman, and Arthur D. Nock, who read and criticized some parts of it, and to Bernard DeVoto and G. L. Haskins, who gave valuable advice. He is also indebted to Miss Helen M. Mitchell, who drew certain of the maps. During his stay in England, the officials of the Public Record Office and the British Museum were unfailingly kind and helpful, as they are to all scholars from overseas. He acknowledges the permission given him by the Ecclesiastical Commission to inspect the manuscripts in its possession which are now on deposit at the Public Record Office. Finally, he must express his admiration for those hundreds of English antiquaries, living and dead, upon whose detailed researches in local history the soundness of a work of synthesis depends.

G. C. H.

CAMBRIDGE, MASSACHUSETTS
April 1, 1940

NOTE ON REFERENCES

SINCE IN THESE DAYS not every scholar has a reading knowledge of Latin, it has seemed best in this book to translate into English all passages which have been cited in the body of the text and come from manuscripts in medieval Latin. But since many of the MSS. cited have never been and probably never will be edited and printed, it has seemed best not to quote from these MSS. in translation only. Accordingly the following policy has been adopted. A passage translated in the body of the text from a MS. which has been edited and printed will have in the notes only a reference to the volume and page where the Latin text of the passage is to be found. A passage translated in the body of the text from a MS. which has not been edited and printed will have in the notes a reference to the MS. where it is to be found and also the Latin text from which the translation was made. In editing these texts, the rules laid down in the "Report on Editing Historical Documents," *Bulletin of the Institute of Historical Research*, I (1923), 6 ff., have been followed in most cases. In particular, abbreviations the meaning of which has seemed in the least uncertain have not been extended but have been represented by an apostrophe. In the use of *v* and *u*, the practice of using the *v* form as initial, the *u* form as medial has been adopted in all cases. In the use of *c* and *t*, which often cannot be distinguished in the MSS., an effort has been made to make each text self-consistent. The use of (*sic*) has been avoided as far as possible. The author begs the indulgence of scholars for his editing of these passages from MSS. In most cases the passages come from manorial court rolls, and these rolls were neither well written in the beginning nor well preserved afterwards. The passages also come from a large number of different rolls from all parts of England. They have had no such uniformity, even if it is only a uniformity in error, as appears in the work of a single clerk in a single MS. For these reasons their editing cannot be a work of consistency and elegance.

REIGNS OF ENGLISH KINGS FREQUENTLY MENTIONED
IN THE TEXT

Henry III: October 18, 1216 — November 16, 1272
Edward I: November 16, 1272 — July 7, 1307
Edward II: July 7, 1307 — January 20, 1327

ABBREVIATIONS

MANUSCRIPT MATERIALS

Add. MSS.   Additional Manuscripts (at the British Museum).
Add. Rolls   Additional Rolls (at the British Museum).
Brit. Mus.   British Museum.
DL   Duchy of Lancaster rolls (at the Public Record Office).
Eccl.   Rolls in the possession of the Ecclesiastical Commission
             and deposited at the Public Record Office.
PRO   Public Record Office.
SC   Special Collection (Class of rolls at Public Record Office).

PRINTED MATERIALS

Bleadon Custumal. E. Smirke, "Notice of the Custumal of Bleadon, Somerset" in *Memoirs Illustrative of the History and Antiquities of Wiltshire and the City of Salisbury* (Royal Archaeological Institute of Great Britain and Ireland). London, 1851.

Chertsey Abstract. E. Toms, ed., *Chertsey Abbey Court Rolls Abstract* (Surrey Record Society). Frome and London, 1937.

Chichester Custumals. W. D. Peckham, ed., *Thirteen Custumals of the Sussex Manors of the Bishop of Chichester* (Sussex Record Society). Cambridge, 1925.

Durham Hallmotes. W. H. D. Longstaffe and J. Booth, eds., *Hallmota Prioratus Dunelmensis* (Surtees Society). Durham, 1889.

EETS   Early English Text Society.

Estate Book of Henry de Bray. D. Willis, ed., *The Estate Book of Henry de Bray* (Camden Society). London, 1916.

Glastonbury Rentalia. C. I. Elton, E. Hobhouse, and T. S. Holmes, eds., *Rentalia et Custumaria Michaelis de Ambresbury (1235–1252) et Rogeri de Ford (1252–1261) Abbatum Monasterii Beatae Mariae Glastoniae* (Somerset Record Society). London, 1891.

Gloucester Cartulary. W. H. Hart, ed., *Historia et Cartularium Monasterii Sancti Petri Gloucestriae* (Rolls Series). London, 1863–7.

Halesowen Court Rolls. J. Amphlett, S. G. Hamilton, and R. A. Wilson, eds., *Court Rolls of the Manor of Hales* (Worcestershire Historical Society). Oxford, 1910–33.

Lyndwood, *Provinciale.* W. Lyndwood, *Provinciale, (seu Constitutiones Angliae).* Oxford, 1679.

Maitland, *Manorial Courts.* F. W. Maitland, ed., *Select Pleas in Manorial and Other Seignorial Courts,* Vol. I (Selden Society). London, 1889.

Neilson, *Customary Rents.* N. Neilson, "Customary Rents," *Oxford Studies in Social and Legal History*, II. Oxford, 1910.

Oseney Cartulary. H. E. Salter, ed., *Cartulary of Oseney Abbey* (Oxford Historical Society). Oxford, 1929–36.

Ramsey Cartulary. W. H. Hart and P. A. Lyons, eds., *Cartularium Monasterii de Rameseia* (Rolls Series). London, 1884–93.

Stenton, *Danelaw Documents.* F. M. Stenton, ed., *Documents Illustrative of the Social and Economic History of the Danelaw, from Various Collections* (The British Academy: Records of the Social and Economic History of England and Wales, Vol. V). Oxford, 1920.

Tusser.   T. Tusser, *Five Hundred Pointes of Good Husbandrie*, W. Payne and S. J. Herrtage, eds. (English Dialect Society). London, 1878.

Wakefield Court Rolls. W. P. Baildon and J. Lister, eds., *Court Rolls of the Manor of Wakefield* (Yorkshire Archaelogical Society, Record Series). Leeds, etc., 1901–30.

Wilkins, *Concilia.* D. Wilkins, *Concilia Magnae Britanniae et Hiberniae.* London, 1737.

BOOK I
FIELDS

CHAPTER I

INTRODUCTION

B^{Y} STUDYING any state of affairs as a whole, as the sum of its parts and something more, we are often able to understand it in a way we could not otherwise have done. This is a commonplace, but like many commonplaces is important and often forgotten.

In what follows an attempt will be made to describe as a whole a social order of the past, that of English villages of the thirteenth century. The story begins with husbandry, with the skills men had learned of making a living from the English earth in the English weather. It goes on to tell how men used these skills, how they lived and worked together as neighbors in a village. And since a villager was not only a neighbor but also a father, or a brother, or an uncle of other men and women, there will be something to say about English families. Especially strong was the feeling that a holding of land ought to remain in the blood of those who had held it of old. Since a villager was also a tenant, there will be something to say about the relations between the lord of a manor and his men. The lord dealt with his men in some degree not as individuals but as members of a community. The story ends with the ceremonies, both those of the folk and those of the Church, which were performed or witnessed by countrymen. Perhaps it is pretentious to say that an attempt will be made to describe the social order as a whole. All that these words mean is that an attempt will be made to consider not simply a few of the important aspects of society but rather as many as possible. The list cannot in fact be complete, partly because the records which tell about villagers of the thirteenth century are necessarily fragmentary and one-sided, and partly because different generations of scholars see with different eyes: the men of the present day cannot tell what the future will find they have overlooked.

There are several reasons for making such an attempt. The facts in themselves are interesting and, in this instance as in others, the process of making as systematic a statement of the facts as possible may bring out certain generalizations which could have been brought out in no other manner. Some of the most fruitful work in the social sciences has been done by anthropologists studying so-called primitive societies, that is, societies which are sufficiently small, simple, and isolated to make possible consideration of every aspect of each society in relation to all the other aspects.

The attempt to describe as a whole the social order of English villages of the thirteenth century is at once in difficulties. For one thing, that description must be built upon the work of many men, on the work of Seebohm and Maitland, of Vinogradoff, Coulton, Stenton, Gray, Gras, and many others, of whom the latest is H. S. Bennett, author of *Life on the English Manor: 1150–1400.* The work done by these men has been distributed unevenly over the different institutions of society in the Middle Ages. Much has been written about the open-field system and the organization of manors, but little, to take two instances, about family customs or the traditional year of husbandmen. No doubt this unevenness will continue, partly because the documents allow students to go further in certain directions than in others, and partly for the reasons which cause other investigations to advance upon irregular fronts. If, then, a man is trying to make a description of the social order of English villages, as a total organization, he will have in some parts of his work little more to do than restate what others already have discovered, and in other parts will have to rely upon his own research. His description will have to mingle much that is well known with something that is new. Such a description is the present one.

There are several reasons for choosing the thirteenth century as the period in which to describe the social order of English villages. One reason is that it is the earliest century from which enough records of the right sort survive to tell us in some detail about the life of English countrymen. All attempts to reconstruct what society was in earlier centuries must start from what it is known to have been in the thirteenth and work backward in history. Another is that the thirteenth century, in town and country, was the one in which the social and economic order of the Middle Ages was most prosperous and least challenged.

There is no particular virtue in the dates 1200 and 1300; there was no dramatic change when the twelfth century ended and the thirteenth began, when the thirteenth ended and the fourteenth began. But limits set to a study are convenient, and ones that are easily remembered, such as the beginning and ending of a century, are the most convenient of all, provided that they are not taken seriously. Most of the documents which will be cited in evidence here date from the thirteenth century, especially from toward the end of that century. Others will pass over into the early years of the fourteenth and even later times than that. Customs did not so change in the Middle Ages, even in the course of generations, that what went on in one year necessarily did not go on a hundred years later. *Piers Plowman*, written toward the end of the fourteenth century, confirms at many points what is known about English plowmen at the end of the thirteenth. Even when there are gaps in our knowledge of early custom, it would be pedantic to refuse to fill them in with what is known of later times in England or even of later times in other peasant communities, if the early and the late are compatible with one another, if they fit together to make a full and coherent description.

No description can take account of every aspect of a situation; it must in some measure be abstract. The present description will be abstract in many respects by bad workmanship or by lack of information, and in at least one respect by deliberate plan. No account will be taken of changes in the social order of English villages. It will be considered as if it were unchanging, or rather as if it were the social order of an island in Melanesia, which an anthropologist can describe only as it exists at the time he lives there. Since the information the islanders give him of their history is rather legend than fact, he can have little to say about the changes which have taken place or even about those which are taking place in the society. Such a description does violence to the facts. Every social order changes. The social order of England was changing less rapidly in the thirteenth century than it was in the time of unrest at the end of the fourteenth century and certainly less rapidly at either of these times than it was in the nineteenth century. But we do not clearly understand what we are talking about when we talk about the rate of social change. All that is assumed here is that the rate of change was not so rapid that information taken from a record of the date 1220 and information taken from a record of the date 1280, and so forth, cannot be put together to make a description which in many instances is equally close to the actual state of affairs at either date, at least so far as concerns social as distinguished from political history.

An attempt will be made to describe the social order of English villages in the thirteenth century — these words are not clear as they stand. What they mean is that many English villages conformed more or less closely to a certain general type of social order and that this type is what will be described. In recent years, however, many studies of the state of affairs in the Middle Ages in different parts of England have made increasingly plain what has always been vaguely understood, that the customs of countrymen varied greatly from one end of the land to the other. Some account will be taken here of this variation by leaving out of consideration the customs of large parts of England. An attempt will be made to describe the social order, not of all English villages, but only of those within what was called the champion country. The customs of countrymen of other parts of England will of course be mentioned, but only in order that they may be compared with the customs of the champion country.

The villages within the champion country may be treated, in a first approximation, as social bodies of the same type. In several respects they were more like one another than they were like the villages and hamlets of the rest of England, but there were important differences of custom even within the champion country. For one thing, the tenants of manors in the North of England, in Lincolnshire and the shires beyond, seem to have been more free from the burdens of working on the lord's demesne than their contemporaries of the southern Midlands and Wessex. Perhaps because of that very circumstance, which made it unnecessary that lords should have elaborate records of the services owed by their tenants, the countrymen of the North are those about whom we have the least information. With a few important exceptions, such as the court rolls of the manor of Wakefield in Yorkshire, there has as yet appeared from the North no such body of revealing documents as those which tell us about the men of the southern shires. Not only are the villages which will be described limited to the champion country but also for the most part to the southern half of the champion country. Even within this part of England, there is no reason for believing that all villages conformed to a single general pattern, and nothing in what follows is to be understood as implying that they did.

The accidents of the original writing of records and of their survival have been such that there rarely exists a set of documents which allow us to make a description of all sides of country life in any particular neighborhood. We may know much about the farming practices of one place, about the customs of inheritance and marriage of another, about the manorial organization of a third, but we seldom know about all these matters as they were in any single district. The result is that we are in fact forced to make the assumption that the social order was in most important respects the same over a certain area, in this case the champion country. Otherwise we are not justified in constructing any coherent description of the social order as a whole by putting together partial information about many different places.

The greatest difference between English villagers of the thirteenth century and the peoples the modern anthropologists have studied is that the villagers are dead, and many important matters will escape any anthropologist who is unable to talk with the people whose social order he studies. But if the student of England in the Middle Ages is unable to talk to the villagers of those days, he is more lucky in his other sources of information than he has any right to be. Like any other people with a great legal tradition, the English have had for centuries the greatest respect for all old papers and parchments, preserving them long after they have ceased to be of practical importance. And English history has been largely free from revolutions in which all records are likely to be destroyed. For these reasons, more manuscripts which give good information about the state of the countryside in the Middle Ages survive in England than probably any other country in Europe, more, apparently, than in France, though France, throughout the Middle Ages, was much the more populous and wealthy country.

Of the classes of manuscripts which have something to tell

about the countryside in England in the Middle Ages, there are two which will especially be cited here: manorial custumals and court rolls. The custumals belong in a body of documents called otherwise registers, extents, rentals, or terriers, according as emphasis was laid on one or another element of the information they gave. A custumal was so called because it recorded the customs, that is, the customary rents and services, owed to a lord by his tenants on one or more manors. In recording the customs, it perforce recorded the amounts of land held by the different tenants, grouped in classes, and the kinds of work in husbandry they performed at different times of the year. A good custumal can reveal in great detail the farming practices and the sorts and conditions of men in a medieval community. Of the custumals which have been edited and printed, the best are those of the Sussex manors of the Bishop of Chichester and those of the manors of the Abbot of Glastonbury, together with the custumal of Bleadon, Somerset, which is the only part yet edited of what must be the interesting custumal of the manors of St. Swithin's Priory, Winchester. Among the important custumals which remain unedited are the two Ely custumals in the British Museum.[1] One thing which becomes clear at once from this list is that the best custumals are custumals of religious houses, especially those religious houses possessing large estates. Before they can be accepted as giving information that is typical of conditions in any part of England, they must be compared with the custumals included in the Hundred Rolls, which are less detailed but describe estates other than those of religious houses.

The second and more important of the two classes of manuscripts which will be chiefly cited here is that of the manorial court rolls. Much has been heard lately about the interest of the *compoti* — the yearly account rolls of the reeves or bailiffs of manors, as drawn up by clerks and then audited. Without doubt they yield a great deal of information to the historians of medieval economics, but Maitland's instinct was right when he urged the publication of court rolls. They are the foremost medieval sources for what is called social history. The court rolls were the records kept of the proceedings in the manorial courts, the hallmotes, the lowest in the hierachy of English courts in the Middle Ages and the only ones in which common villagers often appeared. The business of the hallmotes was diverse, ranging from breaches of village bylaws to suits regarding land, and the hallmotes were registries of deeds and legislative assemblies as well as courts of law. Almost any custom or event which was of great practical moment to a villager must sooner or later have found mention in a court roll. The court rolls, like the custumals, were kept in Latin, a Latin often crude, hurried, and abbreviated.

Unhappily there have so far been found very few manorial court rolls or court records of any kind that date from the first half of the thirteenth century. But for the second half of the thirteenth century and the beginning of the fourteenth they become more and more common. Of the sets of court rolls which have been edited, the most notable are those of Halesowen, on the borders of Worcestershire and Shropshire, and those of Wakefield, Yorkshire. But some of the best of the court rolls remain unedited. The best of all are the court books of certain of the Hertfordshire manors of St. Albans Abbey, most of which are preserved in the British Museum.[2] They are court books, that is, compilations of extracts from court rolls, not court rolls proper, but their entries begin at an earlier date and are continuous for a longer time than any manorial court records which have so far appeared. The rolls of the manors of Ramsey Abbey should also be mentioned. Some of them have been edited,[3] but the larger part remains unedited. They are preserved partly at the British Museum and partly at the Public Record Office. Also the court rolls of Newington, Oxon., and Halton, Bucks., manors of Christchurch Priory, Canterbury, which are the property of the Ecclesiastical Commission and preserved at the Public Record Office. Without question there are a number of sets of court rolls still in private collections. Anyone who helps bring their contents to light will be doing the greatest service to history and sociology. Almost every court roll has something important to tell about the social order of England in the Middle Ages.

The entries in both the custumals and the court rolls were of the nature of sworn testimony, and the testimony was given by the villagers themselves. The custumal of an estate was commonly drawn up from the findings of inquest juries of men of the different manors. The records of such inquests on several of the manors of Ramsey Abbey have survived, although the Ramsey Register which must have been compiled from them has not.[4] (We know a Ramsey Register existed because the court rolls of Ramsey manors several times record that appeals were made to it.) A court roll must have been drawn up by the parish priest or some other clerk, either in the hallmote while it was sitting or shortly thereafter, and many of the cases recorded in the roll were decided on the oath of a jury of men of the manor. Not only were custumals and court rolls of the nature of sworn testimony, but it was of the greatest practical importance at the time they were drawn up that they should be accurate. If a lord tried to increase the services rendered him by his tenants, or if the tenants refused to render services which they had rendered in the past, the injured party might appeal to the record of a custumal or a register. In the same way, the verdicts of manorial juries, as they were recorded in the court rolls, stated the binding custom of the manor in such matters as the inheritance or alienation of land. To be sure the evidence given by these sources is often incidental. What would have seemed to a villager of the thirteenth century the important point in an entry in a court roll may not seem so to an investigator of the twentieth. What is most interesting now is what was taken for granted then. Our only consolation in lacking the sort of intimate acquaintance with countrymen in the Middle Ages which an anthropologist can have of people who are alive and can be interviewed is that custumals and court rolls are probably as sober and trustworthy records of facts, not fancies, as any records of a past time can be.

Many of the men who have written about the Middle Ages have made one or the other of two kinds of judgment about the life of those times. Some have looked on it as a wretched state of misery and oppression. To others it has seemed a kind of Gothic idyll. These judgments of the past are likely to be linked with judgments of the present. If you look upon the present as an age of high fulfillment of the possibilities of the human race, you take the first attitude toward the Middle Ages: the men of the Middle Ages were wretched in so far as they had no experience of life as it is lived in a modern democracy. If you look upon the present age as an age of social disorganization, you take the second attitude: the men of the Middle Ages were happy in that they all were the children of a universal Church. One reason why the two judgments differ is that they are concerned with different sets of facts. Certainly the physical conditions of a husbandman's life were hard, but nothing is more commonplace or more often forgotten than the words: "Man does not live by bread alone." In these pages, matter will be found to confirm both judgments, but the author hopes he has adopted neither as the whole truth.

CHAPTER II

WOODLAND AND CHAMPION

THE STUDY of landscapes is a good beginning for the study of the societies of men, because men must live on and off the land as the first condition of their survival. Landscapes have come to differ as much in their fields, fences, and houses as in their waters, woods, and hills: they are marked by the ways men know of making a living and of working and dwelling in company with their fellows. Since each society has its own ways of carrying on these concerns, each society has its own landscape. The study of landscapes where men live or have once lived is more than the study of geography and geology; it is more than the study of techniques of farming and forestry; it is the study of societies as wholes, in so far as their form is determined by or determines their use of the land.

The landscape which a society has created may become its most enduring memorial. Especially likely to be indelible are the marks left upon the earth by men who know cattle and the plow and the cultivation of grains, because these men clear fields and build fences, and their successors will not afterward find it convenient to undo the work their forefathers have done. Thus the lines of their dry stone walls, built when they dragged from the earth, to make it fit for tillage, the boulders the glaciers had laid down, will be the most enduring memorial of the Englishmen who settled New England. Though the frost leave hardly one stone upon another, their walls will long outlast their white wooden churches, their other most characteristic monument.

The people of Europe in the Middle Ages were busy, almost wholly, with tilling the soil, and accordingly left behind them well-marked medieval landscapes, which must be studied as a part of any investigation of medieval society. To talk about medieval landscape is no more nonsense than to talk about medieval art, because in many parts of Europe we can still look at medieval landscapes just as we can still look at cathedrals. Indeed the landscapes are the older of the two. They are dateless; they are the engraving of societies older than written history.

In England, four hundred years ago, when people first began to take an interest in such matters, they distinguished between two main kinds of English countryside, which they called *woodland* and *champion*. The word *champion* is of course derived from the Low Latin *campania*, by way of the French *champagne* and the English *champaigne*, which was in use, in something like its later sense, at least by the beginning of the fourteenth century.[1] What the travellers of the sixteenth century meant by the distinction between woodland and champion can best be made clear in the landscape of France, which for one reason and another remains closer to what it was in the Middle Ages than does the landscape of England. Around Chartres in the Beauce, or around Rheims, in Champagne itself, the land lies in great open stretches of arable fields, broken only, here and there, by stands of trees and by the buildings of the villages, which cluster around the spire of each parish church. In old times, such land would have been called *champion* in England and *champagne* in France: the county of Champagne got its name because it was conspicuously open country. On the other hand, in western Normandy — if we orient ourselves again by one of the great cathedrals, in the country around Coutances — the fields are small and are surrounded by ditches and by walls made of the earth thrown up in digging the ditches. Hedges and trees grow in these walls, to give this kind of countryside the look of being wooded, at least in the eyes of men who are used to the open fields of the champion land. Such country in France is called *bocage* — it is bosky — and in old times in England would have been called woodland, though of course it was not woodland in our sense of the word, that is, forest. It was not woodland absolute but woodland only in comparison with the champion country.[2]

Observers early and late have made much of the fences which surrounded the small fields of the woodland country. Sometimes the fences were ditches and earthen banks, overhung with trees, as in a green Norman valley: this was the woodland proper. Sometimes they were walls of sod and stones, overgrown with flowering vines, as in Cornwall[3] or in a yellow Irish upland pasture, the blue Kerry Hills beyond. Sometimes they were dry stone walls, and sometimes hedges simple, but whatever the means used, the fields of the woodland country were enclosed, to use the proper technical term, while the champion country was "open-field" country: its fields were not regularly surrounded by permanent fences. Perhaps the walls and small fields of the woodland were useful to fold cattle and protect them in the winter.[4] Perhaps their reason for existence was that, in the absence of positive restraints upon enclosure, small walled fields were the convenient units for the use of the land, under the conditions of old-time farming. But such questions cannot be settled by city-bred people, who have learned about husbandry from books. They can be settled only by a Breton or an Irishman who farms in the old way, and he would take his ancient walls and fields for granted.

The subject of this book is the social order of the champion country in the thirteenth century. Accordingly we must estimate what parts of England were enclosed and what were unenclosed and champion, and we must estimate what these parts were in the thirteenth century. Two difficulties are encountered in making this estimate. In the first place, the amounts of land enclosed and unenclosed have not remained constant through the centuries. Today all of England, save perhaps one or two villages, is in the technical sense enclosed, but, as the world knows, it was not always so. Enclosure movements have changed the face of England. They began early in the Middle Ages, first became important at the end of the fifteenth century, and only in the first half of the nineteenth century came near to completing their work. In the second place, much of our information about enclosures dates from centuries later than the thirteenth. Nevertheless, on the basis of all that is known about these matters, a definite assumption is made here. It is the following: the distribution in England of enclosed and unenclosed land, as it was about 1500, when the enclosure movement first became important, was upon the whole the same as it had been at least since the Norman Conquest.

The roughest but most explicit evidence of the distribution in England of woodland and champion comes from travellers of the sixteenth and later centuries. They could see how the look of the country changed as they rode from Kent to Cornwall.

The author of *A Discourse of the Common Weal of this Realm of England* (written in 1549) asserts: "We se that countries, wheare most Inclosures be, are most wealthie, as essex, kent, devenshire, and such"[5]—naming counties of the West and South-east. Thomas Tusser was an Elizabethan farmer-poet, whose *Five Hundred Points of Good Husbandry*, a book full of good sense and charming doggerel, will be much quoted in the pages to come. His range was the eastern counties, and he recognized that in his day Suffolk and Essex were woodland, while Norfolk was champion, or at least open-field.[6] To come to later observers, a traveller of the nineteenth century says of Devonshire:

The rectangular fields of a few acres each, which we see in Devonshire, were probably once divided into arable strips; but the strips were small, and few of the fields can have been cultivated simultaneously. The tall hedges raised on huge mounds, by which the fields are bounded, look almost as though they had existed from time immemorial and are a prominent feature of the landscape.[7]

Better perhaps as descriptions of the woodland country in old times are those of the landscape of Essex, just north-east of London. To be sure, the whole of the country in the Middle Ages was forest, that is, royal forest. It was a hunting preserve of the king's, but that did not mean that the whole country was in woods even then. The Messrs. Griggs, agricultural experts of the end of the eighteenth century, speak as follows of Essex:

The inclosures, which from time immemorial have almost universally prevailed, make Essex greatly preferable to some of the neighboring counties; here every man enjoys his own the year around. . . . His ditches carry off the water from his land, and the thick hedges of white thorn, which grow upon the banks raised by what is thrown out of them, serve to shelter his stock from the storms of winter, as well as to protect his corn from the intrusion of cattle; and by dividing his land into distinct parcels, enable him to support twice the quantity of stock he could otherwise do; advantages an open country can never enjoy.[8]

Such men as the Messrs. Griggs, practical farmers, writing for practical ends, at a time when the old agriculture was still alive, give us some of our most useful insights into the problems men faced in making a living off the land, and into the ways they solved them in the long centuries when the tiller of the soil was inarticulate. A few years later the historian of the county wrote in the same vein:

The country being inclosed, makes it much more comfortable to live and travel in, than such as is quite open; exposed, without the least shelter, to all the inclemencies of wind and weather: and it also makes every man's property, whether great or little, much securer, and more his own, than where it is unfenced, and liable to the encroachments of every joint commoner, or greedy neighbor. To which add, that the trees in the fences afford a great quantity of fuel; a matter of no small importance.[9]

Such is the testimony of the early traveller, but the modern one is not thereby excused from using his eyes. If he will, he can see that Devonshire, with its small, squarish fields and big walls, has not the same landscape as Oxfordshire, though today the fields of both counties are, in the technical sense of the word, enclosed.

These passages tell us once more the marks of woodland country. Its fields were enclosed, that is, they were fenced in. Though it may sound paradoxical to say so, this does not mean that there was no open country in the predominantly woodland parts of England. Devon was an old-enclosed county, yet we think at once of the Devonshire moors. It means simply that in woodland country land which was regularly under the plow tended to be enclosed. On the other hand, the fields of the champion country were open. Furthermore, the enclosures of the woodland were of a certain kind; they were ditches with earthen walls beside them, crowned with trees and thorn hedges: they were permanent. But the passages tell us much more than this. The men who wrote about the woodland landscape of Essex were not simply describing it but were comparing it with open country to the disadvantage of the latter: "Here every man enjoys his own the year around. . . . It also makes every man's property, whether great or little, much securer, and more his own, than where it is unfenced, and liable to the encroachments of every joint commoner." This is the recurrent theme of English experts in agriculture, from Thomas Tusser in the sixteenth century to Arthur Young at the end of the eighteenth. Evidently the difference between woodland and champion was not merely that the one was enclosed country and the other was not: in the champion country a particular regime of husbandry and property was in force which was unlike that of the woodland country.

The champion regime will be described in detail later, but a first sketch of it must be made now. The fields of a village were divided into two or three great sectors. In these fields, a villager did not have his land in one compact plot but rather in the form of a number of strips scattered all over the fields, intermingled with the similar strips of his neighbors. The two or three great sectors were cultivated as wholes according to a customary rotation of crops, and, finally, at certain seasons the fields were used as the common pasture of all the cattle of the village. This regime is called by modern scholars the "open-field system," but there seems no good reason for using the modern name for the system when an older English name for it exists. By champion country Englishmen meant not simply a country of open fields but one of open fields submitted to this particular customary agriculture. Hereafter the open-field system will be called the champion husbandry. It was this champion husbandry which the agricultural experts were condemning. They felt that it had come to obstruct the introduction of new and improved methods of agriculture. On the other hand, they approved of the farms in the woodland country, because they resembled our farms of today. In the words of the Messrs. Griggs, since every man had his land in distinct parcels and not in the form of strips intermingled with those of his fellows, and since he enjoyed his own the year around, without being forced to submit to a customary rotation of crops or to the right of common pasture, he was able to improve indefinitely his methods of agriculture. But a word of caution is needed here. There is every reason to believe that in early times much of the woodland country, like the champion, was submitted to communal forms of husbandry. The point is that these forms differed from the champion husbandry, and particularly in the fact that they early disintegrated and gave way to something like our own compact farms with freedom of farm management, so that the experts could speak of the woodland as having a progressive agriculture.

The process by which land became enclosed is called enclosure, and might mean any one of several things. It might mean the fencing in of rough pastures, wastes, with an eye to turning them into tillage. This could take place in any part of England, woodland or champion, in Dartmoor as much as in Sherwood

Forest. This was the most prominent kind of early enclosure in England. By the statute of Merton (1235), supplemented by the statute of Westminster (1285), the lords of manors were allowed to approve as much of the pastures appurtenant to their manors as they saw fit, so long as they left to their free tenants pasture sufficient to support their stock. But the kinds of enclosures which are important here are those which involved an attack on the open fields of the champion husbandry. Enclosure might mean the process according to which individuals, by judicious sales and exchanges of their scattered strips of land in the open fields, concentrated their holdings into one or more large compact parcels, and then fenced them in. Our earliest records of villagers' dealings in land, the manorial court rolls of the thirteenth century, seem to show this process already under way at that time in some parts of the country.[10] If villagers forbore to insist upon their rights of common over these enclosed plots, the work could go forward the more safely. Lastly, enclosure might mean the process by which a champion village, as a whole or in part, was redivided into compact plots, which were then fenced in, and the rights of common abolished. At the time of the first great wave of enclosures, at the end of the fifteenth century, this process was often accomplished by landlords who by evicting copyhold and other tenants put themselves in a position to make severalty of the open fields. Their purpose was to turn tilled land into pasture for the profitable business of raising sheep. In the eighteenth century, the process was often accomplished by the common consent of the landholders of villages with the purpose of improving the methods of agriculture and increasing the yield of land. The agricultural experts had convinced people by argument and invective that the champion husbandry was inefficient and that progress in farming was to be hoped for only through the individual management of compact plots of land, unencumbered by communal custom, the regime which now exists generally in the western world.

Of all the enclosures, the last are the ones which are most interesting for the present purpose. They involved the legal rights of many people and they came to be carried out by means of special acts of Parliament or general Enclosure Acts. As a result there are good official records of what villages were enclosed. The land so enclosed was a large part of the whole area which had once been champion country.

If we plot on a map of England, in black, the villages which were enclosed by act of Parliament, we shall find that the black is not distributed at random but is concentrated in a band running diagonally across England from the North Sea coast through the Midlands to the Channel. This is the country which was predominantly champion throughout the Middle Ages. Of course large parts of it were waste, and parts, as will be shown, were submitted to forms of husbandry more primitive even than the champion. Too much emphasis should not be put on the uniformity of practice. But predominantly champion this country certainly was. On one side of this band is left a large area of white to the west and north-west, and on the other side a smaller area of white in the south-eastern corner of the island. To the west are the shires of Cornwall and Devon, all of Wales, and the shires of the North-west from Wales to Scotland: Cheshire, Lancashire, Westmoreland, and Cumberland. To the south-east is the whole of Essex, Middlesex, and Kent, together with parts of Suffolk, Hertfordshire, and Surrey. Of this country, much must have been enclosed for many centuries, or at least submitted to agricultural regimes which favored enclosure. The rest must have formed a debatable ground, where the champion system, if it was ever in force at all, was not so solidly organized as it was in the Midlands. Sales and exchanges by the villagers of small pieces of land may have long been common there and allowed small enclosures gradually to encroach on common field.[11] Economic boundaries are not surveyed lines like frontiers.

Another interesting map can be and has been drawn. From the surveys and extents surviving from the Middle Ages and later times it is possible actually to determine for a large number of villages whether or not they were submitted to the characteristic champion husbandry. When the champion villages are plotted on a map they fall within an area with definite boundaries, and this area, as we should expect, is strikingly coincident with the area filled by villages enclosed by act of Parliament. The only exception is Norfolk, which is without the country of the champion villages but within the country where villages were enclosed by act of Parliament. One reason for the divergence is this: in

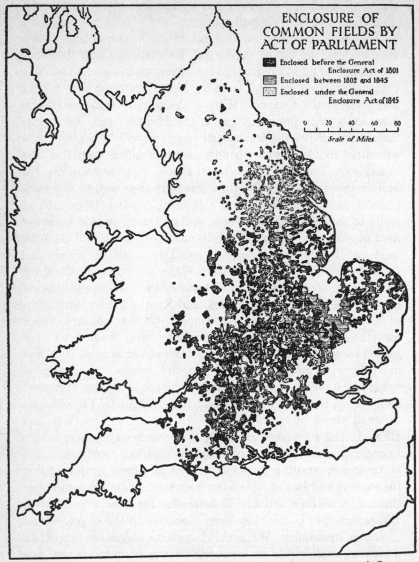

ENCLOSURE OF
COMMON FIELDS BY
ACT OF PARLIAMENT

Enclosed before the General
Enclosure Act of 1801

Enclosed between 1802 and 1845

Enclosed under the General
Enclosure Act of 1845

0   20   40   60   80

Scale of Miles

(Original in G. Slater, *The English Peasantry and the Enclosure of Common Fields*, 73. The present form of the map appears in H. S. Darby, ed., *An Historical Geography of England before A. D. 1800*, 472, reproduced by permission of the Cambridge University Press.)

Norfolk, if any part of a township was to be enclosed, the procedure was to ask Parliament for a nominal redivision of the whole township. In fact the parcels of land to be enclosed were commonly small. The rest had long been enclosed, so that the map of enclosures by act of Parliament gives a wrong impression of the amount of open-field land there had been in Norfolk.[12] The final reason is that Norfolk husbandry always had peculiarities, which will have to be described later.

The testimony of travellers, the map of enclosures by act of Parliament, the map of the distribution of champion villages all agree in this, that in the days before the great enclosure movements there was a broad band of country stretching from the North Sea coast of England to the Channel in which there was practiced a kind of husbandry the most striking mark of which was its wide expanse of open fields. Men called this champion country. On either side of this band, in Devon and Cornwall, Wales, and the shires of the North-west on one hand, and in Suffolk, Essex, Kent and other shires of the south-eastern corner of England on the other, there were in force kinds of husbandry which may have differed among themselves but were alike in this, that they were marked by enclosures.

What is more, champion and woodland were set apart in other ways than simply the character of their fields. To these two different landscapes corresponded two different kinds of human habitation. As before, the observation seems to have first been made by an Elizabethan Englishman and traveller, in this case William Harrison. Harrison's statement is this:

It is so, that our soile being diuided into champaine ground and woodland, the houses of the first lie uniformelie builded in euerie town togither, with streets and lanes; whereas in the woodland countries (except here and there in great market townes) they stand scattered abroad, each one dwelling in the midst of his owne occupieng.[13]

In short, in the champion country were found compact villages; in the woodland was found some kind of dispersed settlement. That this statement has all the convenience and all the danger of what men of science call a first approximation, Harrison surely would have recognized.

The boundaries of landscape are international and intranational. The same contrasts were recognized on the southern shore of

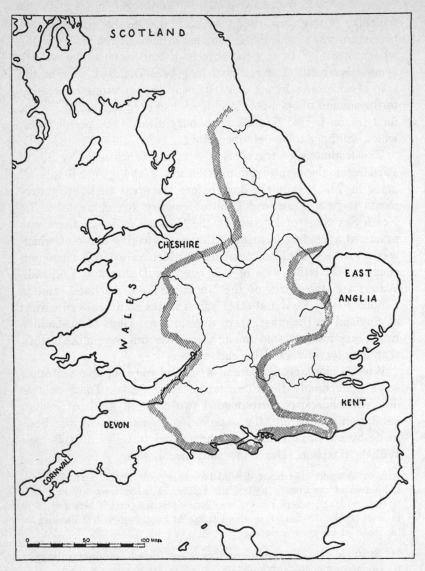

The Boundaries of the Open-Field System in England
(From H. L. Gray, *English Field Systems*).

the English Channel as on the northern, and there today they are much less blurred. *Bocage* and *champagne* were distributed in northern France in much the same manner as woodland and champion in southern England. Over against the woodland of Cornwall and Devon, Brittany and most of Normandy were countries of small, walled fields and scattered settlement. Then, north-east of a line running roughly from the mouth of the Seine to the northernmost bend of the Loire, came the country of the champion husbandry and the big, compact villages, in the Beauce, in Champagne itself, and in Picardy. And just as Kent in England was woodland, so to the east of the *champagne* in France much of Flanders was a land of old enclosures. To say that it was also a land of scattered settlement would be rash. Arthur Young, the most prominent of the agricultural experts of the eighteenth century, noted the eastern boundary of the *champagne* as it was when he visited France, just before the Revolution. His words are these:

Between Bouchaine and Valenciennes, end the open fields, which have travelled with me, more or less, all the way from Orleans. After Valenciennes, the country is inclosed; here also is a line of division in another respect. The farms in the open country are generally large; but in the rich, deep, low vale of Flanders, they are small, and much in the hands of little proprietors.[14]

Outside of France, the country of the big villages and open fields reappeared in Denmark and southern Sweden, and in the lands held or conquered of old by the Germans. In fact, with local variations, it covered most of the plain of northern Europe, as far as the Urals.

Such are the facts of the distribution in north-western Europe, in the centuries before the Agricultural Revolution, of two types of countryside, one marked by big villages and open, common fields, the other by relatively scattered settlement and fenced-in fields. The facts can be established with some certainty; their interpretation, linking them with other observations, is not as firm.

One of the common traits of human beings is that of trying to interpret a set of facts as the effect of a single cause, and they have tried to interpret the distribution of woodland and champion in Europe in this way. According to the fashion, this single cause has often been found in some economic influence; some form of the economic interpretation of history has been applied. One such theory is that of the geographers. The sort of thing geographers have to say about the way men settle on the land can be illustrated in the matter of soils. In France, they point out, or once pointed out, the land of scattered settlements, both in Flanders and in the West, is by and large the land of the soils which hold water. The big villages, on the other hand, lie on the soils which allow rain to soak through them quickly. In the first kind of country, surface water is abundant and habitation can be dispersed, whereas in the other kind of country springs are rare and wells must be sunk deep; accordingly people come together in numbers by the few sources of drink for their cattle and themselves.

Unhappily, the coincidence of soils with kinds of human settlement is only a rough one. The weakness of arguments which trace the differences between woodland and champion landscape to such geographical influences is that woodland is often found on the kind of soil which should, according to theory, have produced champion country, and champion country is found on the kind of soil which should have produced woodland.[15] The problem must be more complicated than the geographers thought.

Of the economic motives in the behavior of men, their desire to make the most of their geographical environment is certainly one. How strong has it been? To be sure, such motives underlie all others, because most men have always been determined to get enough to eat and to keep themselves warm. But once they have worked out techniques which satisfy these needs reasonably well, they are slow to make them more efficient. They do not adopt such of the methods other people use as are better than their own, because they do not hear of them. They do not conceive of the possibility of reflecting upon their methods so as to invent better ones or adapt the old ones more accurately to the requirements of the environment. They neither adopt nor adapt. This was especially true of times when useful information spread slowly, and the feeling that it was wrong to change established custom was stronger than it is now. In those days a farmer would do his work in the way his neighbors did and his father taught him. He would not dream that another way was possible. And when he moved into a new country, he would try to adapt the country to his customs rather than his customs to the country. A proof of this is at hand. The old world contrast between villages and scattered settlement repeated itself in the new world. The earliest colonists in Massachusetts settled in big villages and even tried to establish open, common fields like those of England.[16] In the same way, many centuries before, their Saxon ancestors had brought the ancestors of the English villages across the North Sea from Germany. In time the "commons" had to be abandoned, save in the form of parks — there was that much giving in to American geography — but the big village remained and became the fundamental social and political unit of New England life, the New England town. The first Frenchmen in Quebec, on the other hand, came from woodland country in Brittany and Normandy, and settled, as at home, not in villages but in scattered farms. Villages of course grew up, but only as churches were built and the houses of shopkeepers and tradesmen clustered around these general meeting places. The colonists, at least in the beginning, tried to live as far as possible as they were used to living in the countries beyond the sea. What was true of the French and English in America was true without doubt of their distant forefathers who made the woodland and champion landscapes of Europe.

There would be stronger reason to take into consideration geographical reasons for the distribution of woodland and champion in north-western Europe if there were not facts of another kind with which this distribution can be correlated. If we leave out of account such places as Kent and Flanders and look only at the woodland country of the western rim of Europe: Brittany, Cornwall, Wales, and Ireland, what anyone will say at once is that it coincides roughly with the country in which large numbers of the people we vaguely call Celtic lived throughout the Middle Ages and in modern times. The claim has been made not only that the woodland landscape was the work of the Celts but also that the champion landscape was the work of the Germanic races.[17] Unhappily, as is well known, the word *race* is used in many senses. Does it refer to common blood, common language, common culture, to a set of sentiments, or to a combination of these? There is no need to enter this discussion here, but whatever one of these meanings be assigned to the word *race*, if the woodland of the West covered the same country as the Celtic races, its distribution cannot be explained directly in economic terms. Races introduce other factors.

The same kind of thing can be said of the woodland of the south-eastern corner of England. There is no reason to believe that any large number of Celts survived in a shire like Kent. But the Venerable Bede, who wrote, it is true, a quarter of a millennium after the events, said that Kent was the country overrun by the first Germanic invaders of England, whom he called the Jutes. They seem to have been less like the Angles or the Saxons than either one of these groups was like the other. Throughout the Middle Ages the customs of Kent were peculiar.[18] Once more differences of landscape are found associated with differences of folk.

Furthermore, the distribution during the Middle Ages of customs of inheritance of land coincided in a first approximation with that of champion and of woodland, both in the east and in the west of England. In champion, the custom was likely to be that land descended to one son of the last holder, and only one; in woodland, that it descended jointly to all the sons. There will be a place for details later. Differences in customs of inheritance are sensitive signs of differences in traditional types of family organization.

One feature of the woodland country was the small groups of people by which it was inhabited, in contrast to the big villages of the champion land. But the settlements were not simply small and scattered: they had other characteristics besides. They were not isolated farms, each the home of a man with his wife, children, and hired men, as in the rural parts of the United States. Instead, what the settlements of the woodland may have been in ancient times may be illustrated in one of the woodland countries, Wales. In Wales, as in Cornwall, these small settlements were called *trefs* or, more elaborately, *trefgordds*: *tref* is a common element in Welsh and Cornish place names, as *ton* is in English. According to one of the ancient Welsh laws:

This is the complement of a lawful hamlet [trefgordd]: nine buildings, and one plough, and one kiln [odyn], and one churn [gordd], and one cat, and one cock, and one bull, and one herdsman.[19]

In describing a *tref* in this way the ancient lawgiver was without doubt projecting an ideal. Few actual *trefs* can have corresponded with his description in every respect. But several matters appear in it which are supported by other evidence. The *tref* was not an isolated farm. Neither was it a village. It was something between them in size — nine houses is the number mentioned in the law, and these houses seem to have clustered close to each other. It was a hamlet. It was a hamlet, too, in which the group of people lived who used one plow in common and kept their cattle in a single herd.

The people of the *tref* were held together by economic bonds; they seem also to have been held together by bonds of kinship. They were the group of descendants of a near and common ancestor, working together and perhaps redividing the land of the *tref* from time to time so that every adult male had a share. The *tref* was, to use a technical term of anthropology, a joint family. Today, in out-of-the-way parts of Ireland, the sentiments and ceremonies associated with the kin are more elaborate than they were in the country of the champion villages. But the villagers made up for their falling short in feelings of kinship by their neighborliness in the larger community. After centuries of living in hamlets or villages, many of the attitudes characteristic of each, impressed by the older generations on their children, must still be vigorous even in peoples who have left their old homelands. A New England Yankee, descendant of the original English colonists, does not share with his Irish fellow-citizen a strong feeling of obligation toward his remoter kinsman.

To say that the Welsh *tref* was typical of the social order of all the woodland countries of the Celtic fringe in early times would not be safe. The interpretation of the Welsh texts themselves is uncertain. What is sure is that settlement in small hamlets was the rule in Brittany, Ireland, and Scotland, as well as in Wales and Cornwall. It is sure, too, to take a further instance, that the Scottish "farm," the cell of agricultural life in that country at least until the end of the eighteenth century, was an economic unit resembling the *tref*, its inhabitants being the group of people who held their land and used their plow in common. And in Scotland and elsewhere in the Celtic West, as in Wales, these peculiarities in economic organization were probably accompanied by and linked with peculiarities in the social order.

From what has gone before, it is plain that the character and distribution of such landscapes as the woodland and champion of north-western Europe can be explained not in terms of a single influence or class of influences but only in terms of several influences and classes of influences. According to one convenient scheme, the classes into which the influences determining the character of landscapes are divided are three, to be called geographical, technical, and social. The geographical influences include the terrain, the soils, the minerals, and the climate. The technical influences include the ways in which the people who live on the land make a living from it: what tame beasts they keep and how they care for them, what grains, vegetables, and fruits they raise, what tools they use and how they use them, and so forth. These first two influences are economic. The third class of influences, the social influences, include the customs according to which particular groups of people: tribes, villages, families, work together in making a living and carrying on the other activities necessary to the survival of a society.

Not only must the character of landscapes be seen as the result of several influences, not one, but also none of these influences can be seen as acting independently of the others. The use of the plow is one of the influences determining the nature of human groupings, but the nature of human groupings is one of the influences determining the use of the plow. The geographical, the technical, the social influences are thus in a state of direct mutual dependence, of one upon each of the others. Experience suggests that they are also in a state of indirect mutual dependence in that they are all components of organized wholes or systems, which persist in time. These systems have characteristics which are not those of their components, in particular, the characteristic that a change in one of the components introduces changes in all the components, and they will react so as to reduce the original change. Such systems are found in many kinds of phenomena; those in question here are called cultures, total social and economic adaptations, social systems.

The description of the Welsh *tref* will serve as a sketch of the social order of the woodland country of England, at least in the West. The sketch will not be elaborated. There remains the social order of the champion country, the country of the villages. To describe that, at a particular period in its history, is the matter of the rest of this book.

CHAPTER III

THE PLACE OF THE THIRTEENTH CENTURY

THE SOCIAL ORDER of the champion country of England will here be described as it was at a particular period in its history.[1] That period is the thirteenth century. We all know that one year is very like the year following, even if the two are in different centuries; nevertheless we contrast the nineteenth century with the twentieth and believe that the contrast has some meaning. In the same way we may properly speak of the place of the thirteenth century in history. We may also speak of the thirteenth century in English history, but we shall do well to remember that much of what happened in England was matched by what happened across the Channel. As today, in spite of an increasing economic nationalism, booms and depressions are felt throughout the world, so in the Middle Ages economic and social movements followed parallel courses over great regions. Such a region was north-western Europe: England, France, and the Low Countries. Not even in the Middle Ages did England live in isolation.

In the ninth century of our era, in the days of the descendants of Charles the Great, north-western Europe reached the bottom of a long period of political and economic disintegration which had continued, with waves of recovery, ever since the high tide of the Roman Empire under the first Caesars. If the slope of the downward curve was not as steep and the bottom not as low as they are sometimes said to have been, nevertheless no one will deny that there was a downward trend and a low point. Earlier, the German tribes had penetrated into the Empire. They did not "break through the wall of the legions," but advanced as the legions were withdrawn or disintegrated. Some of the Germans had crossed the sea to England, had rooted out the romanized Britons with some thoroughness, and had founded, so far as we know today, the big villages of the champion husbandry. To the new country they brought the institutions of their homes in northern Germany. Other folk had given France, Spain, and Italy new ruling classes.

The older school of historians described in too lurid terms the disorder which attended the invasions. Before the Germans took political control of the Latin world, they had long been in contact with Romans, and the two cultures had been under the influence of one another.[2] Roman ways had become familiar. The Goths, the Vandals, the Franks, and the other tribes were not responsible for the great economic decline. It had begun before they marched and continued after they had settled in new homes. Instead the Saracens and the Northmen seem to have been to blame, if anyone was to blame, for the decline in its final phase. The Roman Empire was what Graham Wallas would have called a Great Society: its prosperity depended on the exchange over long distances of the goods of different regions. The Great Society withers when its lines of traffic are cut: this result the Saracens and the Northmen accomplished. The Saracen pirates harried all the coasts of the Mediterranean, and at last came near to extinguishing the seaborne commerce of the Empire. Only in the waters around Byzantium was the old traffic safe. In the northern seas, the men of Denmark and Norway systematically plundered the coasts exposed to their raids.

The ninth and tenth centuries were at the bottom of an economic cycle of long term. But if they were at the end of a period of decline which had lasted since the first century, they were also at the beginning of a marvellous period of increasing prosperity which has continued, more or less steadily, until the present. Revival soon followed the depths of the depression. In the Mediterranean, the Italian cities took over the defence against the infidel at sea, and in the Crusades of the twelfth century developed the counter-attack. In effect, the rude and fanatical men of war from beyond the Alps were the instruments of the Italian cities, for the cities were the chief profiteers in the revival of Mediterranean commerce which accompanied the Crusades. In the north, the age of Viking colonization succeeded the age of Viking piracy. The Danes, in the ninth century, descended upon north-eastern England and resettled the country. Iceland and the Isles of Scotland were occupied, and Normandy given vigorous new rulers, by jarls and farmers of western Norway who would not submit to the overlordship of King Harald Fairhair. The age of Viking colonization brought in the age of Viking trade. A northern economic system was developed, its arteries the North Sea, the Baltic, and the Russian rivers, its outposts Greenland and Byzantium.

Under these influences, to the north and to the south, the life of north-western Europe began to quicken. Thenceforward must be observed that interaction of economic development, changes in the importance of different social classes and in their interests and sentiments, and changes in political forms and measures, which has been characteristic ever since. The first development to be observed was the revival and growth of boroughs and cities. These places in many instances began as the seats of bishops or abbots, of kings or counts. The rents of the lands of a great lord were in large part spent in his borough; the goods needed by his many dependents were in large part bought or made in his borough. In this manner a natural nucleus of trade was formed.[3] Another influence was at work besides. There were traders in Europe throughout the Dark Ages, but the early traders were adventurers, who travelled about with their goods where they saw the largest chances for profit. The increase of the volume of trade was accompanied by the appearance of a class of sedentary merchants, established in the centers of trade as the managers, the financiers of trading enterprises. We must not try to find a single dominant influence in the growth of cities. Such things are always a matter of a balanced relationship between many factors.

The commercial and manufacturing cities of Flanders were first in the race for wealth and influence, but even tiny boroughs in England tasted the new prosperity and grew. What the class of merchants wanted who came to the front in the cities was freedom from a feudal regime which had grown up in adaptation to an agricultural civilization. They wanted their real property in the cities to be free from the restrictions and services incidental to the feudal order. They wanted to regulate their own markets, assess their own taxes. These privileges they secured in the course of the twelfth and thirteenth centuries by the clauses of charters granted to the corporations of the boroughs by kings and other lords.

No important economic movement is limited to one field: the economic revival was not confined to the cities. In the countryside, too, population was increasing. New land was being brought under cultivation. Many of the great Cistercian abbeys were deliberately set down in waste places, upland and marsh, so that the monks might make the wilderness to blossom as the rose. On the estates of many of the great landholders, lay and clerical, the system of manorial farming, according to which the demesne lands of a lord were cultivated by the customary services of his villeins, was consolidated and elaborately organized. We should not think of the temper of the towns as being very unlike that of the country. Many of the boroughs began as farming villages and some even kept their common fields. The country fed the towns with men: as early as the thirteenth century husbandmen were sending their sons to be bound apprentices. And names such as John Merchant or William Chapman, appearing in manorial custumals, show that even the country was infected with the spirit of commerce.

England in especial had been fortunate. By force of arms her Anglo-Danish governing class, which had some talent for the arts but little for government, was replaced by the Norman aristocracy, one of the most famous *élites* that has ever ruled. In Normandy the ducal machinery had been operating effectively for a generation; William the Conqueror transferred it to England in its full vigor. By such measures as his shrewd distribution of confiscated estates, he prevented for the future of his new country the appearance of powerful provincial nobles supported by strong sentiments of local loyalty, and thus avoided the difficulties which delayed for so long the unification of France and Germany. Later, at the end of the twelfth and in the thirteenth century, the drastic rulings of a succession of vigorous royal justices consolidated for England a body of simple common law.

We have heard the thirteenth century described as "the greatest of centuries." It was the century of the universities and of the scholastic philosophy. It was the century of the building of the great cathedrals: Chartres, Paris, Rheims, Amiens, Salisbury, Lincoln. They were built by a devout people, united in its ceremonies and its view of the world by the Catholic Church. But let us consider what we imply when we say all this. One thing, at least, which we imply, though the historians of philosophy or of art will tell us nothing about it, is that the thirteenth century was a time of substantial material prosperity. Scholars like St. Thomas cannot be supported, cathedrals like Chartres cannot be built by a poor society. We must think of the bishops who built the cathedrals as most resembling those presidents of universities who, in another prosperous century, delighted in sinking the money of the alumni in bricks and mortar. But when we say that the thirteenth century was the century of Chartres and of St. Thomas Aquinas we are implying much more than material prosperity. Society felt sure of its foundations and confident of its future. In that sense it was an age of faith.

Like other such ages, before and since, it had no reason for confidence. With the beginning of the fourteenth century, economic expansion slowed down. Scholars have little information to use as a basis for estimating the population of England and France in those days, but their best guess is that population, which had been increasing slowly for several centuries, failed to continue to increase. It is not that there was a clear loss, but simply that there was no further growth, and numbers remained nearly stationary until the expansion which accompanied the discovery of America, two centuries later. Population is held to be a good index of the prosperity of a social and economic order. Another index is the price of such important commodities as grain: rising prices are an index of prosperity. We possess good series of English grain prices, and their evidence is that prices increased throughout the thirteenth century and after that became stabilized, or at least did not increase at the same rate.[4]

One reason for the failure to keep up the great advance is provided by the disasters which filled the fourteenth and fifteenth centuries. A severe famine in 1315 was only the beginning of misfortune. The plagues of the middle of the century followed: they are estimated to have killed at least one third of the population of north-western Europe. Peasants' revolts were characteristic of the time of disequilibrium after the shock. They were brutally put down by an upper class still so unshaken by change or by the agitation of intellectuals that it was ready to use force to the utmost to preserve the form of society of which it was the apex. Worst of all, the marchings and counter-marchings of the Hundred Years War devastated France and exhausted England. Except for wars on the borders and the revolt against the weak king Henry III, led by Simon de Montfort, Earl of Leicester, the thirteenth century was a time of relative peace for Englishmen. In the fourteenth and fifteenth centuries, the state of war either at home or abroad was nearly continual.

Much of the stagnation of economic life can be blamed on these disasters, coming, so to speak, from without. More of it came from developments within the structure of society. The great expansion itself generated the forces that checked it. So much can be said in general terms: the actual processes are often obscure. Some of them appear in the history of the cities, especially those of the Low Countries. The class of merchants, the creatures of the revival of trade, had become in many cities by the end of the thirteenth century a closed and ruling oligarchy. It had freed the cities; it now ruled them. And like many such classes, it was inclined to put the money it had accumulated in the active management of commercial enterprises into property, particularly real estate, which would yield a stable income. The oligarchy inclined more and more to be made up of men who had the sentiments of people living from their rents, men who were less closely in touch than their fathers had been with the active productive forces of the community.

Hard upon one class which had arrived, pressed another which tried to gain for itself a more secure station in society, a larger share of power. As in the nineteenth century the winning of social and political power by the financiers and manufacturers was followed by agitation on behalf of the proletariat, so in the Middle Ages the city oligarchies were challenged by a lower class. The growth of the cities as centers of manufacturing had accompanied their growth as centers of trade, so that a large body of handicraftsmen showed itself underneath the merchants and landlords. It was a body organized in craft gilds, designed to control for the benefit of their members the conditions of each mystery. More and more the handicraftsmen and their craft gilds, by means violent or peaceful, challenged the power of the oligarchies. More and more, as they secured a voice in legislation, they put into force ordinances of which the effect, if not the intent, was to check the introduction of new methods of production and distribution in the crafts. Measures of protection were also made law. In many cities, certain articles could be offered for sale in the city only if they had been made there. Just as government regulation of industry and finance succeeded the period of laissez-faire capitalism in the nineteenth century, so in the fourteenth century the period of restriction by legislation succeeded the free mercantile expansion of earlier times.

In agriculture, as in industry, the processes of stagnation in the later Middle Ages are obscure, but in England the change may have been of the following character. The landed aristocrats, whether knights or prelates, commuted the labor services of their villeins, by means of which their lands had been tilled, for money rents, with which they could hire farm laborers. By the end of the fourteenth century, this development was well advanced. But many of the gentry were also setting out at rent even those lands which they had once managed directly themselves. Whereas in the thirteenth century the upper class had been the heart and soul of efforts to improve agricultural methods and manorial organization, by the fifteenth century, the gentlemen, like the members of the city oligarchies, may often have had the sentiments and point of view of *rentiers*. A change came only with the appearance in the country, at the end of the Wars of the Roses, of a new and vigorous, if commercial-minded, upper class. Whatever its explanation, agricultural stagnation in England in the fifteenth century is a fact. Land went out of use, and even the productivity of cultivated land decreased.[5]

To give too much weight to the economic forces in history is easy, because in general more is known about these forces than about others. Probably the most important development of the fourteenth century in England was not the Hundred Years War or the failure to maintain economic expansion but the appearance of John Wyclif and his followers the Lollards. Of course the Lollards cannot be wholly dissociated from the economic situation: no one of the developments of a country's history is independent of the others, but Lollardry was certainly in no immediate manner an economic phenomenon. Among other matters, Wyclif laid great stress on preaching, on the work of parish priests, and on personal acquaintance with the Bible. He

also attacked the doctrine of the Church concerning Transubstantiation in the Mass. The issues he raised were important.
Since they were exactly the issues which the Protestants took up
again more than a hundred years later, they must have
corresponded to certain underlying tendencies of the northern
peoples. But, in the fourteenth century, the grounds on which
Wyclif attacked the Church may have been less important than
the mere fact that he did attack it. He must have made articulate
certain common, if vague, sentiments of discontent with the
Church as it then was. Religious movements like that of the
Lollards often arise in sick societies. This statement is a vague
one, expressing little more than an intuition. The characteristics
of a sick society have not yet been well described, not even for
our own social order. But Wyclif is a sign that in the fourteenth
century medieval civilization was losing something of its old
morale. Indeed there is drama in the fact that the year of the
Peasants' Revolt (1381) was also a year of Wyclif's attack on
the doctrine of Transubstantiation. The famines, wars, and
pestilences of the fourteenth and fifteenth centuries, the economic
stagnation of those years, must not be viewed in isolation from
their social malaise.[6]

The thirteenth century can for convenience be treated as a
single epoch, with its own characteristics. It was a time of peace
and prosperity, the culmination of a movement of economic
expansion several centuries old. It was a time of confidence and
of an unshaken social order, though the very process of expansion
had already begun to undermine that order. Like all times of
prosperity, it was a time of change, though not of change so rapid
as that to which people of modern times are accustomed. But
the thirteenth century in England and France was followed by
two centuries of arrested development — not decline, but arrested
development, or if that phrase seems too strong, say that the
advances made in the earlier Middle Ages were not kept up.
In either case, the statement represents only a general impression
of developments which were complex and have not been well
described. Certainly in some fields these centuries brought forth
new and vigorous institutions: one example is the native English
cloth industry. And the statement can be applied to France and
England only, not to Europe as a whole. No one could say that

in Italy the fourteenth and fifteenth centuries were centuries of arrested development. Whether advance in north-western Europe would have begun again without the discovery of America we cannot tell. In point of fact a new advance did begin therewith, and has continued, in waves, until the present day.

CHAPTER IV

THE SKILLS OF HUSBANDMEN

S TUDENTS HAVE LONG since abandoned the full-blown economic interpretation of history. No successful attempt has ever been made to show that the customs of human societies are wholly determined by the nature of the country where men live and by the skills they have of making a living from the country. None the less there is little doubt that the customs are in part determined by these economic factors. This you could never tell from the work of some anthropologists. In studying any society, they are at once concerned with its more spectacular aspects, its myths and ceremonies, and neglect its practical aspects, its hunting, fishing, farming. We should never know from their work that the men of the society ever had to bother about keeping themselves alive. But most anthropologists are free from one common bent of people's minds. Men of the present day are inclined to think of their own age as the only one which has made great inventions. In the presence of the automobile and the radio, they forget that fundamental inventions have been made from time to time throughout human history. No one who is trying to fix the place of the thirteenth century in history should make the mistakes of the anthropologist or the common man. He should consider as soon as he can the skills by which the people of that century made their living, and he should describe how those skills differed from those used in earlier and later centuries.

When they set up as a pathetic type the man who is honest, but poor and oppressed, the literary men of today make him a worker in industry. Their fellows of the Middle Ages made him a farmer — Piers Plowman. They liked to envisage him actually at his plow, ankle-deep in the fen, his hard hands on the plow-stilts, his four feeble rothers yoked before him and driven by a goad in the hands of his wife.[1] Piers Plowman was the proper object of sympathy of an age when nine men out of ten were tillers of the soil.

But almost everyone who now writes about these tillers of the soil and the way they worked fails of understanding because he has never been himself a dirt farmer. For years the people who wrote about commerce in the Middle Ages repeated the story that the little ships of those days hugged the shore in their voyages, so that they should always be near a harbor in which they could find refuge in a gale. These writers were not seamen but scholars, and therefore did not appreciate that the first thought of the master of a small sailing vessel in bad weather must have been in the Middle Ages, as it is now, to run out to sea for deep water, not inshore for shelter. He knew his ship could ride out any ordinary gale off soundings, but steep, breaking seas, lee shores, and sands were real perils. If medieval ships hugged the coast, the reason was not that they wanted never to be far from a safe anchorage. The city-bred man is likely to make the same sort of mistake in talking about medieval farming. There are things that any experienced seaman or farmer, modern or medieval, knows, and these are the things that most people who write about seamen and farmers do not know, and cannot learn from books. If the division of labor in society is such that the writers must nevertheless proceed with their treatises without waiting for the criticism of practical men, they should do so in the understanding that they are probably making mistakes which would cause any plowboy or foremast hand to call them fools. In this understanding, let us consider what husbandmen of the thirteenth century knew of husbandry.[2]

The husbandman of the Middle Ages, Piers Plowman, was a subsistence farmer, to use an American phrase. He raised crops not so much to be sold in the market as to be consumed by himself, his household, and his stock. And his subsistence was largely of grain, with peas and beans, baked into bread, boiled into puddings, or brewed into ale. Some leeks or cabbages he may have grown in his garden. He kept a few tough, razor-backed hogs, either running half-wild in the woods and battening on the mast of English oaks and beeches, or about the village, ringed or yoked to prevent their rooting up the turf. Swine flesh, salted or smoked, was the flesh Piers commonly ate. He kept hens and geese, too, and sometimes slaughtered a sheep, a cow, or one of his plow oxen. But he cannot have supped every evening on a dish of meat. Bread, throughout the Middle Ages, was the staff of life.

As Iris bears witness in *The Tempest*, the lands of England were

> rich leas
> Of wheat, rye, barley, fetches, oats, and pease.

These were the staples, augmented by the varieties of seeds, such as maslin and drage, which men made by mixing two or more of the basic grains.[3] The important thing to remember about them is that they fell into two main classes, according to the time of year at which they were sown. The first two, wheat and rye, were sown in the fall, in the season between Michaelmas and Christmas which the men of the Middle Ages called winter. These were the winter seed, *semen hiemale*. The last four: barley, vetches, oats, and peas, together with beans, were planted in the early spring. These were the lenten seed, *semen quadragesimale*. Both classes of crops mature at nearly the same time in August and September.

The first man who cultivated grains must have been cast from self-satisfaction to despair when he found that his plot yielded every year smaller and smaller crops. Perhaps it is not right to say that husbandmen have known ever since that fields cannot be cropped continuously without becoming exhausted. It is not a question of exhaustion in the sense that the fields will eventually bear no crop at all, unless as a result of cultivation the top-soil has washed or blown away, something which has happened in parts of the United States. But they will bear much poorer crops than they might otherwise have borne. Piers Plowman knew at least three means by which the fertility of fields which had been under crop could be restored or improved. The first was the simplest of all. He knew that if fields were simply let alone for a time they would bear better crops. This method he called fallowing. The second method was marling. In many parts of England he could dig marl, a soil of clay combined with carbonate of lime, and spread it on the fields. Marl was a fertilizer. The third method was dunging. He could fold his sheep systematically on the fields. Or he could spread on the fields the manure of his cattle, commonly as mixed with straw in the form of compost. In some countries a cow or an ox is more important as a machine for producing dung than it is for any other purpose. Since Piers seldom could get marl in large quantities and never had vast dunghills because of faults in his technique which will appear presently, he was reduced to fallowing as the only means of bringing any large part of his land back into good heart.

So far Piers Plowman possessed a respectable understanding of agriculture. The great gap in his skill was that he did not know turnips or the grasses, such as the clovers and alfalfa, as field crops.[4] Modern farmers employ the grasses in ways which serve either directly or indirectly to keep the soil rich. Directly, a crop like alfalfa grown on a piece of worn-out land and plowed in will restore to the soil the nitrogen it needs to produce grain. Indirectly, grass can be grown as a fodder for cattle; the cattle produce manure, and the manure is spread on the fields. Using judicious combinations of these means, a modern farmer can almost manufacture the kind of soil he requires. The artificial grasses and turnips do not seem to have been introduced into England much before the second half of the seventeenth century and were not in common use until a century later. The introduction of the new methods is called the Agricultural Revolution, which is less spoken of but hardly less important than the Industrial Revolution which took place at the same time. But it is better to put the matter in this way: the important thing the Agricultural Revolution brought in was not any specific method but an idea — the idea that all methods of agriculture could be studied and improved, the idea of a rational agriculture. This idea was new in Europe, at least since Roman times. In the Middle Ages, agriculture was customary. Men farmed as their fathers had farmed and did not dream of anything better.

Piers Plowman did not know the grasses as field crops. He did not know anything about sowing them in worn-out fields in order to bring the land back into good heart. He had only fallowing as a means of making any large part of his land once more able to bear crops, and thus no matter how hard he worked he was limited by the original qualities of the soil. More important, he did not sow the grasses for fodder for his cattle. The greatest difference between medieval agriculture and modern is in this humble but vital matter of hay. The men of the Middle Ages knew nothing of hay deliberately sown as a crop. This notion is a hard one for us to get used to, but it seems to be true. This does not mean that Piers Plowman had no hay. But the hay he had was only such as grew naturally and luxuriantly in the river bottoms and other low, wet places. Again, this does not mean strictly that it grew without any cultivation. Piers' forefathers had to reclaim the meadows from swamp, and Piers himself had to mow them every year and see that the ditches were clean. But he did not sow grass-seed as he sowed corn. Unhappily the amount of water meadow in England is limited, and in the Middle Ages an acre of meadow was worth something like three times as much as an acre of arable land. Piers' hay crop was small, and since it was small his cattle were few. During the summer they could graze in the pastures, but in the winter they had to be fed on hay, together with as much of the spring-corn crop as Piers used for fodder. And since his cattle were few, the amount of dung Piers had to spread on his fields was small also. Husbandry is full of such vicious circles. In still another way, then, Piers was brought back to fallowing as his only large-scale means of restoring the qualities of the soil. From time to time, he simply had to leave the soil alone.

To turn up the sod to prepare it for receiving the seed, Piers used a plow, drawn by a team of oxen or horses. The plow was the most important instrument of agriculture, and the husbandman looked on his labor at the plow as the type of all his farm labor. Piers himself was a plowman. That the work of the plow should go forward, unhindered by frost or bad weather, was his continual worry; "God speed the plow!" was his prayer.

Two main kinds of plows have been used in Europe.[5] One is very ancient. It consists of a crooked stick, which may be shod with iron. One end of this crooked stick forms the hale, the handle of the plow, the other end scratches the earth. Toward the middle of this stick, another piece may be fitted to jut forward, and the plow team is made fast to this. Such are the essentials of this kind of plow: its construction varied somewhat from place to place. This was the primeval plow; it is called by words which have the same root in all European languages. It is the *aratrum* of Latin, the *araire* of French, the *arðr* of old Norse. Since it is light and does not enter the ground deeply, it is most successful where the soil is light, not where there is a heavy turf, as in England. It can be drawn by a small team, an ox or horse or two, a team which can be turned easily. Accordingly the *araire* is adapted to cross-plowing, first drawing the furrows in one direction and then at right angles across them, and so encourages a regime of squarish fields. Such fields are found in southern France and in other Mediterranean countries, where the *araire* has been in use for ages. In the far north, also, this kind of plow lingered, especially as a part of the traditional Norse agriculture. As late as the end of the eighteenth century, its use was observed in the Shetland Islands, and in the Middle Ages this light hoe-plow may have been common in many parts of Europe.[6]

Contrasted with the *araire* was the plow proper, a much more powerful instrument. To the forward end of a long and heavy plow-beam the plow team was made fast. Beneath the plow-beam, fastened to it by stout cross braces, a share-beam hung. This was the part of the plow that went through the earth, and to its forward end was fitted a detachable cap of wrought iron, which broke up and under-cut the sod, the plowshare. Another iron, the sword-like coulter, was driven through the plow-beam to hang a few inches before the share and slice the sod before the share broke it up. Then, behind the share, always built on the right-hand side of the plow, was the wooden mould-board, tilted so as to turn the furrow over to the right after the share had cut it. Lastly, two hales or stilts were fitted to the back of the plow, by which the plowman held it to the proper course and depth. Sometimes to the forward end of the plow-beam a wheel or pair of wheels was attached, to make the plow go more evenly, to keep it to a furrow of a constant depth. But the wheel was not one of the essentials of the plow. These were its strength and weight, which enabled it in heavy soils to break the ground to greater depths than could the *araire*, and its big share and mould-board, which turned over a furrow. The *araire* only scratched the soil.

Such was the plow proper, the plow of Piers Plowman, the common plow of northern Europe during the Middle Ages. The root of the word for the *araire* is common to all the European languages, but there is no common term for the plow. In Low Latin it is called *caruca*, from the wheels with which it often was fitted. (The common Roman plow was of course the *aratrum*.) In the Germanic languages it is plow, *pflug*. If the reconstruction of the *plaumorati* of the text of Pliny as *ploum Raeti* be correct, the first people who are known to have called it by a name of this root are the Raeti in the first century of our era. At that time they were living to the south of the upper Danube. Pliny speaks also of the instrument as being used in Gaul.[7] Surely it is a later invention than the *araire*, and an improvement upon it, which must have replaced the *araire* over wide regions.

One advantage of a plow fitted with a mould-board, which must have commended it to the peoples of northern Europe, is that it can be used as an instrument for drainage. In wet countries like England, it is always a serious problem to free the surface of the soil from standing water so that the grain shall not be drowned. Something can be done by ditching, and dikers and delvers worked hard in old times, but ditching is slow work. One of the great improvements of the improving era in agriculture at the end of the eighteenth century was the introduction of earth drains. These drains, of tile, loosely laid some feet deep in the soil, draw off the surface water. The medieval husbandman knew nothing of drains but arranged for the drainage of his land by plowing it in a particular manner. All over England, where fields which were once under the plow have for long been in grass, you will see them laid out in long, parallel ridges, waves of earth like the waves of the sea, but more regular. A villager speaks of such fields as being under "ridge and furrow." These fields were the work either of plowmen of the Middle Ages or of farmers of later times who still plowed as their ancestors did.

There were several ways of "gathering," as of "casting" and "cleaving," these ridges, but a description of one of them is enough.[8] The plow would enter a strip of land just to the left of its center line and would plow round and round the strip from the center outwards, the mould-board (on the right-hand side of the plow) thereby always turning the earth toward the middle of the strip. At the end of a few such plowings, the earth would become heaped up in a ridge in the middle of the strip, sloping off to the two furrows on either edge. If the plowman thought his ridges had become too high he would reverse the process, entering with his plow just to the left of the furrow and turning all the earth downward. Such were the rigs, ridges, or lands of English speech, the *seliones* of medieval Latin.

Once they had been satisfactorily plowed in, the lands seem to have been maintained, and they became units in landholding, in work at the plow, and in reaping in autumn. A team of reapers would work along the ridge.[9] The customary size of ridges varied greatly from county to county of England.

The manner of plowing land is in three formes: eyther they be great Lands, as with high ridges and deepe furrowes, as in all the North parts of this Land, and in some sothern parts also, or els flatte and plaine, without ridge or furrow, as in most parts of Cambridge-shiere: or els in little Lands, no land containing above two or three furrowes, as in Midlesex, Essex, and Hartfordshiere.

—So says one "I. R." in one of the additions he made in the 1598 edition of Master Fitzherbert's *Book of Husbandry*.[10]

The reason why plowing in ridges was a good method of draining land was that in wet weather the tops of the ridges and the corn upon them would stay dry while the water collected in the furrows or, better, drained down the furrows into a ditch. In land with any slope, the ridges were laid out so that the water should drain in this way. Corn that was low down on the sides of the ridges was likely to suffer, of course. Gloucester Abbey, in the rules it drew up in the thirteenth century for the management of its manors, gave the following order in the matter:

that wherever on the edges of the lands the corn is drowned in winter time, the earth be dug up and seed of another kind there allotted, lest that earth lose its fruit by that mishap.[11]

According to Thomas Tusser, also, the difference in the wetness of the tops and bottoms of ridges should make a difference in the kinds of grain planted there. He advised:

> For wheat ill land
> where water doth stand.
> Sowe pease or dredge
> belowe in that redge.[12]

The plow was a heavy implement and it broke up the earth to some depth. Accordingly, the team that was used to draw it was larger than the one hitched to the *araire*. There is no doubt that the team mentioned most commonly in documents of the Middle Ages in England is one of eight beasts, either of oxen or of horses and oxen mixed, in four yokes in line ahead. Sometimes even larger teams, teams of ten beasts, are spoken of, but they cannot have been as common as smaller ones. Indeed there is no team larger than one of four oxen pictured on the borders of English manuscripts of the Middle Ages. It would be hard to crowd eight oxen into a margin; nevertheless scholars probably do not take the illuminations of manuscripts seriously enough as realistic pictures of medieval life. Perhaps the eight-ox team was the standard of what a proper draught should be rather than the team that was in fact used. Perhaps the full team of eight oxen was divided into two sets of four, working on alternate days.[13] Then too the number of head needed in the team varied with the soils and seasons. But a team of eight oxen or horses is specified in the records so much more often than any other that the presumption is that this was commonly the number of beasts actually yoked to the plow. Such a team seems vast to us, who forget that hay was not plentiful, that oxen were probably given grain only rarely, that much of the time their diet cannot have been better than straw, so that after a winter in the byre or after a hard season of plowing they must have been bundles of skin and bones. Big plow teams were used, perhaps, because oxen were weak and small, but to seek purely economic reasons for working practices is always dangerous. The men of the Middle Ages may have plowed with eight oxen simply because it was the custom so to plow. The economic experts of the eighteenth century certainly held many a husbandman up to ridicule because he plowed with several yoke of oxen when a pair of horses could do the same work.

A single man could not both hold the plow and manage an eight-ox team or even a four-ox one. Two men went with such a team. One was at the plow tail, holding the stilts, or perhaps he "holdeth the plough stilt in his left hand, and in his right the plough staff to break the clods." [14] This was the plowman proper, the *carucator*, the holder of the plow. At the orders of the plowman, who was the boss of the team, was the driver of the oxen, the *fugator*. He walked by the oxen and to their left, shouting to them how they were to go, driving them with a whip or a goad.[15]

The plowman himself or the driver of the plow team was often the oxherd as well. Bartholomew the Englishman described the duties of the oxherd as follows:

An oxherd hight Bubulcus, and is ordained by office to keep oxen: He feedeth and nourisheth oxen, and bringeth them to leas and home again: and bindeth their feet with a langhaldes and spanells and nigheth and cloggeth them while they be in pasture and leas, and yoketh and maketh them draw at the plough: and pricketh the slow with a goad and maketh them draw even. And pleaseth them with whistling and with song, to make them bear the yoke with the better will for liking of melody of the voice. And this herd driveth and ruleth them to draw even, and teacheth them to make even furrows: and compelleth them not only to ear, but also to tread and to thresh. And they lead them about upon corn to break the straw in threshing and treading the flour. And when the travail is done, then they unyoke them and bring them to the stall, and feed them thereat.[16]

The oxherd, says another Englishman of the thirteenth century, must love his oxen and sleep by them at night.[17] In Bleadon in Somerset, the oxherd

when he fastens the cattle of the lord in the byre in winter, must watch over them and get the hay and straw which they must eat, and he will carry it into the byre, and he will have what is left before two oxen, which is called *orte*, for the whole time the oxen of the lord are standing in the byre; and he will have his own ox fastened between two oxen of the lord from Christmas Eve to noon on Ascension Day; and he will watch over the oxen and cows and the other beasts of the lord in the byre day and night and he will give them to eat and will water them when it is needful.[18]

Beside the plowman and the driver of the team, several other men or women might go with the plow. Some with plow-bats might break up the clods. Others might sow immediately after the plow. Plowing was a labor in which many people worked together. Of the symbolic plow-team in *Piers Plowman* we read:

> Now perkyn with þe pilgrims · to þe plouh is faren;
> To eryen hus half aker · holpen hym menye.[19]

People have learned from experience and the study of modern working groups that in any labor where people work together, a set of customs grows up which regulates the behavior of the members of the group toward each other and toward the work.

Such a code must have governed the groups that worked at the plow in the Middle Ages. Custom must, for instance, have regulated when the men rested and what compensations and perquisites they received for their work. But almost nothing is known about this. The passage in *Piers Plowman* goes on to say:

> Atte hye pryme peers · let þe plouh stonde,
> And ouer-seyh hem hym-self · ho so best wroughte,
> He sholde be hyred þer-after · when heruest-tyme come.

Piers Plowman cannot be taken as giving a realistic description of a fourteenth-century plow team at work. The requirements of its allegory prevented such a picture being made. None the less, Piers may have reflected on the plane of allegory some of the attitudes of actual plowmen.

One of the important schemes by which the husbandman oriented himself to his surroundings was built around his work at the plow. As in hose, smock, and hood he went stooping at the plow tail along the side of a land, leaning on the hales so that the share should go at an even depth and cut off an even slice, how did he see himself placed as regards his work and the country? We can learn by talking to modern plowmen, by looking at medieval fields, by studying some of the common words plowmen have used. On the right side of the plow, always, was the mould-board, turning over the sod after the share had broken it up. Why the mould-board, ever since the earliest drawings were made of plows and unquestionably long before that, should have been on the right side of the plow we do not know. Something to do with man's right-handedness must have put it there. Because the right was the side to which the furrow was turned, the side of the black earth already broken up, that side of the plow, as seen from the plowman's point of view, was called the furrow-side. And the left-hand side of the plow, the side of the green unbroken turf, was the land-side. Forward of the plow would go the beasts of the plow team. The plowman would have hitched or yoked his strongest and fastest horses or oxen on the furrow-side, since the furrow-side beasts draw in the furrow, and the footing is not as good there as it is on the unbroken turf where the land-side beasts draw. Up beside the plow team would be the driver with his goad. He too would naturally march where the footing was good, on the turf to the left of the team, the land-side. This customary station of the driver of the team has left its mark on working language. The right-hand beast in any team is always called the off-horse or ox, because he is the further from the driver, and off the land, in the furrow. The left-hand beast is called the nigh-horse, because he is nearer to the driver. Even today, when people no longer plow in the old way, the man who leads any team customarily stands at its left. Of course he thereby has his right hand at the bridle, and this is another convenience.

The ancient manner of plowing made natural the use of certain kinds of measures of land. A team of eight oxen could not conveniently be turned often, but it had to be turned sometime if a field was to be plowed. And from time to time the oxen needed a rest from drawing. There came to be a conventional length for the furrow a team drew before being rested and then turned. Such a length survives in our furlong, as its name shows: it is a furrow-long. A ridge of land might thus be a furlong in length. In its turn the shape of the ridge helped determine that of another measure, the acre. The statute acre was once not simply a measure of area, but an area of a particular shape. It was a furlong (forty rods) in length by four rods in width. It contained one or more of the long, narrow ridges. It may also have borne some relation to the amount of land custom decreed should be plowed in a given length of time. The plow team did not as a rule work all day but only up to noon or into the early hours of the afternoon, and then the oxen were unyoked and sent to pasture or to the byre. Perhaps the half-acre of which *Piers Plowman* and many of the records speak was the amount of land which was expected in custom to be plowed in such a long morning's work. The acre itself, until fixed by statute, varied in size from district to district, from forest land to open country. Furthermore, it is important to remember one thing, that the furlong and the acre were measures of length and of area, not actual lengths and areas. Few plowed strips in the fields were just a furlong in length and four rods in width. Instead, they were more or less than a furlong in length, more or less than an acre in area, according to the soil and the lay of the land. Practical husbandmen could not have made them otherwise.

What happened when the big plow team reached the end of

the ridge? Commonly a strip was left at right angles to a group of ridges, and across their heads, called, indeed, a headland. On this the plow could be turned. The plowman would tilt the plow so that it came out of the ground, and the driver would put his hand on the leading yoke in order to lead the team around. But which way would he turn? If you look at the fields under ridge and furrow in England, you will observe that the ridges are usually not straight but curved and that they are usually curved in the form of a reverse letter S, that is, if you look along the ridges from one end to another, you will see that they nearly always bend to the left at the further end. Other people have observed this fact, have commented upon it, and have as usual found reasons for it. There is no need to go over them here, but one of the most convincing is the following. The driver of the plow team walked with his goad in his hand to the left of the team. What was more natural than that he should lead it around to the left when it came time to turn at the end of the ridge? In using a big team, the turn would begin before the end of the furrow, and in time the ridge itself would become curved.[20] But in the Middle Ages what is practical can never be distinguished from what is customary. Even if at some hypothetical origin the curvature of ridges was dictated by practical considerations, without doubt it was continued simply as a matter of custom. The practical was forgotten in the customary.

All this talk about medieval plows and plowing may be summed up in a curious Old English riddle, found in the Exeter Book, which is thus translated:

My nose is downward; I go deep and dig into the ground; I move as the grey foe of the wood guides me, and my lord who goes stooping as guardian at my tail; he pushes me in the plain, bears and urges me, sows in my track. I hasten forth, brought from the grove, strongly bound, carried on the wagon, I have many wounds; on one side of me as I go there is green, on the other side my track is clear black. Driven through my back a cunning point hangs beneath; another on my head fixed and prone falls at the side, so that I tear with my teeth, if he who is my lord serves me rightly from behind.[21]

The answer to the question "What am I?" is of course "A plow," and anyone who has read what has gone before will recognize the parts of a medieval plow which are described in the riddle, and the way the plow was used.

CHAPTER V

THE CHAMPION HUSBANDRY

SUCH WERE SOME of the important skills, techniques of husbandry known to Piers Plowman in the thirteenth century. So far they have been described simply as available knowledge: there has been little to say in detail about the ways in which they were actually put into effect. Conceivably the possible ways of putting them into effect were many. This we can appreciate from the history of the present time. Americans and Russians today know approximately the same techniques of farming. The Russians are making, as fast as they can, tractors just like the American ones. But the human group which puts the techniques into effect is in the United States what is called the individual farm, in the Union of Socialist Soviet Republics what is called the collective farm. The lesson to be read is that the particular application of any set of skills is determined not only by the skills themselves and by the physical environment in which they are used but also by the sentiments, traditions, ideals of the people who use them. In this way, the particular application of the skills of husbandmen in the champion country of England was determined in part by the social traditions of these husbandmen. For one thing, they live in big villages, of a certain kind, and for another, they lived in small families, of a certain kind. The practice of husbandry in the champion country cannot be considered in abstraction from the traditions of family and village.

First there is something to say about names. An Englishman today speaks of a village as a village. An American, or at least a New Englander, speaks of a village as a town. In this as in other matters he is more archaic in his language than the Englishman, because throughout the Middle Ages the English word for a village was *town*, and a villager was a townsman. The word *village* is no more than a French importation. In another way, too, the New Englander is more archaic than the Englishman. He uses the word *town* when he is thinking of the whole area belonging to a village, whether or not the whole area is covered with houses. He has such a notion as a township; the Englishman has not, unless it be the notion of a parish. But the Englishman's ancestors of earlier centuries would have been quite familiar with the notion of a township, not only as an area within definite boundaries but also as the unit of local government. In fact the reason why the notion is familiar to New Englanders is that, three centuries ago, some Englishmen of the old school came to America and did their best to organize towns like those they had known at home.

But the Englishman of the Middle Ages used the word *town* in two senses. Remember that the two characteristics of the champion country which at once impressed themselves upon travellers were, first, that the houses of men clustered together, and second, that outside this cluster of houses, the arable land lay in a great open expanse. Now the Englishman of the Middle Ages used the word town in the sense of township. But he used it also in a more restricted sense for the village proper, the cluster of houses about the parish church. With town in this sense he contrasted the open country which spread out around the cluster of houses. This he called field. The expression "town and field" became a formula. A man would speak of "all his chattels in town and field," meaning all the chattels he had anywhere in his township.[1] It would be pleasant to use in talking about English countrymen in the Middle Ages the words they used themselves. But most of the work in this field has been done by modern Englishmen, and therefore the custom is to speak of villages and villagers rather than of towns and townsmen.

The order here will be to speak first of the town and then of the field. In many modern English villages, the only medieval building that remains is the parish church. The church was the heart of the village. It was not only the house of God but also on occasion a storehouse, a courthouse, a prison, a fort. It was the strong place of the village. The bell in its tower told the men who were at work out in the fields of any alarm or excitement, as it told them that the Host had been elevated in the celebration of the mass. And just as the house of any man was set in a yard, so was the house of God. In the churchyard the villagers gathered for gossip after mass of a Sunday or for a fair or even for sports. Bishops throughout the Middle Ages denounced the use of the churchyard as a market-place and as a dancing-green for the boys and girls of a village, but they do not seem to have brought about the slightest change in the ancient practices. Here in the churchyard, too, the villagers were united in death as in life.

About the parish church, in the champion country of England in the Middle Ages as in north-eastern France today, clustered the houses of the villagers, sometimes in two long rows on either side of the village street, sometimes in other traditional forms. The present positions of its houses often reveal the ancient plan of a village. This clustering was what William Harrison referred to when he said that in champaine land the houses were "uniformelie builded in euerie town togither with streets and lanes" and were not scattered abroad as in woodland country. But the houses were not built literally together. They were not built wall to wall. Each was set in a narrow messuage or toft, which left some room for outbuildings and a garden. Behind the houses there would be certain closes or crofts, used perhaps by the villagers who held them to supply further herbage for the stock. "Toft and croft" is a phrase common in the charters. Tofts and crofts could be managed by their holders as they saw fit: they were not subject, like the open fields, to the control of village custom.

Such was the town, and now for the field, the open expanse of arable land which spread out around the houses and closes of a champion village. A study of the champion husbandry to which the field was submitted may well be begun by the study of more primitive husbandries which once existed in parts of England. In many regions of the world, it has for ages been the practice of people living by tilling the soil to cut and burn the brush off a piece of land and crop it for a number of years until the yield of grain becomes too small to be worth the effort of cultivation. Then they move on to another plot, and let the old one go back to grass or brush. This is the simplest form of the rotation of crops, and works reasonably well when the land is poor and there is plenty of it to spare.

Another stage of development is reached when some of the land is kept in permanent cultivation, and the rest cultivated as before in patches, each for a few years at a time. The land in permanent cultivation is probably as much as can be kept in heart by manure. In the villages of Sherwood Forest, as late as the eighteenth century, arrangements like this were in force. A small amount of land around the villages was permanently enclosed and kept in continuous tillage or pasture. Outside of this, "the rest lay open, common to the sheep and cattle of the inhabitants and the king's deer. It has been besides an immemorial custom for the inhabitants of townships to take up breaks, or temporary inclosures of more or less extent, perhaps from 40 to 250 acres and keep them in tillage for five or six years." [2] Wherever townships had the use of large tracts of wood or waste, arrangements like this were likely to be found. The system is called that of infield and outfield, these terms being borrowed from Scottish agriculture. In Scotland the infield was the land permanently in pasture or tillage; the outfield, often divided from the infield by a wall, was made up of patches of moor plowed up each for a few years at a time and sown with oats. The infield-outfield arrangements were a feature of the rough northern and western parts of the British Isles, but they were found also in England where conditions favored them. They appeared in Sherwood Forest. They appeared in the Breckland of south-western Norfolk and north-western Suffolk,[3] and *intakes*, enclosures for temporary cultivation, were made on the Yorkshire moors.[4] The words *breck*, *brock*, *brech*, alone or as elements in field-names, appear in many documents of the Middle Ages and mean land newly or for the time being enclosed and cleared.

Where villages were close together, where there was not an abundance of pasture for the support of the sheep and cattle of the township, and where all the soil was reasonably good, a more intensive agricultural regime was in force in England. This was the champion husbandry. It was first described by Frederick Seebohm in his classic, *The English Village Community*, and it has often been described since. Together with the organization of manors, it is that part of the social and economic order of the Middle Ages about which most is known. The only reason for describing it again here is that the other features of society cannot be understood except in relation to it. Even then, any new account of the champion husbandry may give a misleading impression because it must put more emphasis on the varieties of the system and less on its normal forms than would be proper in a first description. There were variations, but the striking thing is how many of the normal arrangements of the champion husbandry were found in all the champion part of England.

Outside the tofts and crofts of champion villages, the arable was divided into several great sectors, commonly into either two or three. These were the fields properly so-called. Often the villagers named the fields with reference to the direction in which they lay from the houses of the town. There would perhaps be a Northfield, a Westfield, a Southfield. These fields, or seasons, as they sometimes were called, were units in the rotation of crops. Suppose a village had three fields, which seems to have been the commonest arrangement. In a given year, one of these fields, all of it, would be plowed up in the fall and sown with winter corn — wheat and rye. At this time every villager who held land in that field would have to plant seed of that kind. As a matter of fact, we need not speak of this as if it were a matter of coercion; it would probably not have occurred to any villager to do otherwise. He would want to sow some grain every fall; the custom of the village simply determined the field in which he was to sow it. In the next spring, a second field would be plowed and sown to spring corn, that is, oats, barley, peas, beans, and vetches. (The spring-corn field was the one where, in the words of the folk-song, "oats, peas, beans, and barley grows." The folk-songs are village songs and reflect in the language of childhood many of the attitudes and interests of the open-field villages of England.) The third field would lie fallow all the year around, that is, from harvest to harvest. In the next year, the field which had been in winter corn would be planted with spring corn; the field which had been in spring corn would lie fallow, and the old fallow field would be planted with winter corn. And so on in succession, year after year and century after century. A husbandman would describe this rotation in his technical jargon as a three-course husbandry consisting of winter corn, spring corn, and a bare fallow.

When the village fields were only two, their management would be a variant of this. In one year, one of the fields would be sown to winter and spring corn and the other would lie fallow. In the second, the old fallow field would be tilled, the old tilled field lie fallow. And in the third year, the field originally tilled would be tilled again, with the difference that the part of the field which had been in winter corn two years before would probably now be in spring corn, the part which had been in spring corn, in winter corn.[5] Whether there were two fields or three, these dispositions gave representation to the two classes of grains known to Piers Plowman: those sown in the fall and those sown in the spring, and they made allowance for the only method he knew of restoring the fertility of any large part of his land. In every second or third year the land was simply let alone. Sometimes, instead of two or three fields, the arable of a village would be divided into a number of sections equal to a multiple of these numbers, such as four or six. The rotation of crops would still be basically in three courses, but it is likely that such arrangements were of late date.[6]

Whether a village was submitted to a two-field or to a three-field course depended in part on the goodness of its soil. The countrysides which stuck to two-field husbandry were upon the whole "the bleak, chalky, unfertile uplands." Where the loam of a village was richer, where it did not require so long a rest between periods of bearing crops, the village was likely to be under a three-field regime. Under a three-field husbandry one-sixth less arable lies fallow through every year than under a two-field husbandry.[7]

Consider now this entry from a book of extracts from the court rolls of Fountains Abbey of the fourteenth and fifteenth centuries. It relates to Marton in Dishforth in the North Riding of Yorkshire:

Richard of Pobthorp, Richard of Eskilby, John Ward on the part of the freemen; John Robynson, Robert Hardyng, Peter Libi on the part of Lord Richard Scrope; Robert Thomson, Robert Dyconson, and William Ysacson on the part of the abbot are chosen with the assent of these men and of all the tenants to do and ordain as best they can to cast the field into three parts, so that one part every year be fallow.[8]

This passage gives no hint of what course of husbandry preceded at Marton this three-field arrangement. Perhaps it was a two-field course; perhaps it was something more primitive. But the passage shows that villages did change their field systems, and that, in this one instance at least, the change was made by a commission chosen with the consent of the tenants, in which the interests of the important landlords of the village were represented.

Several villages are known to have changed a two-field order for a three-field order during the course of the Middle Ages. That was the direction of progress. The records show these villages under one kind of husbandry at one date and under the other at a later date: at some time between the shift must have been made.[9] Many another village must have done the same thing, without its being revealed in any surviving documents. Some villages added a third field to their original two by a long process of clearing land and bringing it under tillage. Others redivided their two fields into three, having decided that soil and skill would be equal to the new demands put upon them. They hoped to make the same area yield more grain.

People are less likely drastically to change the regime under which they live than to introduce small novelties within its framework. A shift from two-field to three-field husbandry was one way of increasing in a village the area under cultivation. But there was another more simple method. That was the practice of sowing every year a part of that field which would in the normal course have lain fallow. This was called making an *inhoc, innam, ofnam*, or *intake*, one name being used in one part of England and another in another part. These words were also used of outfield lands brought into temporary cultivation. *Nam* is the root of an Old English word meaning to take, to seize; an *innam* was a piece of land taken into tillage when it would ordinarily have remained outside, either because it was a part of the fallow field or because it was part of the outfield.

The making of an *inhoc* was a breach in the customary husbandry of a champion village and often was not allowed to pass without challenge. Unusually full records survive of the manors of Ramsey Abbey and they will often be cited in these pages. One of these manors was Broughton, Hunts. An entry of 1290 in the court rolls of Broughton reads as follows:

The names of those who sowed in the fallow where the freemen and bondmen ought to have their common pasture [there follow the names of ten persons who had sown small amounts of land, none of them larger than three roods, apparently with peas]; and whereas the freemen and the whole town-ship testify that the lands aforesaid had been sown when that field was fallow, and that for twenty years past and more, accordingly it is allowed to said men that before the next court they seek the will of the lord Abbot therein, and if they do not, let them remain in mercy.[10]

Unquestionably the lord Abbot of Ramsey would allow his men to continue to sow in the fallow, provided they paid him a fine. At least that is what happened elsewhere.[11] It is well to notice that the lord's court was busy with the maintenance of the farming and other customs of the manor.

Sometimes men thought that their rights had been seriously infringed by an *inhoc* others had made, and trouble followed. So it happened at another Broughton — Broughton Hackett, Worcs. At an inquest held at Worcester in 1287, the following finding was reached:

On Friday after the translation of St. Thomas the Martyr [11 July 1287] at Broughton, the commonalty of the towns of Upton Snodsbury and half the town of Broughton came with their cattle to feed on their common of pasture of Broughton. The men of John Lovet had sown a tilth within the common, that is, in the fallow, and when they saw the cattle feeding on the tilth they came and tried to impound them. A quarrel arose over this, and Simon Fraunceys of Snodsbury, John, son of Osbert of Bryghlaston, and William Kelus of Snodsbury killed Thomas le Blak' in the conflict. Many others were present, but none of them is guilty.[12]

We know little about the way inhocs were made, except that they were commonly sown with spring corn and that they were often made by a minority of the villagers. Individuals who held land in the fallow field might well be glad to have it under crop. Of course they would have to fence the land in. They would have to have enough compost to keep it in good heart under this more intense cultivation. And they would have to have the consent of the neighbors. But inhocs may also have been made by the community as a whole, though if they were we know little about how they were managed. One thing is clear, that the practice of making inhocs, if kept up over a number of years, could lead to a more complicated rotation of crops than that of the two- or three-field husbandry, and perhaps to a redivision of the fields of a village. An inhoc was a relief from the strict champion system. No scheme governing the behavior of men is wholly simple and regular.[13]

Both in Broughton, Hunts., and in the other Broughton, in Worcestershire, the objection found to the practice of enclosing and sowing a few acres of the field that ought to lie fallow was that it interfered with the common of pasture of a village. To understand this objection one must be familiar with one of the most important provisions of the champion husbandry. As we know, Piers Plowman did not plant grasses as a field crop and so was forever short of fodder for his cattle. Such hay as he mowed in the water meadows of the river bottoms went toward feeding his stock through the winter; for the rest of the year the beasts had to go on rough pasture. Some villages, near fen or saltmarsh, near moor or forest, had plenty of pasture. Others had little or none, and what were such villages going to do to fill the lack?

They solved the problem by using their fields for pasture as well as for tilth. Remember that one of the fields of a three-field village was lying fallow throughout every farming year, and that the other two fields were fallow for some part of the year, one of them until the sowing of winter corn in the fall, and the other until the sowing of spring corn in the spring. On the fallows there was much to feed the stock: the stubbles of the last harvest, such grasses and weeds as chanced to seed themselves, and the grass of the parts of the fields which never were plowed — roadsides, low-lying places, other nooks and corners. After the sheaves had been carried in harvest, the cattle of all the villagers were turned onto the fallows. Indeed, the whole livestock of the village was turned onto them, under proper precautions. Cattle, for one thing, were sent on before sheep, because sheep crop close and leave nothing behind. So far as the weather allowed, the beasts ranged in common over the fallow pasture, until the time came for plowing. The winter-corn field was of course plowed in the fall; the spring-corn field was plowed after the winter corn was in the ground and again for sowing in the spring; the third field lay fallow all year long and it was left alone until the late spring and summer months, when the land was given the so-called fallow plowings to destroy the weeds. But by summer the other pastures were green, in wood, or moor, or marsh, and there was not so much need for the fallows.[14] The meadows were used for pasture in the same way as the fields.

After the hay had been cut and carried, at Lammas (August 1), the stock was put on the meadows to feed on the aftermath. From this custom, the meadows were often called Lammas meadows — in the old English farming year Lammas marked the end of hay-harvest and the beginning of corn-harvest. The meadows remained pasture land until early the next spring when the grass began to grow again — Candlemas (February 2) was the traditional time for closing them to the stock. From such meadows husbandmen can have had no rowen.

If people plowed and sowed a part of the fallow field, made an inhoc in it, they would cut down seriously the amount of pasture available for their neighbors' cattle, and the neighbors would be likely to object unless they themselves shared in the inhoc. Cattle would certainly be driven over the young corn and feed on it: this is what happened at Broughton Hackett in 1287. By the device of fallow pasture, a champion village helped solve the problem of keeping its cattle alive. On their part, the cattle that wandered over the fallows helped in some measure by their droppings to restore them to good heart. Even with the help of the fallow pasture, there was a danger that a village might be overstocked and its pastures ruined by over-grazing. Accordingly in many English villages the rule was that only such cattle should be allowed on the pastures as were actually "lying down and getting up," *couchant et levant* on each villager's tenement. Sometimes the actual number of head each villager was allowed to put on common pasture was stinted.

When the lawyers of the Middle Ages spoke of the arrangement which has just been described, they called it common of pasture. All the villagers in common had the right to put their cattle on the pastures of the village, and all the cattle were to feed on all the pastures, as well the natural rough pastures, the wastes, as the fallow pastures, the arable fields during the time when they were lying fallow. We may speak of the villagers turning their cattle onto the range of the village, and when the cattle were on the range, they ran as all cattle do, in a herd, "horn under horn" as the countrymen of the Middle Ages put it, just as they spoke of the intermingled strips in the common fields as lying "acre under acre." Under the champion husbandry, just as the fields were village fields, so the cattle ran in a village herd. And in some parts of England the increase of the herd was provided for just as it is on the ranges today, by allowing bulls to run free with the cows. This gave Chaucer a chance in the *Parson's Tale* to develop a neat simile for lecherous priests. He wrote:

Swiche preestes been the sones of Helie, as sheweth in the Book of Kynges, that they weren the sones of Belial, that is, the devel. / Belial is to seyn, "withouten juge;" and so faren they; him thynketh they been free, and han no juge, namoore than hath a free bole that taketh which cow that hym liketh in the town. / So faren they by wommen. For right as a free bole is ynough for al a toun, right so is a wikked preest corrupcioun ynough for al a parisshe, or for al a contree.[15]

If a literary simile may be taken as an accurate picture of the practice of husbandry, this passage from the *Parson's Tale* tells that a free bull was enough for a town, that he took what cow he liked in the town, and lastly that he was free, as it seems, to wander where he wished. If the free bull appeared only in literature, there would be good reason to be skeptical about him, but he appeared also in matter-of-fact legal documents, and with him was associated another animal of like function, the free boar. Free bull and free boar were technical legal terms. They were franchises: the right to keep a bull or a boar was the privilege of the lord, or one of the lords, of many a village, and the bull or boar was literally to be free. For instance, at Newington, Oxfordshire, in 1279, Robert de Clifford held a fee of five yardlands, with a manse and a mill:

and he has his free bull throughout the township in all fees and places.[16]

Even wider was the range of the free bull and boar of the lord of Eccles in Norfolk. According to an inquisition as to his rights and property, taken there in 33 Edward I:

he has free bull and boar, wherever they shall stray through the whole hundred of Happing, nowhere to be impounded.[17]

Interference with the freedom of the bull was a matter for a law-suit. Such a suit came before the king's justices in Eyre at the Michaelmas Term, 1232, and was thus set down:

Stephen de Haya was attached to reply to William Rossel wherefore he took his beasts and unjustly kept them against gage and pledge; and therein William pleads that although he ought to have in the township of Wickham [West Wickham, Cambs.] one boar and one bull to go freely through the fields and elsewhere, and they did go there as they ought and were accustomed to go, the same Stephen took those beasts unjustly and held them captive against gage and pledge, whence he is damaged, etc.; and therein he says that he ought to have those beasts free in all open land in that township, in meadow, corn, and everywhere else.[18]

The reason for the trouble was that both Stephen and William claimed to have the franchise of free bull and boar in West Wickham, and the case turned on which one of them was in fact entitled to it. There are many things we should like to know about free bull and boar which the legal records do not tell us. They do not tell whether the free bull and boar were used for the increase of the lord's herds only or were kept by the lord for the use of the villagers as well. They do not tell whether or not a free bull was enough for all a town, as Chaucer said. Unquestionably in some towns one was not enough. Jocelin of Brakelond, writing of the revenues of the cellarer of the Abbey of Bury St. Edmunds at the end of the twelfth century, complained:

Moreover the cellarer alone ought, or was accustomed to have, a free bull in the fields of this town; now they [the townsfolk] have many.[19]

Nor do the records tell whether or not any payment was made by the villagers to their lord for the use of his free bull. It is true that they were sometimes willing to pay to be free of the free bull, but the reason may have been that the free bull trampled their growing crops and could not be impounded, rather than that they were sick of paying the lord for the use of his bull. In the years 1309 through 1311, Henry de Bray, one of the chief lords of Harleston, Northants., made agreements with the Abbot of St. James outside Northampton and with Ralph de Bulmere (both were landlords in Harleston) and with the twenty-eight free tenants of the village, by the terms of which Henry was allowed to fence in every year two acres of pasture which had formerly been common every other year, and in return he gave up his "lordship of free bull and boar:"

so that neither the aforesaid Henry nor his heirs shall have henceforward forevermore a bull or boar in the fields of Harleston pasturing in common on corn or meadow.[20]

In later centuries, as perhaps in the thirteenth, the town bull was not kept by the lord of the manor but by a committee of villagers or by the parson. Of a town stallion or town rams there is no word. On all these matters new documents may yet inform us.[21]

If the fields of a village were to be used at one time as pasture and at another as arable, there had to be some means of keeping cattle on the fallows and out of the corn. Two such means were in use: herdsmen and hedges. More often than not, perhaps, each family designated one of its members to be shepherd for its own sheep. At least, the stipulation appears in many manorial cus-tumals that no tenement need send its shepherd to reap and carry the lord's corn: he could not be spared from his job. Sometimes each family may have had its own neatherd and swineherd. But practices varied throughout England, and it was also common for the men of a village to choose village neatherds, village shepherds, village swineherds, to keep the stock of all the village, and the neighbors assessed themselves for the wages of the common herdsmen. Thomas Tusser wrote of the disadvantages of the champion country:

> There swineherd that keepeth the hog,
>   there neatherd, with cur and his horne,
> There shepherd with whistle and dog,
>   be fence to the meadow and corne.[22]

He is speaking of champion husbandry as he knew it in the six-teenth century, but these arrangements were traditional and probably much older.

In some parts of the country and at least in the later centuries, the neatherd went down the village street in the morning early, blowing his horn, and each house along the way sent out its cattle to him. This practice may have had its influence on the form of villages. Many old villages have their houses set fairly close together on either side of the village street, and the street is often much wider than trade and traffic alone ever required it to be. The reason may be that at one time the street was also used as a pen for the village cattle. The herdsman or herdsmen then drove the village herd to pasture, in fen or wood or moor, if the village had pasturage rights in such places, or if the herd was to range the fallow fields of the village, then the herdsman's duty may have been to drive the cattle over all parts of the fields, so that all parts should be equally dunged. In the evening he brought the cattle back to the village, unless perhaps in summer he slept with them in the pastures. In winter, if the cattle were in the byre, his work ceased.

Only rarely do the records open a window on the life of the herdsmen in the fields, and then only by the way, as an incident to more important matters. Here, in an inquest of 1251, the herdsmen of Sudborough, Northants., are seen sitting together at their noon-day meal under a hedge in the field. Their beasts, we can guess, are in the fields around them:

Henry, son of John of Sudborough, the shepherd, says that as he was sitting at his dinner on Whitsunday under a hedge in the field of Sudborough, and with him William, son of the winnower, and William Russel, herdsmen of the cattle of the town of Sudborough, and Roger Lubbe of Denford, cowherd of the lord, his fellow herdsmen, came William of Drayton by them in a tunic green in hue with a bow and arrows; and two others whom he knew not, with bows and arrows, came with William.

He says also that after them came a horseman on a certain black horse carrying a fawn before him on his lap, and he carried venison behind him covered with leaves.

He says also that after them came two pages leading eight greyhounds of which some were white, some tawny, and some red.[23]

These men were suspected of doing evil in the royal forest, and the herdsmen who had seen them were carefully examined before the steward of the forest and the foresters. Here is a scene characteristically medieval: the neatherds of a village sitting at their meal under a hedge in the fields and encountering a party of huntsmen who have been making free with the king's deer.

The second means of keeping cattle on the fallows and out of the corn was hedges. When one of the fields of a village had been sown, hedges were set up around it to keep off the cattle. The records do not make plain the precise nature of these hedges. They were not hedges in the modern guise, live hawthorne hedges, at least not in large part. Instead they were dead hedges made of stakes and brushwood, and many villagers had the right to take wood from their lord's wood for this purpose — the right called *heybote*. For *hedge* was not even the word commonly used in Middle English for such a brushwood hedge, but *haya*, to give it the Latin form. Its descendant in modern English is the word *haha*. A charter (*c.* 1221–29) recording an agreement between William de Hamptone and Oseney Abbey concerning

Hampton Poyle, Oxon., tells us something about these hedges. William granted to the monks:

that the *brecca* next the church of Hampton, by which an entrance is made to the north field of the same town, shall lie open in the fallow time, and by it the beasts of the same canons shall be able always to pass without hindrance when that field lies untilled, as is contained in a chirograph made between us concerning that and other matters. When, however, the field is tilled, then a stile shall be made in the aforesaid *brecca*, by which the men and servants of said canons can always pass without hindrance along the path of that field.[24]

This passage implies that much of the hedge around the open fields of a village was kept standing from year to year. But there were certain gaps, breaches, in the hedge, and these were opened or closed to allow or deny the passage of animals, according as the fields were lying fallow or were under crop.

When a field was sown, each villager had the duty of setting up a certain amount of hedge around its boundary, along the roadways or elsewhere. If we may judge from what was later the practice, he had to set up hedge wherever the edge of one of his own lands was also the edge of the field. Or better, he had to see that a certain amount of hedge was in order and all the gaps in it closed. Many a villein also had to hedge around his lord's demesne a number of perches proportionate to the size of his holding, and fines levied on villagers for failure to close their shares of the hedges appear in the rolls of manorial courts. In a court of 1300 at King's Ripton, Hunts., one of the Ramsey manors, the jurors of the court found:

that Ivo in le Hyrne has an opening toward the field to the damage and hurt of the neighbors. Therefore Ivo is in mercy, 3 d.[25]

Again at Halesowen, Worcs., an entry of 27 March, 1281, in the court rolls records that five people were in mercy and fined:

because they did not close their hedges at the proper time, whence the lord and the neighbors received damage, and they are enjoined under pain of a half-mark that the hedges be reasonably made within one week.[26]

When the hedges were set up around the tilled fields, and the gaps in them closed, began the *closed time* of which the records speak. The fields were then said to have been put *in defence*. When harvest was over, the hedges were thrown down once more, and the livestock of the village was allowed to batten on the stubbles. Then began the *open time*. There were rules about when the hedges were to be cast down as well as about when they should be set up, and breaches of these rules, as usual, were punished by fine in the manor court. At Minchinhampton, Glos., the following appears in the court rolls of 1273:

Alan of Forwood is accused of this, that he had his hedges around the field of Westfield carried off before the term, who replies and says that the reapers and others carried off part of the hedges so that in many places there was an entry, so that cattle had a common entry before he carried off anything.[27]

This entry is phrased even less felicitously than is usual in the country-made legal language of the court rolls, but the charge and the defence are plain enough. Why the fields of the champion country were always spoken of as open fields ought now to be obvious. The fields were in themselves huge. The hedges which surrounded them were in part thrown down as soon as harvest had been carried. Finally, the fields were fenced only at their boundaries. Since every villager sowed the same crops as his neighbors, in the same places and the same times, there was no need for dividing the fields by hedges into smaller units, and such hedging would have taken time. Unhappily for consistency, these statements are too sweeping. There was at least one village — and where there was one which we know of, we may be sure that there were others which we do not know of — which had many small fields, and these fields were enclosed with ditches and live hedges; they were permanently fenced in. At the same time the fields were divided into three groups and submitted to the usual three-course rotation of crops. This village was Tittenhanger, Herts., in the early years of the reign of Edward III.[28] Hertfordshire, to be sure, was on the edge of the champion country, where a mixture of champion practices with enclosure might well be found. In a purely champion country, like Oxfordshire, the fields may have been more nearly open.

When there were unwarranted breaches in the hedges, when cattle strayed and got through the hedges into the corn, it was the duty of one of the most important officers of a village to see that the breach was mended, to impound the cattle. This officer was the hayward, the warden of the hedges, in Low Latin the *messor*. He corresponded to the fence-viewer of old-time New England towns. But the hayward's duties included more than this, and there will be time to consider him later in his joint capacity of village official and servant of the lord.

The champion husbandry articulated the management of the fields of a village, the management of its cattle, and the management of its hedges. The seasonal changes in these elements fixed the rhythm of the year in the countryside, and in an agricultural civilization like that of England in the Middle Ages, that was the rhythm of all life. From the end of harvest, about Michaelmas (September 29) — Michaelmas was in fact held to mark the ending of the farming year — let us follow what happened to each of the three fields of a champion village as the months went by. Few changes are needed to make this description fit the cycle of a two-field village. It is Michaelmas; all three fields are lying fallow, two of them with new stubbles. The beasts of the village are ranging over all three fields. At some time in October they are driven off the field that lay fallow throughout the year past; it is plowed and sown with the winter corn: wheat and rye, and the hedges around the field are closed. It is put in defence. Two fields are still fallow pasture. At some time in early spring — Candlemas (February 2) is the traditional date — the beasts are driven off one of these fields, that is, the one which was in winter corn the year past. Indeed they may have been driven off earlier, when this field was given a preliminary plowing before Christmas. In any case, it is now plowed and sown with spring corn, and the hedges around the field are closed. The two fields which are under crop will remain in defence until after the harvest has been carried in the autumn. There remains one field, which will continue as fallow pasture until October, except for two fallow plowings, perhaps in May and July. So the farming cycle ran, year after year, century after century, and to it the holiday and ceremonial cycle of the people became intimately bound.

CHAPTER VI

THE HOLDING AND THE COMMON PLOW

THE FORM of the champion husbandry was determined jointly by the skills of making a living from the land which were known to Englishmen of the thirteenth century and by the traditions according to which these Englishmen lived and worked together. So far the traditions by which men worked together as fellow villagers have been considered. A champion village has been described as if the village itself was the farming unit. And so in a sense it was: the fields were village fields; the cattle ran in a village herd; the herdsmen and the hayward were village officers. But this notion of the village as the cell of life in the country is clearly a fiction, useful only in a first approximate description. The village itself was made up of smaller cells — families. Next to be considered are the traditional dispositions whereby each family shared in the work and partook of the fruits of the village fields.

Perhaps the subject can be reached more surely in the end if it is approached from a distance, by way of a closer inspection of the open fields of a champion village. So far they have been considered as two or three great units in husbandry, but they were themselves divided into subordinate units. First, they were plowed into ridges. The ridges varied greatly in width from one part of England to another and somewhat also in length. Though they seldom ran to just one furlong, they were of that order of magnitude. But the furlong was not only a length; it was also an area. A group of ridges lying parallel and next to each other, so that they formed a squarish plot of ground, was called in some places a *furlong*, in others a *shott*, a *wong*, or, in Latin, a *cultura*. Across the head of the ridges in such a furlong, at right angles to them, a *headland* would often be laid out, which allowed the great plows room to turn and the villagers access to the different ridges. The headland would be the last part of a furlong sown and the first reaped.

The system of laying out fields had to be flexible enough to fit the natural features of the village. The furlong was a measure of length but not a measure of area. It was only the name of an area. Any group of contiguous and parallel ridges was called a furlong, but furlongs in this sense were most unequal in size, containing more ridges or fewer, longer ridges or shorter, as the lay of the land permitted. Sometimes if a piece of good land was to be taken into tillage, it could not be plowed as an oblong ridge, but only as a long triangle, tapering toward one end. Such a plot was called a *gore*, and the word gore has come to be applied to anything in the shape of a triangle with a short base and long altitude. In like manner, a *butt* was a ridge that did not run to the proper furlong in length, but stopped abruptly. A furlong, to accommodate itself to the terrain, would often contain gores and butts as well as proper ridges. The furlongs were the main subordinate divisions of the fields, and each furlong would be given a name of its own. A people who live close to the soil become conscious of every local variation in landscape and are rich in field names.

The means of measuring land used in the Middle Ages were in intimate relation with the way fields were laid out under the champion husbandry. And, at bottom, measures of land were measures of the amount of plowing to be done. When the teams went out in the morning to the fields to plow, the man whose duty it was to oversee their work, if it was work for the lord of the manor, measured out the land that they ought to plow in the day's or the morning's work. At least we must assume that this was what happened, because according to a roll of 1285 of a hallmote of Sevenhampton, Wilts.:

all the plowmen of the lord are in mercy because they suffered the plows to stand, contrary to the measure.[1]

Again, at Houghton, Hunts., in 1313, Geoffrey Lacy was fined 3 d. at the hallmote:

because without the licence of the lord and the bailiff he measured the land of the lord with his yard in contempt of the bailiff at the boon plowings.[2]

Geoffrey was probably setting his own standard of how much work was to be done instead of accepting the lord's.

The two ways of measuring land were with a rope, which

was the less common, and with a wooden pole, a rod, yard, or perch. From the means used in measurement came the names of the measures. The rod as a measure of length departed in one place or another from the sixteen and a half feet of the statute rod, but it was always of that order of magnitude. Each neighborhood had its customary rod. *Yard* originally meant any pole, a sail-yard for instance, and when it came to be used of measures there were a number of different yards. Our present yard comes from the cloth-yard, the yard used in measuring cloth. There was another yard used in measuring land, the land-yard, which was commonly of a length with the rod, and perhaps the customary and convenient size of the ox-goad set the length for both.

Since the length of any plot of land to be plowed was the length of the ridge, and that was conventionally one furlong, the area of such a plot was known to a very rough approximation when its width was measured. Accordingly in England the names of several measures of width became the names of measures of area as well. The rod is sixteen and a half feet long: the rood is that area which is a rod in width and a furlong in length. The same thing was true of the yard as a measure of area: it was a thin oblong of land, a strip in the open fields, one land-yard in width and a furlong in length, and therefore of the same area as the rood, because the rod and the land-yard were commonly of the same length. That the acre, the most important measure of area, may have borne some relation to the amount of land that custom decreed should be plowed in one day has already been argued, but its size was also related to the traditional system of measurement with rods, since there were regularly four roods in an acre. People have since generalized the use of these measures, until they are measures of any area, but they began by being the measures used in a particular system of laying out fields, the system of the champion husbandry.

This essay on surveying in the Middle Ages is in preface to the main matter. A villager of a champion township, with his family and household, was principally supported by the crops grown on a particular part of the land of the village, which was called his holding. Or by a direct translation of the word *holding* into Latin, it was called his *tenement*. It was spoken of as if it were something the villager actually held, like his sword or his plow. He himself was a holder, a tenant. The holding of a villager was the land which he and the members of his family tilled, in coöperation with his neighbors, and the land the crop of which he harvested, again in coöperation with his neighbors. To speak of his holding as his property is misleading. The word *property* has reference to the particular legal system of such countries as Great Britain at the present time; in speaking of the different legal system of the Middle Ages we must use the conceptions which then were current.

The farm of a modern husbandman is almost always a compact plot of land; a holding in a champion village was not. It consisted of several separate and separated parcels. One parcel was the site of the husbandman's house in the town proper, with the land around it or behind it, next to the houses of the other neighbors. This was the messuage or, as it was called in the North of England, the toft. Besides his toft, a villager would be likely to have somewhere near the houses of the town another close or croft. This, unlike his strips in the fields, he might manage as he wished. He might use it as pasture for his own stock, or plant it with what crops he pleased. The arrangement was a natural one. Nobody is comfortable if all his labors are determined by a plan, whether that plan be set by hallowed tradition or by a dictatorial government. A man must have some room to do the things he wants to do as an individual.

But the larger part of the holding did not consist of toft or croft. It consisted of a certain definite amount of arable land, which again was not in a single plot but lay in the form of strips scattered all over the great fields of the village. The parcels of land were strips because each was made up of one or more of the long ridges made in plowing. Between the strips of one man and those of his neighbors would lie only the furrows between ridges. Under these conditions a man who was un-scrupulous in plowing might easily guide his share so that it cut into his neighbor's strip and gathered land to his own. In *Piers Plowman*, Avarice is describing himself as if he were a villager. Said Avarice:

> And yf ich ȝede to þe plouh · ich pynchede on hus half acre,
> Þat a fot londe oþer a forwe · fecchen ich wolde,
> Of my neyhȝeboris next · nymen of hus erthe.
> And yf y repe, ouere-reche · oþer ȝaf hem red þat repen
> To sese to me with here sykel · þat ich sew neuere.[3]

One of the charms of *Piers Plowman*, and one of the things which substantiate its value, is that the abuses it condemns can often be illustrated by actual events as they were recorded in legal documents. Thus at a hallmote of 1287 at Alrewas, Staffs.:

An inquest says that Ralph Quintin cut down two oaks of Geoffrey, Hugh's son, unjustly, and removed a mete between them and occupied two furrows unjustly of his land and therefore is in mercy, and said Geoffrey, because he occupied for himself one half-foot, is therefore in mercy.[4]

In champion villages the question of bounds was always acute. In the absence of hedges or ditches separating the strips of the neighbors, stakes or mearstones were let into the soil at the ends of the strips, to mark their boundaries. But bad neighbors would move bounds; boundary disputes were constantly coming before manorial courts. At Upwood, Hunts., one day in 1318, several people were fined for placing bounds "without precept of the court." The entry in the court roll goes on:

And the bailiff and the reeve are ordered to take with them the whole homage of the lord, as well of Great Raveley as of Upwood, and go thither. And let them oversee until each of the aforesaid persons has his lands as he ought by right to have them and then let them place between them sure metes and bounds, so that henceforth no complaint or quarrel be made therein.[5]

The people of a village of England in the Middle Ages were divided not only into families, but also into social classes, of different degrees of wealth and consideration. In fact the notion that at any time in their history the Germanic tribes consisted of a mass of substantially equal freemen — a theory which was once a favorite — has gone the way of other similar theories, for instance that of primitive communism. In most villages the number of the main social classes was two. There will be much more to say on this matter later, but a first sketch must be made now. The more substantial villagers were called the *husbonds*, or at least they were so called in north-eastern England. They were the bonds who had houses, in contrast with the villagers of the poorer sort, who were called cotters or cotmen, because their dwelling-places were only cots or cottages. In the thirteenth century a husbond was not simply a married man, but a man of a certain class, a substantial farmer. From this second meaning of the word we derive of course the word *husbandry*.

This division of villagers into two main classes seems to have been common in many parts of Europe under the old peasant social order and to have been determined fundamentally by an economic cleavage. In ancient France, for instance, the two classes were called the *laboureurs* and the *manouvriers*. The laboureurs were the substantial farmers, who had tenements large enough to enable them to keep plow-oxen; the manouvriers were the poorer peasants, who had only their hands with which to work. The laboureurs would lend the manouvriers their oxen for use in tilling the small holdings of the latter. And in return the manouvriers supplied the laboureurs with the spare hand-labor which the latter required on their larger lands. A considerable amount of mutual help between the two classes was maintained, together with a considerable amount of mutual distrust.[6] The relation between the husbonds and the cotters of England may have been much like that between the laboureurs and the manouvriers of France.

One of the most interesting facts of the social order of medieval England must now be considered. In many a village the tenements of villagers fell into definite classes according as they were larger or smaller, and what is more, the tenements within each of these classes tended to be equal in size. There were standard tenement units, and we know that they were recognized as such by the villagers, since they were called by special names. In the first approximation — and in any exposition of something complex we must proceed by successive approximations — it is safe to say that there were two main classes of tenement units, as there were two main classes of villagers. These two main classes were also the two recognized in the first instance in the language of the people. To take first the terms used in champion villages of the South of England, the large tenement units were called *yards* or *yardlands*, in Latin *virgatae terrae*. Though the size of the yardland varied from village to village — each village had its own standard yardland — a good average size to remember is thirty acres. The men who held each one yardland were often called *yardlings* (*virgatarii*).[7]

The smaller tenement units were the *cotlands*. These were of the order of five acres or less in size, each having little or no land in the open fields and in the village proper only the cot or cottage from which this class of holding took its name. The cotlands were held by the cotters, the cotsetles, the cotmen, as they were variously called — the poorer sort of villagers. Often there were sub-classes of tenements, as half-yardlands and quarter-yardlands, or the tenements were of irregular sizes — this is the correction which brings the first statement closer to the reality.

The yardland was the name for the standard tenement in champion villages in the southern part of England; the *oxgang* (*bovata*) was the name of the standard tenement in the North. (Scholars have got into the habit of using derivatives of the Latin names for the tenement units, of speaking of virgates and bovates, but there are old English names for them, yardlands and oxgangs, and the sense of being close to the villagers' point of view may be heightened by using the words they used themselves.) The oxgang tended to be smaller than the yardland; in other respects its position in the village economic organization was the same. The oxgang of one village might be larger or smaller than the oxgang of another, but within any given village all oxgangs were of a size. Each of the more substantial villagers, the husbonds, would hold one oxgang, or more often each would hold two.

The yardland and the oxgang divided between them the part of England which in the Middle Ages was strictly champion country. If you plot on a map the area in which the documents show that the common tenement unit bore one name and the area in which it bore the other, the map will reveal that, upon the whole, the oxgang ruled in the country north of a line drawn from the Wash to the Mersey.[8] Lincolnshire, northern Leicestershire, Derbyshire, and the shires north of them were oxgang country. The rest of champion England was yardland country. Between, a narrow debatable land was found, where there were both oxgangs and yardlands. The line between the two may go back to a boundary between ancient Anglo-Saxon kingdoms, but it is not important in later social history. Substantially the same social and economic system reigned in southern Leicestershire as in northern.

In the customs of land measurement in medieval England, the oxgang and the yardland were both fixed parts of larger units.

In the North eight oxgangs made a *plowland* (*carucata*), and in the South four yardlands made a *hide*. Since the plowland and the hide were of the same order of magnitude — 120 acres is a good average figure to remember — the oxgang tended to be about half the size of the yardland. Plowlands commonly went with oxgangs, and hides with yardlands, but not always. Sometimes plowland was simply another name for hide. The area assigned in different places to the plowland and the hide varied with a number of circumstances in a way which has never been satisfactorily worked out. The most important circumstance was probably that the plowland was the amount of land which one plow team was expected in custom to till in one year's work. Agricultural experts of the thirteenth century spoke as if this was the case,[9] and the name of the plowland seems to confirm them. As such, the size of the plowland must have varied with the character of the soil of a village and with the field system in force there, whether two-field or three-field. Perhaps its size also depended on fiscal considerations: it was a unit for the assessment of taxes and other charges. What is more interesting, *hide* may be derived from an old word meaning *family*, and before the Conquest the hide may have been thought of as the customary allotment of one family. But in the thirteenth century the hide and the plowland were important as measures of the size of large estates, not as holdings of individual villagers. Only a few wealthy villagers would hold so much land. The origins of these units may seem important to us; they were not to the townsfolk.

Disregarding for the moment the yardland and the hide, let us consider the oxgang and the plowland. The agricultural writers of the thirteenth century spoke of the plowland as the amount of land which could be properly tilled by one plow team in a year. And the commonest plow team of the thirteenth century was one of eight oxen. In view of these facts, is it not significant that the oxgang and the plowland bore the names they did and that there were eight oxgangs in every plowland? Early in the investigation of the champion husbandry, people suggested that the oxgang was that tenement which supported one ox and sent it to a common team of eight oxen, and that the plowland of eight oxgangs was tilled by this common team made up of one ox from each oxgang. The same sort of thing was said of the yardland, that each yardland sent two oxen, a yoke, to the common team of eight from the hide.

Whatever may have been the original dispositions, in point of fact in the thirteenth century such a neat regularity is almost never recorded, though there are sometimes hints of it. In an extent of the manors of Baldwin Wake, taken in 10 Edward I, the services due to the lord from his bondmen in Bransdale in Kirkby Moorside, Yorks., are detailed. There William Gondi held a messuage and two oxgangs of land. The entry continues as follows:

And his three neighbors with their oxen, joined to himself and his oxen, shall plow for one day at the winter sowing, and his work is worth a penny. . . . He shall plow at the Lent sowing for two days in the manner as above.[10]

Each of William's three neighbors held two oxgangs, like himself, so that in this instance eight oxgangs in fact made up one plow team between them. Whether or not each of the neighbors sent just two oxen to the common team does not appear.

That one of the common village holdings, a yardland or an oxgang, could not usually support a full plow team, even if the team were of less than eight oxen, is plain, though there are exceptions even to this rule.[11] A husbandman had to pool his oxen with those of his neighbors to make up a common team, or he had to borrow or hire oxen. All of these arrangements were common practice, and something must be said about each of them, in their many variations. But this must first be remembered, which is true of all sorts of information about villagers in the Middle Ages: the documents tell us for the most part what a villager was bound to do when he was working for his lord. That he worked in the same way when working with his neighbors or on his own account is an assumption. Occasionally, though only occasionally, it is supported by facts. For instance, there is no doubt that the standard set by a husbandman when he was working for himself was often the standard of what his work for the lord ought to be. He was expected to plow the lord's land only in the weeks when he was plowing his own, or to come to plow the lord's land with as many head of oxen as he yoked in plowing his own.

When a husbandman was unable to make up a plow team from

the beasts of his own tenement, there was no rule about how many of his fellows he went into partnership with. Sometimes two, sometimes three, sometimes four, sometimes eight villagers formed a joint team.[12] The evidence suggests that the commonest team was of eight oxen, but there was no regularity as to how the team was made up, no regularity as to the number of head furnished by each tenement. This is but natural. The accidents of husbandry would be likely to prevent a yardland from being able to send just one yoke, no more and no less, to the common team, year after year. An able yardling in a good year would be able to send more, a poor yardling in a poor year would not be able to send as many or would be unable to send any at all. The statement of the services of a yardling at Barton-in-the-Clay, Beds., in a Ramsey inquest of 39 Henry III, puts the case:

Each Friday, however, in the aforesaid time [Michaelmas to Christmas], if he has his own plow team he will plow a half-acre, and when it shall have been sown, he will harrow it. If, however, he does not have a full plow team of his own, he will plow the land of the lord with as many beasts as he plows his own with. Four men or eight, if need force them, may indeed be joined at the plow, if their means reach no further, and they will be quit of the plowing of a half-acre as if said common plow was that of one man.[13]

Sometimes when four tenements are making up an eight-ox team in the neatest possible way, it nevertheless turns out that they are not yardlings but half-yardlings, so that a plow team is being made up out of a half-plowland, instead of out of a whole plowland, as it should be to correspond with theory. Thus on one of the manors of the Bishop of Ely, Horningsea in Ditton, Cambs., one of the entries of the bishop's custumal of 1277 runs:

Roger Holdeye holds fifteen acres which make a half-yardland. . . . And furthermore he will plow within the same time [Michaelmas to August 1] every Monday until noon for one work, in such manner that he and three other men, his fellows, will make one plow team with eight beasts.[14]

Lastly, on some of the manors of Ramsey Abbey, the number of men who pooled their plow beasts to make a common plow team varied with the season of the year. More men joined together in partnership in spring and summer than in winter, that is, the medieval winter, before Christmas. Perhaps after the cold weather, after a winter in the byre, the cattle were weaker and more of them had to be hitched to the plow. Perhaps, as winter came on, the husbandman slaughtered one or more of his plow oxen, because he was not going to be able to feed them through the winter. Then he would have fewer oxen in the spring, and more men would have to join together to make a full team. These are speculations; what the real reasons were, whether these or others, we do not know. But the fact is plain. At Upwood, Hunts., for instance, among the services of a yardling in 1252 were these:

At wheat sowing he will plow one land alone without a fellow, for his yard-land, and at barley sowing, as his plow team is joined with others, he will plow one land and harrow it; and thus he himself and his partners will be quit of the plowing of said land.[15]

The disputes which arose about joint plowing are often the means of revealing to us that joint plowing existed. Breaches of covenants men had made to plow jointly with their oxen or horses gave rise to suits before manorial courts. For instance, an entry in a court roll of 1338 of Alton, Hants., is this:

Nicholas Upechepyng was summoned to answer Henry Astil in a plea of covenant. And the same Henry complains therein that said Nicholas did not keep a covenant with him, in this that he agreed with Henry, in the village of Alton on Monday next after the Feast of All Hallows in the eleventh year of the reign of King Edward who now is, that he would find three horses for Henry's plow from the Monday aforesaid until the Christmas following in the same year, which covenant he broke to Henry's damage of 20 s., and thereupon etc. And said Nicholas defends etc. and wholly denies the aforesaid covenant and thereupon he wages his law six-handed.[16]

So it was in the South, and so also in the North. At a court held at the Bridge of Rastrick, in the West Riding of Yorkshire, in 1286, among the proceedings were these:

It is found by an inquest of neighbors that Richard of Tothill was the companion of Roger of the Wood to plow jointly with his plow, and at the time of plowing cast him off, so that his land lies untilled. Therefore, let him make satisfaction to him for the damages, which are taxed at 10 s.[17]

People were, as is natural, unwilling to plow with neighbors who did not bear a good character. In 1275, at the time of the taking of an inquest for the Hundred Rolls, John of Fulbeck complained of injustices which had been done him by Geoffrey de Turnai, bailiff of the Isle of Axholme in Lincolnshire, saying, among other things:

Such hurt did he do him that this John could not find in the town of Belton a single neighbor who dared yoke one ox in a plow with him because of his [the bailiff's] forbiddance and power.[18]

What happened to the poor wretches who had no plow cattle of their own and so could not join with neighbors in making a common team? Such might be those men whose holdings were not large enough, whose rights of common of pasture were not extensive enough to allow them to support plow oxen. But through misfortune or mismanagement even villagers who were potentially more wealthy might be in this case. Even yardlings were sometimes without plow oxen. An entry in the court rolls of 1293 of King's Ripton, Hunts., is this:

John William's son is attached by the pledges of John Dyke and Nicholas in the Nook because he does not come to the lord's plowing, which John comes into court and says that he has no beast of his own wherewith he can plow but only borrowed beasts, wherein he says and alleges that so long as he borrows beasts for plowing he is not bound to answer to the lord for any plowing, and thereupon he puts himself upon the Ramsey Register. And therefore let the Register be inspected before the next court.[19]

The Ramsey Register was the book in which were entered all the rents and services owed to the abbot by his tenants. John William's son was appealing to it for confirmation of his claims, and other tenants are to be found doing the same thing. The Register has not survived, but some of the inquests, made by juries of villagers, from which the Register was compiled were included in the Ramsey Cartulary, and this has come down to us. The reason why the tenants showed such confidence in the Register may have been that it was based on the sworn testimony of men of their own class.

Sometimes there were suits involving damages done to plow beasts while they were in the hands of a borrower. At a hallmote of Polstead, Suffolk, in 1292:

Robert le Coc comes and complains of the aforesaid Philip [Denelind] and says that the aforesaid Philip received a certain horse from him in a certain covenant, namely, that the aforesaid Philip should keep the aforesaid horse and pasture it and harness it in the plow. Moreover he says that Philip beat the aforesaid horse and bound a stone onto the ear of this horse, and he ought to render to the aforesaid Robert one day's work of plowing.[20]

According to the last clause, either Philip had agreed to do some plowing for Robert in return for the use of the horse or he was bound to make up the damages by doing plowing. The fact that the amount of land a team was expected to plow in a day was everywhere fixed in custom made it easy to use plowing as a sort of payment in kind. Fines in manorial courts were often levied in the form of so many days' work in plowing. Why the rock was tied onto the poor horse's ear is dark to us.

Sometimes the borrowing of plow oxen was not with the consent of their owners, but without such consent and by stealth. An entry in the court rolls of Newington, Oxon., for 1278 is the following:

They say [that is, all the villeins] that John Grug and Geoffrey his brother took without consent the beasts of good men by night on the eve of Michaelmas and plowed two acres and a half, that is, with three plows. An inquest is taken to find whether or not Richard of Berwick lent these two his plow, and the inquest says: not in that time.[21]

How plowing was done successfully at night is again beyond those of us who are not dirt farmers, but other evidence confirms that people did plow at night and by stealth.

If a man could not borrow beasts of the plow, and had money, he could contract with other men to plow his land or even to do the plowing services he owed his lord. In its specification of the services owed by the tenants of Somersham, Hunts., the Ely custumal of 1222 laid down this rule:

And be it known that if by chance anyone holding a yardland has nothing in a plow team because of his poverty, he is bound to plow with his pence nine acres a year.[22]

Even a yardling might be short of oxen. On the other side we are told of men who "take money for the plowing of other people's land." [23]

But what, at last, of the man who was so poor that he was able neither to support plow oxen on his holding nor to hire them? Perforce he delved up his land with a spade. If a man's holding was small, he could prepare all of it for seed with a spade. Adam, who, as the father of mankind, stood in medieval mythology for the ordinary father of a family, was a delver. As usual we must guess, from what he did for his lord, what the husbandman did for himself when he lacked plow oxen. At Banstead in Surrey in 1325, the services due by villagers to the lord were such that:

if he does not have a plow team each tenant of a yardland ought to delve four dayworks.[24]

The possibility is once again contemplated that even a yardling might not have plow oxen. The *daywork*, like the acre and the rood, was a measure of area, but it was a smaller area than these, because it probably represented the amount of land customarily delved, not plowed, in one day.

What certainly has not been established by all this evidence is that each oxgang sent one and only one ox to a common team of eight oxen for the plowland, each yardland one and only one yoke to a common team of eight oxen for the hide. Such a neat and seemly arrangement was found sometimes, but only rarely. In the thirteenth century, the varieties of common plow teams were many, whatever they may have been at an earlier age. But the important thing is the fact of common plowing, not the forms of common plows, and this fact cannot be contested. There were plenty of husbandmen, even the more substantial ones, who were not able to support on their tenements a full draught of oxen apiece. Such husbandmen, in groups of two or more, would become partners, or *marrows*, as men would have said in the North,[25] and pool their oxen to form common teams, which then plowed the lands of all the partners. This was one of the practices which made it a matter of indifference whether a villager had his land in a single parcel or in scattered strips: the common plow team had in any case to move about from the lands of one of the partners to those of the others.

In any community where people are poor and the struggle to make a living is hard, mutual help must be a matter of course if the community is to survive. In a community of husbandmen, lending tools or animals and working in company with neighbors to get a job done which is beyond the resources of a single family are among the most familiar practices. In old New England, there was the custom of holding bees, according to which a man might call in his neighbors to help him do some heavy piece of work, such as raising the frame of a new barn. In the same way, in English villages of the Middle Ages, coöperation in farm work was the basis of village life. And inasmuch as plow beasts were the most important single means of carrying on husbandry, their hiring, borrowing, and the customs of joint plowing were a large part of this coöperation. A complicated code of borrowing obtains in most farming communities, even though it is formulated only half explicitly. For the loan of a tool, an animal, a day's work, a neighbor expects to be able to ask and receive at some later time a service to be done for him, not necessarily a service of the same sort. The reciprocities are not strictly measured, but are based on what is felt to be customary. Without these traditions of exchange of help, making a living from the soil would have been much harder than in fact it was. They must have been supported by strong sentiments of confidence and good will among neighbors — neighborhood (*vicinitas*) as the villagers of England called them.[26] In champion country, the village was the social group on which these customs of mutual help were binding.

CHAPTER VII

VILLAGE PLANS AND PLANNING

WITHIN THEIR DIFFERENT classes, the tenement units of villagers tended to be equal in area. This equality may have been accompanied at one time by a sentiment on the part of the villagers that the tenements ought to be equal, but expressions of such a sentiment do not appear on the records. Here is one instance of the disadvantage in which the student of a dead society finds himself as compared with his colleague who can talk with the people he is describing. The latter could easily bring such a sentiment to expression, if it existed in villagers of the present time. But the equality of the village tenements, class by class, was not solely a matter of the area of arable land belonging to each tenement. It was a thoroughgoing equality in the use of all the resources of the village. The arrangement may be described in this way: the resources of the village were divided into shares; one man might have more of these shares than another, but the shares themselves were equal.

For one thing, there was the matter of *assarts*. So far villages have been described as if their fields were fixed in size once and for all. Of course this was not the case. During the early Middle Ages, up through the thirteenth century, great efforts were made to bring new land under the plow, in fen, in moor, in wood. People were making what they called in French *assarts*, in English of the North *riddings*. They were clearing land.[1] Assarts were sometimes made wholesale, through the efforts of enterprising and wealthy landlords, such as the great Cistercian abbeys, founded in the twelfth century. They made whole districts profitable. Sometimes the lord of a manor enclosed and reclaimed a part of his waste. If he did so, he was bound by the statutes of Merton and of Westminster to leave pasture sufficient to support the beasts of his free tenants. Sometimes individual villagers assarted, with the help or permission of the lord. But sometimes also a village made a community enterprise of the work of clearing land and bringing it under tillage.

Thus in the Estate Book of Henry de Bray, an entry of 1308 describing certain pieces of land in Harleston, Northants., speaks of:

the whole portion of heath, when by agreement of the community of the township it shall be broken up, which I kept by me of one half-yardland which belonged to Beatrix, daughter of Richard the clerk.[2]

This heath was pretty clearly not an assart in the strict sense of the word. Rather it was an intake, a piece of land cultivated for a few years and then allowed to go to grass. But it is likely that many assarts began by being treated as intakes and only in course of time became permanently arable. The important facts which this entry reveals are that the cultivation was undertaken by agreement of the community of the township and that a half-yardland had the right to a definite "portion" of the land cultivated.

Sometimes, when the lands held by the men of a village are described in a custumal, many or all the villagers are shown to have held each a small bit of *forlond*, that is, in a common meaning of the word, assart. Each of them was bringing a small piece of land under tillage. Sometimes these pieces of land, though all small in size, were not in proportion with the tenements to which they pertained. But sometimes they were, and sometimes the documents make it clear that when a man made an assart, all his neighbors holding like tenements were allowed to make assarts of the same size.[3] In the time of Henry II, an oxgang of arable in Spaldington, Yorks., was granted to the nuns of Ormsby, with the following provision:

If it happens that the bounds of the tilled land be extended further than they now are, their oxgang will be increased as much as the other oxgangs are increased.[4]

Just as a half-yardland at Harleston had a right to a definite portion of the heath when it was taken under cultivation, so an oxgang at Spaldington shared equally with the other oxgangs in any increase of the tilled land of the village. The tenement units were equals, class by class, not only in the land of old arable but also in any new opportunities for economic exploitation. By these arrangements, assart land could easily be brought within the scheme of the champion husbandry. Each villager would have a small piece of new land, presumably a strip, which could be incorporated at once, if convenient for other reasons, with the other intermingled strips in the open fields. One hypothesis, indeed, explains the scattering of the strips of a tenement as the result of a long period in which the fields of a village were extended by assarting. Another thing to be noticed is that no new oxgangs or yardlands would be formed by assarting. The old tenement units would simply grow in size.[5]

In the treatment of meadow, too, the equality of the tenement units in economic opportunity was maintained. For reasons which have been considered, hay was scarce in the Middle Ages. It was not a cultivated crop. It grew only in natural meadows, as in the river bottoms, and was worth at least twice as much per acre as arable land. With each oxgang or yardland would go perhaps two acres in the meadows of the village. But often, unlike the strips of the arable, these two acres would not be a particular two, year after year. Often they were the two acres which fell to the holding every year by some scheme of drawing lots. Whether or not this arrangement was determined by the great value of meadow land, acting in concert with a sentiment that all holders of tenements of a certain class ought to be economic equals, we do not know. Nor do we know whether it was further supported by the consideration that hay-fields were neither tilled nor manured, so that there was no question of robbing a man of the fruits of his enterprise if he were assigned a different piece of meadow every year. Villagers probably never expressed such sentiments, but took the arrangements for granted, as part of a settled order. The fact is beyond doubt that village meadows were often lot-meadows.[6]

Besides his messuage, his arable, and his meadow, a villager had various other rights of use over the lands of the village. He sent his cattle to graze on its pastures, his pigs to batten in its woods of beech and oak. In the open time, all his livestock, from plow oxen to geese, wandered over the stubbles of the village. In its woodlands he cut wood for house, hedge, and fire. He dug peat in its turbaries. He had also the right to hunt over the village lands.[7] Within the village boundaries he expected to find what would meet most of his needs.

Accordingly, in an age of subsistence farming, villages were laid out so that they should be so far as possible self-sufficient. Villages are no longer units in farming and government and so no longer have definite boundaries, but parish boundaries often follow the ancient village boundary lines, and they have much to tell about the old village economy. Thus Ewell, in Surrey, was shaped as a rough rectangle, stretching from the top of a ridge of downs to the bottom of a river valley, so that the village contained within its limits both upland pastures and low-lying meadows, with sound arable in between.[8] Like reasons, in a different setting, determined the bounds of Fleet in the south-eastern corner of Lincolnshire. The houses of Fleet were set on the low ridge that rises between the Wash and the Fens, and the village lands lay in a long strip across the ridge, from the salt marsh on the sea side to the Fens on the other, the tilth lying in between.[9] At the forgotten day when the boundaries of the villages first were set, they were set so that each village would contain a measure of each of the assets of the environment.

In any primitive or in any ancient and stable society, the behavior of men may fall into patterns which appear to be more elaborate than there is any need for them to be. To an observer, the patterns often look as if they had been elaborated for their own sake, though of course this is not a satisfactory way of describing how in fact they were developed. In the Middle Ages, this tendency may be illustrated in the matter of village plans. Today by town planning we mean the process of making rules to which a town shall conform in its future development in order to make the most of the beauties and resources of its site. In the Middle Ages there are signs that villages were laid out less by logic than by custom. Fixed in the minds and sentiments of men, and related both to their economic interests and to their ways of conceiving the world, was an arrangement of houses and holdings to which, men felt, all proper villages should approach. To put the case more carefully, the founders of many English villages may have had some traditional village plan in mind and laid out the villages originally in accordance with it. Their descendants preserved the arrangement more or less well. By the thirteenth century,

NOTE TO ACCOMPANY THE FOLLOWING MAPS

These maps of the village of Elford, Staffordshire, as it was in 1719, are developed from a map printed in *Collections for a History of Staffordshire* (Wm. Salt Arch. Soc.), 1931 vol., to accompany H. R. Thomas, "The Enclosure of Open Fields and Commons in Staffordshire" in the same volume, pp. 61–99. The map is reproduced by permission of the Staffordshire Record Society, and acknowledgment is hereby made of Mr. Thomas' kind assistance. The map is of late date, but there are few village maps which date from earlier than the seventeenth century, and any map of a village, made before the village was enclosed, shows in essentials what the village was throughout the Middle Ages. The first map printed here shows the strips in the open fields and various other features of the village of Elford. The distribution of the land of one tenant is also shown. The second map shows the approximate boundaries of the four open fields. The manor house seems to have been situated on the river beside the church, and the demesne lay partly in compact parcels and partly in strips intermingled with the other strips in the open fields. These details have been left out of the maps for fear of overburdening them with detail. Mr. Thomas believes that there were originally only two fields: Parke and Ridgeway, and that Up Field was added later, to form a three-field system. Down Field was of still later date and consisted of "irregular encroachments on what was primitively common or meadow."

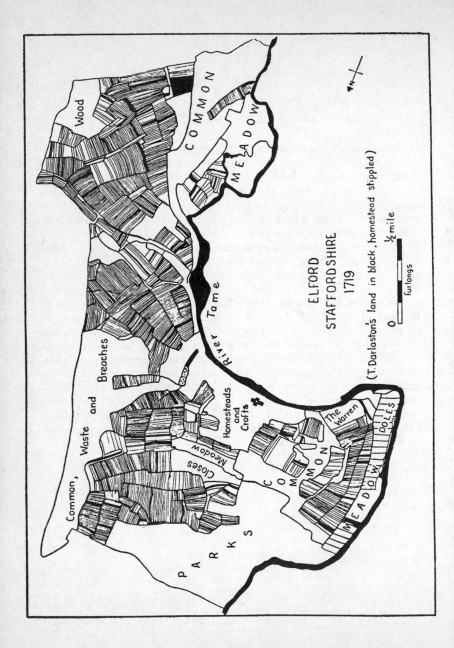

ELFORD
STAFFORDSHIRE
1719

(T. Darlaston's land in black, homestead stippled)

furlongs
0   ½ mile

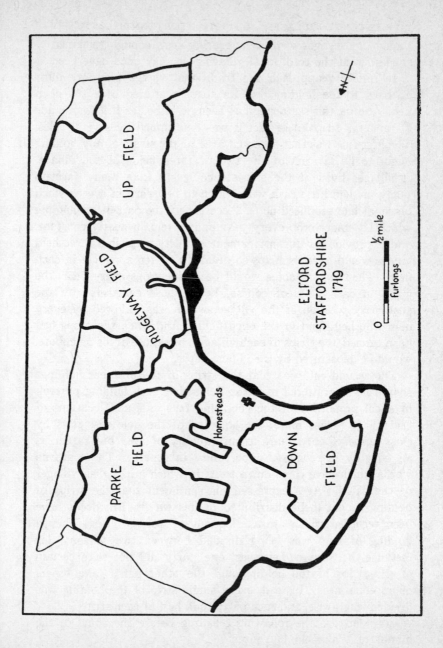

UP FIELD

RIDGEWAY FIELD

PARKE FIELD

Homesteads

DOWN FIELD

ELFORD
STAFFORDSHIRE
1719

0   Furlongs   ½ mile

though its vestiges were disappearing fast, enough remained to suggest what the traditional village plan may once have been.

In order to approach the traditional village plan, we must go back to the holding and its strips scattered over the open fields. So far this scattering has been described as if it were made at random. In point of fact it was determined by several rules. The first rule was that an equal area of the strips of any holding ought to lie in each of the two or three fields of the village. A villager lived at the subsistence level. Like many farmers today, he had little cash with which to buy corn in a year when his lands had produced none. Accordingly the part of his holding which lay under crop every year had to remain nearly constant, and to provide for this, a tenement of thirty acres in a three-field village would have its strips so divided that ten acres lay in each field. Then twenty acres would be under crops every year, the crops in each field, of course, being those called for by the customary rotation of the village, which was followed by every man who held land in the open fields. And when the crops had been carried, the strips of each villager, like those of his neighbors, would be depastured by the village herds.

The second rule was that the strips of the different holdings should lie so scattered over the fields that each holding partook in equal proportion of the good and bad soils and locations of the village. Once more, the equality of the holdings, class by class, appears not simply as an equality of area but rather as an equality in economic opportunity in general. There are no words which have come down to us in which an English villager of the Middle Ages expressed his sentiment that the strips of holdings ought to be distributed in this way.[10] But deeds have been recorded which are as eloquent as words. Often, when a holding of land was being divided between two persons, for instance, between co-heiresses, one party did not take certain of the strips of the holding and the other party take others of an equal area. Instead, every single strip of the holding was divided lengthwise, and each party took half of each strip.

Consider also the following pleading before the court of the manor of Wakefield in 1297:

Alvirthorpe . . . Robert Daneys complains of William Attebarre, and says that when he bought an oxgang of land from Adam de Neuton, William

Attebarre, who had previously bought another oxgang, gave him the worse part of the said two oxgangs and took the best part. The defendant says that when he bought his land Adam certified him where the said oxgang lay in the fields, and he took no other land. They refer to an inquisition of the neighbors, . . . who find for the plaintiff. The said messuage [*sic*] is to be divided between them according to the quantity of their land, and the land likewise, according to what belongs to their oxgangs.[11]

This is a revealing passage. It shows Adam de Neuton pointing out to the buyer where his oxgang lay, as it lay presumably in scattered strips in the fields of Alverthorpe. It shows the strips of the different oxgangs so intermingled that they could easily be confused. And there is at least a hint that the oxgangs were so distributed that each contained good and bad land. The offence of Attebarre was that he had tried to arrange that his oxgang should contain only good land.

Like the other arrangements of the champion husbandry, the scattering of the strips of the different holdings was not as queer as it looks at first glance to one who has been brought up to modern conditions. Under the circumstances it was wholly natural. Since they did not know the techniques of today, villagers of the thirteenth century had only dung and marl with which to increase the fertility of their fields, and these only in small amounts. They could have no escape from, no way of progressively improving upon the original qualities of their soils. It would be no wonder, then, if they, or their forefathers who originally laid out the villages of the champion country, insisted that the different holdings should share proportionately in the areas of the village in which good and bad soils were found — not to speak of the matters of exposure and drainage — and such sharing would necessarily mean that every holding would consist of a number of parcels scattered over the fields. This explanation is of course based upon a premise: that the land of a village was to be divided into tenement units, and that these units were to be equal, class by class, in economic opportunity. The premise itself has yet to be explained.

The strips of a holding were to be distributed equally in the two or three fields of the village and proportionately in the good and bad locations. But in founding a village it would not be an easy matter to carry these rules into effect for any large number of holdings. Unless there was some simple method by which a roughly equitable distribution of the strips of the holdings might automatically be reached, the villagers would fight and wrangle endlessly about their shares. Traces of such a method are found. Scholars have observed that, in particular villages, the strips of a certain holding had as neighbors on one side or the other in an overwhelming number of instances the strips of the same other holding. For one example — others could be brought forward — in the middle of the fourteenth century in the village of Winslow, Bucks., the yardland of John Moldeson consisted of 72 half-acre strips, of which 66 were next the strips of a certain John Watekyns.[12]

When documents survive recording the position of every strip of a holding by reference to the strips of other holdings, one can tell by inspection whether this holding had the same other holdings as its neighbors in most of the furlongs of the fields. But such documents are rare. Happily there is another kind of record which mentions the fact that a certain holding was everywhere next to a certain other holding, while saying nothing of the position of particular strips. Thus, in a memorandum of lands held by Henry de Bray in the early years of the fourteenth century in Harleston, Northants., a certain yardland is described as:

one yardland which throughout the field lies by half-acres next to the lots of the Doddeford fee.[13]

Observe that both in Winslow and in Harleston the yardlands lay in half-acre strips; the half-acre was a common standard of a job of plowing. In many villages, though far from all of them, the tenements may have lain in the fields in strips all of a size.[14]

From such evidence, students of the champion husbandry have gone on to infer that, in some villages, the strips of the different holdings were arranged in a regular order of rotation, so that the strips of every holding would be likely to have, on one side and on the other in every furlong of the village fields, the strips of the same two other holdings. There is more evidence of the sort that has been given. The difficulty with such evidence is that it shows only that a regular order of rotation of strips existed so far as the two or three holdings named in each document are concerned, and we may find an explanation for this fact without assuming that such a regular order of rotation applied to all or most of the holdings of a village. When open field land was being divided, a common practice was to split every single piece of land lengthwise. The strips of two or more tenements might conceivably lie next to each other in consequence of such a division, without there being a regular order of rotation of the strips of all the village holdings.

The best reply to this objection is that such divisions were usually made in the lands of a lordship, the fee of some member of the feudal gentry. The yardlands and oxgangs within the fee, held of the lord by husbandmen, would be kept intact in spite of the division. The records show for some villages a regular order of rotation in the strips of some of these standard tenements, and there is no reason to believe, if there was such a regular order of rotation among some of the holdings, that there was not a regular order of rotation among them all.

If the assumption is made that this regular order of rotation was in existence, some interesting deductions follow. A plowland, for instance, would consist of the eight oxgangs, the strips of which lay next each other in the fields in the same order of rotation. To put the case in another way: in any furlong the area pertaining to any given plowland would be a compact block of land made up of the eight contiguous strips belonging to the component oxgangs. This arrangement would clearly be convenient if the men who held the eight oxgangs of a plowland were also the men who sent each an ox to a common team of eight oxen. When the strip belonging to one oxgang had been plowed, it would not be necessary to move the plow and team to a strip perhaps a long way off in the fields. Instead the plow could begin work on the strip of the next oxgang in the same furlong.

We may also conceive of the practical convenience of this arrangement in putting into effect the canons of the division into holdings of the land of a village. If the strips of the holdings of Tom, Dick, Harry, and their neighbors fell in turn in the same order everywhere in the village fields, a roughly equitable distribution of the strips would automatically be made. Simply as a matter of probability, the strips would be nearly equally divided among the two or three fields and over the good and bad locations.

There is another curious fact to be observed. In many documents, the wording of which clearly points to the existence of a regular rotation of the strips belonging to different holdings in the open fields of a village, the position of such holdings relative to the position of other holdings is stated in expressions which use the word *sun*. One oxgang, as compared with other oxgangs, especially with the oxgangs of any larger holding of which it is a member, is said to lie *against the sun, on the sunny side, nearer the sun*. (In Latin: *versus solem, ex parte solis, propinquior soli*). Or the oxgang is said to lie *against the shade* (*versus umbram*). The directions against the sun and against the shade are regularly contrasted.

For example, by a charter dating from the early years of the reign of Henry III, Roald, son of Cospatric de Bereford, made a grant of an oxgang in Barforth-on-Tees, Yorks., described as follows:

an oxgang of land at Bereford on Tese, that is, that one of two of his oxgangs which lies against the sun in all parts of the whole field.[15]

Many other instances of this sort might be cited. The use of phrases involving *sun* and *shade* was common when land was being divided. A final concord of 1234 provided that a holding of two oxgangs in Harlaxton, Lincs., should be divided into moieties. The description of one of the moieties is interesting as it brings in the two great fields of a common type of village. It was:

that moiety which lies everywhere in the fields of Northfeld and Suthfield toward the sun.[16]

One other instance will suffice. In 1302, a settlement was made whereby two yardlands in Althorp in the parish of Brington, Northants., were divided equally between two parties, two women on one part, and Henry de Bray on the other, in the following manner:

Moreover the said Agnes and Isabel will have a moiety of one yardland lying within the demesne lands of Hamo de Vieleston and a moiety of one yardland lying in the common fields of Althorp, that is, a moiety of each parcel of both of the aforesaid yardlands, on the sunny side.[17]

The settlement then goes on to describe in exactly the same terms the moiety of the two yardlands which is to go to Henry de Bray, with the exception that his moiety of each parcel is to lie on the shady side (*ex parte umbrali*).

The question now is: what is the meaning of the expressions *versus solem, versus umbram,* and the like as used in the documents cited? Do they mean simply "to the south," "to the north?" Probably not, or not always, and for the following reason. Village maps show that the groups of parallel strips which made up the furlongs of a champion village did not generally lie all in one direction, though they may have done so in some instances. The strips of some furlongs stretched nearly at right angles to the strips of other furlongs, and so on. Now suppose that a charter described an oxgang of land, made up of scattered strips in different furlongs in the open fields, as lying everywhere next the strips of another such oxgang and "nearer the sun." "Nearer the sun" could mean "nearer the south" and make sense only if all the strips in the fields lay in nearly an east-and-west line. But if, as was usually the case, only a certain number of furlongs were made up of strips with this orientation, while others were made up of strips stretching in length in a generally north-and-south line (or in other directions), then "nearer the sun" could not mean simply "nearer the south" and make sense. Instead, "nearer the sun" would have to be given a more general meaning, such as "nearer to the south and to the east (or west)."

There is no adequate evidence, but there are hints that expressions such as "toward the sun" often mean "toward the south and east," the directions from which the sun comes, with the dawn and with the spring. Conversely, "toward the shade" would mean "toward the north and west." Rarely, in place of the more usual expressions, phrases are used which suggest that this was the case. For instance, at some time before 1262, Henry Dyve settled upon his son, when the latter married, a moiety of his holding in Little Brampton, Northants., namely:

a moiety of the whole holding in Little Brampton on the eastern and southern side.[18]

Here, the expression *ex parte orientali et australi* might just as well have been *ex parte solari*: that is the contention. Again, in

1208, two oxgangs of land in Bucknall, Lincs., were divided, and Gilbert de Tointon and Ivetta, his wife, received

a moiety of the said land toward the north and west.[19]

Here, the expression "toward the shade" might just as well have been employed. Unfortunately no documents seem yet to have appeared which directly equate *versus solem* with *versus orientem et australem*.

The assumption that, in the minds of Englishmen of the thirteenth century, the south was linked with the east as the sunny side of their world, and the north with the west as the shady side, is supported by the fact that they thought of good things as situated in the south and east and of bad things as situated in the north and west. In one of the opening visions of *Piers Plowman*, the fiend and his fellows and the hold of hell are seen on the north side.[20] They took the place of the giants, whose home under heathendom had been in the north: these beliefs are ancient and wholly natural to peoples who saw the light of the sun always to the south and low in the sky. On the sun side, over against Lucifer, sat Christ, and in the east was heaven:

> And alle þat han wel y-wroght · wenden þey shulle
> Eastwarde to heuene · euere to abyde.

Remember that, because of the customary orientation of churches, men in the Middle Ages, as now, looked eastward to the sanctuary. Again, in the very first vision of *Piers Plowman*, the tower of Truth was seen in the east and the dale of Death in the west:

> Esteward ich byhulde · after þe sonne,
> And sawe a toure, as ich trowede · truthe was þer-ynne;
> Westwarde ich waitede · in a whyle after,
> And sawe a deep dale · deþ, as ich lyuede,
> Wonede in þo wones · and wyckede spiritus.
> A fair feld, ful of folke · fonde ich þer bytwyne.[21]

The pairing of the directions south and east and of the directions north and west as two contrasted halves of the horizon was a part of popular cosmology.

There is the stronger reason to guess that there was once in England a system of laying out the strips of the different holdings in a regular order of rotation, and that the order was related to a conventional conception of the direction and course of the sun, in the fact that such a system is known to have been in force until recent times in villages of Denmark and Sweden which had the general characteristics of English champion villages.[22] There it was called *solskift*, which may be translated as "sun-division." The tofts, the house sites, as they might lie in two rows on either side of the village street, were considered as falling in order in a clockwise direction about the village. This clockwise ordering of the tofts is significant, because the course of the sun as seen from any point toward the northern parts of the earth is clockwise, and a belief common in folklore is that the lucky way to make any circular motion is clockwise. Accordingly, "in the North of England, a funeral procession, when arrived at the churchyard, must move in the sun's course." [23] Conversely, to move contrary to the sun's course, the direction called in English *withershins*, was considered unlucky. Folk said that the devil could be approached only by turning withershins.

The order of the tofts in the village was that of the strips belonging to these tofts in the fields. To use the Danish expression, "the toft is the mother of the acre." [24] Thus every villager would be likely to have, in every furlong of arable land, the same neighbors holding strips on the one side and on the other of his own strip as held tofts on the one side and on the other side of his own toft in the village. He had everywhere the same two neighbors. Furthermore, the direction in which this regular order of rotation was applied was a particular one. The strips fell in order from east to west or from south to north, according to the orientation of the different furlongs. Evidently this arrangement, like the ordering of the tofts, was related to a conventional interpretation of the course of the sun. In Denmark the *solskift* has been described as "a division determined by the course of the sun: it followed in fact the movement of the sun, from east to west and from south to north." [25]

The following, then, seem to have been the important characteristics of the *solskift*:

The holdings of the different villagers in the land of the village were arranged in a regular order of rotation.

In particular, the order of the arable strips in the furlongs was that of the tofts in the village to which these strips pertained.

The direction in which this order was applied was that of a conventional direction and course of the sun.

Clearly, two of the characteristics of the *solskift* — the regular order of rotation of the strips of holdings and the relation of this order to a conventional direction of the sun — are like, if not identical with, the arrangement disclosed by English documents of the Middle Ages. But there is little evidence that in England the other feature of the *solskift* was present, that is, that the order of the tofts in the village determined the order of the strips in the furlongs. Occasionally there is something to suggest that if two or more holdings were neighbors in the village fields, the tofts pertaining to these holdings were neighbors in the village proper, but the evidence is scarce. The documents are not of a sort to reveal whether or not this was a common arrangement. Yet, for one instance, Robert de Tolebu granted to the Canons of Guisborough, in Cleveland, Yorks., a plowland in Yarm, in the following terms:

one plowland in the township of Yarm, of my demesne, that is to say, that one which lies nearer the land of Robert de Lestria, with half my meadow which lies next to the meadow of the same Robert, and with a toft which is next to the toft of the same Robert.[26]

According to old Scandinavian laws, the *solskift* was more than a simple regulation of the position of the tofts and the holdings of arable. It was a complete village plan. The *solskift* was a *quadrata divisio*; solskift townships were called *villae quadratae*. Four roads were supposed to run out of the village, the *by*, at right angles to each other, and the boundaries of a proper village were supposed to make a rough rectangle.[27] If this was the case, certain expressions in Lincolnshire charters may be of significance. A charter of the time of Henry II granted:

the township of Legsby, whole and entire, with all the appurtenances which are contained within the four boundaries of the same township.[28]

Again, a charter of the same reign granted to the nuns of Ormsby:

one oxgang in the territory of Spaldington which I have taken from my demesne and have measured and have given them in four quarters in the field of the aforesaid Spaldington.[29]

SCHEMATIC PLAN
of a
SUN-DIVISION VILLAGE
of
2 PLOUGHLANDS = 16 OXGANGS

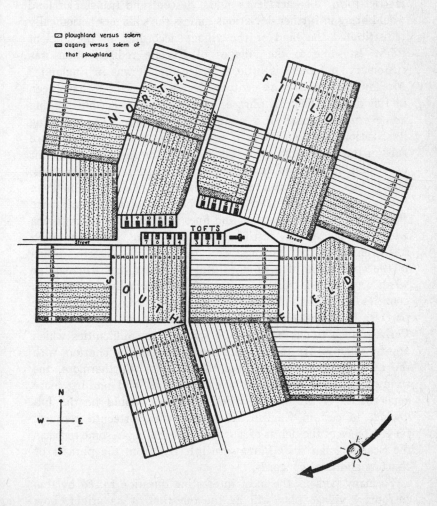

If there was once, in some of the champion villages of England, a scheme like the *solskift* governing the position of the parcels of land belonging to the different holdings, that scheme was full of irregularities, at least by the thirteenth century. A *solskift* is elaborate. In rugged country it would be hard to apply it in a strict form. The accidents of the descent and transfer of land would bring in further deviations, unless the villagers periodically redistributed the land of the village according to the ancient rules. In some of the villages of Europe redistribution was customary, but there is little evidence that it was in England.[30] Already in the thirteenth century the system seems to have been in full decay. That is, phrases showing that a certain holding lay everywhere next to a certain other holding, or describing its position with reference to the sun, become more and more rare in the documents, probably because the increasing amount of dealing in land, in that prosperous century and later ones, had in fact overwhelmed any regular order of strips. But even the hypothetical reconstruction of an English *solskift* by inference from the language of charters and fines has rested on assumptions which are not always justified. For one thing, the assumption has been made that oxgangs were made up of scattered strips in the open fields of a village. But we know that oxgangs, or what were called oxgangs, were often, especially in northern counties like Yorkshire, compact lots of land or lay in a few large parcels. In at least one village all the oxgangs were of this sort.[31] Perhaps such things account for some of the difficulties which appear when we try to reconcile the phrases of the charters with the existence of a scheme like the *solskift*. Furthermore, the sunny side was often simply the south side, and nothing more generalized. A properly guarded statement would be the following: in certain English villages of the thirteenth century, the existence of the debris of a scheme resembling in some respects the Scandinavian *solskift* may be inferred from the phrases of charters and final concords.

To many persons the most interesting question raised by this customary village plan will be the question of its origin: how did it get to England? It is true that the phrases which can be interpreted as revealing such a plan appear in numbers only in documents relating to villages of north-eastern England, especially Lincolnshire and Yorkshire, and these were the shires in which the Danes in the centuries before the Conquest settled in greatest force. It is also true that Denmark was one of the countries in which *solskift* villages existed even into modern times. It would be comfortable to hold the theory that the Danes brought an ancestor of the *solskift* with them into England as part of their cultural inheritance, and laid out in accordance with its rules the villages they founded in the new country. Unhappily phrases of the same sort as those found in documents from Lincolnshire and Yorkshire are found also, though more rarely, in documents relating to such counties as Warwickshire, Oxfordshire, and Buckinghamshire, and these were not Danish counties. Perhaps the customary village plan was part also of the cultural inheritance of peoples who were in England before the Danes.[32] The most interesting thing, however, about any sun-division is not its origin but its evidence of the scheme according to which the northern peoples conceived their world: their division of the world into things good and bad, lucky and unlucky, and their association of this dichotomy with the quarters of the heavens and the course of the sun. What is more, their cosmology took a part in the day by day work of their lives. The very way they plowed their fields was determined by their philosophy.

The champion husbandry has been described as if it worked automatically, simply by the repetition of ancient custom. Much was settled in custom, an enormous amount in the eyes of people of the present day, who are used to changing their methods rapidly in response to changes in economic conditions, but in no society can everything be left to custom; there is always a time when men must take thought and come to a decision of their own. Even champion husbandry had to be adjusted to conditions which varied from year to year: for one thing, farmers have never been able to take the weather for granted. Villagers had to decide when hedges were to be closed and opened; they had to choose such village servants as the herdsmen and make regulations about the common herd. A man's strips of arable lay intermixed with those of his neighbors, open and unfenced. Villagers had to provide that a man should not trample the corn on his neighbor's strip or steal his neighbor's sheaves in harvest. As we have seen, they also had to determine when and in what manner an intake or an assart was to be made. The meetings at which they agreed upon these matters, and also, be it noted, the rules made at these meetings, were called *bylaws*, or *byrlaws*. Sometimes the bylaw of a village must have been held in conjunction with the hallmote, the lord's manorial court; sometimes it must have been held separately, but in either case it dealt with the same matters: the conduct of village husbandry.

In the thirteenth century the bylaws were rarely entered in the rolls of the manorial courts. References to the bylaws were made, and breaches in the bylaws were fined, but the bylaws themselves were never set down. The memory of the villagers about what they had agreed upon was enough. In the fourteenth century it became more and more the practice to write out the bylaws on the roll of the hallmote, and particularly to write them out in English, while the other entries on the roll were kept in Latin. The bylaws were the particular concern of the English-speaking husbandmen; the rest was the business of the clerks.

The making and enforcement of bylaws was especially necessary for the anxious time of harvest. The court rolls of Halton, Bucks., contain, enrolled in Latin, some of the earliest examples of codes of harvest bylaws. The first code appears in 1325, but that of 1329 is fuller and illustrates many of the ordinances typically found among bylaws. It runs as follows:

It is ordained by the lord's bailiffs and by the community of the whole homage, as well the freemen as the villeins, that no one shall glean who can get for a day's work a penny and his food. Also, that the gleaners shall glean as well and faithfully as their youth or age will allow. Also, that no one shall take in outsiders or natives who behave themselves badly in the gleaning or elsewhere. Also, that no one may have a way out from his close over the land of another, and if he has a way out over his own land he shall save his neighbors without damage. Also, that no one may go into the fields with a cart after sunset to carry corn. Also, that no one may enter onto the stubbles with sheep or other beasts before they have been depastured by the beasts of the plow. Also, that no one may tether horses in the fields amid growing corn or corn that has been reaped where damage can arise. Also, that no one may make paths, by walking or driving or carrying corn, over the corn of another to the damage of the neighbors, by night or at any other time. Also, that no one hereafter may gather in the fields beans or green peas save between half of prime and prime. And these ordinances are to be observed under pain of 6 s. 8 d. And Philip atte Lynch [and five others] are sworn in to see that these ordinances are observed, to attach offenders against said ordinances, and to present them at the court following, as many and as often as they are found.[33]

For the most part these rules explain themselves. No able-bodied man, one who was able to earn wages for farm work, was allowed to glean. Gleaning was reserved for the young and the old, and women who were poor and old seem to have been the chief gleaners. Elsewhere bylaws provided that gleaning should not begin until the sheaves had been carried, or that no one should glean in a furlong until the reaping of that furlong had been finished. Sometimes, in order to give the gleaners a chance, the village live-stock was not allowed on the stubbles for some days after the corn had been carried. The village was always short of hands at harvest time, and it tried to maintain a monopoly at least of its own supply of labor by promulgating bylaws to the effect that no man who lived in the village might go to another village for work in harvest. When the strips of men's holdings lay intermixed in the fields, unscrupulous persons had endless opportunities to reap corn that belonged to others or to steal sheaves. Accordingly the bylaws provided that the greatest publicity should be given to all the works of harvest. That was the reason for the rule that no one should go into the fields by night to carry corn and the rule that no peas or beans should be gathered save between certain hours. The bell high up in the tower of the parish church was often used to regulate work in common. Accordingly some bylaws ordered that no corn was to be carried in night time "between bell and bell." Cattle were regularly allowed upon the stubbles before sheep, because sheep crop close and leave nothing behind them. Another common bylaw ordered that swine should be yoked or ringed to prevent their rooting up the sod.

Full codes of bylaws begin to appear in the rolls of the hall-motes only with the fourteenth century, but particular rules which later formed part of these codes are found much earlier, and fines levied in the hallmote often make it clear that a bylaw such as those enrolled at later times was in existence and had been broken. For instance at Therfield, Herts., in 1278, Edith Ordinar was fined:

because she carried her corn at night against the statutes of harvest.[34]

That bylaws were in existence early in the thirteenth century is shown also by an entry for the manor of Wilburton, Cambs., in the custumal of 1222 of the manors of the Bishop of Ely. The entry is the following:

It is to be known, that the lord shall have of the forfeitures of the Belawe, and of the sale of rushes, half the pence.[35]

Indeed bylaws, under that name or another, written or unwritten, must have been made during the whole life of the champion husbandry.

Aside from the content of particular bylaws, the enforcement of bylaws and the organization of the bylaw as a deliberative body are matters of interest. The bylaw, or byrlaw as it was called there, was most prominent in the North. In parts of Yorkshire, indeed, a bylaw was a distinct territorial district, a unit for the purposes of local government, and often included several manors.[36] There too the bylaw was not held in conjunction with the manorial court but was a separate gathering. Commonly bylaws were made by the whole community of a village, bond and free, with the consent of the lord of the manor or his officers. They seem to have been made by unanimous agreement. The procedure in primitive deliberative bodies is not usually by vote. What happens is that everyone who is interested expresses his views until at last, out of the discussion, something like a consensus of opinion emerges. No long continued disagreement among the members of the group is tolerated. In England, a man might be fined if he was unwilling to agree with his neighbors in a bylaw.[37] A bylaw would also elect its own officers, whose duty was to watch for breaches in the rules and present them before the hallmote or before the bylaw itself. In the North, these men were called byrlawmen or byrlawgraves, and in the South, in several villages, *custodes statutorum autumpni* were elected to keep the special harvest bylaws.

Breaches in the bylaws were punished by fines. Sometimes these fines were levied in the hallmote and therefore went to the lord of the manor. At Wilburton, we have seen, half of the forfeitures of the bylaw went to the lord. Elsewhere the fines went to the parish church or even, perhaps, to the community itself. Some bylaws are found awarding damages to the people injured by breaches of the rules. At a court of Wakefield, in the year 1297, German Filcok complained that four men had seized his horse. The defendants answered as follows:

They say that the seizure was made for 4 d. awarded to them by the community of the byrlaw for trespass committed by it (the horse) in the fields of Stanley. German says that they took the horse off his own ground, and not in the fields of Stanley put in defence.[38]

The horse evidently had been suspected of having damaged growing crops in the common fields of Stanley.[39]

It should be clear by now why the early travellers always described the fields of the champion villages of England as open fields. They were in fact broken only by hills and woods, and by the hedges around the two or three great fields, not by the many walls and fences which must surround small enclosures. It should also be clear why the travellers spoke of the houses of the villagers as being gathered in one cluster, why the houses were "uniformelie builded in euerie town togither, with streets and lanes." The holding of a villager lay in the form of narrow strips scattered over the fields. He had no compact plot on which to build an outlying farm; he was forced to live close to his neighbors in a central place. But this statement of the case is poor because it suggests that one characteristic of the social order was determined by others rather than that they were all in a state of mutual dependence. Especially in a champion village, all the arrangements and dispositions: the fields, the rotation of crops, the herd, the hedges, the holdings, and the cluster of houses which was the town proper — all were intricately interdependent, as is proved by the fact that one part of the system could not be disturbed without disturbing all the other parts. Indeed the interdependence of its elements was one reason for the great stability of the champion husbandry, century after century. The history of the enclosure movement shows that open-field villages had to be changed drastically if they were to be changed at all.

Such was the system of customs which was called the champion husbandry. We must not think of any such system, even one so intricate, as being imposed on people and felt by them as a constraint. Most men feel actively unhappy if they are prevented from acting in accordance with custom. Furthermore, the work of villagers was not simply a matter of acquiescence in tradition, even if the acquiescence was willing. Villagers worked together successfully in carrying on the various affairs of their community, and people work together not usually because they recognize that it is to their advantage that there be such coöperation, but because they feel certain active sentiments which make them able and willing to coöperate with their fellows. As he grew up, these sentiments were induced in every villager by reason of his contact with his parents, his contemporaries, and the other members of his community. Villagers even had a name for these sentiments: they called them *neighborhood*. Of course, in any particular village, neighborhood might break down into mutual distrust. Perhaps it was always in danger of breaking down, and perhaps when it did so the bitterness was all the greater because of the closeness of the contacts between men. But if we can judge by farming communities in modern times, the traditions of coöperation were probably so well established that they could survive a great deal of petty bickering. Neighbors groused at one another but worked together just the same.

The bylaw, in particular, displays the champion husbandry as a matter of active collaboration. A village formed what we call a community not only because all its members were submitted to the same set of customs — because the land of every villager lay in the form of strips intermingled with those of his neighbors, because every villager followed the same traditional rotation of crops and sent his cattle to run in a common herd. A village formed a community chiefly because all its members were brought up to consent and act together as a group. In fact the detailed rules of the champion husbandry could never have been maintained if a village had not formed a community in this more important sense. The bylaw was the community, not simply following the customs handed down from a hallowed past, but actively considering how to make provision for a successful future.

BOOK II

FAMILIES

CHAPTER VIII

PARTIBLE INHERITANCE OF LAND

IN THE CHAMPION COUNTRY of England, husbandmen lived in big villages, of a certain kind, and in small families, of a certain kind. The social order of the big villages has already been examined; also, to some extent, the relation between family and village: the lands of a village were divided into family holdings. The next chapters will be concerned in more detail with the bond between the family and its holding, especially as it is revealed in the customs of inheritance and marriage, and these customs will in turn have something to say about the maintenance of the village organization. We should like to be able to pursue the study of husbandmen's families in the Middle Ages beyond the customs by which they held land, but these are the only matters which are described in detail in the surviving records, which are for the most part legal documents. In the absence of a great contemporary novel about husbandmen, we cannot follow them into the intimate life of their homes. We shall be concerned, then, with the blood and the land.

In theory, a villager, if he was also a villein, held his tenement at the will of his lord. His lord could oust him at any time at pleasure. In practice nothing of the sort happened. If the villein rendered his customary services and paid his customary rents, he was secure in his tenure. When he died, he was succeeded in possession of the holding by the person who was his heir according to the custom of the manor. The heir had to come into the manorial court and pay a fine to the lord — called also the relief or *gersum* — for having entry into the holding. He also had to render to the lord a *heriot*, commonly the best beast of the deceased, and perhaps to the parson of the parish the second best beast as well. He also had to do fealty to the lord. But once he had fulfilled these duties, his seisin was secure, and in this course the holding descended from generation to generation in a family line.

A villager was not free to bequeath his holding to whom he would. Its descent was fixed by custom and that custom was local custom, varying from place to place. A holding in any manor descended according to the custom of that manor. The customs of inheritance of villagers' holdings are revealed by court rolls. They record the names of men who paid fines for entry into particular tenements after the deaths of the last holders, and thus show how these tenements did in fact descend. They record how disputes over inheritance were in fact settled. The customs of inheritance are also revealed by custumals, which state what the customs of inheritance of different manors were said to be. According to these sources, two main customs governing the descent of villagers' holdings prevailed in England in the Middle Ages. These two customs will here be called, for convenience, the customs of partible and impartible inheritance. Only tenements in villeinage and in socage are in question, the two tenures by which husbandmen held their lands, since the rule of descent in tenements held by military service was always primogeniture.

According to the custom of impartible inheritance, a villager's holding — a yardland, an oxgang, a cotsetle, or whatever else it might be — went at his death to one of his sons and one only. By the custom of some manors, the eldest son inherited, by the custom of others, the youngest — the Borough English rule. Possibly in some villages the father chose which of his sons should hold his land after his death. In any case, one of his sons and only one inherited. In default of sons, one of his daughters was the heir, or the holding was divided among the daughters. And in default of heirs of his body, the holding would commonly descend to a brother of the deceased. In different manors, different customs, but the governing canon of descent was that a villager's tenement should descend to one of his sons.

Of the customs of partible inheritance, the most prominent was that of gavelkind, which was the custom of Kent. According to the custom of gavelkind, if we accept the statement of its provisions which is said to have been allowed by the justices in Eyre in 1293,[1] a tenement might be divided equally among the sons of the last holder. In default of sons, then among the daughters. The messuages might also be so divided, provided that the covering of the hearth should remain to the youngest son or daughter.

J. E. A. Jolliffe, in his book *Pre-Feudal England*: *The Jutes*, has had much that is important to say about the ancient constitution of Kent. Some of his arguments must be reviewed. He points out that when we talk about gavelkind or other customs like it, we are not talking about one thing, but about two, which may become confused. Either the tenement was physically divided among the sons and each of them then lived of his own, or it was held jointly by the sons as a group of co-heirs, living in common. As will be shown, there is a considerable difference between these two events.

In Kent, the documents show, holdings often were not split up when the holder died, but were held by the heirs in common. Of brothers in Oare it was said that they "lived in common on that land."[2] At the manor court of Lewisham, Kent, in 1301:

Walter, Robert, Richard, and John, the sons and one heir of Gerard Ate Pirie, pledged their amercement for contempt etc.[3]

and later made relief to the lord for their father's holding, which they now held, and swore to do whatever they ought to do therein. There were several sons, but they were the one heir of their father — this was the common expression. They held his land jointly and undivided. In like manner, if one of the sons died without issue, all his brothers were the one heir of his interest in the common tenement. In the legal phrase, it accrued to his brothers. In the Lewisham court rolls, in the same year, there is the entry:

Richard, and Richard, (*sic*) and William, the brothers and one heir of Henry le Lung, offered themselves to do after the aforesaid Henry whatever by right they ought to do. And they pledged the relief and did fealty.[4]

Observe that there is no mention of Henry's holding any particular amount of land. How the holding descended to the third and later generations, and how the fruits of the common holding were divided among the heirs are questions still unanswered. The answers would reveal the social organization of Kentish families in the Middle Ages. All that is clear is that tenements held by successive groups of *heredes* often were maintained undivided for many years. In one case, the *heredes Hamonis de Ghelde* held a tenement undivided for at least eighty years in the thirteenth century, and perhaps for much longer, inasmuch as there is no telling when the eponymous Hamo lived.[5]

Too seldom do people try to interpret the economic and legal facts of medieval manuscripts in terms of the social order underlying them. The customs of inheritance of a place are one of the best signs of the kind of family organization that prevails there. The Kentish families of the thirteenth and early fourteenth centuries must have resembled those that still existed in Auvergne, the Nivernais, and other parts of France in the nineteenth: descendants of a common ancestor, living in one large house or in a small group of adjoining houses and holding a domain in common and undivided. Passing through the hands of successive generations of joint heirs, some of these family domains preserved their integrity for centuries.[6] Of course such families were not to be found only in France, but scattered all over Europe and in all ages. The most famous of them probably is that Icelandic family of the tenth century which was burned to death in its homestead at the climax of the greatest of sagas, that of Njal.

According to the custom of gavelkind, a tenement might be held by a group of heirs in common, but the custom also allowed an action at law for the measurement and physical partition of the tenement among the heirs. Many such partitions were in fact carried out during the thirteenth and fourteenth centuries, before the manorial and other courts. If we can judge from what happened at other places and other times, these partitions involved more than a simple division of holdings. They involved the dissolution of family communities which were also self-sufficient farming units, and led to the formation of a large class of small holders, who in the course of successive partitions might find themselves without enough land for their support. A charter of 4 Edward I, by which the king disgavelled the lands of John de Cobham in Kent, states the situation as it was then. (Disgavelling was the process of changing the rule by which a tenement descended from that of gavelkind to the primogeniture of the common law.) The charter reads in part:

According to an ancient custom of the county of Kent concerning the division and partition of lands and tenements which are accustomed to be held in gavelkind, it often happens that lands and tenements which in certain hands, undivided, were accustomed decently to suffice for the subsistence of many men, to the great stay of the realm, afterwards are separated and divided into so many parts and parcels among coheirs, that to none of them does his part then suffice for his subsistence.[7]

In reading this, we might as well be reading Frédéric LePlay's complaints that the legislation of the French Revolution, allowing an action for the division of a deceased person's property among his children, had led in time to the partition of the family domains of Auvergne and the Nivernais, that with the partition of the domains the life of the family communes had been dissolved, and that the final result was the appearance of a large class of poverty-stricken small landholders. The processes, though occurring in different countries and six centuries apart, are parallel.

In thirteenth-century Kent, as in nineteenth-century France, a family holding continued being held in common by the heirs, unless one of them wanted to force a partition. In France, the motives that led a man to make such a move were various: a feeling that he would be richer as an individual farming his own private holding, an irritation with the leaders of the commune, and so forth. We do not know the motives of the Kentishmen who asked for a partition of gavelkind tenements, but presumably they were of the same kind. The thirteenth century was a time of prosperity and change in economic affairs, and the experience of the last century has shown how quickly in such a time ancient loyalties may weaken and the ancient social order disintegrate.

The most famous of the customs of partible inheritance was the custom of Kent. But partible inheritance was by no means limited to Kent. Students have not paid enough attention to the facts which show that customs like gavelkind governed the descent of tenements in socage and villeinage in other parts of England. For instance, an entry for 1317 in a court roll of West Newton, Norfolk, reads:

Robert Kempe, William Kempe, and Alan, son of Geoffrey the miller, seek against Alan, son of William Scholer, one messuage with its appurtenances in West Newton as the right of the same Robert, William, and Alan. And they say that a certain Robert Spondrift, their forefather, was seised of the aforesaid land with its appurtenances as of right. And after the death of said Robert the right descended and ought to descend to Richard Kempe and Geoffrey Hauche as two sons and one heir. And from the aforesaid Richard and Geoffrey the right descended and ought to descend to Robert Kempe, William Kempe, and Alan, son of Geoffrey the miller, who now sue. And they seek for an inquest that such is their right.[8]

The inquest found for the demandants, but no reasons for the verdict are given on the roll, nor is it explained how Alan, son of William Scholer, had entry. What is clear is that the rules of inheritance of land in West Newton were like those of gavelkind. The inheritance descended to the two sons of Robert Spondrift as two sons and one heir — the very phrase is the same as that used in the Lewisham court rolls. After their deaths, the inheritance descended to the two sons of one of these brothers, that is, the two Kempes, and to the one son of the other brother, that is, Alan, son of Geoffrey the miller. (A reasonable assumption is that Geoffrey Hauche was the same person as Geoffrey the miller.) And apparently the inheritance descended jointly. Furthermore, elsewhere in England, as in Kent, if a man died without issue, his lands accrued to his brothers or to his uncles, his father's brothers. An entry in the court rolls of Sutton, Lincs., for the year 1306, reads:

Robert, son of Simon Horman, who held of the lord one messuage and two acres of land in villeinage is dead without an heir of his body, and thereupon came Geoffrey, Peter, and Thomas, sons of William Horman, brothers of the aforesaid Simon, and they beg to be accepted to pay the heriot for said land, and they give the lord 10 s. for entry.[9]

What is more, if all the heirs in the first generation, the brothers, were dead, the land of a man dying without issue accrued to his first cousins. At least, in the following entry in the Sutton rolls for 1310, the persons concerned were all Dods and probably first cousins:

Nicholas, son of Geoffrey Dod, who held of the lord one messuage, a half-acre, and eighteen perches of land in villeinage, whereof a half-acre and nine perches were held in the name of dower, is dead. And thereupon come John, son of William Dod, and William his brother and John, son of Fulk Dod, as nearest heirs and beg to be accepted to pay the heriot for said land, according to the custom of the manor.[10]

Such is the evidence of court rolls, that customs of inheritance like those of gavelkind were in effect outside of Kent. The existence of such customs may also be inferred from entries in extents and custumals. In the 1222 custumal of the manors of the Bishop of Ely, there is the following entry in the description of Walpole, Norfolk:

Richard, son of Hildebrand, and Adam his brother and Richard their nephew hold sixty acres for 10 s.[11]

Or in the Ely custumal of 1277, under Wisbech:

Mayner, son of John Gocelin, and Adam and Peter, his nephews, hold one messuage.[12]

Other entries of this sort occur in the Ely custumals, and it is hard to believe that they do not refer to holdings which descended jointly to the descendants of a common ancestor. We are lucky, in this regard, to have these two Ely custumals, both of the thirteenth century and spaced fifty-five years apart. Family names in the thirteenth century were very unstable, but comparison of the names of those who held a tenement in '22 with the names of those who held what was obviously the same tenement in '77 often shows that the *participes* who held the tenement in '77 were descendants of the *participes* who held it in '22, and that these *participes* perhaps were kinsmen. This statement can be made of tenements in Tydd, Cambridgeshire, Terrington and Walton, Norfolk.

All this material shows that in parts of England other than Kent holdings descended, undivided, to groups of heirs who held them in common. Nevertheless, as in Kent again, some such holdings, in the thirteenth century and the first part of the fourteenth, were being physically partitioned. For instance, in the Sutton, Lincs., rolls for 2 Edward II we read:

Robert Denyel gives the lord 12 d. in order that he may have a reasonable part of his father's land according to the custom of the manor, and that it be measured by good and lawful neighbors. And it is ordered that it be measured and divided between himself and his brothers before the next court.[13]

Yet the very fact that Robert Denyel took this action at the hallmote suggests that commonly an inheritance in land was not divided among brothers but was held by them in common. After a holding had been split up, the usual customs of inheritance were unquestionably applied to the component parts. For instance, the divided share of a man who died without issue would still accrue to his brothers. Some of the entries which have been cited probably refer to cases of this sort. As soon as it became common practice to divide tenements upon the death of their holders, a multitude of small, even tiny holdings would of course appear in other parts of England, as in Kent.[14]

Partible inheritance of villagers' holdings was the custom in England in the Middle Ages outside of Kent as well as in that shire. The next question for investigation is: Where was it the custom? For one thing, historians have remarked that customs of partible inheritance were common in East Anglia,[15] and it is possible to confirm this observation in detail. Partible inheritance may be assumed to have been the custom of any manor where any one of the following conditions obtained: where manorial extents show that tenements were being held jointly by groups of three or more kinsmen, or were divided among kinsmen; where more than one son regularly paid his relief in the manorial court for the father's holding; finally where, in any document, partible inheritance was explicity stated to be the custom of the manor.

When the villages of the East of England where, by any one of these tests, the custom of partible inheritance obtained are plotted on a map, their distribution proves to be interesting. The most prominent group of villages clusters on the northern edge of the Fens, between the Fens and the Wash: Sutton and Fleet in Lincolnshire, Wisbech and Tydd in Cambridgeshire, Walpole, Walton, Tilney, and Terrington in Norfolk. But the custom was also found commonly in Norfolk, in such widely distributed townships as Brancaster, Whissonsett, Martham, Carbrook, and Tivetshall, in several Suffolk townships, more rarely in Essex, and, perhaps, at Stevenage in the neighboring Hertfordshire.[16] These villages of course do not exhaust the list of those where the custom obtained. They are only those found in a first gathering and unquestionably form an inadequate sample.

The interesting thing about the distribution of the villages where partible inheritance was the custom in the Middle Ages, in Kent and in other shires of the East of England, is this. With a very few exceptions, which will be considered later, they are all to the east of the eastern boundary of the country where the strict champion husbandry was in force [17]— the regime in which the fields of a village were divided up into two or three great sectors, about equal in size and submitted to a customary rotation of winter corn, spring corn, and fallow, and in which a villager's holding lay in the form of a number of strips, scattered everywhere over the village fields.

Kent was of old a country of enclosures. East Anglia, and in particular Norfolk, including the townships which lay between the Fens and the Wash, was not famous for its enclosures. Nevertheless its customary field and tenement dispositions were unlike those of the champion country. In East Anglia the arable of a village was not divided into two or three great fields. In the sixteenth century and no doubt much earlier, a three-course husbandry was in force, but it was applied to the holdings of individuals and not to the village as a whole. A holding commonly lay in the form of strips, but the strips were likely to be concentrated in one part of the village fields. The customs of partible inheritance, working through the generations on a holding which lay in a single parcel or a few large parcels, may account for this arrangement, especially if we assume that often a separate division among the coheirs was made of every different kind of land within the holding. Just as the holdings of East Anglia were unlike those of the champion country, so were the names given to them. There were tenement units, but they were not called yardlands or oxgangs as in Wessex, the Midlands, and the North. They were called in some places *eriungs*, in some *plenae terrae*, in some simply *tenementa*, and already in the thirteenth century they were likely to be units merely for the assessment of rents and services. As a result of the customs of partible inheritance, accompanied perhaps by a large amount of buying and selling of small pieces of land, they had become split up among a large number of parceners, and some men were parceners in several different tenement units. The prominence of sheep-farming and special ways of managing sheep-folds complete the peculiarities of the social and economic order of East Anglia.[18] Our understanding of it is still far from firm, and being outside the country of the champion husbandry it is also outside the scope of this book.

Thus far only the East of England has been in question. But

just as customs of partible inheritance obtained to the east of the eastward boundary of the champion husbandry, so they obtained to the west of the westward boundary. The custom of Wales and of Ireland was partible inheritance. Indeed when the English conquerors of Wales observed this fact, they remembered the custom of Kent and spoke of Welsh gavelkind. The local customs of inheritance in other parts of the old-enclosed country of the West have not been sufficiently explored, but a reasonable guess is that such shires as Cornwall resembled Wales in this as in other respects.

Though the villages where partible inheritance was the custom were concentrated outside the boundaries of the two- and three-field systems, there were also a few within its boundaries. Partible inheritance was the custom in at least two great sokes of the Danelaw, that of Rothley in Leicestershire and that of Oswaldsbeck in Nottinghamshire, and without doubt elsewhere.[19] Sometimes it was alleged at law that all tenements held in socage were partible, but this notion arose simply because socage tenements descended according to local custom instead of going always to the eldest son like tenements by military service.[20] In some parts of England, socage land was partible; in others it was not. But anyone who has worked extensively in the court rolls of the thirteenth and fourteenth centuries will agree that, within the parts of England where the strict champion husbandry prevailed, the rule was that only one son paid relief in the manorial court for his father's tenement. There were irregularities, as there are bound to be in any matter of custom. If the father's tenement were a large one, he might arrange that it be divided between two of his sons.[21] But the prevailing custom was that a villager's tenement descended to one of his sons, and one only.

Nor can it be contended that everywhere to the east of the eastward boundary of the two- or three-field husbandry customs of partible inheritance were the rule. For example, in a court roll of Stratford St. Mary, Suffolk, of 1293, we read of the death of Robert Sebrith, a villein who held twelve acres of land, and we read further that:

John, younger son of the same Robert, is nearest heir of the same Robert according to the custom of the manor.[22]

This is not partible inheritance, and Stratford certainly is to the east of the eastward boundary of the strict systems of champion husbandry. There were many other villages of southern and western Suffolk and of Essex where the descent of tenements to one son was the custom.[23] No, Norfolk and Kent were the only two shires where the partible inheritance of holdings in villeinage and socage was general. They were also shires full of numbers of small and perhaps impoverished landholders, and the two shires where the revolt of 1381 held most violent sway. It is not hard to see a connection between these three sets of facts. But to make a more guarded statement, the present contention is only the following. There is a correlation between the area where the champion husbandry was in force in the Middle Ages and the area where the custom was the descent of a villager's holding to one of his sons, and this correlation is probably significant. There is also a correlation between the area where other field-systems were in force and the area where the custom was partible inheritance, and this correlation is probably significant.

Grant that two main customs governing the descent of villager's holdings obtained in England in the Middle Ages. There is good evidence both ancient and modern that different customs of inheritance correspond to different types of traditional family organization. Frédéric LePlay, who was the first sociologist to study the underlying social order of Europe, observed that these types were two in number, which will here be called the stem-family and the joint-family. According to the stem-family organization, a man's farm or his shop descended to one of his sons and one only; the other children had to leave their home if they wanted to found families of their own. According to the joint-family organization, a man's land descended to all his sons jointly. They and their descendants would hold and work the land in common, and dwell together in one great house or in a small cluster of adjoining houses. The Welch *trefs* were such groups, or the big farms of the sagas, or the family communes of Auvergne and the Nivernais. From time to time as the population of joint-families increased, they would be likely to split or bud and so found new families. In certain circumstances the customs of the joint-family were in danger of degenerating into mere rules of law allowing an action for, or prescribing, the division of a man's land at his death among all his sons. Then in time men would hold as individuals pieces of land too small to be individually worked. This degeneration seems to have been taking place in Kent as early as the thirteenth century. Without doubt the division of European families under the old social order into stem-families and joint-families is only to be tolerated in a first approximation. Perhaps also the two forms of family organization were more like one another than they seem when thus crudely described.[24] But the important thing to recognize here is that the evidence of customs of inheritance must be interpreted as showing that representatives of both the stem-family and the joint-family lived in England in the Middle Ages.

Grant now that the stem-families and joint-families of medieval England settled in separate parts of the country. How is their distribution to be interpreted? The inhabitants of Kent were a peculiar people, the Jutes. There is some evidence that they were akin to the Franks, in partible inheritance as in other respects. The custom of the kings of the Franks was certainly partible inheritance, witness the partition of Charlemagne's empire. But the problem remains of accounting for the likeness of the inheritance customs of Kent to those of East Anglia and, worse, to those of Wales and Ireland. There is no reason to believe that any large number of kinsmen of the Welsh survived in either Kent or East Anglia. Why were the customs of these widely separated regions more like one another than they were like the customs of the champion country? All we can say is that in many parts of Europe, in ancient and modern times, both kinds of inheritance existed and both kinds of family organization. Even a country like Norway, which we think of as culturally homogeneous, was in old times divided between the two. In western Norway the land of a family was partible but was often in fact held in common by a group of joint heirs. In eastern Norway the land of a family descended to one son of the last holder.[25] What were the forces effecting such a distribution, in Norway, in England, elsewhere in Europe? We do not know, but we have the stimulus of believing that the question may be important.[26]

CHAPTER IX

IMPARTIBLE INHERITANCE OF LAND

THE CUSTOMS of the partible inheritance of villagers' holdings have been described only to be disregarded. They obtained outside the borders of the champion country of England. Within, the governing custom of an overwhelming number of villages was that a man's land descended undivided to one of his sons and one only. Since what is to be studied here is the social order of the champion country, the customs of impartible inheritance are the ones which must be considered in detail.

The words villagers used go far to reveal their attitudes. When villagers of the thirteenth century spoke about inheritance, they used their own English expressions instead of the Latin ones adopted by the lawyers. Where we should say that a man had a right of inheritance in a piece of land, they would say that he had *kind* in that land. *Habere kendam* is the expression found in many of the court rolls from some parts of England.[1] Thus *gavelkind* meant, perhaps, the right of inheritance (*kind*) applying to lands paying rent (*gafol*). (By the end of the thirteenth century Kentish holdings were rendering few labor services or none and were almost wholly at rent.) In another use of the word, a man's *kind* was made up of his blood relatives. *Kin* and *kindred* are related terms. The important thing to notice is how closely kinship was associated with the inheritance of land.

Another word which villagers used in speaking of the inheritance of land, and used much as we use it today, was the word *blood*. The people among whom a man's heir was to be found were his blood kinsmen. According to the schemes that clustered about the idea of the blood, kinship was reckoned by degrees of descent from an original mated couple, a man and a woman. Thus a son was "nearer by blood" (*propinquior sanguine*) to inherit a tenement than was a nephew. The only occasion when the lord of a manor was in fact as well as in theory free to choose who was to hold a villein tenement was when it had escheated to him *pro defectu sanguinis*, that is, when the last holder was dead leaving no one of his blood to succeed him.

Sometimes the phrase "the blood of the village" was used to mean members of families who had always held land in the village, and there is at least one case in which a man of the blood of the village was preferred as heir of a tenement in the village over persons who were nearer to inherit by the blood of the family, but were not of the blood of the village. Thus at the court of King's Ripton, Hunts., in the year 1307–8:

The whole village says that Thomas Arnold, clerk, who acquired a messuage and fourteen acres of land in the village of King's Ripton, has died seised of the whole of the aforesaid holding. And they say that after his death a certain Ralph Arnold, his brother, is the nearer heir by blood, but they say that by the custom of the manor Nicholas, son of John in Le Hyrne, is the nearer heir of the said Thomas to have the aforesaid holding according to the custom of the manor, in that said John in Le Hyrne, father of the said Nicholas, who was of the blood of the village, married Margaret, sister of the said Thomas, born at Bury by Ramsey, upon whom he begot Nicholas, who now sues.[2]

Clearly the village is saying: "Thomas Arnold was not a member of one of the old families of King's Ripton, but was an outsider who 'acquired' land therein. He had a brother Ralph and a sister Margaret. Ralph, being a brother, would by all ordinary rules be Thomas Arnold's heir, in default of heirs of his body, but Ralph was no more of the blood of the village than was his brother. Margaret, the sister, however, married John in Le Hyrne, who was of the blood of the village, and they have a son, Nicholas. He is the nearer heir by the custom of the manor." Thus the sister's son of the last holder was preferred over the brother. This would never have happened, had not the one been of the blood of the village and the other not.

Whether or not the men of a particular village thought of themselves as being all blood kinsmen we do not know. In the thirteenth century a man whose daughter married outside the manor was usually bound to pay a small fine to the lord. Conceivably this custom was a survival of days when every village girl was expected to marry a boy of the same village, when the villages were endogamous units. If they were, the villagers would soon be of one blood, and even if there was no formal rule in the matter, a man's daughter must often have married his neighbor's son. In any event, the men of King's Ripton felt that no one ought to be a full member of the community whose forefathers had not been members. The same families must in fact have lived for centuries in the same villages, or such sentiments would have had no chance to become established. That the steward or other official who was presiding in the court of King's Ripton was not easy in his mind over the verdict of the township is shown by the fact that he gave the parties a day before the Abbot of Ramsey, lord of the manor, and in 1310, contrary to the verdict of the township, Ralph Arnold became secure in his possession of his brother's holding.[3] The important matter, however, is not what actually became of the tenement but the sentiments expressed by the men of King's Ripton.

The most familiar and perhaps the commonest of the rules of impartible inheritance of villagers' holdings was primogeniture. According to primogeniture, a tenement descended to the eldest son of the last holder. He was the son and heir. If there were no sons, the custom of some manors was that it descended to the eldest daughter, but more commonly it went to all the daughters as coheiresses — only in this case was the tenement divided.[4] If there were no children to inherit, then the tenement descended to the eldest brother of the last holder, and so on, according to well known canons. As will be shown, a number of customary life interests might prevent the possession by the heir of some part of his inheritance, but at least his right of inheritance, his *kind*, fell to him by these rules.

The canons of descent by primogeniture are familiar; those of the custom of Borough English, to call ultimogeniture by its proper name in English law,[5] seem strange. As in primogeniture, the tenement descended to one son of the last holder and one only, the son and heir, but this son was the youngest son, not the eldest. He was also the youngest son of his father's first wife.[6] Sons of a second wife were disregarded if sons of a first wife survived. If there were no sons, the tenement was either divided among the daughters, or the youngest daughter inherited. And in default of heirs of the body, the tenement went to the brother of the last holder nearest to him in age, his youngest surviving brother. In short the custom of Borough English was like primogeniture, except that the right of inheritance began with the youngest son or daughter and moved toward the eldest, in ascent, as the lawyers would have said. In some places, not all, the custom of Borough English was a matter of status: only tenements in villeinage descended by that rule.

By the working of the custom of Borough English, a man might well die leaving an heir who was under age. Then there was sometimes the strange spectacle of the elder brother's taking over the younger's land until the latter was old enough to have seisin. An entry in the court rolls of Alrewas, Staffs., of 1273 is this:

To be remembered: that Henry, son of Hering, gives the lord 13 s. to have his father's land until his brother's coming of age, namely Robert, heir of said land. And when said Robert attains full age, he shall enter his land without any claim of the lord of the fee. Moreover said Henry took two acres of the lord until said term and at this term said two acres shall revert to the lord of the fee.[7]

It cannot have been easy for Henry to give up to his brother, when the time came, land which had absorbed years of his labor.

Even where the custom of Borough English existed, arrangements could be made to get around it, as indeed arrangements could be made if necessary to avoid any custom of inheritance. The custom of the manor of Bucksteep in Warbleton, Sussex, was Borough English; nevertheless in 1299 the following entry was made on the court roll:

Heloise who was the wife of Robert le Capel comes into full court and surrenders to the lord two parts of the whole tenement which said Robert formerly held in villeinage, and said two parts of said tenement are granted by the lord to Philip, son of said Robert, to perform therein for the lord all the due and accustomed services as the aforesaid Robert was accustomed to do, and he gives the lord 6 s. for having entry . . . and Stephen, younger son of said Robert Capel, comes and granted to said Philip, his brother, for 5 s. 6 d. all the right which he had or could have in said tenement, and thus seisin is given to said Philip, and he gives the lord 8 d. for the relief.[8]

In a word, the younger son, in return for a cash payment, surrendered to the elder son his right to inherit the holding. The consent of the heir was commonly required if a tenement was to be alienated in any way from the customary line of inheritance. We are not told why, in this case, the heir thought that selling his birthright was worth his while, nor what pressure was brought upon him to make him do so. Perhaps he was hopelessly sick in mind or in body and so in fact unable to hold the tenement. We can think of a number of reasons why it might be necessary that a tenement should not descend to the man who was designated in custom as its heir. At Bucksteep, the custom was that the widow held all of her late husband's tenement until her youngest son, the heir of the tenement, was fifteen years of age. That was the reason why Heloise was in a position to make a surrender in court of Robert le Capel's tenement. Without question the reason why she surrendered only two-thirds of the holding was that she had determined to keep one-third in her own hands as her widow's bench.

Countrymen of the Middle Ages had no occasion to speak of the advantages or disadvantages of their customs. Either they did not think about their customs at all or they took them as part of the nature of things. People of the present day may reflect and divine the influence of customs of primogeniture or of Borough English on the life of country families, but they may divine quite wrongly, because considerations which would have been of the first importance to villagers have not occurred to them. The custom whereby the holding descended to the first-born son had this advantage, if it was an advantage, that at the father's death the heir was likely to be of full age and ability to manage the holding. The custom of Borough English may have had advantages which are less obvious but no less real. If they were to acquire land with which to support themselves and found families, the sons who did not inherit had to leave their father's holding. Under primogeniture these sons were the younger sons; under the custom of Borough English they were the older sons. Accordingly, under the latter custom, the sons who did not inherit were those who were best able to find land for themselves. Again, there is evidence that the heir of a tenement did not marry until he actually held it, either after his father's death, or after a settlement whereby the father turned over the tenement to his heir, on condition that his heir support him in his old age. An heir who was a youngest son would be likely to be able to marry earlier in life than an heir who was an oldest son. But in default of statements by the villagers themselves, all this discussion is hypothetical.

Villagers did put themselves on record at least once that they felt the custom of Borough English to be to their disadvantage. The men of Bookham, Surrey, in 1339, told the steward of Chertsey Abbey (the Abbot of Chertsey was their lord) that:

Of old it was usage in that manor that after the death of each holder the youngest-born son was accustomed to succeed his forefathers, to the grave hurt and detriment of the whole homage and of their holdings.[9]

They did not give the reasons why they felt the custom was hurtful, but they petitioned the Abbot and Convent that it be changed for primogeniture, and offered them forty shillings for doing so. The custom was changed at Bookham, and later the homages of other Chertsey manors came and made the same successful request.

Elsewhere a change in the opposite direction was made, from primogeniture to the custom of Borough English. This is alleged in a suit at the court of Graveley, Cambs., in 1316:

Walter, son of Gerard le Koc, who took himself off the fee of the lord for a long time without licence, now comes and demands that he be admitted to that half-yardland which William Koc, his first-born brother, holds of the lord for a gersum formerly made therein, by reason that this Walter is the later-born son of said Gerard, wherefore he says that he has more right in said land than said William who now holds it. And the aforesaid William says that he demands that land unjustly in that he himself (William), forty years ago in the time of William de Gomecestre then Abbot of Ramsey, made fine for it according to the use and custom of the manor, since he says that then the custom was that the first-born brother should make fine for, have, and hold unfree land after the death of his ancestors, but that William of Washingley, at the time when he was the lord's steward, changed that custom, and that his right is such he seeks an inquest.[10]

Clearly William of Washingley, at some time at the end of the thirteenth century, changed the custom of Graveley from primogeniture to that of Borough English. In his defence, William le Koc admitted this fact, but pleaded that he had been given seisin of the half-yardland as his father's first-born son before the change had been made and that the change could not be made retroactive. There is no record of why the change was made, whether to please the tenants or to secure some advantage for the lord which we cannot now divine. The ease with which a change was made, both in this instance and in that of Chertsey Abbey, shows that the difference between inheritance by primogeniture and inheritance by the custom of Borough English was not an important one. Changing from one to the other does not seem to have radically altered the social order of a village. The important difference was between either one of these customs and the custom of inheritance by a group of joint-heirs.

The geographical distribution of the custom of Borough English confirms this impression. Unlike the customs of partible inheritance, it was not concentrated in particular parts of the country, but scattered over every part of the area within which inheritance by one son was the rule. Villages where Borough English was the custom of the manor would be neighbors of villages where primogeniture governed the descent of holdings. Perhaps it was commonest in the South-east — in Sussex it was particularly plentiful — and least common in the North, but even there, in four of the Five Boroughs of the Danelaw: Derby, Leicester, Nottingham, and Stamford, the custom of Borough English was the rule. The same was true of Germany, where in old times districts in which peasant holdings descended by primogeniture lay intermingled with districts in which the custom was *jungsten recht*. If the differences in the canons of inheritance had been part of a drastic difference in the general forms of the organization of society, such intermingling would scarcely have been found.

A third custom, besides those of primogeniture and Borough English, whereby a villager's holding descended to one of his sons and one only must now be considered. In parts of England, custom may have allowed the holder of a tenement to choose for himself which one of his sons was to be his heir, and to hand over his tenement during his lifetime to this son. Only if the holder died without having made such a choice would the heir be determined by the custom of the manor. The record of a suit of the year 1306 before the hallmote of Barnet, Herts., a manor of St. Albans Abbey, shows that, in that village at least, such a choice might be made. It shows also what the consequences might be.[11] Walter Bartholomew had three sons, named, in order of their ages, Walter, Robert, and John. Walter the elder gave his tenement, by licence of the lord, to John Bartholomew, his youngest son, and John held it for his lifetime. When John died without leaving an heir begotten of his body, Robert, the next youngest son, entered and held the tenement. In the meanwhile, Walter, the eldest of the three sons, had begotten a son of his own, named Thomas. This Thomas brought action against Robert, his uncle, saying that Robert was unjustly deforcing him of the tenement, unjustly because after the death of John, to whom the tenement had been given, "the right ought to return to the issue of the elder brother." To this Robert replied that "by the custom of the village of Barnet, he entered said tenement justly after the death of said John, his younger brother, because of nearness of blood in ascent." Both parties asked for an inquest, which found that:

> By the custom of the village of Barnet and the hallmote therein, tenements given as is said above to any younger son, if there were several brothers, ought always to revert to the brother nearest by birth because of nearness of blood and not to the elder brother or his issue. And this they hold and use according to the custom of their hallmote and not according to common law.

Accordingly Thomas was judged to have lost his suit.

Pretty clearly, if the tenement had not been deliberately given by Walter Bartholomew to his youngest son but had been allowed to descend according to the custom of the manor, it would have gone to the eldest son. Otherwise Thomas, the son of the eldest son, would have had no color of right to bring a suit. But granted that the tenement had been given to the youngest son, the question at issue was: When that son died without issue, did the tenement revert to the eldest male line, or did it go to the next older brother of the deceased? The inquest found that according to the custom of the village of Barnet it went to the next older brother. This rule, of course, was the one that applied when similar situations arose under the custom of Borough English. But the interesting points are not those at issue but those on which both parties were evidently agreed. Neither party denied the right of Walter Bartholomew to make whichever one of his sons he pleased his heir, no matter what the usual rule of the manor might be, or the right of that son to transmit the tenement in his turn to one of his children, and the inquest accepted the gift of a tenement to "any younger son" as a common happening, with consequences for which provision had been made in custom.

Consider now the following entry, of the year 1269, from a book of extracts from the court rolls of Park, Herts., another one of the St. Albans manors:

John of Eywode surrendered into the hands of the lord the whole land which is called Julian's land to the use of John, his son, and the lord seised him of the aforesaid land with all its crop to hold according to the custom of the hallmote, doing etc. And he gives a half-mark for seisin. Afterwards comes said John, son of the aforesaid John, and grants the aforesaid land with its appurtenances to said John his father to hold all his life.[12]

At first glance, this transaction seems to have been a rather silly one. John of Eywode surrendered the land into the hands of the lord only to have the lord at once give his son seisin. This was simply a matter of form: a surrender followed by a regrant was the form taken by any transfer of land before a hallmote. When the surrender had been made, the lord, or rather the lord's steward, presiding in the hallmote, did not regrant the land to whom he would, although in theory he had the right to do so. He granted it to the person the last holder wished him to grant it to. Thus John of Eywode surrendered his land into the hands of his lord "to the use of" his son. Furthermore, it seems silly that a father should hand land over to a son, only to have the son turn the land over to his father again, for the lifetime of the latter. But the transaction was not as absurd as it looks. By a settlement of this sort, the permanent rights in the land were transferred to the son. To use the language of the lawyers, he became tenant in chief; his father was only tenant for life. After his father died, the tenement would revert to him and to his heirs. The settlement was literally "to his use." By this means a father could arrange during his lifetime how the whole or a part of his land was to go after his death. He could choose his heir. Walter Bartholomew may have made some such settlement when with the licence of the lord he "gave" his tenement to his younger son John and to his heirs.

Customs which preserved the principle that a tenement ought to descend to only one son of the last holder, while allowing the holder himself to choose which one of his sons was to be heir, seem much more sensible than the rigid rules of primogeniture or the custom of Borough English. In Germany in old times such customs were found besides customs that fixed the descent of peasant domains to eldest or youngest sons. Even in communities where all men were born and bred husbandmen, not every one of a man's sons would have the ability or character to manage the family holding prosperously, not every one, perhaps, would want to take the job upon himself, and nothing made it certain that the ablest son would be the eldest or the youngest. If the father was free to choose his heir among all his sons, the chance of his having a satisfactory successor would be greater than if the heir was fixed in custom.

But it is too early to say that settlements such as that cited from the court book of Park preserved the principle that a tenement ought to descend to only one son of the last holder. Sometimes they did the very opposite: they did not preserve the principle but got around it. Such a settlement was sometimes used to provide that a tenement should be divided among the sons, where in the absence of any settlement the custom of the manor required that land should descend to one son and only one. Consider this entry from the court book of Barnet, Herts., under the date of 1306:

Thomas Freysmouth surrendered a messuage with a curtilage and other appurtenances, as it lies between the holding of Henry Geffrey on one side and Gunnildewelle on the other, abutting on St. John's churchyard in Barnet. And the lord seised William son of said Thomas of the main part of said house and messuage, with a solar and a room, to hold to himself and his, doing thereof etc. And also the lord seised Geoffrey son of said Thomas of two rooms and a solar of said house and messuage to hold to himself and his, rendering yearly to said William his brother 1 d. and to the lord the other due and accustomed services thereof. And he will not make waste. And he gives the lord for seisin 2 s. Pledges etc. And the form of the seisin is such that said Thomas and Agnes his wife will hold said messuage to their lives' end.[13]

Freysmouth's house was a substantial one. It had a number of rooms and at least two stories. (A solar was an upper room.) What we are told about the rudeness of villagers' houses in the Middle Ages must often be revised in the light of the facts. To be sure, Barnet seems to have been a large and prosperous village. The house was to be divided between Freysmouth's two sons. This arrangement seems strange to us, but it was common in those times. Was a common household maintained in spite of the formal division? We do not know.

These are incidentals. The important point is that by this settlement the two sons of Thomas Freysmouth were made the nominal tenants of his messuage. Nevertheless he retained a life interest in it, so that, in effect, what the settlement did was fix how his messuage was to descend after his death. If Thomas had died without having made this settlement before the hallmote, we may suspect that his son William would have had the whole messuage, since primogeniture seems to have been the normal custom of the manor of Barnet. As it was, he got the main part of it, and his nominal supremacy was recognized in the penny a year of rent which his brother was to pay him. Save only that he had to secure the consent of the lord, settlements such as these which have been cited allowed a man to make the same sort of free disposition of his land that he could make in later times by will. But all of these settlements were made before courts of the Hertfordshire manors of the Abbey of St. Albans. In few villages did custom allow a man to settle so freely the descent of his land. Commonly the consent of the man who was designated in custom as the heir was required before a holding was alienated in any way.

In some villages, if a man had no heir of his body, he could come into the hallmote and designate someone as his heir, and this person would be admitted after his death as the holder of his tenement. Thus in 1298 before the court of Halton, Bucks.:

Richard Hychman gives the lord 12 d. to have an inquest whether Geoffrey Leuwyne made this Richard his heir after the death of this Geoffrey of the holding which the same Geoffrey holds in Halton. . . . The inquest comes and says that the same Geoffrey came into full court and led the said Richard by the hand and said in full court: "Since I have no heir of my body and the aforesaid Richard is my sister's son, I make and constitute him my heir after my life of this tenement." [14]

As we shall see, the fact that the person designated as heir was a sister's son may not be without significance.

According to each of these customs, whether primogeniture or Borough English or that whereby a father was allowed to choose which one of his sons was to be his heir, it was the family holding which descended to the heir. In some manors the family holding was not simply all the land held by the father of the family, but only such land as had descended hereditarily in the blood. Assart lands, or lands he had "acquired" in any other way, the father was free, subject to the consent of the lord, to grant or leave to whom he would.[15] In this case he was not bound by the custom of inheritance of the manor. Only such land descended to the heir as had descended to a line of heirs before him. A family holding, villagers felt, was not to be diminished by alienation, nor was it to be increased by acquisitions. These might properly be used for the support of children other than the heir. The holding ought to be constant in size from generation to generation.

CHAPTER X

CHILDREN NOT INHERITING

THE CUSTOM of the usual champion village was that a holding of land descended to one blood kinsman of the last holder as his heir, who in the common course of events would be his son: his eldest son, his youngest son, or the son he chose to succeed him. The next question is: What provision was made in custom for the children who did not inherit? Two distinctions must be made in answering this question. First, there is the distinction between sons and daughters. The provision made for sons and that made for daughters were similar but not identical. Second, there is the distinction between immovables (land) and movables. The person who was called the son and heir was the prospective inheritor of the family holding of land. Provision could not be made for the other children out of land, not at least in the sense of their becoming tenants of the holding. They had to be provided for out of their father's movable possessions: his goods and chattels.

Custom governed the descent of goods and chattels just as it did that of land. According to one common custom, if a villager died and he was a villein, his goods and chattels were disposed of as follows. His best beast was taken by his lord as a heriot, and if he had no beast, money or some valuable tool was taken in its place. His second best beast was taken by his parish priest as a mortuary. In theory it evened accounts for the tithes which, it was assumed, the deceased had failed to render during his life. Then, after his debts had been paid and the expenses of his wake and burial, a number of tools and utensils needed for husbandry and housekeeping were bound to remain on the holding for the use of the heir. Sometimes the best example of each kind of tool was expected to go with the holding. These were the *principalia*, in English the heirlooms.[1] (*Loom*, in old English, meant *tool*, any tool.) Sometimes a list of the *principalia* was inscribed on the court roll when a man inherited a tenement and was given seisin, as at Wotton Underwood, Bucks., in 6 Edward II, where the *principalia* on a holding of a messuage and somewhat more than five acres of land included a coulter, a plowshare, a yoke, a cart, an axe, a cauldron, a pan, a dish, and a cask.[2]   Finally, the remaining goods and chattels of the deceased were divided into three equal parts, of which one went to his widow, one to his children, and one to the dead man himself.[3]   The part that went to the children was divided equally among the sons and daughters with the exception of the heir. The part that went, as the language of the time put it, to the dead man himself was the part which custom allowed him to bequeath by his last will and testament to whom he pleased. If there were no children, the goods and chattels were divided into two parts, one of which went to the widow, and the other to the dead man.

The statement that one third of the goods and chattels of the deceased was divided equally among his children with the exception of the heir must at once be modified. Here the church records become our chief source of information. For reasons which are of no present importance, the Church claimed the right to protect and execute the last will of the dead man, and throughout the Middle Ages bishops and councils of the Church made rules governing the behavior of their subordinates in these matters. For one thing, a man's last will was properly made in the presence of the parish priest and of two other trustworthy witnesses. In the case of a villein, his lord sometimes required the presence of the reeve or bailiff as well, on the theory that a villein's goods were the property of his lord.[4]

Among the most interesting of these rules of the Church is the chapter of the acts of the Synod of Exeter (1287) which deals with testaments, particularly the paragraph which describes the division among the sons of the part of their father's goods which fell to them. The paragraph reads:

If indeed the testator previously provided sustenance for any of his sons out of his own goods, and there is another son or several sons for whom no provision was made, we forbid by statute that those for whom provision was made, heirs of the testator (if they have as much by this provision as their portion would be if they were admitted to the division with the others), be admitted on any account to the portion to be divided among the sons, but let them remain content, inasmuch as provision was made for them by the testator or by his rightful successor, and let not the portion of the others be by them diminished.[5]

This passage shows that often sons did not have to wait until their father's death before getting their share of his goods but were given their share in his lifetime. The situation the church-men must have had in mind is one which is common in English story. One of the sons of the family was to inherit the father's land or shop. As for the others, their father from time to time as they came to manhood made them up "portions" out of his goods and chattels and sent them out into the world to seek their fortunes. Every son had the right, in custom, to expect a portion, but once he had received it he had no further claims on his father's estate. At the father's death only those sons still without portions were entitled to a share of his goods.

The sons who were not to inherit the family holding might leave it and seek their fortune. (The fate of the daughters remains to be considered.) One might go to school and then into the Church. If he did so, his father would have to pay the lord a fine, as indeed he would whenever one of his sons left the manor permanently for any reason. The Church was the poor boy's surest avenue to high position. Most of the bishoprics and abbacies went to men of gentle birth, but not all. If he had ability and luck, a poor man's son who took orders might rise to any office. Robert Grosseteste, the great Bishop of Lincoln, was said to have been born a villein. Another son might go to the wars or into the household of a nobleman. More important, the thirteenth century was a time of expansion in industry and commerce, and the centers of industry and commerce were growing. Many a country boy, then as in later centuries, must have left his family holding to seek his fortune in the nearest borough or, like Dick Whittington, in London. Already in that century, the neighboring counties were sending lads up to London to be bound apprentices.[6] This circulation of man-power from country to town has been going on from that day to this. The countryside feeds the city with men as with food.

Some of the sons who did not inherit might choose to cleave to the life of husbandry to which they had been born and bred. Since the family holding could not be theirs, they would try to obtain other lands so as to be able to marry and found families of their own. In the course of a lawsuit concerning a half-hide of land once held by Reginald de Bradebroc in Garford, Berks., it was stated that:

This man had four sons, and the youngest of them remained in that land as in villeinage, and the three others took land elsewhere where they could.[7]

One way to take land was to marry an heiress. The husband of a woman who held land in her own right had himself the right, by the custom called the curtesy of England, to hold this land after her death for his lifetime. Whether or not he survived his wife, such a man was established for life. There will be more to say on this matter hereafter.

But the supply of land was limited, and many of the men who were forced to seek for holdings cannot have found them. Such men must have become farm laborers. In the East of England, the custumals and court rolls speak of a class of people called *anilepimen* and *anilepiwymen*. An anilepiman had no permanent stake in a village. He might be allowed to keep a few cattle or sheep on its pastures, but he held no land.[8] At least he held no land immediately of the lord of the manor. Instead he was boarded or given a cottage on the tenement of a man who did hold land, and he must have received food and wages in return for helping in farm work.[9] He was the counterpart of what we in America should call the hired man. Many of the anilepimen were members of the floating population which wandered about the country helping to get in the harvest, the medieval forerunners of our harvest stiffs. The men who made up the extent of Leverington, Cambs., for the custumal of 1277 of the manors of the Bishop of Ely observed:

The sum of the boon-works in harvest is twelve score and eight, counting the reeves, and not counting the coterells, undersettles, and anilepimen, who cannot be numbered, because sometimes they increase and sometimes decrease.[10]

In any society where husbandry is nearly the only means of subsistence, a man's status as a landholder or a landless man is in close relation with his status as married or single. So it was in England in the thirteenth century, as the word *anilepiman* shows. *Anilepi* is an early form of the word *only*. *Anilepiman* means single man, unmarried man, but an anilepiman was also a landless man. Other words have had a double meaning of the same sort. One of them was the word *maid*; another was the word *husbond*.[11] *Husbond*, the Middle English form of our *husband*, meant then what it does now, but it was applied also in northern and eastern England to one of the middle class of villagers, to a man who held a substantial tenement. In the country in the Middle Ages a man could keep himself alive by taking work as a farm laborer, but he could not keep a wife or found a family unless he held land. No land, no marriage — that was a rule which names like anilepiman and husbond prove was acknowledged by countrymen.

Instead of taking his portion and going out into the world, a son who was not to inherit his father's holding might properly choose to stay and live on the holding. In this case he was not simply unable to take a wife; he was not allowed to take one. Consider this entry in a court roll of 1287 of Sevenhampton, Wilts.:

Six pounds from Reginald Damemalde as above for the fine of one yardland formerly of Maud, his mother, of the holding of John de Seinte Elene. And the same Reginald grants to Walter his brother a house and every year at Michaelmas one quarter of wheat, so long as he remains without a wife and on this domain. And he granted this before the full court.[12]

What had happened here? Maud had died, and her son and heir, Reginald Damemalde, who must have taken his name from his mother, was paying the fine for entry into her holding. Reginald had a brother Walter who was not the heir but wanted to remain on the holding, and accordingly Reginald arranged for his support, at least in part, by giving him a house and promising to find him in one quarter of wheat every year. Probably Walter would work as a farm hand, either for his brother or for the neighbors, but if he left the lord's domain, or if he married, he lost his house and his wheat.

In other shires, far away from Wiltshire, arrangements of the same sort were usual. At Oakington, Cottenham, and Drayton, in Cambridgeshire, in the early years of the fourteenth century, the custom was that the son who inherited the family holding granted a small piece of it — for instance, a half-acre in each of the fields of a two-field village — to each of his brothers to be held by them for life, unless they moved away or married.[13] The landless brothers had the right to expect this much: they had a right at least to their keep if they remained on the family holding, but they had no right to marry. A cardinal principle of the social order was that a family holding ought to descend undivided, generation by generation, from one representative of the blood of the holding to another. By following this principle, at least one married couple and their children were sure in each generation of having their subsistence from the holding, but the principle would be in danger if brothers who were not to inherit the holding were allowed to remain on the holding, marry, and beget children. A skeptic will say that it is naïve to think that because a man remains unmarried he does not beget children. The only answer that can be given to the skeptic is that the facts are sometimes against him, though plainly not always. In Ireland at the present time, where the custom is that one son takes over his father's holding, the sons who do not inherit, if they remain in the neighborhood and without land, do not marry and in fact beget very few bastard children, such is the strength of sentiment established in the community and supported by the Roman Catholic Church that people who are not married ought to be chaste.

Great store must be set by these arrangements at Sevenhampton and at the three Cambridgeshire manors. Others like them have not yet been reported for medieval England — that is true.[14] But almost nothing is told in the court rolls about the fate of sons who were not heirs, nothing about provision of any sort being made for them. When what is done is clearly specified, the facts are important. Probably provision was often made for them informally, no agreement being registered before the hall-mote. Furthermore, Wiltshire and Cambridgeshire are far apart: though the custom was not mentioned often, it was not confined to one part of England. Aside from all these considerations, the particular form of the arrangements — that the landless sons were to be given support on the family holding so long as they remained unmarried — forces itself on the mind as of some significance, because identical customs obtained in countries where the customs of inheritance were like those of champion England. In Germany, as late as the last century, wherever the custom was that a peasant *hufe* descended to one son of the last holder, the *onkel* was an institution. The *onkel* was the brother of the head of the family, who had chosen to remain on the *hufe* and unmarried.[15] Today we are familiar with the maiden aunt but not with the maiden uncle. We also, members of a society which feels itself bound to find subsistence for every one of its members, are likely to expect every man to get married. At least we do not expect economic or social forces seriously to hinder his getting married if he has set his heart upon it. But when nearly everyone had to make his own livelihood and make it by tilling the soil, these attitudes were not the common ones. Society regulated the increase of its population even before the invention of modern methods of birth control. Customs like those of Sevenhampton and the three Cambridgeshire manors must be borne in mind by anyone who discusses the slow increase during the Middle Ages of the population of countries like England.

The fate, then, of the sons who did not inherit a holding may be summed up in this way. Either they were given a portion of their father's goods and left the holding to seek their fortune elsewhere, or they stayed on the family holding, with the right to their keep but without the right to marry.

The fate of the daughters of the house was parallel to that of the sons. If there were no sons, one of the daughters inherited the holding, or it was divided between them, and the future of any woman who held land in her own right was secure: she was sure to find a husband. There was no lack of men looking for land, and they would marry to get it, whether or not they had fallen in love with the heiresses. But commonly there was a son and heir. Then the same possibilities lay before the daughters as lay before the sons not inheriting. They might take their portions of their father's goods and go out into the world, perhaps to become *anilepiwymen* like those spoken of in the Ely custumals. The court rolls of some villages show that strange women, outsiders, appeared in harvest to work in the fields and to glean afterwards. They were useful, but were looked upon with distrust, as likely to steal and do other evil. Sturdy beggars, both men and women, were always common on the roads of old England.

To be sure, the commonest way for a girl to leave her family holding was to be married from it. Then, just as a boy leaving the holding expected his father to give him his portion of the father's goods and chattels, so a girl expected to take with her from the holding, when she married, her marriage portion, her dower. The dower was a vital consideration in the making of any marriage in Europe under the old order. If what happened in England in the thirteenth century was like what happens in the parts of Europe where the old peasant culture is still established, careful and determined haggling went on between the head of the boy's family and the head of the girl's before her dower was agreed upon, and the agreement might be an elaborate one. Something of this sort must have been common, inasmuch as the withholding of a dower upon which two parties had agreed was, like any other breach of covenant among villagers, a cause for a suit before a manorial court. For instance, at the hallmote of Broughton, Hunts., in 1294:

Henry John's son acknowledged that he was bound by promise to give to William Aleyn with his (Henry's) daughter in marriage one dress, worth a half mark, and one pan, holding two gallons, worth 16 d., and one "urtiol" holding a half gallon, worth 16 d., and two carpets, worth 2 s., and five silver shillings to repair a cart with iron, and six shillings of the silver given by them to the church; sum: 22 s. 4 d., of 9 s. of which said William discharged him. And for unjust detention said Henry is in mercy, 12 d.[16]

Another good example is found in the court rolls of Belper, Derbyshire, for 1312:

Richard Maud's son was summoned to answer to John Wade in a plea of detention of chattels. And the same John complains therein that said Richard withholds from him unjustly to his damage of 20 s., one cow, worth 10 s., and one dress, worth one mark, which goods he (Richard) agreed to give him (John) with his daughter at the time when this John married her etc.

But this was not all Richard had promised. There was another plea:

Richard Maud's son was summoned to answer to John Wade in a plea of covenant. And the same John complains therein that said Richard unjustly went against a covenant, unjustly in that they agreed among themselves on Friday after the feast of the Invention of the Holy Cross in the year [   ] in the town of Duffield that the aforesaid Richard would build for the same John within a year from the day of the aforesaid covenant a certain house on the ground of the aforesaid John and of Avis, his wife, in the village of Holbrook, worth 40 s., which house said Richard has not yet built, whence said

John is hurt and has damage to the amount of 60 s. and thereupon he brings suit. . . . By licence of the court the aforesaid John and Richard are reconciled so that for all quarrels, actions, and matters foregoing said Richard Maud's son agreed to give at once to the same John a cow with a calf, worth 13 s., also a surcoat, worth 5 s., or 5 s. in coin, also three sheep, worth 4 s., or 4 s. in coin.[17]

These dowers were all in money, or houses, or livestock, or utensils, or clothes. This was probably the rule in the matter of marriage portions in the champion country of England. Dowers were not generally made in land, unless in the form of a grant of land for a term of years. That entries are found in the court rolls recording the gift by fathers of land with their daughters in marriage is true, but where villagers had strong feelings that a tenement ought to descend as a whole to one son and heir of the last holder, dowers must usually have been made out of the father's goods and chattels.[18]

If a girl was married with her father's goods, a common custom required that she be then excluded from making any subsequent claim to inherit her father's land, so long as there was another sister who had not received a marriage portion. Perhaps this custom was linked with a sentiment that sisters ought to get married in order of their ages beginning with the eldest. An entry in the court rolls of Dunmow, Essex, for 1315 shows a decision being made in accordance with this custom:

John Russel de la Penne and Annis his wife, daughter of Robert Osbern, come and say that said Annis is the daughter and nearer heir of the aforesaid Robert, villein of the lord, who died seised of one messuage and twenty acres of villein land. They give to the lord for an inquest. . . . Whereupon the whole court is charged and sworn to say whether said Annis is the daughter and nearer heir of said Robert according to the custom of the manor or whether she was ever alienated outside the homage of the lord or married with the goods and chattels of her said father, since she has several sisters; and the court says unanimously that said Annis is the nearer heir and that she never was alienated or married with the goods of this Robert whereby she ought not be admitted to obtain said inheritance. And seisin is granted them, saving the right of anyone else.[19]

At Dunmow, if the last holder of a tenement had no son and heir, it clearly descended to one of his daughters, and a daughter who, with a portion from her father's goods and chattels, had either married or left the manor was excluded from inheriting if there were other daughters who had not married or left the manor under these conditions. The words of the court roll force us to assume that such was the custom; elsewhere it was explicitly stated, as at Bray and Cookham, Berks., in the year 1224. There, if a tenement was to descend to the daughters of the last holder, then the daughters who had been married out of the tenement with their father's goods and chattels were excluded from the inheritance in favor of the daughter who had remained, as it was said, on the hearth. In this as in other cases, there was a prejudice in favor of the *astrier*, the child who had remained on the *astre*, hearth.[20] Customs of this sort, if applied to sons, might easily end in a Borough English rule.

Finally, if a girl remained on the holding and unmarried, she had the same rights as her brothers had under these circumstances. The heir was bound to provide for her sustenance. Accordingly, at Over, Cambs., one of the Ramsey manors, the following entry appears in a court roll of the year 1300:

Roger Syward and Alan Syward are the pledges of Margery Syward for paying 2 s. to the lord Cellarer that she may have the judgment of the court as to the portion which belongs to her while she lives without a husband out of one villein yardland which was her father's who is now dead. And the village comes and says that said Margery and Avis her sister will have, according to the custom of the manor, their lodging and one ring of corn, namely one half of wheat and the other half of peas, of which Roger Syward their brother will supply them with half and Alan, their other brother, with the other half, because the land is now divided between the said brothers.[21]

Just as at Sevenhampton, Wilts., and and Oakington, Cottenham, and Drayton, Cambs., a son who was not to inherit his family's holding was entitled to his support from it so long as he remained unmarried, so here at Over a daughter who was not to inherit had the same rights. Incidentally, Over is within the country where the usual custom of descent was that a tenement descended to only one son of the last holder, but in this instance the yardland was divided between two sons.

To sum up: in the champion country of England in the thirteenth century the custom generally was that a tenement descended to one of the sons of the last holder and one only. It was also a custom that the daughters of the house and the sons not inheriting either left the tenement, and in leaving took with them their portions of their father's goods (in the case of the girls who married, their dowers), or stayed on the tenement, and in this case had a right to their keep but no right to marry. Plainly these two customs were adapted to one another so that from generation to generation an orderly and expected disposition was made of holdings in land and of the men and women born and brought up on the holdings. Today, we might speak of social security. In the way of material goods most men could look forward to having very little, but of that little they were sure.

HAVING DETERMINED the fate of the children who did not inherit the family tenement, we must return once more to the relations between the holder and his heir. Thus far we have assumed that the heir did not take over the tenement until its last holder died, when he came into the hallmote and made fine for the tenement as the nearer heir according to the custom of the manor, or claimed the reversion of the tenement according to the terms of a settlement made by the last holder during his lifetime. We must move now from the less to the more complex disposition. Often an heir did not have to wait for the death of the last holder before obtaining the tenement: while the last holder was still alive he handed it over to the heir. Consider the following entry of the year 1294 from the court rolls of Cranfield, Beds., one of the manors of Ramsey Abbey:

Elyas of Brickendon surrendered in full court one messuage and a half-yardland at rent in Cranfield, with a wood appurtaining thereto and with all its other appurtenances, and three acres of forland in the same, to the use of John, his son, and this John comes by William LeMoyne of Barnwell his attorney and makes a fine with the lord Abbot of three silver marks for having that land. [The terms at which the marks shall be paid are then specified, and pledges are found for their payment.] And the aforesaid Elyas until Michaelmas next will have all said land properly tilled and sown at his own cost, of which land he and Christiana his wife will fully receive half of the whole crop. And for the rest, the aforesaid John will find for the same Elyas and Christiana his wife honorable sustenance in food and drink so long as they live, and they will dwell with the aforesaid John in lodging on the chief messuage. And if it chance (which God forbid) that quarrels and discords arise in time to come between the parties, so that they cannot dwell together peaceably in one house, the aforesaid John will find for the same Elyas and Christiana, or for whichever one of them survives the other, a house in his courtyard, with a curtilage, where they can honorably dwell, and he will give every year to the same Elyas and Christiana, or to whichever one of them lives the longer, six quarters of hard corn at Michaelmas, namely three quarters of wheat, a quarter and a half of barley, a quarter and a half of beans and peas, and a quarter of oats. And moreover said Elyas and Christiana, according to the covenant made between the parties, will have wholly in their possession all the goods and chattels of said house, movable and immovable, which were theirs on the day when said Elyas surrendered into the hands of the lord his land aforesaid.[1]

By this settlement, a father handed over all his land to his son. Thenceforward the son was to manage the tenement. In return the father stipulated that he and his wife should be cared for in their old age, and the details of the treatment they were to receive were carefully recorded. We should say that the father was arranging for his retirement. The transaction took place before the hallmote, and was entered on its rolls, so that it might be enforced there. One fact incidentally revealed by this settlement should be noticed, that a farmstead of the Middle Ages might have in its yard a dependent cottage, in which the husbandman's old father and mother might live or, perhaps, a married couple of farm laborers, his *undersettles*. Settlements of this sort, though not usually recorded in such detail, are common in the court rolls of the thirteenth and fourteenth centuries of all parts of England.[2]

Another example will show some of the other common provisions of this form of settlement. It comes from the court rolls of Dunmow, Essex, for 1320:

Inasmuch as it was ordered at the last court to seize into the hand of the lord a half-yardland in villeinage which Petronilla of Teye demised to John her son, without the licence of the lord as was found at the last court, it was agreed at this court between the aforesaid Petronilla and John that the aforesaid Petronilla should surrender into the hands of the lord the whole half-yardland aforesaid to the use of the aforesaid John, to whom the seisin is given to have and to hold to said John and his, of the lord in villeinage at his will, for the due and accustomed services, to wit in the following form, to wit that said John will find for said Petronilla for said Petronilla's lifetime reasonable victuals, in food and drink, as befit such a woman, and moreover said Petronilla will have a room, with a wardrobe, at the eastern end of said messuage, to dwell therein during said Petronilla's lifetime, and one cow, four sheep, and a pig, going and feeding on said half-yardland as well in winter as in summer during said Petronilla's lifetime for her clothing and footwear.[3]

Besides its general form, there are two points of interest in this agreement. For one thing, Petronilla was not to have a separate house, as in the last example, but only a room of her own at the end of the house, presumably running across the end. This room at the end of the house appears in other covenants of the kind.[4]

When John took over the holding, did Petronilla move from the room which had been hers to one at the end of the house, further perhaps from the life of the house? For another thing, it is interesting that the cow, the pig, and the sheep, which were to be Petronilla's and were to be fed on the half-yardland, were specifically set apart to provide her with clothes and shoes. Was the wool of these same sheep, the hide of this same cow to be made directly into the proper articles, or was the income from these beasts to be used to buy them? Agreements of this kind have more to suggest about the details of the life of husbandmen in the Middle Ages than any other class of record.

In the commonest form of these settlements, a father or a mother handed his or her holding over to one of the children, bargaining at the same time for sustenance in old age. But like covenants were made in other situations. A man who was poor and old, unable to keep up his holding, and childless, might turn his land over to another in return for his keep. An example of 1332 appears in the court book of Barnet, Herts.:

John in the Hale surrendered into the hands of the lord one messuage and all the land which he held in East Barnet with all its appurtenances. And John ate Barre came and made fine with the lord for holding said messuage and land to himself and his, doing the due and accustomed services thereof, under this form, that the same John ate Barre acknowledges that he will find for the aforesaid John in the Hale yearly so long as the same John in the Hale lives, one new garment with a hood, worth 3 s. 4 d., two pairs of linen sheets, three pairs of new shoes, one pair of new hose, worth 12 d., and victuals in food and drink decently as is proper. And the aforesaid John in the Hale will work for the same John and serve him in proper services to the best of his ability. And the aforesaid John ate Barre satisfied the lord for the heriot of said John in the Hale by one mare, with which the bailiff is charged. And he gives as fine for having entry 3 s.[5]

The provision that John in the Hale would work for the new holder of his tenement is uncommon. Usually the stipulation was that the new holder was to care for the man who had surrendered the tenement to him. So it was in the settlement which gave rise to a suit recorded in the court rolls of Hemingford, Hunts., for 6 Edward II. The case is not strictly relevant to the main thread of argument but is interesting for its own sake:

Henry Edmond and Simon his son complain of Adam Hog that at the feast of the Purification two years ago they agreed between themselves and the aforesaid Adam, to wit that the aforesaid Simon would dwell with the aforesaid Adam in his house from the feast of the Purification aforesaid until the end of the life of said Adam and that after the death of the aforesaid Adam the aforesaid Simon would have one yardland of the land of the same Adam. And for the fuller and firmer observance of this covenant and for the greater security of this matter the aforesaid Adam surrendered the land aforesaid into the hands of the farmer of the village to the use of the aforesaid Simon to hold after his death as is aforesaid and the aforesaid Henry father of this Simon gave a half mark as a fine for holding said land in the aforesaid form. Afterward, indeed, said Adam drove the aforesaid Simon out of his house at the feast of St. Peter's Chains next following and broke the covenant to the damage etc. And the aforesaid Adam well acknowledges the covenant in the form aforesaid but he says that the aforesaid Simon ought to stay with him in his household and ought to serve him well and honestly as his son, and when he had stayed with him from the feast of the Purification aforesaid until the Gule of August, the aforesaid Henry came and enticed from him the aforesaid Simon his son by his counsel and incitement. And he seeks an inquest that it is so, and the others likewise. The inquest is thereupon taken by the twelve jurors aforesaid who say that the aforesaid Adam did not break the covenant with the aforesaid Henry and Simon as they complain, because the same Adam was ready to lodge the same Simon in his house and to keep the covenant, if the aforesaid Simon had not left against the will of said Adam, and he still was ready after he had left if he had wanted to come back. Therefore it is judged that the aforesaid Simon have none of said land after the death of said Adam and that he and his father are in mercy, 6 d., for false complaint. And said Adam goes *sine die* without claim of the said Henry Simon.[6]

Seemingly Adam had no heir and was ready to make Simon heir of his yardland if the latter was willing to live with him and serve him as his son. To confirm this agreement Adam went before the hallmote and made a settlement in a common form whereby Simon was to have the reversion of his yardland after his death, while he himself was to be tenant for life. We are not told why Simon and Henry his father were willing to run the risk of losing the yardland: sometimes medieval court records stop at the most interesting point in the story. The farmer (*firmarius*) of Hemingford was of course the man who had agreed to pay the Abbot of Ramsey, lord of the manor, a fixed yearly sum for the manor in return for the right to collect the rents, services, and other fruits of the manor.

When people handed over their tenements to their heirs and bargained in return for their keep, the matters about which they were most concerned appear plainly in these examples. They required in the first place food and drink. Sometimes the amount of grain they were to be given yearly is specified: grain, in the form of bread or puddings, was the staple food of countrymen. Sometimes the means of obtaining a supply of food were in part kept in the hands of the old folk. Just as a son who was not to inherit but wanted to stay on the family holding was sometimes given a couple of acres of it to hold so long as he remained unmarried, so the old folk sometimes kept for their own use a couple of acres of the holding, or insisted on the right to keep a cow, a pig, or a few sheep. Next in importance after food came clothing. Exactly what garments were to be found for the old folk were entered in the covenant. Lastly, they stipulated that they should have a cottage or at least a room in which to spend the rest of their days.

As usual, besides the specific instances recorded in court rolls and other documents, there is a contemporary statement recognizing that fathers were in the habit of settling during their lifetime some or all of their holdings on their sons. In an account, probably made early in the fourteenth century, of the customs of the bond tenants of Vale Royal Abbey in Darnhall, Cheshire, the following appears:

And whereas some of them have been accustomed to give part of their land to their sons, so that it came about that after their death their sons have by the carelessness of the bailiffs of the place been received as holding those same lands without doing to the lord anything for their seisin in their father's time; those sons who hold land ought to do suit of court, or obtain the lord's grace to redeem the suit at the will of the lord, on account of the great loss which has by this means been suffered by the lord.[7]

At Darnhall, then, the custom was that a father turned over only a part of his holding to his heir rather than the whole of it. The entry is not well phrased, but it seems to complain of the following offence. Villeins who held land were bound to attend sessions of the lord's manorial court. This service was as definite as any other they owed their lord, and they could be amerced if they did not appear. At Darnhall, the bailiffs had not insisted that a son who had received a part of his father's holding should, during the father's lifetime, do suit of court for this land, and the lord had been the loser thereby. The suggestion has been made that the reason why a tenant made his holding over to his heir was that the heir thereby escaped paying the heriot and fine for entry which he would otherwise have had to pay after the death of the last holder. But the entries of many court rolls show that as a matter of fact these payments were not usually avoided by these means.

We have seen that the prospective holder of his family's tenement, who was called the heir, might acquire actual possession of the tenement in one of three ways. After the death of the last holder of the tenement, he might come into the manorial court and be given seisin as nearer heir according to the custom of the manor. Or, again after the death of the last holder, he might come into the manorial court and claim the tenement according to the terms of earlier proceedings before the court, in which he had become tenant in chief and the last holder tenant only for life. Or the last holder during his lifetime might relinquish the tenement to his heir before the manorial court, requiring only that the heir find him in food, clothing, and shelter. In moving from the less to the more complex disposition, we must now consider the relation between the heir's marriage and his acquiring land in one of these ways. There is evidence that the heir's marriage was often dependent on, or even coincident with, his acquiring the whole or a part of the family tenement.

Consider first the following entry of the year 1296 from the court rolls of Amberley, Sussex:

Mabel of Middleton, who held of the lord a certain villein holding, is dead. And the lord has as heriot one mare. And Richard son and heir of said Mabel comes and gives for entry and has seisin and did fealty and found pledges for maintaining the holding and the services. And he gives the lord 12 d. for licence to marry.[8]

Here the last holder was dead, and as soon as the heir had seisin of the tenement he got licence to marry. There is no reason to believe that he married at once: he was simply making provision for the future. But there is a presumption that he could not have thought of marriage before he held the land. On many manors a girl's father, if he was a villein, had to make a payment to the lord when she married, especially when she married outside the manor. This was the customary payment called *merchet*. But customs differed widely in this matter, and on some manors, among which Amberley was one, men as well as women had to pay for licence to marry. Such manors are of great interest to scholars, because only on their court rolls will be found records of the marriages of men.

Consider next this entry in a court roll of 1310 of Hindringham, Norfolk, a manor of the cathedral Priory of Norwich:

Catherine Leman surrenders into the lord's hands one acre and three parts of one rood of land, with one messuage thereupon, and one rood of herbage, to the use of Roger Grilling and Agnes, daughter of this Catherine, and the heirs of the body of this Agnes. And if said Agnes dies without an heir of her body, let the said land revert to the heirs of this Catherine. And for this surrender said Roger and Agnes agree that said Catherine may hold all said land while she lives. And after her death it may remain to said Roger and Agnes in the form aforesaid. And in this form seisin is delivered them, to hold in villeinage at the will of the lord Prior etc., saving etc., and they give etc. And said Roger and Agnes give 5 s. for having seisin and for licence to marry together.[9]

For the most part, this entry is of a familiar kind. By going through a common form of procedure before the hallmote, Catherine Leman determined how her land was to descend at her death. What is new is that she settled the land on her daughter and her daughter's bridegroom just before the couple were married. There is no question here of a marriage at some time in the indefinite future: the marriage was already arranged. We do not know whether Roger and Agnes were to have some use of the house and land, even though Catherine was tenant for life. At least they were sure of having them after her death, and it is likely that, unless they had been provided with land, they would not have felt able to marry.

Consider now another kind of settlement, for example, one recorded in the court rolls of Snetterton, Norfolk, for 1279:

Adam Waryn surrenders into the hands of the lord one messuage and seven acres of land, with all the lands and holdings which he has in Snetterton, to the use of Robert Waryn and his heirs, for the aforesaid Robert and his heirs to have and to hold in villeinage for the due and accustomed services thereof, saving the right etc., and he gives for entry. [He finds pledges, whose names are given.] And the aforesaid Robert agrees and binds himself and his heirs and all the holdings aforesaid to find and keep said Adam to his life's end in food and clothing and all other necessaries.

And the same Robert made fine for licence to marry.[10]

In the margin of the roll is the note that Robert's fine for entry and for licence to marry was 13 s. 4 d. Once more, the first part of this entry is perfectly familiar. Adam Waryn made over his holding to a man who was probably a kinsman — he bore the same name — and in return this kinsman agreed to find Adam in food and clothing for the rest of his life. What is new is the last sentence. As soon as Robert had the land, he paid a fine to the lord for licence to marry. He may not have married at once, but again there is a presumption that he would not have felt free to marry before he held the land.

The manors in which a man had to make a payment to the lord for licence to marry were limited in number, but among this number were the Hertfordshire manors of the Abbey of St. Albans — luckily, because the court books of some of these manors, consisting of extracts copied from the court rolls, have survived as one of the most magnificent sources of English social history.[11] In these court books, many entries are found like the following of the year 1245 from Cashio, Herts.:

Walter le King gives the lord in gersum 10 s. for his father's land and for taking a wife.[12]

Entries like this one are short and business-like and do not tell us much about what actually happened. Perhaps the father had died, and Walter his heir was making his fine for entry into the tenement and at the same time preparing to marry, now that he had land on which he could support a wife and children. More probably Walter's father was still alive but had turned over his tenement to his son and heir on the understanding that the son would keep him in his old age. The son would have to pay his gersum in this case just as surely as he would if he were inheriting the tenement after his father's death. There are more detailed entries in the court books of the St. Albans manors which show that transactions of this general sort in fact took place, for instance the following entry of the year 1325 which refers to Park, Herts.:

Gilbert Hendigome surrendered into the hands of the lord one ferthling of land which John Hugh once held, which land said Gilbert had by grant of the lord. And William, son of said Gilbert, made fine with the lord for holding said land to himself and his, doing the due and accustomed services thereof, and he will not make waste. And he gives as a fine for having entry and for licence to marry 2 s.[13]

Without question many of the shorter entries in the court books would have read much like this one if they had been expanded. A ferthling was, as the word suggests, a fourth of a yardland. In this instance it is clear that Gilbert was still alive when he surrendered the land to his son. In fact an inspection of other entries in the Park court book shows that he had other holdings which he did not surrender at this time. The important point is that as soon as his son had the land he paid the lord for having licence to marry.

Entries like the two which have been cited are extremely common in all the court books of the St. Albans manors. More than a hundred will be found under the reigns of Henry III, Edward I, and Edward II, and there may have been many more in the original court rolls from which the court books were compiled. The regular custom of inheritance in these manors was descent to one son, and in these entries from the court books it is regularly one son of the last holder who makes fine both for seisin of the tenement and for licence to marry. Our conclusion must be that the son and heir was the person who took over his father's tenement and at the same time prepared to take a wife. The other sons married only if they acquired land or some other means of livelihood elsewhere: they were not married with a part of the family's tenement. Our conclusion must also be that the son and heir did not marry until he had the land, either after his father had died or after his father had made over the land to him. Such was a common practice on the Hertfordshire manors of St. Albans Abbey. Such was a common practice in other parts of England, as the earlier entries showed. It may have been more common than we can tell, since in the court rolls of most manors there are few records of the marriages of men. In any case we can speak of it only as a common practice and not as a rigid rule. It was not followed as a matter of course and under all circumstances.

To go on to still more detailed records, there is an interesting passage in the court rolls of Newington, Oxon., of 1306. It is the following:

Agnes ate Touneshende widow of Stephen ate Touneshende came into full court and said that she was powerless to hold one messuage and one yardland of servile condition which formerly she held according to the usage of the manor of Newington after the death of said Stephen. And an inquest is made concerning the kind of this land by the whole court, which says that Agnes who was the daughter of Nicholas ate Touneshende has nearer kind of that land according to the custom of the manor, doing for the lord whatever by right she ought to do for entry. And by the death of the same Agnes the lord will have 5 s. as heriot, because she has no live beast. And afterward said Agnes came and made a fine of a half-mark for entry. And afterward came Henry, son of John Aleyn, and made a fine of a half-mark so that he could take said Agnes to wife. Pledges of the pair, all the tenants of the lord. And whereas the aforesaid Agnes surrendered said land into the hands of the lord so that Agnes, her son's daughter, could enter, therefore said Henry and Agnes agree that to the end of the life of the same Agnes they will find for the same Agnes food and clothing, according to what her station requires. And if this does not satisfy the same Agnes they will give yearly to said Agnes three quarters of grain, namely two of wheat and rye, and one of barley, namely at four terms . . . . And if they fail of payment at said terms in whole or in part, they agree that they are bound to pay the lord a half-mark and said Agnes likewise a half-mark for her damages.[14]

Agnes ate Touneshende, then, surrendered her land in favor of Agnes her grand-daughter. The younger Agnes was about to take a husband, and the couple agreed to support their grand-mother. This was common practice. What is chiefly interesting here is that the younger Agnes was definitely spoken of as the heir of the land. She had the "nearer kind," as the men of Newington said. A good guess is that at Newington, as in the St. Albans manors, the person who took over the holding and then married was the person who would in any case inherit the land after the death of the last holder.

Many examples of this kind of transaction must be given, because it carried into effect a change which may have been more important in family feeling than any change made by death. Consider then the record of a case tried before the king's justices in Eyre in 1227:

An assize comes to determine whether Anseline of Illegha, Richard of Illegha etc. unjustly etc. disseised Hugh de Muntchesney and Alice his wife of their free holding in Illegha, after etc. And Anseline comes and says nothing.

The jurors say that the aforesaid Anseline gave the aforesaid Alice, his daughter, to the aforesaid Hugh, and it was agreed among them that he (Anseline) would give him half of all his acquisitions in Illegha and that they would dwell together in one house, so that the same Anseline would dwell in one room and they in another. And the same Anseline went out of the house and handed over to them the door by the hasp, and at once begged lodging out of charity, and ever afterward remained in seisin, so that that land was tilled with the plow of this Anseline and the corn was used in common, so that he treated his land as his own as before. And whereas the aforesaid Anseline never was out of seisin, it is judged that Hugh and Alice may take nothing by the assize.[15]

This case came before a royal court, because it concerned a free tenement, but the arrangements it revealed are obviously like those made before manorial courts. Anseline agreed to give his daughter to Hugh, with half of his land. Furthermore the father-in-law and the married couple were to live together in one house. The house does not sound like a large one. All this is familiar, but there is much that is new. First, the arrangements to be made were agreed upon between the father and his prospective son-in-law before the marriage. In the Latin phrase, *prolocutum fuit inter eos*. A marriage bargain was made. This fact is interesting, because it suggests that other settlements of this sort were made as a result of marriage bargains, even if nothing was said about such bargains in the court rolls. The hallmote simply registered an agreement made beforehand between the parties. Second, as we should expect in England in the Middle Ages, there was a ceremony. Anseline went out of the house, handed over to the married couple the door by the hasp, and then begged lodging out of charity. The ceremony must have been meant to symbolize that Anseline gave the couple the house and that he was to be no more than their lodger. In many of the other cases which have been cited the position of the father must have been of this sort. But the law expected a real change in management to accompany the grant of the land, and here Anseline had in fact treated the land as his own after the grant as before. Accordingly the court found that the son-in-law had never had seisin of the land and could not recover it.

Medieval literature confirms the evidence of legal documents that it was common for a man as he grew older to make over his tenement to his son and heir, and that the son married only after he had the land. Such confirmation is something which medieval literature, in Latin, French, or English, is rarely able to give. With a few exceptions the men of letters were too much concerned with piety or romance to bother with the lives of common folk. One of the exceptions was the author of *Piers Plowman*; another was Robert Mannyng of Brunne, author of *Handlyng Synne*, written about 1303. In *Handlyng Synne* the following passage occurs:

> Of a man þat sum tyme was,
> Y shal ȝou telle a lytyl pas.
> Of hys sone he was gelous
> And ȝaue hym alle hys land & hous,
> And al hys catel in toune & felde,
> Þat he shulde kepe hym wel yn hys elde.
> Þys ȝong man wax fast, & was iolyfe,
> Hys cunseyl was to take a wyfe;
> He wedded one, & broght here home
> With alle þe myrþe that þerto come;
> He badde here fyrst, loude and stylle,
> To serue hys fadyr weyl at hys wylle.[16]

But as soon as a boy was born to him, he began to think that his father was too heavy a burden, that his father had been alive too long, and he began to mistreat him. At last, when his father was shivering with cold, he bade his young son cover him with nothing more than a sack. The boy cut the sack in two, covered his grandfather with half of it, and showed his father the other half, to signify that just as his father had mistreated his grandfather, so the boy himself when his turn came would mistreat his father in his old age and cover him when he was cold with only half a sack. Rough treatment of this sort cannot have been the common fate of fathers at the beginning of the fourteenth century, or they would not have been as ready as in fact they were to hand over their lands to their sons. Mannyng had said earlier:

> And oþer men also y see,
> Þat ȝyue here chyldryn boþe lond & fee
> For to fynde hem systynaunce
> Yn here age, for alle chaunce.

And he used the horrible tale he told to warn men against this practice, which reversed the natural order of things by making fathers subject to their children. The important point here is not of course the moral, but Mannyng's statement that it was common practice in his time for a man to make over to a son his land, his house, his chattels in town and field, and that in return the son was supposed to find him sustenance in his old age. Another feature of the story is that the son's marriage followed hard upon his getting the land. The arrangements might have been taken straight from a court roll.

Robert of Gloucester in his *Metrical Chronicle*, written at some time in the last decade of the thirteenth century, used the traditional story of King Lear to point a similar moral. Shakespeare has made the story familiar to us, but not the meaning it had for men of the Middle Ages. Lear had no sons, and as he grew old he determined to divide his kingdom among his three daughters. Cordelia, of course, was denied her share because she would not make protestation of her love for her father, but the other two sisters took the land on the understanding that they were to support their father in his old age. As soon as they had the land, they married. But instead of finding their father honorable sustenance, they neglected him and ill-treated him without pity. Robert of Gloucester applied the moral not to daughters but to sons, not to kings but to simple franklins. At the end of his story of Lear he wrote:

> Þis men mowe her ensample nime · to lete hor sones wiue
> & ȝiue hom vp hor lond · al bi hor liue
> Vor wel may a simple frankelein · in miseise him so bringe
> Of lute lond wanne þer biuel · such cas of an kinge.[17]

This passage tells us that countrymen, simple franklins of little land, were in the custom of giving up their lands during their lifetimes to their sons, and the marriages of the sons seem to have been coincident with their acquiring land, just as Goneril and Regan married as soon as their father had given them their shares of his kingdom. It tells us also, what we might have guessed from the entries in the court rolls, that fathers could let their sons take wives, or prevent them from doing so, by giving them land or withholding it from them. We do not know what motives brought a father around to giving his son and heir his tenement and allowing him to marry, but we can guess that among them were the desire for a grandson, the desire to see the son settled in life, the desire to be rid of the responsibility for the tillage of the tenement, and perhaps the fear of what the neighbors would say if the son were kept waiting beyond what was considered a proper age. Robert of

Gloucester's treatment of the story of Lear confirms once more the fact that a father who had turned his tenement over to one of his children expected in return to be supported in his old age. Indeed he confirms at every point what the court rolls have revealed. And he feels with Mannyng of Brunne that fathers in this case were in danger of hard treatment.

The custom by which a man as he grew older made over his land to a son and heir, whereupon the heir took a wife, and not before, is not limited to medieval England. It was and is common in parts of Europe where descent of peasant holdings to one son was the rule. To take one instance, such is the custom of rural Ireland to this day.[18] Modern legislation has changed the rule of inheritance of countrymen's lands in Ireland from the ancient Celtic joint inheritance to inheritance by one son, who is the son the father of the family chooses as his heir. The other sons must leave the family land if they wish to marry and found families of their own. As he gets on in life, the farmer decides that it is time for the heir to have the land and to marry. He does not marry earlier: inheritance and marriage are parts of a single transaction. The changes in the the status of the son, from bachelor to married man, and from landless man to man of property occur together, and make this event the most important in the life of a family.

The time when the change is made is an anxious one. Not only is the father displaced in the management of the holding, but the man who displaces him is his son. He is hard put to it to keep himself from interfering with what the new manager determines to do, especially when the latter is one who has hitherto been subject to him in all the businesses of life. Furthermore, a new woman is brought into the house: the son's wife displaces his mother in the kitchen and at the head of the women's work. The old couple continue to live with their son, but they move into the room which in the traditional farm house is reserved for the old folk, the room called in Ireland the "west room." In time they become used to their new position and adopt new attitudes, but there is always a period of transition. In reconstructing any ancient society, our knowledge of what happens today must give flesh and blood to the dry bones of records: in medieval England, sentiments and behavior like those of

modern Irish countrymen must have accompanied the retirement
of the father and the marriage of the son. The court rolls tell
us nothing about these matters, except sometimes to admit
that discords might arise between the new husbandman and
the old so that they would not wish to dwell together in one house.

We must not take the rule of no land, no marriage to have
been a strict one. A man might marry in expectation of land, or,
as at least one instance will show, a father might settle his
son and his son's wife in a dependent cottage on his tenement,
without making over to them the tenement as a whole. But there
is plenty of evidence that in some parts of England in the
thirteenth century, as in Ireland today, the son and heir did not
in fact marry until he held his father's land. And if a man had
to wait until his father died or gave up his holding, he would
be likely to marry rather late in life. Marriage is late in Ireland
today; it is said to have been late in England in the sixteenth
century,[19] when the social order had not greatly changed from
what it had been in the thirteenth century. And lateness of
marriage may have some effect on the number of children born.
Certainly the families of upland England in the Middle Ages
were not so large as, say, those of New England in the seventeenth
and eighteenth centuries, when work and livelihood in opening
a continent could be found for everyone.

In an age when nearly everyone made his living by tilling the
soil and raising crops, and these not for the most part to be sold
in a market but to be consumed directly, land was a possession
which had an importance all its own. Only if he had land was
a man sure of his livelihood. To this hard fact of economics the
social order had become adapted. The sentiments and customs of
men first specified who was to possess land: land was divided
into tenement units and each of these descended from one man
to another in the blood of the family, the governing custom in
champion country being that a tenement descended to one son
of the last holder. This arrangement was hard on the men who
did not inherit, but it insured that on each tenement in every
generation at least one married couple and their children would
enjoy a decent subsistence. The sentiments and customs also
asserted that only men who held land were to marry. It made
no difference, of course, that an unmarried man had failed to

go through a certain ceremony, but it did make a difference that he did not have a wife and children to be supported on his family's tenement. The working of the rule, no land, no marriage, had two aspects. First, men and women who were not to inherit a family tenement did not marry unless they could secure land for themselves. Second, in many places, the man who was to inherit the tenement did not marry until its last holder was ready to turn it over to him. In this manner the sentiments and customs of men secured a stable adaptation of society to its economic conditions. Despite the logic of Malthus, they limited the number of persons who pressed on the land for subsistence.

CHAPTER XII

TROTHPLIGHT AND WEDDING

M UCH HAS BEEN SAID about the relation between marriage and the holding of land. Now it is time to describe the actual process by which a marriage was contracted: the making of the marriage bargain, the troth-plighting, the wedding at the church door, and the festivities which followed. We can only consider here what may have been one common way of making a marriage. Without doubt, custom in this matter varied greatly from place to place.

There is a passage in *Piers Plowman* which seems to describe how wedlock was wrought in the country in England in the Middle Ages:

> And þus was wedloke ywrouȝt · with a mene persone;
> First bi þe faderes wille · and þe frendes conseille,
> And sytthenes bi assent of hem-self · as þei two myȝte acorde.
> And þus was wedloke ywrouȝt · and god hym-self it made.[1]

First, a man could not marry without his father's consent. According to Robert of Gloucester, it was within the father's power to let his son take a wife or prevent him from doing so. The son and heir could not marry until his father was ready to turn over to him the possession and management of all or a part of the family holding. Once he had decided to give up his land, the father would look about for a suitable match for his son, without question among the daughters of men of his own class and substance. When he had hit upon one to his son's liking and his own, he would open negotiations with the father of the girl to lead to a marriage covenant. Bargaining went before marriage in all the old peasant communities of Europe, and the first move was to send a go-between, a "mean person," to make a proposal to the girl's father. If he was found willing to go further in the matter, the young couple would keep company for several months, to see how well they were matched. Then one day, when they were agreed and contracted together, the father of the girl would take her over to the house and tenement which the young man was to have, in order to find out if all was in good order and to their liking. As in a country wedding in Ireland today, a view was made of the man's land, and at once thereafter the two fathers would thrash out the terms of the marriage covenant. The matters which would be discussed were the amount of the dower the girl's father would give with her to bring to her new home, the kind of settlement of land the boy's father would make upon the couple, and the endowment the groom would make to the bride at the church door.[2]

The next thing for the boy's father to do was to go before the hallmote. There he would surrender his land to the lord to the use of his son, and the son would make fine for having entry into the tenement and for having licence to marry, if the custom of the manor was that he ought to pay such a fine. Sometimes the marriage covenant was entered on the rolls of the court. For instance, under the year 1289 in the court rolls of Newington, Oxon., the following entry appears:

It is thus agreed between William le Toter' of Warborough on the one hand and James West on the other, to wit that said James will marry Alice daughter of said William, and said William will acquit said James toward the lord of a fine of eleven marks and will give this James other chattels, as is agreed between them. Therefore said James granted to this William the whole profit of his land from Michaelmas this year until the end of the four years following, and the latter will remove no goods out of the fee of the lord, and will maintain and mend the houses, and will keep said James throughout said time. And in the fifth year he will have for the same James at the Gule of autumn his land under crop, together with hay and all other fruits of that year.[3]

What is involved in this agreement is plain enough. Even when the actual terms of a covenant had not been entered in the rolls of the manorial court, but had been left to common knowledge, any breach of covenant was a cause for an action before the court. This held true of marriage covenants as of any others. Accordingly, in the court rolls of Houghton, Hunts., for 2 Edward II, the following entry is found:

It is found by the jurors that Stephen the reeve broke a covenant with Andrew the reeve in that they agreed among themselves that the aforesaid Stephen ought to have kept Agnes daughter of said Andrew and to have lodged her in his house, or to have found proper lodging for her within his yard, together with all things needful to her, by reason that Stephen son of said Stephen married the aforesaid Agnes. And this Stephen (the father) afterward drove the aforesaid Agnes out of his house contrary to the aforesaid covenant. Therefore the aforesaid Stephen is in mercy 40 d. Pledges, John Mareschal, Alexander the reeve, Robert le Hyrde, John le Porter. And for these pledges the aforesaid Stephen the reeve will keep the aforesaid Agnes with her husband in his house or will find proper lodging for her within his yard, together with all things needful to her, etc.[4]

Here is a case in which the father agreed to keep his son's wife and allow the couple to live with him or in a dependance in his farmyard. But clearly he kept control of the holding himself. This arrangement is unlike the custom whereby the marriage of the son and heir was accompanied by his taking over management and possession of the family holding. Marriage settlements cannot be reduced to one form. Clearly also the marriage settlement was the result of a covenant made between the father of the bride and the father of the groom. Bad feeling later arose in the joint household. We should much like to know what its cause was.

A father must always have been preoccupied with making good matches for his children. Was there an heiress to whom he could marry his son? Was there a young man with land to whom he could marry his daughter? According to the passage in *Piers Plowman*, the consent of the young man and woman was expected only after their fathers had made the match, not before. Many fathers decided whom their children were to marry without even waiting until they were of age. So long as a good match could be made, it made no odds when it was made. Thus in the court books of Cashio, Herts., under the year 1294, the following entry occurs:

Walter, Ailrich's son, came and made fine for the land which belonged to Ailrich his father. And thereupon came Adam Irman and took said land and said Walter the heir until he is of age, so that in the meanwhile he will build and will maintain the land and the holding and will give Helen daughter of said Adam to said Walter. And he will do the due and accustomed services. And he gives, for the fine and for the term of years and for the licence to marry, a half-mark.[5]

In short, Adam Irman took the wardship of Walter and the management of his land until he was of age. But Adam did not propose to let Walter or his land go out of the family later, and therefore Walter was to marry Adam's daughter.

When marriage was a means of getting possession of land or

goods, many a father was not content with arranging a marriage to take place at some time in the future, but made sure of his gains by having the young couple joined in wedlock at once, even if they were still in childhood. Robert Mannyng of Brunne, in *Handlyng Synne*, denounced the practice of making child-marriages:

> ȝyf þou dedyst euer swyche outrage
> To wedde chyldryn or þey hadde age,
> Þare-of may come grete folye
> ȝyf þey so ȝunge to-gedyr lye.[6]

He later explained the reasons for these matches:

> Also, for men by-hete hem largely,
> Are chyldryn wedded ofte for-þy;
> For þyr are many wedded for gode,
> And for no stedfast loue of blode.[7]

According to Mannyng, children were often wedded simply as a result of the large promises their parents made about the goods the children would bring with them in marriage. He maintained that when couples married in childhood grew up they often wanted to break off their marriages:

> Many one weddeþ euery deyl
> For þe loue of syre kateyl;
> Whan hyt ys go, and ys alle bare,
> Þan ys þe weddyng sorowe & kare;
> Loue ande catel þan ys awey,
> And 'welaweye' þey cry and sey.[8]

But good fathers cannot have wholly disregarded their children's inclinations in marriage. And there is at least one entry from a court roll in which two fathers arranged for the marriage of their children, and made other agreements to accompany the marriage, but the lord's representative in court, in giving his licence for the marriage, expressly provided that the young couple must consent.[9] In forbidding child-marriages, the position of the Church, as it was expressed in the Constitution of St. Edmund Rich, Archbishop of Canterbury, was that where there was no consent there was no *coniugium*.[10]

But we are speaking too soon in speaking of marriage, if we mean by marriage a ceremony performed at church and by a priest. In Miles Coverdale's translation, of about 1541, of a work of Bullinger's under the title of *The Christen State of Matrimonye,* there is the following interesting passage:

After the hand fasting & makyng of the contracte, the church goyng & wed-dyng shulde not be deffered to long, lest the wicked sowe hys vngracious sede in the mene season. . . . For in some places ther is such a maner, wel worthy to be rebuked, that at the hand fastynge there is made a great feast & super-fluous bancket, & even the same night are the two hand fasted persones brought & layed together, yea certayne wekes afore they go to the church.[11]

This text is of the sixteenth century, and we have so far discovered nothing to reveal customs of precisely this sort in the thir-teenth. Nevertheless, these words of Coverdale's at once carry conviction as a description of the behavior of countryfolk throughout the Middle Ages. They tell us that when the marriage covenant had been made, a ceremony took place. Coverdale called it the hand-fasting; it was also called the troth-plight. Its names show that in the ceremony the man and the woman at least joined hands and plighted their troths one to another. The ceremony was celebrated with a feast; that same night the couple were bedded, and only certain weeks later did they go to church.

Nothing has yet been discovered which directly reveals the existence of such customs in the thirteenth century, but there is much evidence which is compatible with their having existed. For one thing, there is the matter of bastard children. At common law, bastards were excluded from inheriting land; the question came on the definition of a bastard. In the Council of Merton in 1236, the barons of England made their famous declaration: *Nolumus leges Anglie mutari,* in refusing to allow that the subsequent marriage of their parents made legitimate, so far as concerned their inheriting land, children who had been born out of wedlock. But the barons' protest determined only what the common law in the matter was to be. The customs of some manors, and particularly of their bond tenants, continued to be more lenient and to allow children born out of wedlock to inherit under certain circumstances. Consider, for example, an entry of the year 1271 in the court book of Park, Herts.:

Simon, son of William atte Leye, gives the lord 12 d. to have an inquest whether he is nearer heir than William his brother. And the same William gives 18 d. for the same. And the inquest says that the same William is nearer heir than said Simon his brother, since the same William was the first born, and his father had plighted his troth to his mother before the same William was born, therefore etc. And the same William came and made fine for the land of the said William his father, doing thereof etc.[12]

In this entry nothing is said about whether William was born before the marriage of his parents. The inference is that he was: otherwise there would have been no excuse for a lawsuit. But the statement is made that his father plighted his troth to his mother before William was born: *pater suus matrem suam affideuerat antequam idem Willelmus genitus fuit.* In the eyes of the hallmote, the trothplight, not the wedding, was the important ceremony. So long as he was born after trothplight, nothing in the custom of the manor prevented William from inheriting his father's land as his father's eldest son. Another case, in which the fact is made plain that the birth of the son came after the trothplight but before the marriage of his parents, occurs in the court rolls of 1286 of Wakefield, Yorks., at the other end of England from Park:

Robert, son of Richard de Rissewrth of Wakefeud, and John his brother, come and crave the land of Thomas, son of Nigel de Wakefeud, as his heirs. John says Robert ought not to be heir, because he was born before marriage solemnized at the church porch, but after the plighting of troth privately between them. Robert, the elder brother, says it is the custom on the lord's land in these parts for the elder brother, born after trothplight, to be heir, and he therefore prays to be admitted as heir.

The bailiffs of the lord, the Earl of Warenne and Surrey, wished to be sure of their ground. Accordingly an inquest was taken by six graves: a grave in the North Country was nearly equivalent to a reeve in other parts of England. The six graves said on their oath that the facts were as stated and that by the custom of the countryside (*patria*) Robert ought to be heir.[13] In 1315 a case of exactly the same kind came before the manor court of Wakefield, but at that time the bailiffs were still more uncertain and decided to consult the council of the lord Earl.[14] They must have been disturbed by the contrast between the common law and the custom of the countryside. But it is clear that in earlier days at Wakefield, whatever the rule of the common law may have been, a man who was born before the wedding of his mother and father but after troth plighted between them was not disbarred from inheriting their land.

Both at Park and at Wakefield, the eldest son was born after his parents had plighted their troth but before they had been joined in wedlock by the Church. On the other hand, the second son must have been born after his parents had gone to the church to be married, or he would have had no grounds for an action before the hallmote. Plainly these events of the thirteenth century are consistent with what Coverdale said about the marriage customs of countryfolk in the sixteenth. The trothplight was the important ceremony, and may well have marked the making of the marriage covenant. After the trothplight the couple were bedded, and only certain weeks later were they married at the church.

Both at Park and at Wakefield, the certain weeks of delay after trothplight before the couple were married at the church became in fact a delay until their first child was born. This fact is interesting, because according to the customs of countryfolk of more recent times both in England and on the continent, a man did not marry a woman until a child had been born to them, or at least until he had gotten her with child, but was under an obligation to marry her then. As late as the last century, this was the custom of the Isle of Portland in Dorset:

It has been the custom of the island from time immemorial that they never marry until the woman is pregnant. The mode of courtship is that a young woman never admits the serious addresses of a young man but on the basis of a thorough probation. When she becomes with child it is then considered the proper time to be married, which then almost invariably takes place.[15]

Customs of the same sort are likely to have obtained in Park, Wakefield, and other English villages of the thirteenth century. They differed from our marriage customs but were not loose or promiscuous. We cannot tell what reasons countrymen gave for their existence, if indeed they gave any. One may have been that a man ought to make sure he was not marrying a barren woman. Children were an economic necessity to a subsistence farmer, and in a society where people felt strongly that a holding of land ought to descend in the blood of a family, the lack of an heir was a disaster.

We have seen that a trothplight was often the proper and

accepted beginning of a relationship which eventually became a marriage. But often it was something like the opposite. A man would go through the ceremony as a means of having his will of a woman he had no intention of marrying. Once more we are enlightened by a book of the sixteenth century. In the second edition (1537) of Richard Whitforde's *A Werke for Housholders* the following passage occurs:

For many men whan they can not obteyn theyr vnclene desyre of the woman wyl promyse marryage, & thervpon make a contracte promyse, & gyve fayth & trouth eche vnto other sayenge. Here I take the Margery vnto my wyfe, I therto plyght the my trouth. And she agayne, vnto hym in lyke maner. And after that done, they suppose they maye lawfully vse thyr vnclene behauyour, and somtyme the acte and dede doth folow, vnto the great offence of god & theyr owne soules.[16]

This passage tells us something about the actual form of a trothplight. It consisted at least of words of the present tense in which the two persons took each other as man and wife. People must have felt a sentiment that such a trothplight did in fact make a good marriage, that the words were in fact binding, and that after they had been pronounced it was permissible to proceed at once to the act of kind without waiting for marriage at the church. Otherwise women would not have been so easily deceived by men who were willing to plight them their troth.

In the thirteenth century trothplights were abused in just the same way. Mannyng of Brunne condemned the practice in harsh words:

> A werse spyce ȝyt men holdes,
> To begyle a womman with wordys;
> To ȝyue here trouþe but lyghtly
> For no þyng but for lygge here by;
> With þat gyle þou makest here asent,
> And bryngest ȝow boþe to cumbrement.[17]

Again, in the Constitutions of Richard Poore, Bishop of Salisbury, dating from about 1217, it was forbidden that

anyone encircle the hands of a young woman with a ring of rush or of any other material, vile or precious, in jest in order to fornicate with her the more freely, lest while he (or she) thinks he jests he avoid the honors of marriage.[18]

This statement completes our knowledge of the ceremony of trothplight. It consisted of a solemn joining of the hands of the man and the woman, the giving and receiving of a ring, and the saying of words of the present tense in which the man took the woman as his wife and the woman took the man as her husband. Perhaps some of these elements would be omitted if the trothplight was performed privily, by the man and the woman without witnesses.

Obviously these features of the trothplight were also features of the marriage ceremony of the Church. There is little likelihood that the trothplight took the form it did in imitation of the church marriage service. Instead, the Church took over the form of a secular marriage service which was ancient in Europe, and in the Middle Ages this secular marriage service, the trothplight, still maintained some degree of independence of the Church.

In the thirteenth and later centuries a sentiment existed that a troth plighted between a man and a woman, privily or before witnesses, was a proper beginning of a permanent union. As a matter of fact, the Church asserted that in her eyes as well such a troth made a valid marriage. The strength of the sentiment accounts in part for the action of the Church; the action of the Church accounts in part for the strength of the sentiment. According to Canon Law, if a man and a woman said that they were man and wife, if there was an espousal using "words of the present tense," they were married, without more ado. If the marriage was not consummated, it might be dissolved, by papal dispensation or by the taking of religious vows by either one of the spouses. And if a man and a woman said that they would thereafter become husband and wife, and such an espousal using "words of the future tense" was followed by intercourse, this act also, without further ceremony, constituted a marriage. Of course there would be difficulty in proving that the espousal had taken place, if it had taken place when the man and the woman were alone and either one of them later wanted to deny it. The Church much preferred to have the marriage service performed by a priest, after due publication of the banns, but by her own canons these formalities were not essential.[19]

If countryfolk felt that it was not wholly improper for a man and woman to proceed to the act of kind after they had plighted their troths privily to one another, we cannot be surprised if some bastards were born and much fornicating went on which was a matter of common knowledge. If a woman fornicated, she, or her father, or the man in question was bound on many manors to pay the lord a fine, which was called *leyrwite*. And if she bore a child out of wedlock she was bound on some manors to pay *childwite*. These fines were levied at the manorial court, and on the rolls of some manors they are often recorded. But, as we should expect, there is evidence that the man in question sometimes married the woman. In a statement of the services owed by the holder of a half-yardland in Horningsea, Cambs., in the Ely custumal of 1277, we read the following:

Also if this man's daughter fornicated with anyone and is cited for it, then he will give 32 d. for leyrwite. And if the man with whom she fornicated afterward married her, then he will be quit of the gersum.[20]

He would not have to pay the usual marriage fine. Being cited for fornication meant being charged with it before the ecclesiastical court, which had jurisdiction over this form of misdemeanor.

There is no reason to believe that a man and a woman lived together for an indefinite period with nothing more than a trothplight to mark their union. In some places, the opinion of the countryside may have allowed them to do so, but in most it must have expected them to be married in church sooner or later, when the woman was with child or when she had borne a child. Let us suppose, then, that their fathers had arranged a marriage between a man and a woman, that they themselves had consented, and that the marriage covenant had been made. Whether or not they had gone through the form of a trothplight, whether or not they had lived together, they would decide one day to go to their parish church to be wedded.

The manuals which are our authorities for the order of the marriage service of the English Church in the Middle Ages are brief and uncertain at several points or differ among themselves. When there are differences, what appears to be the oldest Sarum manual will here be followed.[21] Before the priest married the man and woman, the banns were to be published. That is, the priest had to announce to his congregation the forthcoming wedding and ask anyone who knew any impediment why the couple might not lawfully be joined together to speak or forever after hold his peace. The banns were to be published between celebrations of the mass on three solemn and distinct days, a feast day to intervene between each two of the three. Until the banns had been published, the priest was not to allow the man and the woman to plight their troths.

The marriage service fell into two parts. The first and most important part took place at the church door. Everyone will remember the Wife of Bath's boast:

> Housbondes at chirche door I have had fyve.

The second part of the service took place within the church. Let us suppose that the man and the woman are standing at the church door before God, the priest, and the assembled company. Around them would be ranged their kinsfolk and perhaps their bridesmen or bridesmaids. Thereupon the priest inquired once more, first of the man and the woman themselves and then of the assembled company, if they knew any impediment why the couple might not lawfully be joined together.

The groom then named the dower which he gave to his bride.[22] We mean one of two things when we speak of a dower in the Middle Ages. We may mean the goods and chattels which the bride's father gave with her in marriage. Properly speaking, this was her marriage portion. On the other hand, we may mean the endowment given by the bridegroom to the bride at the church door, which she would enjoy after his death for her support. According to the lawyers of the time, the groom either named the particular dower he gave his bride, or if he named no particular dower and spoke only in general terms, he was understood to have endowed her with that share of his possessions with which it was customary in the neighborhood for husbands to endow their wives. As we shall see, dowers were commonly in land. Besides his announcement of the dower, the groom made an immediate gift to the bride. He placed gold or silver and a ring on a shield or book, together with pence to be distributed to the poor. The money and the ring would be delivered to the bride later in the wedding service.

The priest then inquired if the man and the woman consented to their marriage. In a form much like the present one, he asked the man whether he would have the woman as his wife, and the man answered, "I will." In the same manner the woman was asked her consent and gave it. Thereupon the bride's father or some other near kinsman gave her to the groom, who took her right hand in his, and the couple may then have spoken the words by which they plighted their troths each to the other. In later centuries they would have plighted their troths at this point in the service, but the manuals of the thirteenth century do not make it certain that they did so in those days. What is certain is that words of the present tense spoken by the groom saying: "I take thee Margery as mine," or some formula of the sort, and similar words spoken by the bride, had some part in the wedding service of that century.[23]

Next the ring was blessed and asperged. Taking the ring from the priest, the groom placed it on the bride's middle finger and said: "With this ring I thee wed." And then, giving her the money, he said: "And with this gold I thee honor." According to some uses, the dower was announced at this time instead of at an earlier point in the service. Thus after the placing of the ring on the bride's finger, the York manual prescribes: "Let the priest ask the woman's dower. Then if land is given to her in dower, let her fall at the man's feet." [24] The gift to the bride of the ring and the money was held to be the outward and visible sign of the endowment which the groom gave her. This is made clear in a manuscript manual of Salisbury use, which specifies that after the priest had blessed the ring and had given it to the groom to put on the bride's finger, he said to the groom: "Lo! this gold and this silver is laid down in signifying that the woman shall have her dower, thy goods, if she abide after thy decease." [25] The gift of the money and the ring in fact determined the name of the ceremony at the church door. The groom made the gift to his bride as a *wed*, that is, a gage or pledge, of the fulfillment of the marriage contract. In the words of the old ballads, he wedded her with a ring. The ceremony was a *wedding*.

Three things were involved in this part of the marriage service: a rite, a statement, and a practical arrangement. The rite was the solemn gift to the bride by the bridegroom of money and a ring. This gift was said to stand for the endowment, commonly in land, which the groom announced he gave to the bride. This endowment had no immediate practical consequences, since the husband continued to possess and manage all his land and goods. Only if he died and his wife survived him did the endowment go into effect. Then the wife had, as we shall see, a legal right to hold during her lifetime those lands which her husband had given her at the church door. A strong sentiment of countryfolk might be expressed in this way: "A widow ought to enjoy a certain portion of her husband's land after his death, because he endowed her with it at the church door when they were married." The endowment was a measure of social security.

The gift of the money and the ring, together with the words which accompanied the gift, may have seemed to countrymen the most important part of the marriage service. It was in fact the climax of what took place at the church door. After the priest had given his blessing to the couple, they moved from the church door into the church itself. There, at the steps of the altar, a nuptial mass was celebrated. Nothing remarkable occurred in this ceremony until near its end. Then, after the *Sanctus*, the couple knelt in prayer, and a pall, the care-cloth, was stretched over them. According to a letter of the great thirteenth-century Bishop of Lincoln, Grosseteste, there was a custom in use before his time, according to which any children that had been born to the couple before marriage were placed beneath the care-cloth at this point in the service and were held to be legitimated thereby. This custom also obtained in Germany and France.[26] The care-cloth remained over the bride and groom until the end of the mass. Then the groom received the kiss of peace from the priest, and in turn kissed the bride. Thereafter the Church had no more to do, except perhaps to bless the bridal bed. Countrymen must have felt that the second part of the marriage service, the mass within the church, was must less needful than the wedding at the church door. The wedding was what they meant when they spoke of a marriage; the rest was an addition. Perhaps for a poor couple no special mass would be celebrated.

After the wedding there would be merrymaking. Without doubt in the thirteenth century it took in the main the form it does now, of a bridal feast with a bridal cake. There was a bride-ale. Then the newly married couple would be bedded. But we know almost nothing in detail about the marriage festivities of the Middle Ages. One little thing we do know, that in some parts of England a villein was bound to give a dinner on his wedding day to the workmen on his lord's demesne. Thus at Wistow, Hunts., in 1294 we see a man fined in the hallmote for not doing so:

Robert Juwel was convicted by the jurors of this, that by custom he ought to have given a meal to all the servants of the Court of Wistow on the day when he married his wife, and he did not do so. Therefore he is in mercy for unjust detention, 12 d., pledge, Robert atte Broke. And by the same pledge he will satisfy the same servants for the aforesaid meal.[27]

Another story, which suggests that wedding festivities in the thirteenth century were not unlike what they are today, is the following. One day in 1268, a newly married couple and others of the wedding party were stopped in Byram, near Ferrybridge, Yorkshire, by a certain William Selisaule, who demanded of them a ball, which, the record says, "is given out of custom." The wedding party had no ball but gave a pair of gloves as pledge for the ball. Later, other men of the village of Byram came up and demanded a ball. The wedding party told the truth, that they had already given a pledge for the ball, but they were not believed. A brawl arose in consequence, and the men of the wedding party, who were "somewhat drunk," assaulted the men of Byram with hatches, bows, and arrows. Many were wounded, and one man was killed.[28] Wedding parties, then as now, were likely to be somewhat drunk. But in those days every man went armed, so that if there was trouble, the trouble was usually bad. The custom of demanding a ball of the bridegroom has had a long history. It was common in Germany, was well established in the coal-mining districts of northern England not long ago, and perhaps is still.[29]

Much has been said about marriage. Something should also be said about divorce, although when men of the Middle Ages spoke of a divorce they did not mean what we mean today. They meant either a separation of the couple because their marriage was held to be invalid or a separation from bed and board. They did not mean the dissolution of what was held to be a valid marriage, allowing both parties to remarry. The Church did not tolerate such a divorce. An example of a separation from bed and board, with a settlement for the support of the woman, is found in the court book of Cashio, Herts., under the year 1301:

Reginald atte Lee by licence of the lord granted that Lucy his wife might hold, as long as she lived, all the land, with one house and with all other appurtenances except the rent of Watford, which Sarah atte Lee, mother of the aforesaid Reginald, held in the name of dower after the death of her husband, doing the due and accustomed services thereof, and she will come and go in such a way as not to enter the close or the doors of said Reginald. And said Reginald granted that said Lucy might hold the aforesaid land with a house and other appurtenances, as aforesaid, although a divorce between them be celebrated. And said Lucy granted that if she prevented a divorce between them from being celebrated in lawful manner, and that too at the suit and cost of said Reginald, from then on said covenant might be held for null, and he might have his land back without hindrance.[30]

Reginald literally did not want his wife to darken his door again, although his close plainly was near the land he was giving her. And in order to make sure that she would not stand in the way of his getting a divorce before the ecclesiastical court, he provided that if she did so she would lose the settlement he was making upon her.

We must remember the circumstances in which a marriage took place. The man who was getting married was often the heir of a holding in the village. If his brothers married, they married only when they acquired land or other means of support for themselves elsewhere. The heir himself did not marry until he could keep a wife. Either his father was dead, and he had inherited the family holding, or his father was ready to surrender the holding to him in whole or in part. In this instance, the heir's taking over the management of the holding coincided with his marrying and bringing home a new woman, so that this crisis was the greatest in the life of a family.

The making of a marriage was attended at every moment by considerations of lands and goods. What would the woman's father give with her as her marriage portion? What part of the holding would the man's father settle upon him? What endowment would the groom give his bride at the church door? No wonder that making a match was a matter of bargaining, and that the persons who made it were the persons in control of the possessions which would change hands — the father of the woman and the father of the man.

When the marriage covenant had been made, the man and the woman plighted their troths. In some parts of England the trothplight was celebrated with solemnity but outside the church. Only after the woman was with child or had borne a child did the couple go to church, and whatever the rule of the common law, the custom of some hallmotes and of the villeins under their jurisdiction was that a child born after the trothplight of his parents but before their marriage at church was entitled to inherit their lands. In fact the Church itself allowed that espousals using words of the present or future tenses made good marriages. But the feeling that a trothplight was a binding ceremony made it easy for a man to take advantage of a woman by going through the ceremony with her privily, so that he could afterwards deny, if he wished, that it had ever taken place.

Sooner or later, after the marriage covenant had been made, the man and the woman went to be married at church. The most important part of the service was the first, the wedding at the church door. The ceremony was symbolic. When we say it was symbolic we mean that in the ceremony certain acts were performed, certain words were said, which those present recognized as referring to matters outside the immediate situation. The woman's father gave her to the priest to be married to the man: her master would in fact no longer be her father but her husband. The man and the woman joined hands and said that they took each other as husband and wife: they were in fact to live together thenceforward. The man gave his wife money and a ring and proclaimed her dower: she would in fact hold a part of his land and goods after his death.

Men are likely to mark with a ceremony any great change in their condition. For the bride and the groom, the marriage marked a change in their status. For the bride's family, it marked the loss of a member, for the groom's family, the gain of one, and often it marked the retirement of the groom's father and mother. For the community at large — the wedding at the church door was a public ceremony — it marked the establishment of a new married couple. We may go on to say that the reason why men are likely to mark with a ceremony any great change in their condition is that they thereby express in action the sentiments connected with that change. We assume that men have a tendency to express their sentiments in actions. We assume also that a ceremony performs a function: that it brings about a useful reorganization of the sentiments of men and that by evoking certain sentiments useful to the stability of society it strengthens them. The marriage service, by giving solemn recognition to the change it marked, made the readjustment of their attitudes easier for the married couple, for their families, for the whole community, and reaffirmed in everyone the traditional cluster of sentiments associated with marriage.

CHAPTER XIII

FREE BENCH, CURTESY, AND WARDSHIP

A<small>T THE CLIMAX</small> of the wedding at the church door, the groom placed a ring on the bride's finger and made her a gift of money. These things were held to be symbols of the endowment of the bride by the groom. According to one use, the priest said to the man: "Lo! this gold and this silver is laid down in signifying that the woman shall have her dower, thy goods, if she abide after thy decease." This sentence speaks of goods, and there is no doubt that a groom might endow his bride with his goods, in the sense of his movable possessions. She probably would not be endowed with all of them: as we have seen, a common custom was that the widow received one third of her late husband's movables, if there were surviving children. But a dower was usually a matter of land, and when people spoke of a dower made at the church door they meant in the first instance a dower in land. If what was true of the free tenures was true of the others, a groom at the church door might either endow his bride with certain specific lands, which he named, or if he named no particular lands and spoke in general terms, he was understood to have endowed her with that part of his holding with which it was customary, either in his tenure or in his neighborhood, for husbands to endow their wives. The endowment at the church door made no practical change in affairs at the time. The husband continued to be master of all the possessions of his household. But when the husband died, his widow had a claim to enjoy for her lifetime a part of his land, on the strength of the fact that he had endowed her at the church door. She claimed "in the name of dower."

It appears that at common law a woman had no right to her dower after her husband's death unless in fact he had wedded her at the church door. Before the king's justices, in the Michaelmas term of 1225, Alice, widow of James de Cardunville, sued Hugh of Welles, Bishop of Lincoln, for a third of two plowlands with their appurtenances in Chislehampton, Oxon., as her dower, "with which said James endowed her on the day he wedded her." The record of the case goes on as follows:

And the bishop comes and says that he does not understand that she ought to have dower therein, since she never was married in the face of the Church, but indeed it may well be that he (James) betrothed (*affidavit*) her in the sickness whereof he died and in his house, but he (the bishop) well knows that while he was healthy and about he always kept her in swinkage as his lover, and he (the bishop) seeks judgment whether he ought to give her dower by reason of such a trothplight (*pro tali fide*).

And Alice says that indeed she was wedded to the same James in that house in his sickness, so that he placed a ring on her finger, and afterwards he recovered and went about from place to place, and she says that the banns were published at three neighboring churches for three Sundays before he wedded her, and he wedded her in the aforesaid manner in his house on the morrow of St. George and he died afterwards on the day of the Nativity of St. John the Baptist, and she likewise seeks judgment whether or not she ought to have dower therein. And whereas she herself acknowledges that she was not wedded at the church door, nor endowed there, it is deemed that the bishop be quit therein and Alice be in mercy, and that she have no dower therein, because the troth which the same James gave, he gave for the safety of his soul and in peril of death.[1]

James de Cardunville, like many men after him, had married his mistress in expectation of death. There was no denying that they were married. True, they had plighted their troth one to another in James' house and not at church, but the Church held that such a trothplight made a good marriage. The point at issue was not whether James and Alice had been married, which, by the way, would have been determined by an ecclesiastical, not a royal court, but whether their marriage was of such a sort as to give Alice the right to her dower after her husband's death. The justices ruled that she had no right to her dower because she had not been wedded at the church door. "At first sight," Maitland says, "the lay tribunal seems to be rigidly requiring a religious ceremony which in the eyes of the Church is unessential." But it is likely that the justices demanded the wedding at the church door not because it was a religious ceremony but because it gave publicity to the endowment. A clandestine marriage did not. On this rule of the common law the Bishop of Lincoln was relying when he disputed Alice's right to dower out of James de Cardunville's lands.

Consider now the following entry, one of many of the kind, from the court book of Park, Herts., of the year 1313:

William of Smaleford surrendered into the hands of the lord his whole tenement which he held. And said William and Benedicta le Knyghtes give the lord 2 s. for said tenement with its appurtenances to hold to themselves and to the heirs of said William after the death of said William and Benedicta, doing the due and accustomed services thereof, and they will not make waste. And they have licence to marry together. And they will not take their chattels out of the lord's fee.[2]

Why did William go through this transaction, making himself and his wife joint tenants of his holding in place of himself as sole tenant? It is not likely that he did so in order to fix the descent of the holding to their heirs, because it would have gone to them in any event. Probably he did so in order that Benedicta might keep the holding after he, William, died. At least this possibility must be borne in mind. Observe also that the settlement was made immediately before the marriage of William and Benedicta.

Consider next the following plea as it is recorded in the court book of Barnet, Herts., under the year 1303:

Alice of Rallingbury comes and seeks the land which she had until her life's end by licence of the lord of the gift of Gilbert Edward once her husband, which land Richard Snouh holds, unjustly as she says. And said Richard says that he is nearer heir and was seised thereof by licence of the lord and that said Alice never was seised thereof until her life's end or otherwise, and he seeks that this be inquired. And said Alice likewise. The inquest says that said Alice had said land by gift of said Gilbert at the church door, and since that endowment was held as null without the licence of the lord, said Alice came at that time and made fine with the lord to hold said land to the end of the life of the same Alice, and that after the death of the same Alice it should revert to the true heirs, doing thereof, etc. Therefore it is deemed that said Alice hold etc. in the form aforesaid.[3]

Here the statement is made in so many words that a man endowed a woman at the church door at the time they were married with land which she was to hold after his death. But at Barnet such an endowment was null and void without the licence of the lord, and therefore Alice came into court and made fine with the lord to hold the land to the end of her life. A good guess is that the settlement was much like the one from Park which was cited earlier, that Gilbert Edward surrendered the land to the lord and that the lord regranted it to Gilbert and Alice as joint tenants. Alice's interest in the land was a life interest. That is, after her death it was not to descend to her own heirs but was to revert to the heirs of her dead husband, although of course these might be children of her husband and herself. In this instance, Richard Snouh, the nearer heir of the land, does not seem to have been a son of Alice and Gilbert.

Both at Park and at Barnet, the widow held her late husband's land after his death as a result of a specific settlement made before the hallmote and registered on its rolls. Park and Barnet were among the manors of St. Albans Abbey, where such settlements seem to have been particularly common. On most manors no such elaborate procedure was necessary. The part of her late husband's tenement which a widow might claim to hold after his death was fixed, like so many other things, by custom, and on such manors the husband probably did not make a specific endowment to his wife at the church door but made his endowment in general terms, allowing the custom of the countryside to take effect. The most frequent custom was that whereby a widow had the right to hold one third of her late husband's tenement after his death, just as she took one third of his chattels, and this was also the rule of the common law. Elsewhere the widow had the right to one half of the tenement or even the whole of it — custom in this matter varied greatly — but in any case the amount was fixed. The widow's interest in her share was no more than a life interest. At her death it reverted to the holder of the rest of the tenement. She might not permanently alienate it. The tenement was not permanently divided.

When a widow made claim to her customary part of her late husband's land, she was sometimes said to claim "in the name of dower," that is, on the strength of the endowment he had made to her at the church door. But sometimes she was said to claim the land as her "free bench." Without question this name for the widow's part referred at one time to the special seat by the family hearth which the widow enjoyed as her right, but by the thirteenth century it had become merely a technical term of law. Whether the documents speak of dower or of free bench, they are speaking of the same thing.

It is well to return to particular cases. An entry which gives the essentials of most customs of free bench appears in the court rolls of Bucksteep in Warbleton, Sussex, of the year 1322:

Philip Capel died, who held of the lord six acres of land in bondage, for which he rendered yearly 12 d. and customs. Of his death the lord will have as heriot one little pig worth 8 d. And Alice who was the wife of the same Philip comes and seeks said tenements according to custom, etc. which is such that widows ought to hold tenements in bondage as their bench until the younger son is fifteen years old, and then widows ought to surrender to the younger son, as heir, a moiety of the inheritance. And they will hold the other moiety as their bench if they remain widows etc. And in the form aforesaid the aforesaid Alice has entry and gave security for the relief, 12 d. Pledge, Richard le Berd. And she made the accustomed oath, and she may keep the aforesaid tenement according to custom.[4]

Non-essentials may be cleared away first. The custom of inheritance in Bucksteep, like so many other manors in Sussex, was the custom of Borough English. And the age of fifteen was a common time for boys to come of age to hold tenements in bondage. As for the customs of free bench, it is obvious that at Bucksteep they were the following. If the heir was not of age, the widow held all the tenement until he was and acted as his guardian. When he came of age, she took the part of the tenement which she might claim as her free bench and surrendered the rest to the heir. At Bucksteep she took one half; more commonly she took only one third. It is likely that the legal division of the tenement did not mean that it was managed as two separate holdings. The heir must often have tilled the widow's part as well as his own. After her death the whole tenement was his.

Another feature of free bench is mentioned in this Bucksteep entry. According to the custom of some manors, the widow lost her bench unless she remained unmarried and chaste, that is, to use the words of the Bucksteep rolls, unless she remained a widow. To be sure, the Church did not look with favor on second marriages, but this custom was determined by practical considerations and not by the Church. If a widow remarried, her second husband might have land of his own: in this case she would be sure of her sustenance. She would not need to keep her bench and so deprive her first husband's heir of the enjoyment of a part of his tenement. Furthermore, if a widow had kept her bench when she remarried, her second husband might have tried to keep it in his turn even after her death. But we must be wholly clear that the rule that the widow lost her free bench as soon as she ceased to be a widow applied only in certain English manors. In others, as we shall see, she kept it in spite of her remarriage, and the second husband even acquired certain definite rights in the land.

Sometimes the court rolls allow us to see what did in fact happen if a widow holding her bench did not remain a widow. An entry of the year 1281 in the rolls of Mapledurham, Hants., runs as follows:

Lucy, widow of Walter le Hurt, comes and gives the lord 2 s. to have an inquest whether she has greater right in a certain land which Richard le Hurt holds than Richard himself who is the holder. [The names of the members of the inquest are given.] These say on their oath that the aforesaid Lucy in her widowhood let herself fall into fornication and thereupon marry, without licence of the lord. And therefore William of Fawkham, at that time steward, decreed the aforesaid land to be forfeit and committed the land to Richard, brother of said Walter once husband of said Lucy, and thus it remains.[5]

The first point to observe in this entry is that Lucy remarried without the licence of the lord. We cannot tell whether she lost her land simply because she remarried or because she did so without his licence. The custumals of other villages make it plain that a widow might keep her bench if the man she married was acceptable to the lord.[6] When Lucy forfeited her land, it naturally reverted to the nearest heir of her first husband, for such in this case we must suppose his brother to have been. Observe also that the lord's steward made judgment in the hallmote in accordance with the findings of an inquest of the suitors of the court. Every entry from a court roll, no matter for what reason it is cited, has something to tell about procedure in manorial courts.

A matter of experience in many fields of investigation is that the things which vary least are the most important. If the temperature of our bodies varies from normal by so much as a degree we are sick. The customs of English villages of the champion country were nearly uniform in such fundamentals of their social organization as the descent of holdings to one son and heir. In matters of a second order of importance, such as the customs of the widow's bench, the variety was great, and only a selection of the more interesting customs need be made here.

One of these is mentioned in a suit before the hallmote of Newington, Oxon., in 1285. Newington was a manor of Christchurch Priory, Canterbury. The following is the entry in the court roll:

Robert, son of Robert the thatcher, appearing, comes and gives the lord 2 s. to have an inquest concerning the demand of a half-yardland with its appurtenances in the manor of Newington, and in this land he claims to have right after the death of Robert his dead father, tenant in chief of the lord Prior. And he agrees to do the services and customs thereof, according to the use of the said manor, by the pledges of Robert Tornepeny and Richard West. [An inquest is then taken by sixteen jurors, whose names are given.] These say on oath that said Robert, son of Robert the thatcher, has no right in said half-yardland with appurtenances while Agnes, wife of said Robert, father of said Robert, is alive. Nevertheless said Robert will receive yearly from said land a half-quarter of hard corn, half of winter corn and the other half of lenten corn, during the lifetime of said Agnes, his step-mother.[7]

The word of the text which has been translated as step-mother is *matertera*. In classical Latin, *matertera* meant mother's sister, but the clerk can hardly have used it in this sense here, unless, indeed, the father's second wife was also the mother's sister, and such a marriage was uncanonical. In any case, the widow at Newington held the whole of her late husband's tenement.[8] The heir got no part of it until she died, but was entitled in the familiar manner to support from his inheritance. This custom seems unduly hard on the heir, but other entries in the Newington rolls leave no doubt that it was the custom.[9] We cannot tell whether actual behavior mitigated the letter of the rule. Perhaps the sustenance which the court allowed the heir out of his inheritance was of the nature of a minimum. The widow may in fact have given him a much larger share of the profits and the management of the holding.

Another village where the widow's dower was all of the land of her late husband was Halton, Bucks., like Newington a manor of Christchurch Priory. An entry in the court rolls of Halton of the year 1303 refers to the custom and suggests among other interesting matters that the letter of custom was mitigated in practice. It runs as follows:

Thomas of Merdene, who held of the lord one yardland and a half and one ferthling of land, entered the way of all flesh, by which the lord has as heriot two oxen. Afterwards came Hugh, first-born son of said Thomas, and offered himself to do for the lord those things which he rightly ought to do for said holdings. And he entered said holdings by the heriot of said Thomas his father and did fealty. And Alice who was wife of said Thomas is endowed with all the lands and holdings which belonged to said Thomas, according to the custom of the manor, as the whole court testifies, and the whole messuage at Merdene remains in the possession of said Hugh, and the same Hugh will give to said Alice two marks and a half of silver and three ash trees of the better sort at Merdene in order to build a house on the messuage that is called Stotkeslond. And said Alice will stay in the chief house at Merdene until said house, at the discretion of the lord and bailiff, is ready.[10]

According to the words of the roll, Hugh, the son and heir, paid the heriot and had entry into the land, but Alice, the widow, was "endowed" with all of it. Does this statement mean that Hugh became tenant in chief and Alice tenant for life? It looks as if Hugh had the actual management of the land. Even though Alice was "endowed" with all of it, she was not going to live in the chief house of the holding but in a "dower house" to be built especially for her. Her son was to supply her with ash trees for timber and with money for labor and the other materials of the house. If she was the tenant of the holding in the sense of having its management, is it likely that her son would supply her with these things? Perhaps being endowed with all the lands and holdings meant merely having the right to support from them, and perhaps some such practice as this mitigated for the heir the seeming harshness of the custom at Newington.

So far we have been concerned with the rights of widows in lands which had been held by their husbands. We must next consider the rights of widowers in lands which had been held by their wives. Here a clear distinction must be made between women who held land in their own right, as of inheritance, and women who held the whole or a part of the lands of their late husbands in the name of dower. The customs which applied to the widower of a woman of the first class were in general, as we should expect, more liberal than the customs which applied to the widower of a woman of the second class. Let us consider the customs in this order.

On the manors of St. Albans Abbey, a definite marriage settlement was made when a man married an heiress, just as one was made when a woman married a man with land. Some of these settlements are interesting and important, for example, one which appears in the court book of Park, Herts., under the year 1285:

Alice atte Forde surrendered into the hands of the lord one tenement with appurtenances in le Parkstrate. And the lord seised Henry le Blund thereof, so that if they have legitimate offspring between them, it may descend to their heirs. If indeed they die without an heir begotten between them, and said Henry survives said Alice, he will hold said tenement all his life, and after his death said tenement will revert to the heirs of said Alice, and he gives 12 d. for having seisin and also for licence to marry.[11]

In spite of the clumsiness of the phrasing — if we take this entry at its word, Henry was able to die and yet survive — what this settlement provided is plain. Henry was marrying an heiress, and she was making over her land to him. If they had offspring, the land was to descend to these heirs of their bodies. If they had not, Henry was to remain tenant of the land for life, and after his death it was to revert to his wife's heirs.

Another interesting settlement appears in the court book of Cashio, Herts., under the year 1306:

Elias Huwe comes and gives the lord 10 s. for licence to marry with Sarah atte Grove, widow of Adam Payne, and to enter the land of the same Sarah and hold it to his life's end, if he begets a boy of her. And if it happens that said Sarah does not have a son with the aforesaid Elias, then after the death of the same Sarah let the land wholly revert to Joan, daughter of said Adam and Sarah, who will do the due and accustomed services thereof.[12]

Elias Huwe was marrying a widow and getting her land. But he was taking a chance of being left without support in his old age, because unless he begot a male child of Sarah, he would not after her death remain tenant of the land for his lifetime. The entry says nothing specific on the point, but its implication is that if a boy were born he would inherit the tenant after the death of his father, Elias. In short the son by the second husband was preferred as heir over the daughter by the first. Joan, daughter of Sarah by her first husband, Adam Payne, would not inherit unless Sarah had no son by her second husband. This provision must imply in its turn that Sarah held the land from the beginning in her own right and not simply as her free bench after the death of her first husband. Otherwise we should expect that the son by the second husband would have no right to inherit the tenement. The blood of the tenement would have been the blood of the Paynes, and Joan, the daughter of Adam Payne, would have inherited to the exclusion of all others.

In these instances, the right of the widower to hold his late wife's tenement rested on specific marriage settlements. We have seen that such settlements were common on the St. Albans manors. In most manors the right was recognized as customary without any specific settlement. When widowers held land in this way they were said, both at common law and by the custom of manors, to hold "by the law of England" (*per legem Anglie*) or "by the curtesy of England." The former is the older phrase; the latter became customary towards the end of the thirteenth century. According to the common law, a widower held the whole of his late wife's land and held it for his lifetime. Just as the widow's interest in a tenement was a life interest, so was the widower's: at his death the tenement reverted to his wife's heirs, though to be sure his wife's heirs might be his own children. According to common law, too, a widower held all of his late wife's land for his lifetime, whether or not he remarried, provided only that a child had been born to them, and the customs of many manors were more or less similar to the common law in these respects. In particular, the widower at Cashio and many other manors did not hold his late wife's land unless a child had been born to them. The judges who developed the common law worked towards rules which were simple and uniform. Manorial custom remained more varied and more elaborate. It also remained more archaic, and this circumstance is what gives it its interest in the eyes of historians of the law.

One good statement of a custom of curtesy is that of Bramford, Suffolk, in the custumal of 1277 of the manors of the Bishop of Ely. It describes the customs suitable to the tenant of two hundred acres of land in Bramford, but it expressly states that they applied to all men who lived in the village. Suppose, the entry says, that the heir of the holding is a woman:

And if that heir is a woman, then she is allowed to marry without licence of the lord provided her husband is suitable. And if the husband dies during the woman's lifetime, then nothing is given for heriot. . . . And her husband aforenamed ought wholly to leave [the tenement] immediately after the death of the woman, or if she dies during her husband's lifetime, and she has an heir begotten of herself, then nothing will be given for his relief, but her husband will remain in all the aforesaid tenement for all his life, and after his death the better beast of the house will be given for the relief.[13]

The provisions which were made in custom for the widower of a woman who held land in her own right, an heiress, are less important for their own sake than for what they imply in general about the organization of English families in the Middle Ages. In the first place, the fact that there was an heiress is important. There was no such emphasis put on descent in the strict male line as there came to be in later times and among the gentry. If the last holder of a tenement left no sons, his land went to his daughters rather than to any brother or other male kinsman. In the second place, all custom conformed to the sentiment that a certain blood ought to remain in possession of a certain tenement, whether that blood was represented by a man or by a woman. If a man married an heiress and did not beget a child of her, ne lost her land to her heirs when she died. If he did beget a child, he held the land for his lifetime, and at his death the land went to this child, who was considered to be his wife's heir rather than his own. In any case the land remained in the blood of those who had held it in the past. The principle was even reflected in family names. Among husbandmen in the Middle Ages, family names were unstable, and usually little can be learned from them. But in one respect the very way they changed is significant. Elsie Toms, writing of the entries in the fourteenth-century court book of Chertsey Abbey in Surrey, points out as a remarkable fact that:

when heiresses marry, they so often keep their maiden names, while their husbands change theirs to their wives' names. . . . In one entry, a woman takes her husband's name, but when her father dies and she inherits his property, they both change to the father's name. Hugh atte Clauwe of Thorpe appears quite often as Hugh le Kach or Keach, because of his marriage to Alice le Keach; and when John atte Hethe of Cobham marries Lucy atte Grene, the remark is added 'He is now called atte Grene.'[14]

To use the words of modern Irish countrymen, the family felt that they ought to keep 'the name on the land.'

Before we take up the second case, that of the widower of a woman who held land not in her own right but only as her bench after the death of her first husband, we may turn briefly to the general question of the remarriage of widows. There was no possible objection to the second marriage of an heiress. All her children, no matter by what husband she had them, were of the ancient blood of the holding, and no ancient lineage was put in danger of being disinherited. In fact, there was every reason why she should marry. If she did not, she might become a charge on the lord of the manor. The belief was that a woman would not be able to carry on the husbandry of a large holding of land and would fall into poverty. She could escape only by marrying a good husbandman. Accordingly on some manors, if a villein heiress did not get herself a husband, the lord exercised the right of ordering her to marry, amercing her if she did not, and even picking out the man she was to marry. Though this practice wounds our modern sentiment that there is something wrong about a marriage of convenience, in the Middle Ages it may have seemed a necessity of the successful management of property in land. In several sets of court rolls, entries occur like the following, from those of Chatteris, Cambs., of 1289:

Agnes Seynpel who holds of the lord eight acres of land gives the lord 12 d. by the pledge of John Hugoun in order to have respite until Michaelmas to choose herself a husband who can maintain the land aforesaid.[15]

More human is this one of 1279 from the rolls of Halesowen, Worcestershire:

Thomas Robynes of Oldbury was summoned and comes and is ordered to have Agatha of Hales as his wife, who says that he wants to pay a fine. Thomas Brid of Ridgeacre was summoned for the same reason and distrained because he wishes neither to pay a fine nor to take a wife.[16]

Thomas Robynes would rather pay a fine than take Agatha. Thomas Brid was wholly stubborn and would neither marry nor pay.

There was no possible objection to the second marriage of an heiress, but there might well be one to the remarriage of a woman who held land not in her own right but only as her bench after the death of her first husband. At least there was an objection to her continuing to hold the land, and on many manors she lost it if she remarried or was unchaste. On others, she was allowed to remarry and keep her free bench, provided she got the lord's licence, and the question arises of the rights her second husband acquired in her land. If we think of the wife as being at one remove from the ancient blood of the holding, the second husband was certainly at a second remove. We should expect that custom would provide for him after his wife's death even less well than for a man who had married an heiress. This expectation is sometimes, but not always, fulfilled. The court rolls of Newington in Oxfordshire are uncommonly interesting and detailed in their recording of custom, including the customary rights of widowers in land. The following is the account of an inquest held there in 1288:

The whole court, charged, say on their oath that Walter Goneyre, who married a certain widow, namely Isabel Bolt, will have after the death of the same Isabel, lately deceased, one cottage with a small curtilage and three acres of land of one yardland which the same Isabel held, namely in each field one acre, the best but one, and for said messuage and land aforesaid he will do for the chief tenant all the due and accustomed services of said messuage and land, and will find for the lord one man at the great boon-work, and after the death of the same Walter a heriot will be given.[17]

In this instance, the widower did not hold the whole of his wife's tenement after her death but only one acre in each of the three fields of a champion village. The explanation of this poor provision lies in the following circumstances. We learn from an entry in the Newington rolls of ten years earlier [18] that Isabel was at that time a widow and that she probably held the yardland not as her hereditary right but only as her bench after the death of her first husband. At that time there was an heir of the yardland, one Thomas Bolt, whose relationship to Isabel is not disclosed. He was to receive from her one quarter of corn a year so long as she held the land. Presumably he was the "chief tenant" who held the land after her death. This arrangement whereby the widower was assigned a few acres of a larger tenement unit is obviously much like those described earlier whereby younger sons were supported so long as they remained unmarried. A man with such an assignment would naturally have to do his share of the services owed by the tenement to the lord.

Consider now the following account of an inquest made at the hallmote of Stratton, Wilts., in 1279:

An inquest is made by the men of Grundewelle. They say that if anyone is a widower and there was a son born on the hearth, while he is a widower let him have the whole tenement, and if he wishes to marry, let the son of the hearth have part of the land to live by. And they consider that the son of Adam Selverlok ought to have six acres of his father's land when John who married his mother wants to take a wife, and should answer to the latter according to the amount of the land.[19]

The court rolls were probably written out on the spot, in the hallmote, and therefore in a hurry. They were written by clerks whose command of Latin was feeble. For these reasons what the clerks wrote was often jargon, and this entry is an example of their workmanship at its worst. But there can be little doubt about the meaning of the entry at most points, although the Latin cannot be translated both literally and grammatically. The men of Grundewelle laid down a general rule of custom and then applied it in a particular case. Adam Selverlok held land and married. He had at least one son by this marriage. Adam died; his widow held the land, and took as her second husband a certain John. Clearly Stratton was not one of the manors in which a widow holding her late husband's land as her bench lost it as soon as she remarried. In this instance the widow died after her second marriage, and the question arose of the disposition which was to be made of the land in case John, her second husband, remarried in his turn. Accordingly an inquest was taken of the men of Grundewelle, who said that so long as he was a widower, John ought to hold all of his late wife's land. But if he remarried, he ought to give Adam Selverlok's son six acres of the land on which to support himself, and the son ought to answer to John for these six acres — or, perhaps, John ought to answer to the son: on this point the entry is not clear — that is, he ought to do his share of the services, pay his share of the rents due from the chief tenant of the holding, so much as pertained to six acres.

This finding settled for Stratton a question which may be put in the following way: what disposal was made of a tenement when a man wanted to remarry, who held it by the curtesy after the death of his wife, who held it as her bench after the death of her first husband? Villagers asserted that they had rules of custom to apply even in questions as intricate as this, which can have arisen only rarely. Observe that Adam Selverlok's son and heir was called the son of the hearth, *filius de astro*. He was the son who stayed on the tenement, by the hearth, because he was his father's heir — or, conversely, was the heir because he stayed on the hearth — while the other sons left the tenement to seek their fortunes.[20]

There are two provisions in the customs relating to widows and widowers which bring forward another matter. On some manors, a widow lost all or a part of the free bench which she held after her husband's death when the heir of the tenement, born to her husband and herself, came of age. And on some manors, a widower did not hold his late wife's land by the curtesy of England after her death unless an heir had been born to them. One reason for these arrangements must have been that the widow or the widower was expected to bring up the heir of the tenement and keep his land for him. In fact entries in the court rolls are common which made specific provision for the custody of their heir and of his land until he came of age. One example appears in the rolls of Minchinhampton, Glos., under the year 1276:

Adam Gene enters into the land and tenement which his father was accustomed to hold, and he gives as relief 2 s. 6 d., and Felice mother of the same did fealty until the coming of age of the same Adam, who now is two years of age. Pledges, Walter Spilemon and Alexander de Rod', for payment on the Sunday after Martinmas [the court was held the Saturday before] and for the maintenance of the houses, garden, and other things without detriment. Also Thomas de Lupeg' husband of said Felice for licence to enter said tenement, 2 s.[21]

Although Adam was only two years old, the court spoke of him as having entry and paying his relief for his father's land. Actually Felice was going to take care of the land until her son came of age, and at the time the court sat she had already taken a second husband.

In feudal law, the exercise of the custody of an heir and his land until he came of age was called wardship, and we may call these village customs by the same name, although in the typical feudal tenements, those held by military service, wardship was exercised by the feudal lord of the heir rather than one of his kinsmen. Among villagers, the guardian was commonly and naturally the heir's mother, and if the mother was dead the wardship passed in some places to the mother's brother, or to use the word for maternal uncle which was employed in the Middle Ages but has since disappeared, the *eme*. The statement of the custom made by the hundred of Milton in Kent before the king's justices in Eyre, in the 43rd year of Henry III, is a good one:

It is a custom throughout Kent that when anyone dies who held land in gavelkind, and his heir is under age, the mother, or the nearest kinsman of this heir on the mother's side, ought to have the wardship of this heir and of his land to draw the profits of the same land and answer for them to the aforesaid heir when he shall come of age, and that without any fine being taken therefor.[22]

The heir's nearest kinsman on his mother's side would usually be his mother's brother. The lawyers spoke of this custom, which was by no means limited to Kent, as a custom of tenements in socage. They did not necessarily mean that the custom was found only in socage tenements. For the most part, the lawyers were concerned with the free tenures, and socage was a free tenure, the one by which free husbandmen held their lands. Of villeinage and its customs the lawyers took little account, and it is possible that the rule that the heir's guardian was his eme applied to the holdings of countrymen, bond as well as free, in several parts of England.

Anthropologists will naturally prick up their ears when they hear of the wardship of a child being exercised by his nearest kinsman on his mother's side, who would commonly be his mother's brother. An earlier generation would have spoken of survivals of a "primitive matriarchate." The present one will recognize that a specially close relation exists between mother's brother and sister's son in a large number of patrilineal societies scattered all over the world from Polynesia to Europe. It seems to be a natural concomitant of the emotional tensions obtaining in the small family: the mother's brother acts as a kind of male mother. Tacitus speaks of such a relation among the Germans, and the sagas show that in Iceland there was a tendency to send children to their mother's brother to be fostered.[23] In the case of the English custom of wardship, there may be no question of a survival from early Germanic society. The lawyers of the time observed that material interests furnished reason enough for the custom. They said that the wardship ought to belong to the nearest of kin to whom the inheritance could not descend, the nearest of kin who would have nothing to gain by the death of the heir. Since land regularly descended from male to male in the blood line, this person would be on the mother's side of the family. We must remember, however, that the lawyers may have invented this theory simply for the purpose of explaining a custom which they encountered but did not understand, a custom more ancient than all their learning.

Rarely in medieval England, as often in other peasant societies, a man would give his son to another man to foster. There is one English instance in which the foster-father was granted a piece of land in return for his services. Consider the following entry of the year 1306 in the court book of Barnet, Herts.:

John, son and heir of John le Clerk, appeared against John Saly and Agnes his wife in a plea of land, and he seeks against the aforesaid John and Agnes one messuage and five acres of land with appurtenances in Barnet, which he claims to be his right and heritage, since he says that the aforesaid John le Clerk, his father, whose heir he is, was seized of the aforesaid messuage with land, and that the same John his father gave said messuage with the land aforesaid to a certain John le Bor with a certain Paine, son of said John le Clerk, to hold only for the lifetime of the same John le Bor in return for the nutriture of said Paine, who ended his days within this term. After whose death came said John le Clerk and sought said messuage with the land aforesaid of the aforesaid John le Bor to be given back to him because of a defect in the nutriture of said Paine. And the same John le Bor refused to give back said messuage with the land aforesaid, but wanted to keep said messuage with land to his life's end according to the form of the covenant, since the defect of nutriture was not his fault, as he said.[24]

John de Bor succeeded in keeping the land until he died, where-upon John Saly and his wife, who were being sued, entered, by what right is not recorded. Three years later John, son of John le Clerk, finally won his suit.

In the customs of free bench, curtesy, and wardship, the same principles were at work as we have found at work elsewhere in the customs of families in the champion country. First, land was the paramount means of getting a living. If a man had no land, he had no economic security. He would have to live precariously by wages or charity. Second, a tenement descended undivided from one man to another in the blood line. A sentiment naturally existed that the widow or the widower of the person who held the tenement ought to be supported from it, and accordingly she or he was allowed to keep the whole or a part of the tenement. They were provided with land. But their interests in the tenement were only life-interests: after their deaths their shares reverted to the heir of the blood. They might not transmit them to heirs of their own. The tenement was not permanently divided or permanently alienated.

CHAPTER XIV

ALIENATION

I<small>F WE MAY PROPERLY</small> speak of a main principle governing the organization of families in the champion country of England, this principle was that an established holding of land ought to descend intact in the blood of the men who had held it of old. The holding of a villager descended to one of his sons and one only. Only in default of sons was it divided among his daughters, and not always then. In many villages the holding descended to only one of his daughters, and if there were no children, it descended to one of the brothers of the last holder. Assart land or land "acquired" in any other way could, in many villages, be left freely by will, but an established holding descended according to these rules. Furthermore, none of the persons who got their living from the holding acquired permanent rights in it, except the heir. A brother or a sister of the heir might be given a few acres of the holding by which to live, but he lost them if he married. The widow of the last holder might hold a part of it as her dower, but in many villages she lost her dower if she remarried. If the holder had been a woman, her husband might hold the whole tenement by the curtesy of England after her death, but in many villages he lost it unless a child had been born to them. In any case, none of these tenancies was more than a tenancy for life. In the course of time the separated shares reverted to the heir and the holding remained a unit.

Men of the Middle Ages would have summed up these facts by saying that no part of an established holding ought to be "alienated." There was a strong sentiment against what was called "alienation." It applied as much to the demesne of the crown as to a yardland in a village of the Midlands. The king ought not to grant to other men those manors which he and his forefathers had held in their own hands for their own sustenance. The king ought to be able to "live of his own." In fact, he often alienated lands of the royal demesne, but the sentiment persisted that he was wrong in doing so. In the same way a yardland might have descended from father to son for several generations. It would be called by the name of the blood which held it.[1] If anything happened which would prevent its descending intact to the person who was designated in custom as the heir, the neighbors would feel that a wrong had been done.

In order that a holding should remain intact through the years, the customs of inheritance and of life tenancies were necessary. But they were not sufficient in themselves. For instance, they did not restrain the heir from leaving a diminished holding because he had given away or sold parts of it. Accordingly on some manors there were rules for the positive prevention of alienation. Consider the following request for a statement of custom, as it appears in the court rolls of Halton, Bucks., in the year 1296:

Thomas le Chapman of Weston comes and gives the lord 6 d. . . . for having an inquest of the court as to this: if any tenant of the lord demised his land for a certain term, and the tenant died within the term, who ought to fulfill the covenant after the death of the grantor? And the whole court is charged as to this. And it comes and says that no tenant of the lord can demise his land except for his lifetime, and that the heir is not bound to warrant.[2]

Thus at Halton, just as the rights of bench and curtesy were enjoyed only for a lifetime, so the holder of land could make no lease of it that ran longer than his lifetime. The heir was not bound to warrant, that is, guarantee the lease. Clearly this custom would prevent any permanent alienation of land from villagers' holdings.

A similar rule was stated by an inquest at the hallmote of Burley, Rutland, in 1299:

To this court comes Richard ate Mere and gives the lord 2 s. for having an inquest as to whether he is the true heir of the land which Juliana Joye bought of William ate Mere. [The names of the members of the inquest are then given.] They say on their oath that said Juliana bought said land, had it, and held it throughout her lifetime, but that she could sell it, bequeath it, or assign it to no one after her death. Therefore the seisin is granted to the aforesaid Richard and his heirs.[3]

Juliana Joye was said to have bought the land, but she certainly did not acquire the rights which go with a purchase in our modern use of the word. She held the land only so long as a widow might hold her bench, for her lifetime. After her death, it was to revert to Richard ate Mere, the true heir of the land and evidently a relative of the man who had sold it: they bore the same name. Thus at Burley alienations were limited to the lifetime of the grantee instead of the lifetime of the grantor, as at Halton. But the important point is that they were limited.

Another common situation is illustrated by the following suit before the hallmote of Park, Herts., in 1280:

Margaret who was the wife of Geoffrey atte Sloo seeks against John le Bedell two acres and three roods of land, in which he has no entry save through said Geoffrey, her late husband, whom she could not gainsay in his lifetime. And John says that he has entry through the lord Abbot who now is, and he calls him to warrant therein.[4]

The case was held over for a later meeting of the court, in order that the Abbot of St. Albans, lord of the manor, might be consulted. Clearly the point at issue was the alienation by a husband of land which was of the right of his wife. Margaret was claiming that her husband might alienate such land only for his lifetime. After his death it ought to revert to her as the true heir. The phrase "whom she could not gainsay in his lifetime" (*cui in vita sua contradicere non potuit*) was regularly used in cases of this sort. The wife and her property were at the command of the husband.

What has been established is that on many manors land could be alienated only for the lifetime of the holder of the land, or for the lifetime of those to whom it was alienated. After their deaths, it reverted to the true heir. A further development of this principle was that land could be permanently alienated by its holder, provided the consent of his heir was secured at the time of the alienation. A long entry from the court rolls of Newington, Oxon., in 1293, will illustrate this point:

Thomas le Northerne by the pledges of John West and Hugh David offered himself in a plea of land against Walter le Rouwe and Maud his wife, attached by Samuel le Northerne and Nicholas Trys. And the aforesaid Thomas complains that the aforesaid Walter and Maud unjustly deforce him of a half-yardland in Brookhampton which is his right, and that John le Northerne his father demised it to them for the lifetime of this John, and after his lifetime it ought to descend to the aforesaid Thomas as son and heir according to the custom of the village, and to this end he brings suit. The aforesaid Walter and Maud are present and deny the right of the aforesaid Thomas, etc., and they say that they have right in the aforesaid land for the reason that John le Northerne father of the aforesaid Maud surrendered the land aforesaid into the hands of the Prior [of Christchurch, Canterbury, lord of the manor] and they themselves took the same land from the hands of the Prior to themselves and theirs to hold by the due services and customs thereof, and they say likewise that the same Thomas who now sues came into full court together with John his father, and surrendered the right that was his into the hands of the Prior, and took for this one ox from the aforesaid Walter and Maud, and thus they have greater right in their tenure than the aforesaid Thomas in his demand, and they ask that inquiry be made. And the aforesaid Thomas says that the aforesaid John his father according to the custom of the village could neither surrender nor in any other manner alienate the land aforesaid save only for his lifetime, and he agrees that he came into full court together with his father and because of his threats dared not gainsay him in his time, but that he never surrendered his right and for this reason has more right in his demand than the aforesaid Walter and Maud in their tenure, and he asks that inquiry be made. And an inquest is made by oath. [The names of the jurors are given.] They say on their oath that said Thomas never surrendered into the hands of the lord his right of that land.[5]

Thomas recovered the half-yardland. Here Thomas, the demandant, cited the rule which we have seen in force on many manors, that the holder of land might alienate it only for his lifetime. At his death, it reverted to his heir. But in Newington, and in many other villages, this rule could be circumvented and the land permanently alienated, provided the heir came into the hallmote and gave his consent. In this instance, Thomas, the heir, had given his consent and had been paid an ox for doing so by those who were to have the land. But he now asserted, and apparently the court believed him, that he gave his consent only out of fear of his father. Therefore his action was void. The accessory circumstances of this attempted alienation are interesting. Pretty clearly it was a marriage settlement. John le Northerne was trying to settle the half-yardland upon his daughter Maud, her husband, and their heirs. The form of the transfer — the surrender of the land into the hands of the lord Prior by one party, followed by the other party's receiving the land at his hands — is well recorded. The rolls of Newington were among the best kept of court rolls.

One other form of these restraints on the alienation of a holding outside of the blood which had held it of old is illustrated by an inquest held before the hallmote of Halton, Bucks., in 1292:

An inquest is made by the whole court concerning the land which Thomas Hemmyng holds by grant of Alice, widow of Richard le Wodeward — whether the aforesaid Thomas has better right to hold said land as he holds it for the lifetime of said Alice than Richard le Wodeward who is the true heir of that land after the death of said Alice and claims to be nearer than all others to hold said land by giving as much as anyone else wishes to give. And the aforesaid inquest says that said Richard has better right to hold that land than anyone else, by giving as much as any outsider wishes to give.[6]

This entry gives a very compressed account of what had happened and what was going forward. The double mention of Richard le Wodeward is confusing. Actually there must have been two Richards, for at the time of the inquest one of them had a widow and the other was still alive. The second Richard was probably the son or in some other way kin of the first, for he bore the same name and was the true heir of the land which the widow of the first Richard held. Alice, this widow, obviously held the land as her bench and not as her inheritance. Obviously also she was still alive at the time of the inquest. She had granted the land to Thomas Hemmyng, and Thomas had expected to keep it while she was alive. But the rule at Halton was that if the widow transferred any part of her bench, she might transfer it only to the true heir of the tenement, and not to any outsider. Two phrases of this entry reveal that here at Halton one form of what the Anglo-Norman lawyers called *retrait lignager* was in force. According to the custom of *retrait lignager*, if land was to be sold or transferred in any other manner, the members of the blood which had held the land had the right to a first refusal of it. They could have the land, provided they were willing to pay as much for it as any outsider was willing to pay. Richard le Wodeward seems to have claimed the land in question against Thomas Hemmyng on the grounds that Alice ought to have granted the land, if she was going to grant it at all, to him, Richard, as the heir, rather than to any outsider, provided he was willing to give as much for the grant as any outsider.[7]

The next point to be considered is not strictly related to alienation, but it throws further light on the attitudes villagers took towards established holdings of land. In the court rolls of Hemingford, Hunts., of 6 Edward II, the following entry appears:

William, son of Peter the miller, gives the lord 12 d. by the pledge of the reeves to have the judgment of the court concerning a croft which the aforesaid Peter holds. And he says that he has greater right in said croft than the aforesaid Peter, etc. An inquest is taken therein by the aforesaid twelve jurors, who say that the aforesaid Peter holds a croft of his own inheritance and a half-yardland of the right and inheritance of his wife. And whereas the custom is such that no one ought to hold two lands, therefore he is in respite until he comes before the lord, etc. And afterwards it is found that said William made fine for that land. Therefore he is quit.[8]

The men of Hemingford said that no one ought to hold two lands, but this statement cannot be taken as an expression of a sentiment against the accumulation of land by villagers. What it meant in the context was that if a man held two distinct tenements, one in his own right and the other in the right of his wife, he ought not to keep both of them in his own hands but turn one of them over to his heir.

The customs of the villagers themselves were one force tending to keep established holdings intact. But there was another force at work as well: the lord of the manor may have had good reasons for wishing to restrict the alienation of the lands of his tenants. As everyone knows — it is the feature of the social order of the Middle Ages which has been studied most thoroughly — many of the tenements in many villages were charged with customary services which their holders were bound to do in tilling the demesne of the lord of the manor. These were the tenements in villeinage. The holder of such a tenement would have to work for the lord for a certain number of days a week throughout the year, would have to plow the lord's land at a certain number of boon plowings, and so forth. The services were of great variety and are described in detail in the manorial custumals. Furthermore the distribution of services was intimately related to the distribution of land in a village. Land was divided into tenement units which tended to be equal in size, class by class, and persons who held the same amounts of land had to do the same services. The regular practice of the custumals is to describe the rents and services which John Doe had to do for his yardland and then to say simply: "Richard Roe also holds one yardland for the same services as John Doe." And so on for the other yardlands.

In any of these tenants permanently alienated parts of their lands, holdings would soon become unequal in size. The equitable repartition among them of a bewildering variety of days of work and other tasks done for the lord would become excessively difficult, as would the business of seeing that the tasks were done. One method of solving the problem was to determine the rents and services due from a given unit of land and make all the people who held parts of the unit collectively responsible for the performance of these services. This method was commonly used where customs of inheritance were such that the subdivision of holdings was the rule, as in Kent and parts of East Anglia. In other parts of England customs whereby land descended to one son of the last holder would automatically keep holdings intact. If the holdings had originally been equal in size and had done the same services, they would remain so, that is, they would remain so provided there was no alienation. Perhaps, therefore, the interest of the lords of manors was to prevent alienation. Certainly an inspection of manorial custumals suggests that holdings which were charged with heavy services were more likely to be all of a size, class by class, than those which only had to pay a money rent. The former tended to be of standard, the latter of irregular size. This fact can be explained by the theory that renders in money could be more easily reapportioned than renders in work; accordingly the alienation or subdivision of rent-paying land was more likely to be tolerated than that of workland. But too much weight should not be given to this argument, since there were manors where the holdings were equal class by class, although the tenants paid money rents and scarcely performed any work services at all.[9]

If the lord wished to prevent alienation by his tenants, he naturally had the power to do so. Transfers of land from one villager to another took the form of a surrender into the lord's hands before the hallmote, followed by a regrant. The lord might give his licence to such a transfer or withhold it, as he wished, and if he gave it he would be paid for doing so. In point of fact there is almost no evidence in the court rolls that the lord of a manor ever did refuse this licence. But the explanation of this fact may be that if the lord did not approve of a proposed transfer of land, he let his displeasure be known before the parties ever went before the hallmote.

We have considered the forces which tended to prevent

alienation; we must now look at those which tended to favor it. Chief among these forces were the economic interests of men. The thirteenth century in England was a time of peace, prosperity, and economic expansion, and one of the forms the expansion took was an increase in the amount of dealing in land, an increase which reached even the lesser countryfolk. Any active traffic in land is clearly incompatible with the prevention of alienation. Among other things, leases were common. They were for terms of only a few years; they were not long leases like those known to modern capitalism. Accordingly they did not permanently break up holdings, but they are properly considered here as one form of the speculative interests in land which affected villagers.

The following is an example of the sort of lawsuit which might arise out of a common form of medieval lease. The entry appears in the court rolls of Methwold, Norfolk, of the year 1272:

Lyna, daughter of Hugh le Coylynr, appeared against Nicholas Attefen, and an inquest made by the neighbors says on their oath that the same Nicholas gave to the same Lyna and William her brother a certain half-acre of land for a term of three years to sow at champart and that when the same Lyna and William had sown said half-acre of land in the first year the same Nicholas came and sold them his part of said crop, and that the same Nicholas afterward sold all said crop to John Querbec and Martin Clut and gave them said land and more at farm contrary to his first covenant, and he took from them [i.e., Lyna and William] said corn and their term. Therefore Nicholas is in mercy, and because he is poor it is condoned, and Lyna may recover her damages.[10]

The lease at *champart* (*ad campi partem*) was one of the commonest kinds of leases among villagers. A man would agree to till and sow a piece of land and take a part of the crop, usually a half, leaving the holder the other half. It was share-cropping, though not organized as we know it in the United States today. In this instance, Nicholas, instead of taking his share of the crop, sold it to Lyna and William and then sold all the crop and leased all the land a second time to other parties. When medieval records speak of a piece of land being a farm (*ad firmam*) they mean that one or more people took it from its holder for a definite or indefinite period, paying him a fixed rent for it. In the original sense of the word, a farmer was not simply a man who tilled the soil but a man who took land at farm.

What would permanently alienate land from a tenement were

sales of land or gifts of land to be held by the donee and his heirs. As a typical example of the form such transfers took before manorial courts, we may consider the following entry, of the year 1298, from the court rolls of Burley, Rutland, a royal manor:

Simon Aunsel came into full court and surrendered into the hands of the lord one croft of land to the use of Walter Morel and his heirs, doing therefor the due and accustomed services pertaining to that land, paying yearly to the lord King 2 d. which ought to be allowed in the rent of the aforesaid Simon. And the aforesaid Walter gives the lord 12 d. of fine for having entry into the aforesaid land, pledge, Augustine the clerk. And he did fealty.[11]

This entry probably records the sale of a piece of land, but it makes no mention of a sale, no mention of the price paid for the land. Indeed we cannot tell whether Simon sold Walter the two acres of land or simply gave them to him. Transactions in this form have been cited which were in fact gifts. In this form a father would make over his holding to his son and heir. There is no doubt that many others represented what were in fact sales. One party surrendered his land to the lord, who at once regranted it to the second party. Such was the regular form taken by the transfer. Of course it had been agreed beforehand who the second party was to be. In this instance, Simon Aunsel surrendered the croft *ad opus Walteri Morel*. Thenceforward Walter was to pay 2 d. of rent for the land directly to the king, the lord of the manor, and accordingly that much was to be taken off Simon's rent. Such a form of transfer maintained inviolate the feudal theory, which did not know of purchases and sales of land, but only of grants and surrenders.

Besides sales, exchanges of land are sometimes recorded. Of a man who held in 1252 a hide of land in Upwood, Hunts., it was said that:

He exchanged two worn-out ridges with William Pykelere, a villein of the lord, for two ridges of land, better, nearer, and more convenient for him.[12]

As this entry suggests, one of the motives for buying, selling, and exchanging small bits of land was the desire of villagers to concentrate their holdings, instead of having them as bundles of strips scattered over the open fields. Once a man had built up a compact plot, the lord and his neighbors might allow him to hedge it in with a ditch and a live hedge. Some of the parts of England which were enclosed early may have been those where the restraints on dealing in land were weak.

Whatever were the forces which prevented alienation or encouraged it, the balance between them differed greatly in different parts of England. At on end of the scale were the Hertfordshire manors of St. Albans Abbey. Their court records are the earliest known. They show that the men of these manors enjoyed unusual freedom to come before their hallmotes and demise land as they wished. They show that sales and other alienations of small amounts of land were already being made in large numbers in the first half of the thirteenth century. They show that questions concerning hedges repeatedly came before the courts, a hint that enclosure had already made some progress, perhaps because the ease of dealing in land had allowed villagers to consolidate their holdings. Hertfordshire was also at the eastern boundary of the champion country and near to the center of commerce — London, in short just where we might expect the social order to be in rapid change.

At the other end of the scale were two manors of Christchurch Priory, Canterbury: Newington, Oxon., and Halton, Bucks. Their court rolls were beautifully kept and date from the end of the century. As we have seen, they show that the customary restraints on alienation were strict at both manors. They record little selling of land, and the pieces of land involved in suits before the courts were for the most part compact tenement units, yardlands and half-yardlands. Both Newington and Halton were in the heart of the champion country, where we might expect its customs to be in most vigorous effect.

The impression of a person who has read a large number of thirteenth-century court rolls is that traffic in land was more active in south-eastern England than in the Midlands, and particularly active in Kent and East Anglia, where the customs of inheritance encouraged the subdivision of holdings into small lots.[13] But this is only an impression. It would be useful but difficult to get quantitative information on this matter from the court rolls. Where dealing in land was reasonably unfettered, the accumulation of holdings by able and energetic villagers could go forward rapidly. In 1279, John Durant, whose ancestor in 1222 possessed only one yardland in Caddington, Beds., pos-

sessed eight or ten tenements at least, which had formerly been
held by other persons.[14] The status in village society of a man
like Durant must have risen nearly as rapidly as he accumulated
land. If there were many like him, the social order was unstable.

For some villages there is a means of making a guess as to
how far holdings were maintained intact. The Abbots of Glastonbury caused to be drawn up two custumals of their manors in
the West Country, one in the year 1189 and the other in about
the year 1235. In like manner, there are two custumals of the
manors of the Bishop of Ely, one of the year 1222 and the other
of the year 1277.[15] There may be other pairs of custumals. A
custumal recorded the amount of land every tenant of a manor
held and the rents and services he had to render for his holding.
A comparison of the earlier custumals with the later with respect
to the number of holdings of the different classes in each manor
ought to reveal how far holdings had been maintained intact,
over a period of forty-six years in the case of the Glastonbury
custumals, over a period of fifty-five years in the case of those
of Ely.

Unhappily there are circumstances which make the comparison
less satisfactory than it might have been. The manorial juries
which swore to the facts and the clerks who drew up the custumals
made no special effort to make the terms and classifications used
in the later custumals consistent with those used in the earlier
ones. There was no thought of pleasing social historians when
they were written. We are prevented from knowing whether
holdings in fact descended as units from one man to another
in the blood of a family by the fact that in the thirteenth
century a villager did not necessarily bear his father's last name,
so that there is often no way of judging whether a man who is
recorded in the later custumal as holding land was a descendant
of a man who held land half a century earlier. And if the number
or size of the holdings in a particular village, class by class, differed
at the later date from what they were earlier, there is commonly
no way of being sure that this fact was not the result of assarting
or the granting of tenements out of the demesne rather than the
result of the accidents of inheritance and alienation. But in spite
of these circumstances, the comparison does leave the impression
that in some villages the number of yardlands, half-yardlands,

ferdels, and other holdings varied little over a long span of years. In such villages the individual holdings must have remained undivided.

The question just discussed brings up the question of the interconnectedness of phenomena. The stability of the relations between the family and the land made an important contribution to the stability of the social order in general. Earlier, the husbandry of champion villages was described, and the elaborate arrangements whereby the economic equality of the villagers' holdings, class by class, was assured. We shall later consider the hierarchy of social classes which went with the classes of holdings. The point which must be made here is that the maintenance of the holding, intact and in the hands of one man, generation by generation, was an important means of maintaining in their turn both the arrangements of the champion husbandry and the social classes of champion villages. If the economic resources of a family remained equal to those of its neighbors, the reason was that the family holding was kept free from sale or division. If the social position of a family remained the same from generation to generation, the reason again was that the holding, on which its position depended, remained intact. We do not know when the yardlands and oxgangs which existed in villages of the thirteenth century were first laid out. We do not know when the village social classes were first constituted. But whatever their origin, the maintenance of both features of society and accordingly of the constitution of society in general was provided for in part by the maintenance of the integrity of holdings. When holdings were frequently partitioned or land was alienated, the other characteristics of village society were liable to change at the same time. This point can be proved in one simple instance. We have seen that the places where there was most freedom in dealing in land, for instance, the St. Albans manors, were also the places where the champion husbandry was in most danger of being dissolved in enclosures.

We must not underestimate the subtlety of the relations between the family order and the social order in general. In England there was a close correlation between the champion husbandry and what has been called the stem-family: briefly, the family organization in which land descended to one son. But this correlation was not universal. In Russia, until the recent formation of collective farms, the agricultural regime was in most essentials the same as the champion husbandry. In fact this regime once dominated the plain of northern Europe. But the typical family organization was not a stem-family. A Russian peasant family resembled one of Kent or Norfolk much more than one of the Midlands. It belonged to the class of joint-families: a group of descendants of a common ancestor, the brothers inheriting jointly and living in one community. The existence of such families produced one feature of the Russian village organization, the *mir*, which differed sharply from English custom. The joint-families naturally tended to increase in size, but at different rates. After a period of time, the amount of land one family would have for the support of each of its members would be small; the amount of land another family would have would be large. Accordingly in a Russian village, all the land was redistributed every few years, and redistributed in proportion to the number of persons, or working males, in each family. There is no evidence that such redistribution took place in medieval England. The adaptation of English village families to the champion husbandry took the form of established tenement units and a hierarchy of relatively fixed social classes. The adaptation of Russian families of a different sort took the form of redistribution and social levelling.

CHAPTER XV

THE FAMILY IN CHAMPION COUNTRY

THE LAST CHAPTER in this study of the families of villagers in the Middle Ages must be a miscellany. It must fill in details; it must summarize; it must generalize. In the first place, the family cannot be seen apart from its setting: the house and the household. Besides his acres of tillage scattered over the open fields, a villager would have a messuage beside those of his fellows in the village proper. A messuage had at least enough room for a house and yard, outbuildings, and a garden. Houses were poor things, of a timbered framework filled in with wattle and daub — the ancestors of the English half-timbered houses. They were easily built and easily moved, since the posts and beams were the only materials which were costly enough to be worth moving. They were easily destroyed: we read of a burglar "digging through" the wall of a house in order to make a theft.[1]

But the smallness and wretchedness of the houses of villagers can be exaggerated. For instance, the specifications of a house are given in the court rolls of the year 1281 of Halesowen, Worcs.[2] It was to be thirty feet long between the walls and fourteen feet broad, with corner posts, three new doors and two windows. Such a house was not large, but it was a house of a peculiar sort. It was to be built by a man for his mother when she retired and he took over her land. In short, it was a "dower house," a dependance. The main house on the holding may have been much larger.

Houses varied, in the thirteenth century as today, with the wealth of their owners. In fact the members of the village social classes often took their names from their houses. The villagers of the lowest class were called cotters after their cotes, which may have been not only smaller and poorer than the houses of the more substantial villagers but also different in plan. In some places the villagers of the middle class were called husbonds:

that is, they were the bonds who had houses rather than cotes. Even in the house of a yardling in a prosperous village, most of the members of the household may have eaten and slept together in the room which was dominated by the hearth. But such houses must have had other rooms. We have seen settlements made before manorial courts in which the holder of a tenement would agree that his aged father and mother should have a room at the end of his house in which to dwell in their old age. The holder himself and his wife must often have had a room of their own.

After looking at the house, we must look at the household. The household, rather than the family, was the actual working unit. The person who held the tenement, the holder, the *husbond*, was the head of the household and directed the husbandry of the tenement. He must have been responsible, after his father's death or retirement, for marrying off his sisters and providing his brothers with proper portions out of the profits of the tenement. Anyone who lived on the tenement, who took meals there, was his *mainpast*. That is, the husbond was held responsible for the good behavior of the members of his household. If they did evil, he was bound to produce them in court and even answer for the damages they had done.[3]

Next in consequence after the husbond came the housewife, the head of the women's work in the household, and after her the husbond's father and mother, if they were still alive. If any of his brothers and sisters had decided to remain on the holding and unmarried, the husbond was bound to find them sustenance and must also have put them to work. Of the husbond's children, the most important was the son who stayed on the hearth, the son and heir. As he grew older, he must have become more and more closely associated with his father in the management of the holding, until at last his father was ready to retire and leave him in entire control. The other children fell into two groups, more distinct in men's minds then than they are today: those who stayed at home and had their sustenance from their father, and those who were making their own living. In widely separated parts of England, the latter were called by a special name, as if they were recognized as a separate class in the community. They were called *selfodes* or

sulfodes. The derivation of this word is unknown — it may
have come from such form as *selfhood* — but its meaning
is made plain in the following passage from a statement of the
customs of Cirencester, Glos., dating from about 1209:

Villeins of Cirencester, that is, of the lord King, while they are under the rod
and power of their fathers, and at mainpast of their fathers and mothers,
their parents will acquit by the bidreaps which the latter do for the lord King
or his farmer. But as soon as the same villeins have their own free power,
and live by their own labor, and are made *sulfodes*, then each of them ought
to do three bidreaps for the lord King.[4]

These bidreaps (*precarie*) were the days in harvest when everyone
in the manor was bound to turn out to reap the lord's corn.

The customs of the bidreaps, as they are recorded for different
manors, have much to tell about the parts played by the various
members of a village household in the economy of the holding.
For one thing, some members of a household were released from
the duty of coming to the bidreaps. Presumably their other
work was so important that it could not be neglected. Foremost
among them was the housewife. Another person often exempted
was the family shepherd. Some villages supported common
shepherds, but in others each holding must have had its own.
Other persons sometimes exempted were the "nurse" and the
"marriageable daughter." Perhaps these two were in fact the
same person: that is, one of the older daughters of the family
had the duty of taking care of the younger children. Still another was the "master servant." [5] These exemptions give some
hint of the size of households and the number of duties to be
performed on a large holding.

Besides the children and other kinsmen of the holder, two
classes of servants, or *hewes*, to give them their old English name,
might be members of a village household. One class was made
up of those servants who slept or took their meals in the main
house of the holding. Whether men-servants or maids, they were
likely to be unmarried. We must remember the *anilepimen* and
anilepiwymen, the single men and single women who are
mentioned in the custumals as hired farm hands. These house
servants would be allowed food, clothing, and lodging, besides
perhaps being paid something in coin for their work.

The other class was made up of those servants who were given dependent cottages on the messuage. They might well be married and keeping house for themselves. They were commonly called *undersettles*, that is, they were settled under the holder of the tenement. Such a name shows how medieval people thought of society as a hierarchy of classes one above the other, the members of the lower class holding their lands of members of the one next higher. This scheme of thought was most elaborately worked out in the customs of the members of the military classes and is now called the feudal system, but the feudal system in its main lines was the scheme of thought of all members of society.

The undersettles were sometimes called coterells, lesser cotters. Such men had to do a share of the works owed to the lord from the holding. In a custumal of Aldingbourne, Sussex, drawn up in 1257, the statement of the services due from a yardling at the lord's works in harvest specifies that:

He shall send to the oat boonwork all his hands, and anyone who holds a cottage of him shall come with his hands to the boonwork.[6]

Again, at the harvest works of Haddenham and Cuddington, Bucks.:

All the villeins ought to come with their entire households except their wives and shepherds. And if the tenant has two men, he ought not work; if he does not have two, he will work. And if any one of them has an undersettle, let him come to the first bidreap.[7]

That is, if the tenant had two able-bodied men in his household, he was exempted from working himself. At Brandon, Suffolk, the arrangements were similar, according to a passage in the Ely custumal of 1277:

It is to be known that every undersettle or anilepiman or anilepiwyman, holding a house or a *bord*, no matter of whom he holds it, will find one man at each of the three boonworks of harvest, at the lord's food.[8]

The *bord* of this entry links these men with the *bordarii* of Domesday Book, where it is hard to distinguish between the *bordarii* and the cotters (*cottarii*). A *bord* was a small house, a cottage. These special words for houses suggest that there were various traditional kinds of villagers' houses, differing in plan as well as size.

It is possible that the position of an undersettle resembled that of a Scotch cotter in later centuries. If it was, the holder of the tenement on which the undersettle lived gave him a cottage and an acre or two of land and helped him in the tillage. In return the undersettle worked for the holder as a farm hand. But often an undersettle was simply a man who leased a house or land from the holder of a tenement. So he was in 1326 at Littleport, Cambs., in the Fen country, when the following entry was made in the court rolls of the village:

The jurors present that outsiders who come in and hire their houses of various people and hold nothing of the lord common in the fen with their beasts and take other benefits in common, and these are called undersettles.[9]

These undersettles were outsiders, holding no land directly of the lord of the manor. Yet they enjoyed rights of common which ought to have belonged only to true villagers, and the court wanted to know by what warrant they did so. It appeared that each of them reaped in harvest half an acre of the lord's corn and did other light services in return for his privileges. Any person who occupied a small part of a tenement held by another man and rendered his share of the rents owed to the lord from the tenement may have been called an undersettle. Under this definition, the heir's brother or sister on whom he had settled a few acres of the family holding would have been an undersettle.[10] Such sub-tenants are often mentioned in manorial records. For instance, at Pavenham, Beds., about 1279, John, son of Robert Cerne, held one yardland and had as tenants William West, Simon West, William Reyn', and others.[11] How could the yardland support all these men, besides the chief holder and his family? We do not know, but we know that this yardland was nothing exceptional. The Hundred Rolls show that many another holding of that size or even smaller was crowded with minor sub-tenants.

Four classes of persons, then, might have lived on a village holding in champion country. There was the immediate family of the holder: himself, his wife, and their children. There were others of his kin: his mother and father, his unmarried brothers and sisters. There were the serving-men and maids boarding in the house. And there were undersettles. On any particular holding, one or more of these classes might not be represented, and if a holding were small its population would be reduced. But many a yardling must have kept a numerous household.

One way of summarizing the traditional organization of families in the champion country of England during the Middle Ages will be to compare it with a similar traditional organization in another time and country. For this purpose a good description exists of peasant families in the Luneburg district of north-western Germany as they were in the middle of the last century.[12] A typical family of prosperous peasants in the Luneburg possessed a compact holding of land with a house and farm buildings upon it, the *hof*. Such a holding was supposed in custom to be indivisible, and some of the *höfe* had in fact remained undivided and in the hands of the same families for many centuries.

It was through the working of the customs of inheritance of the country that the *hof* remained in the family which had always held it. The customs provided that the *hof* should descend at the death of its last holder to one of his sons, and in default of sons to one of his daughters. In some places, the eldest son inherited, in some the youngest; in some the peasant himself selected the son who was to have the *hof* after his death. Commonly the eldest son succeeded.

If he had the right to choose, the peasant selected his son and heir in good time and associated this son with him in the management of the farm. Often the choice of an heir and the heir's marriage went together: the two were parts of the same event. To understand what happened, we must bear in mind the arrangement of the rooms of the *hof*, which was traditional and determined by the family customs. The door of the house opened into a large room which served as kitchen and living-room for the whole household. On the left of the kitchen was the "grandfather's room," the room occupied by the former head of the household, and another room where prayers were said and family meals were taken. On the right were the rooms of the peasant and his children and those where the servants slept. When the heir married, his father moved from his former quarters into the "grandfather's room," and the heir and his wife took over the rooms his father had left.[13] From that day on, the father took a smaller and smaller part in the management of the farm and left more and more to his heir. Thus each generation in its appointed time took a definite place both in the house itself and in the household.

Families were large. When the brothers of the heir, those who were not to inherit the land, came to man's estate, they could do one of two things. They could leave the *hof* to seek their fortunes or they could remain in the *hof*, but if they took the latter course they had to remain unmarried. For all those who left the *hof*, the peasant felt bound to provide portions out of the savings of the farm. In the same way he provided dowers for the daughters of the house when they married.

There were many likenesses between this family and household of the Luneburg of north-western Germany in the nineteenth century and a typical villager's family and household in the champion country of England in the thirteenth. Some of the phrases of the English court rolls even suggest that, in that country as in Germany, when the father turned the holding over to his heir, he moved from the room which he had formerly occupied into another one traditionally reserved for the old folk. The chief difference between the Luneburg family and that of medieval England is that the land belonging to the one was a compact area, while the land belonging to the other was made up of strips scattered all over the fields of a champion village. The custom of both families was that the holding was not to be divided or alienated. These likenesses are only what we should have expected to find. From north-western Germany came the Angles and Saxons who settled the champion country of England. From north-western Germany they brought their language and their social order. This order was still nearly intact in the England of the thirteenth century. In later times it changed considerably, while in the German homeland, in a district which remained somewhat isolated and entirely given over to husbandry, it was preserved much longer. Nor were Germany and England the only places where families of this sort were to be found. They were at the heart of the ancient social order in many parts of north-western Europe.

This traditional family organization had great virtues. There is a danger of considering the rules of inheritance, life-tenancies, and alienation simply as rules of law in abstraction from the conditions under which men live together. When the rules are studied as they were followed in village life, they are seen to fall into a consistent system of custom, according to which the rights of every member of a family in the means of subsistence possessed by the family were established from birth to death and from generation to generation. Every child knew what he had to expect and knew that if he were once given the means of making his living he was secure in holding them. Some certainty and security for the future are necessary to men if they are to be useful members of society.

But presumably there is more than one traditional family organization — indeed we know there is — which provides this certainty and security. The particular family organization which we are studying had virtues of its own. Adapted to a society in which land was the paramount source of wealth, it insured that in every generation of a family at least one man, his wife, and their children had a decent subsistence from every established holding of land. But it retarded any further increase of population which would press upon the means of subsistence: the sons who were not to inherit a holding had to get out or remain unmarried. It preserved a stable social order at home. We have already seen how the intricate dispositions of a champion village were preserved in part by its customs of inheritance. If all went by rule, the same holdings, whatever their rank, would remain in the same families generation after generation. At the same time it supplied plenty of men for the rough work at the frontiers of society. The great French sociologist Frédéric LePlay felt that families of this particular type, which he called stem- or root-families (*familles-souches*) because like the root of a vine they were continually sending forth new shoots, which were continually cut back — he felt that these families had been one of Europe's great sources of strength. LePlay observed that these families steadily provided, for colonization, for trade, for war, landless men with their fortunes to make. And so far as we can tell from its history or judge from similar instances, this admirable organization was not thought out by some primitive Lycurgus and imposed by him on his countrymen, but must have been the product of a long train of interactions between the interests and sentiments of men and the external conditions of their lives.

In some societies the family relationships are extended and generalized until a man considers himself in some way kin of every other member of the community. If a stranger cannot show that he is a kinsman, he is regarded as an enemy and treated as such. Thus in ancient China a village was also a clan. The English place-names in -*ing* suggest that English villages may once have been of this sort: Reading means Red's people or descendants. And the court rolls sometimes speak of "the blood of the village." But upon the whole there is little evidence that the inhabitants of an English village in the thirteenth century thought of themselves as a body of kinsmen. Indeed the stem-family organization may have emphasized the distinction between the family and the community. When the marriage of the heir customarily coincided with his taking over the management of the holding, the history of the blood which held the tenement became the history of a single sequence of small families, each pulsing in its time, each dying away. Since in every generation the sons who were not to inherit land either left the holding or did not marry, the number of actual kinsmen could not increase rapidly. In inheritance the immediate family was favored at the expense of what later became the aristocratic tradition of descent in the strict male line: in default of sons, a tenement was often divided among the daughters of the last holder, and only if the last holder left no children did it go undivided to his brother.

The terms used to reckon and indicate kinship often reflect the facts of family organization. Accordingly in north-western Europe they supported the emphasis put upon the small family group consisting of a man, his wife, and their children. In reckoning closeness of blood relationship, men reckoned by degrees of descent from an original mated couple, a man and a woman. In like manner, the terms for distant kinsmen were made merely by adding prefixes to the terms for persons closer to the small family. There were then, as there are now, great-grandfathers and grandfathers, great-uncles, grandsons, and cousins of different degrees. The point is that the small family was the unit to which the terms for more distant kinsmen were referred. This method is not the one used in many societies.

There was some extension of terms of kinship to unrelated or distantly related members of the community. Friends of the family are still called uncles, aunts, or cousins by courtesy, and in medieval England a pleasant old fellow was probably the uncle of every boy in the village. But this process was carried less far in the stem-family organization than it is in some societies. A further circumstance which may have weakened in the thirteenth century a man's consciousness that he had a large body of kinsmen was the instability of family names. A man was by no means sure of bearing the same last name as his father and his brothers, but was likely to be called Hugh's son, after his father, or Reeve, after his office, or Marden, after his home village, or Atwell, after the place of his house in the village, or Turnpenny, after some personal characteristic, without regard for the names his ancestors had borne. It is true that in that century and later ones the use of family names became more and more settled. Indeed many of the present English family names date from the thirteenth century.

In some societies, then, the larger social groups, the village, the clan, the tribe, are extensions of the family group. They are in fact, or are held to be, groups of kinsmen. In the society of the champion country, family and village tended to be two bodies different in kind. Better than many another society could have prepared them, this society prepared western Europeans and their descendants for the social isolation in which many families live in the great urban agglomerations of today.

The distinctions which were made by English lawyers in the Middle Ages between the different tenures and between common law and local custom have obscured the fact that most men lived under rules which were alike in essentials. If Kent, parts of East Anglia, and the West be left out of account, the different systems of family law were all much alike. Any tenement, a barony or a burgage as well as a yardland, descended to one son of the last holder. In default of sons, it was divided among the daughters. It was subject to the life-tenancies of free bench and curtesy. In their main lines, the rules of family law were the same for the earl and the husbandman, and for the burgess too, though he was somewhat more free than the others to sell or devise his holding. Where the rules differed, it was only in non-essentials, such as the particular fraction of the holding the widow was to enjoy as her bench. In important matters they were the same, and in particular they all held to what we have seen as the central principle of the organization of medieval families: the permanent association of a given blood line with an established tenement unit.

Any member of society, bond or free, belonged to a family much like all other families in its organization. In what concerned his family's tenement, whether that was a cotland or an earldom, he felt the same sentiments as other Englishmen and thought in terms of the same schemes. How strong a force this uniformity was in holding together the classes of society, in maintaining society as an organism functioning harmoniously, we cannot estimate. But certainly the constitutional historians have not been sufficiently concerned with the fact that in ancient and stable societies the organization of the government is often a reproduction, with a difference, of the organization of the common family. Thus in Norway, where the custom of much of the country was that land was held in common by the sons of the last holder, the kingship also in ancient times was held in common by all the sons of the last king. Naturally the system engendered periodic warfare. In England, on the contrary, the realm descended to one of the king's sons and one only, just as any man's tenement descended to one of his sons. Clearly this factor will not sufficiently account for the establishment in England and other countries of the principle of primogeniture in the descent of the kingship, but it must at least be taken into consideration. The constitutional historians speak of the anxiety engendered by the king's alienation of some of his rights or a part of the demesne of the crown as if it were simply a fear of the taxation which might become necessary when the king could not live of his own. There was more force in the anxiety than this theory accounts for. When the king made an alienation, the subject felt a little of the irritation he would have felt if his father had alienated a part of his family's tenement. A king of England, then as now, had to take care to avoid doing violence, not only to the persons and possessions of his subjects, but also to their moral sentiments.

We have been concerned here with the rules governing the disposition of family possessions. These matters are the only ones which the surviving records — for the most part legal records — can reveal in detail. As a result, we understand the main lines of family organization, but much remains unknown. Court rolls have little to say about the day-by-day life of the family, about the play of the children, the work of the men and women, the company around the hearth, the behavior of the family in the births, marriages, and deaths of its members. They have little to say about the language people used in addressing their kinsmen and in talking about family affairs. They have little to say about the relations between the family and the rites of the parish church, although the central object of worship in the Middle Ages was a holy family: a compassionate mother, a stern but just father, and their son. This kind of knowledge is likely to be forever barred to the student of a dead society.

BOOK III

MANORS

CHAPTER XVI

AN EXAMPLE

FROM THE GENERATION of Seebohm, Vinogradoff, and Maitland onwards, the manors of England have been the department of research in medieval social history to which most energy has been devoted. On this subject the man who tries to describe society in the Middle Ages will have least to say that is new either in fact or in interpretation, although he will have to say something if he wants his description to be comprehensive. One question indeed may be disregarded. A large part of the energy of scholars has gone into a search for the origin of the manor and has produced much learning but few solid conclusions. The question which will be studied here is not that of its origin but that of its characteristics at a particular period in its history, the thirteenth century. At that time it was nothing new. As the *Consuetudines Singularum Personarum* shows,[1] manors much like those of the thirteenth century were already in existence in England before the Norman Conquest. Unhappily *manor* became early in the Middle Ages one of those words which are useful because they can be made to mean almost anything, and the labors of all the Monkbarns since that time have not narrowed its meaning. The word is still convenient and its meaning is still vague.

In these circumstances, the sensible thing to do is to turn to things rather than to the words that are given them. In making a beginning of the study of manors, we can find an estate which was certainly called a manor and describe what it was. For this purpose, the manor of Spelsbury, in Oxfordshire, has been chosen, as it was in the year 1279.[2] In that year King Edward I caused inquests to be made concerning the holders of land in his kingdom and the franchises they exercised, with the object of recovering prerogatives of the crown which had been alienated without warrant. This investigation was the most elaborate one of its kind made in England since 1086, when William the Conqueror sent out commissioners to gather the material of Domesday Book. The findings of some of these inquests, called the Rolls of the Hundreds, have survived and have been printed. The most detailed are those which refer to a few of the shires of the East Midlands. They make up the most important single source for a knowledge of the social and economic order of thirteenth-century England. From these Hundred Rolls the description of Spelsbury has been taken.

Spelsbury has been chosen not because it was a typical manor — there was no such thing — but because it failed of being typical in ways which make it a good example with which to begin the study of manors. Its structure was more simple than that of most manors. It had features which were common to many manors but would rarely have been found, as they were at Spelsbury, united in any one manor. Furthermore, Spelsbury was in the heart of the champion country of England, and its description is not an ideal reconstruction but is taken from a contemporary inquest. For these reasons, Spelsbury is a good point of departure, especially when social relations are to be studied rather than economic or legal arrangements.

In 1279, Angareta de Beauchamp held the manor of Spelsbury as her dower of the inheritance of the Earl of Warenne and Surrey. At her death, the manor was to revert to the earl. It was held of the Bishop of Worcester, and the bishop held of the king. Such was the chain of subinfeudation which bound Spelsbury, like any other piece of land in England, to the king. To the lady of the manor belonged the advowson of the parish church, that is, she had the right to name whatever priest she wished as parson of the parish. In the words of later centuries, she might present him to the living. She also exercised the rights of *waif*, that is, of appropriating abandoned property, and of *forefeng*, that is, of taking a reward for the rescue of stolen cattle, besides the rights of having her own gallows and holding the view of frankpledge. The jurors who took the inquest did not know by what warrant she exercised these rights, since they belonged to the king or to his officers unless specifically alienated. There was also woodland in the neighboring forest of Wychwood appurtenant to the manor.

Three plowlands of the manor were in demesne, that is, they

were tilled under the direct management of the officers of the
lady of the manor, by the work of her servants and of her
villeins. The rest of the land was in the hands of her tenants.
These, according to the classification used in the inquest, were
of three kinds: freeholders (*libere tenentes*), villeins (*villani*),
and cotters (*cottarii*). There were six freeholders. The most considerable of them was probably William of Colthurn, who held
a mill and six acres of land, for which he paid a yearly rent of
20 s. 4 d., which freed him from all services except that of
coming to the view of frankpledge on the two days a year when
it was held. Next in consequence after William was perhaps
Thomas le Venur, who held three yardlands and a half, and
did what was called suit and forinsec service, by which was
meant suit at the manorial court and services due from the
manor to the lord king, particularly suit at the royal courts
of hundred and shire. John the Fraunckelein held two yardlands
together with six acres of assart, likewise for suit and service.
We must note his name, Fraunckelein, and the fact that he was
a substantial freeholder. There will be something to say later
about franklins. Henry of Richel held one yardland for a rent
of 3 s. and suit and service of the lord king. Thomas Smith also
held one yardland, for which he was bound to make the irons —
the coulters and the shares — for three of the lady's plows,
out of her iron. He was free from all other services save suit
to the hallmote. Lastly, Robert le Duk held a half-yardland,
for which he rendered 4 s. 6 d. in rent, 6 d. worth of plowing,
boon works in harvest worth 3 d. and four hens.

With the end of the list of freeholders and the beginning of
that of villeins, the irregularity of the size of holdings ended
and heavy labor services began. Thirty-three persons held each
one yardland in villeinage. Three of them were widows and one
of them was called Thomas Reeve. The reeve was a village
and manorial officer whose duties will be described later. Each
of the thirty-three had to do the following services: he had to
do sixty works (*opera*) between Michaelmas (September 29)
and the Gule of August (August 1). These works were in tilling
the lady's demesne and in doing other labor for her profit. Beside
this, each yardling had to do four special days' work of plowing
on the lady's demesne with his own plow and one day's work of

mowing her meadow. Between the Gule of August and Michaelmas, that is, in the harvest season, the rate of work was increased. In that time, a yardling had to do thirty-six works, and three bidreaps (*precarie*) besides. These bidreaps were days chosen by the lady when she had the right to call upon the villagers to come to reap her corn. Such were the yardling's services in farm work. He also had to collect nuts in the lady's wood for three days and render her a bushel of wheat at Martinmas. "Against Christmas" he was bound to give her a hen in return for having dead wood. That is, the hen secured for the yardling the right of gathering dead wood and windfalls in the lady's wood. We must remember that she held woodland appurtenant to the manor in the forest of Wychwood. He also gave her at Christmas a "present," worth one penny. What it was is not specified. On top of all these dues, a yardling was tallaged every year at the will of the lady. That is, she took every year what portion she pleased of the money and goods of her villeins.

Ten villeins held half-yardlands. Two of them were widows, and one was called Richard Bedell. The bedell was like the reeve a manorial officer, but one of lower rank. Each half-yardling had to do thirty manual works between Michaelmas and the Gule of August (half as much as the yardlings), three plowings, and five works in hay-making. In harvest time he did twelve works and came to three bidreaps. At Martinmas he gave the lady three hens. And he was tallaged.

The poorest class of Spelsbury people was that of the cotters, of whom there were six, three of them women. Each of them held a *cottagium*, the size of which is not specified. A cotter had to do forty works a year, plus five works making hay, plus three *precarie*. He had to give four hens. At this point the description of Spelsbury ends, with the information that the total yearly *valor* of the manor to Angareta de Beauchamp was £ 30, 19 s., 10 d.

If Spelsbury was a manor, what were the characteristics of a manor? In the terms of feudal law, it was a holding, a tenement, and was held *of* someone, but this statement is not of great significance, since any piece of land was a tenement or part of one. In particular Spelsbury was a free tenement, and not only was it a free tenement, but Angareta who held it was plainly a gentlewoman. It was also a compact tenement. The manor of Spelsbury was also the village of Spelsbury: there was none of Spelsbury that was not in the manor. There were two parts of the manor, a greater part, which was in the hands of tenants, and a lesser part, the demesne, which was managed by officers of the lady of the manor and tilled by her servants and her villeins. On this demesne there was probably a manor house and court, with farm buildings, and in the hall of the manor house the hallmotes would be held. According to the amounts of land they held and the rents and services they rendered in return for their land, the tenants were divided into classes, which were called by special names. Among the tenants also were men who held particular positions in the economy of the village or the government of the manor: the miller, the smith, the reeve, the bedell. Lastly, besides having her rents and services from her tenants, the lady exercised certain other rights over them, especially the right of holding a manorial court. They had to attend it, and she took the profits of its justice.

Spelsbury was not a typical manor, but it corresponded closely to what, thirty years ago, was conceived to be a typical manor. The typical manor was born of a study of the custumals of a few great religious houses. Later investigation of the organization of estates in all parts of England has allowed few of the characteristics of the typical manor to stand as typical. The typical manor was supposed to be coincident with a village. But there were manors which were larger than a village and manors which were smaller. Some estates which were called manors included several subordinate villages. An example is the Earl of Warenne and Surrey's manor of Wakefield in Yorkshire, the court rolls of which have often been quoted here. Sometimes two or more persons held manors in the same village — this arrangement was especially characteristic of the Danelaw — or there was a complicated structure of subinfeudated holdings. The typical manor was supposed to have both land in demesne and land in villeinage, that is, land held by villein tenants who owed labor services. Indeed, the size of the demesne and the number of labor services must have borne some relation to each other. More services cannot have been exacted than were needed for the cultivation of the demesne. But in the matter of the demesne any actual estate might differ from the typical manor in one of two ways. It might have no demesne but present a complex of free tenants holding of a lord and paying rent. On many manors, even when there was demesne land, parts of it from time to time would be rented out to tenants. Or the estate might consist entirely of demesne, without villein land.[3]

Clearly we cannot specify, by any large number of characteristics common to all of them, what manors were. Estates which might have been called manors covered in the thirteenth century most of the land of England. They differed greatly in their composition, but the word was broad enough to include them all. Even now its meaning does not need to be defined strictly. People use the word *manor* not for complicated logical operations but only for convenience, to show that they are going to talk about one of a large and diverse class of things. But if *manor* is undefined, *village* is not. Whatever the complex of manors which divided its soil between them, a village was a distinguishable unit. It was a unit in that two or more great fields, submitted to the customs of the champion husbandry, surrounded it and belonged to it, that the houses of the villagers were clustered in one group, and that the villagers thought of themselves and behaved as a distinct social body. The royal government laid upon the village and not upon the manor its burdens of local police. We are interested here in manorial organization not for its own sake but only for its effect on village society.

But when all reservations are made, certain characteristics do remain to define a manor. That a manor was a free tenement still holds, and that it was a tenement of a certain order of magnitude. No one would mistake a yardland for a manor. It was also a tenement concentrated in one place, not scattered over several shires like some great honor. There were at least two classes of men on most manors: a lord, and tenants under him who owed him rents and services. It is true that even a yardling might have tenants, that is, undersettles. The difference lay not in the tenants but in the control exercised over them. If the tenants of the lord of the manor were villeins, their goods were in the eyes of the law not their own but the lord's. They owned nothing but their bellies — so men said when they wanted to put the case as plainly and as brutally as they could.[4] The lord might increase the rents and services of his villeins as he wished; they had no remedy. He might drive them penniless away from their homes. More important, the lord of the manor set up some kind of manorial government, and in particular held a court which most of his tenants were bound to attend, the lowest in the hierarchy of English courts. No court, no manor — that is a good rule, especially in a study which relies heavily on the information furnished by the rolls of manorial courts.

For the student of society, the most interesting question which can be asked about a manor is that of the relations between the lord and his tenants. The first thing to be said about these relations is that they were permanent. As long as he lived, the lord was likely to have the same families of tenants; as long as they lived, the tenants had the same line of lords. The two were bound together for better or for worse. A free tenant might leave the manor whenever he wished, a villein after paying a fine to the lord and agreeing to pay a small sum called *chevage* (head-money) every year that he remained away, but no tenant would leave the manor without strong inducement, since leaving meant losing his land. The relations between lord and man were permanent but they were seldom a matter of face-to-face contact. If the lord held many manors, he probably would not reside at any one of them for more than a week or two during the year. The custumals always say that the tenant must render such and such rents and services to his lord and that the lord must give such and such benefits to his tenant, but this assumption of direct relations between the lord and his man was nothing more than a manner of speaking. Unless the lord was a very petty lord indeed, a steward or bailiff was an intermediary between him and his tenants. In the same way at the present time, the official documents often describe the relations between a workman and the company which employs him, when as a matter of fact his only face-to-face contact with the company organization is his contact with his immediate supervisor. This fact does not, of course, prevent the workmen and the upper members of the management from having strong feelings of loyalty or distrust towards one another.

Just as we must take into consideration at least two classes of men on a manor: a lord and his tenants, so we must begin by considering at least two factors determining their relationship: their interests and their sentiments. The economic and other interests of the two parties are obvious, as are most economic interests, and perhaps this obviousness is one reason why the science of economics is further advanced than the other social sciences. If his tenants did not render their rents and services, the lord would not have the wherewithal to keep up his household, pay his officers and retainers, dower his daughters. His state in the world was maintained by the income he received from his manors. He wanted to continue receiving it and if possible to increase it. But even when he had the legal right, as he did over his villeins, to exact what rents and services he pleased, he did not intend to press his tenants so hard that they would run away from the manor. Then the land would lie untilled and no revenue at all would derive from it. Even if the tenants did not leave the manor, oppression might drive them to a kind of passive resistance which would in the long run be just as damaging to the lord's interests. On the other hand, the tenant's possession of his means of livelihood, his holding, was dependent on his rendering to the lord the due and accustomed rents and services of the holding, and there was good positive reason for his remaining on good terms with the lord, since many favors were in the lord's power to confer. Finally, the tenant had the future of his family in mind and wanted to be sure that the tenement would descend to his son and heir.

But to think that the economic interests are the only factors involved in a relationship such as that between a lord and his tenant is always a mistake. Even when the two parties talk as if their economic interests were the only factors involved, when they talk about exploitation, a wise man will look for other forces at work. The situation may be revolutionary; it will seldom be revolutionary for the reasons envisaged by Marx. In point of fact, strong sentiments entered into the relations between landlord and tenant. To say what these sentiments were would be rash in anyone who had not been brought up in England and in the country. All that a historian can say is that for many, though not for all periods in English history there is evidence in the behavior of landlords and tenants towards one another that the two parties felt much mutual loyalty and understanding. The landlord was not simply a landlord. He was in charge of local government and in some manner responsible for the general well-being of the people in his neighborhood. His duties demanded a traditional realism in looking at social relations, traditional because it was not a matter of study or clear expression but was born in the young men as they listened to their fathers talk and strengthened in them later by their own experience. It was realism because it never forgot, not even in the great age of economic theory at the beginning of the nineteenth century, that more than economic interest was involved in the constitution of society. This tradition was the one — we may call it the Tory tradition, though the Whig families were as well trained in it as the Tories — which led Disraeli to believe that the common people would rather trust their destinies to the landed gentry, the gentlemen of England, than to the new plutocracy of manufacturing. For centuries, in politics and war, the common people were in fact ready to follow the lead of their landlords. To be sure, the tradition did not prevent landlord and tenant from being very much alive to their special interests. Indeed they may both have taken the tradition so much for granted that they were seldom consciously aware that anything beyond economic interest was at stake. Furthermore, men of ill will on either side might violate the code. But if it were solidly enough established in the community, even such persons would be driven to conform. There is such a thing as being a gentleman in spite of oneself.

There is reason to believe that these non-economic factors in the relationship between landlord and tenant are old in England. As the French would say, the more the relationship has changed, the more it has remained the same thing. To describe it as it is today or was in the nineteenth century would be difficult enough. To describe it as it was in the thirteenth century, a man must cling to a few hints, a few inferences from the records, and these will tell him only about practices which had hardened into common customs; they will tell him little about the active attitudes of landlords and tenants. Nevertheless the description is worth attempting. Though the treatment of other matters may often obscure it, the importance of the non-economic factors in the relationship between lord and man is the theme which will be pursued in the pages to come.

CHAPTER XVII

THE SORTS AND CONDITIONS OF MEN

IN ALL THE HIGHER civilizations, men are divided into classes, each class having a different degree of social rank. But in the western world of today, the lines between the classes are wholly indefinite: the array of persons from those of highest consequence to those of lowest is nearly a continuum. We talk of a ruling class, a middle class, a proletariat; in fact there are no generally accepted signs by which all the men of one class may be divided from all those of another. The reasons for this condition are at least two. The circulation of men from the lower levels of society to the upper has been and is fast, so that the membership of classes has never come near to being closed. And the range of occupations has been so great and has been changing so rapidly that the degree of social consideration attaching to each occupation has not been settled. A man's business no longer reveals unmistakably the class to which he belongs. But in a relatively stable and simple society, such as the society of England in the thirteenth century, the classes were fairly distinct, and in the speech of the time they were given definite and long-established names.

There were distinct classes even within a village, but a difficulty arises in describing them. Two other classifications of the sorts and conditions of men intersected the classification according to social rank. The first classification was legal: it was developed by the lawyers of the royal courts as one part of their consolidation of the common law. The second classification was economic: it spoke of men acording to the parts they played in the economy of a manor. Each of these schemes had its own terminology; each coincided with the rest at some points and cut across them at others. Furthermore, the facts themselves were of great intricacy, and the words used to describe them very numerous, varying according as the clerks wanted to lay emphasis on one element in a situation or another. Both the legal and the manorial classifications will have to be described before the social classification, which is the one of greatest interest to a student of society, can be brought into the open.

The legal classification has often been described and is brilliantly described by Maitland,[1] upon whose work the present brief outline must rely. Men were divided according to their personal status and according to the tenures by which they held their lands. Both schemes made a primary distinction between freedom and villeinage, between free and villein tenures, between freemen and villeins. A classification both by status and by tenure may seem to have been over elaborate, but it was actually in use in the thirteenth century. In those days it was quite possible for a freeman to hold a tenement in villeinage, a villein to hold a free tenement. Sometimes a doctrine that a man was free if he held free land began to appear. At a court held in 1275 in Wakefield, Yorks., a manor of the Earl of Warenne and Surrey, presentment was made that John the smith of Stanefeud was the earl's villein, but held free land, and the order was given: "He is to be distrained to answer how and wherefore he went out from villeinage into freedom." [2] But such a doctrine would have been foreign to the royal courts.

Tenures were either free or unfree, that is, villein. If they were free, they were protected by the royal courts. If they were unfree, they were at the will of a lord and protected only by the custom of the manor as administered in the lord's manorial court. The free tenures were four in number. Frank almoigne, the tenure by the duty of giving alms, was the tenure by which most of the religious houses held their lands. Tenure by military service was the great feudal tenure. Tenure by sergeanty was that according to which a man held land by doing one of a great variety of services, not necessarily military, such as the service of being hereditary steward of a great lord. Socage was the residuary class of free tenures. Socage land was not subject to the rights of wardship and marriage in their feudal form, and suits regarding such land were decided in many instances by local custom rather than common law. Socage was the tenure of the lesser freeholders.

Land held in villeinage was subject to the jurisdiction of the manorial, not the royal courts. Accordingly the lawyers of the royal courts, who developed the common law, made no distinction between different villein tenures, except in one case, that of land which had once been part of the ancient demesne of the crown but had later been alienated. Ancient demesne was defined as land which had been before the Conquest in the hands of Edward the Confessor. On a manor of the ancient demesne, a distinction was made between two sorts of villein tenures: villeinage proper and villein socage. The peculiarity of villein socage was the following: a man who held by this tenure might have to do for the lord of the manor the work services which were characteristic of villeinage, but he was protected against the lord in his tenure. He did not hold, like other villeins, at the will of the lord. If a villein sokeman was injured in his tenure by his lord or one of his fellow villagers, he could secure in a royal court a writ, the "little writ of right close," directed to the bailiffs of the manor and requiring them to do full right according to the custom of the manor. The manorial court was then to decide the matter on these terms. Again, if a lord increased the services of the body of his villein sokemen beyond what had been customary, they could secure the royal writ which began with the word *monstraverunt*. It was directed to the lord and required him to cease his exactions. If justice were not done under the little writ of right or the *monstraverunt*, there were other writs which would remove the cases into the royal courts. Thus the little writ of right protected the villein sokemen as individuals in the possession of their tenements, and the writ *monstraverunt* protected them collectively against the exaction of new services.[3]

The word socage, then, meant not one thing but several. It meant a free tenure. It meant a privileged tenure on manors of the ancient demesne. And occasionally, on other manors, men who by all legal tests were villeins but who rendered money rents to their lords rather than work services were called sokemen. This variety of meanings arose for two reasons. Before the Norman Conquest, sokemen probably formed a definite single class. Later, when the lawyers tried to draw a hard line, which had not existed in the older England, between freedom and bondage, the sokemen fell into two divisions, one on one side of the line and one on the other. To complete the confusion, the lawyers used socage as a convenient term for a number of free tenures, including some which would have been recognized before the Conquest as those of sokemen as well as many which would not. In the thirteenth century the words socage and sokeman were principally in legal use. A scholar who is studying society in general rather than the law in particular need not concern himself with them.

Men, like tenures, were either free or bond. In their great work of simplification which made the common law, the lawyers of the royal courts were impelled to draw a line between the bond and the free. For many reasons it was a convenience, but unhappily the lawyers could not found on a clear social distinction the distinction they made between bondmen and freemen. It is true that there had once been such a distinction. There were slaves in England at the time of the Conquest, though they were few even then and disappearing. What the lawyers did was take from the Roman law the doctrine that men were either serfs or freemen and try to apply it to the distinction between men who held land in villeinage and those who held land by other tenures. According to Roman law, a serf was the mere chattel of his master, and the lawyers were prepared to envisage a villein as a serf. But custom was too stubborn for them. A villein, even apart from the land he held, was sometimes sold by one lord to another. He held his land, in theory, at the will of his lord. His goods, in theory, were his lord's property. Nevertheless, so long as an English husbandman was a man who did customary services for his lord, tilled his own holding and handed it on to his son, and settled his disputes in the hallmote by the judgment of his neighbors, he could not be looked upon with conviction as a Roman slave.

In the lack of any clear distinction between freedom and bondage, such as had existed in Roman law, the lawyers set up a series of tests to determine whether a man was by status a villein. A man was naturally held to be a villein whose mother and father before him had been villeins and had held villein land. But this rule only pushed the issue back into the past. The most obvious test was that of week-work. A man who worked for his lord for several days in the week was surely a villein. The Hundred Rolls speak of villeins *de sanguine suo emendo*, villeins who buy their blood. By this phrase people meant that a man was a villein who paid merchet when his daughter married outside the manor and paid a fine when, for any reason, his son left it permanently. The Hundred Rolls also speak of villeins as holding their land by uncertain services. According to legal theory, the lord of a manor could change at his will the amount of rent and the number of labor services which his villeins were bound to render him. On the other hand, the rents and services of a freeholder were fixed and "certain." As a matter of fact, although increases in the services of villeins were sometimes made, the services were generally fixed in local custom, and custom was as certain as anything in medieval life. Even the tallages of villeins, which were always described as being particularly subject to assessment at the will of the lord, were commonly fixed at a customary amount. Another test of whether a man was a villein was whether he had served as the reeve of a manor. Reeves were commonly villeins. But the circumstances of any given case might make many of these tests inapplicable. In order to understand what the men of the thirteenth century understood by the word *villein*, we must take into consideration the economic organization of manors and the social classes recognized by the villagers themselves.

A villein was made free by entering religion or by dwelling for a year and a day on the royal demesne or in a borough having a royal charter. He was made free by marrying a free woman, though it is doubtful whether his children would be free. He might also, if his lord were willing, buy his freedom. Such a manumission appears on the court rolls of 1274 of Minchinhampton, Glos.:

Hugh Carter seeks to be freed from serfdom. And he gives the lord 13 s. 4 d. for having liberty, and 2 d. of chevage a year.[4]

The payment of chevage, that is, head-money, was a regular feature of manumission.

Whether or not the Roman distinction between a freeman and a slave could be strictly applied to English conditions, the lawyers had done their work so well that people felt that a villein was something degraded. Villein itself was a French word, applied by a Norman lord to his English tenant. Already in the thirteenth century it was beginning to acquire the kind of meaning it had later. Villagers resented being called serfs, neifs (*nativi*), or villeins even if they were such. In the manorial courts this offence, like any other libel, was punished by fine. The truth was no defence. The record of a hallmote held at Halesowen, Worcs., on October 5, 1300, speaks of such a libel:

Robert, son of Christine of Illey, is distrained for the default which he made against Thomas Amys, with whom he settled out of court, and to answer to the lord for this, that he said that he was of higher condition than said Thomas Amys.

And just three weeks later, that is, at the next court, the same Robert was amerced "because he called his neighbors villeins." [5]

Perhaps for the reason that the Abbot and Convent of Halesowen were oppressive masters or at least, as we shall see later, were steadily on bad terms with their tenants, the question of freedom and serfdom was acute there. Two other cases recorded in the court rolls of the manor illustrate this point and also reveal the organization, as estates, of the villeins and the freemen. The first case came up in the court of April 22, 1297:

An inquest of all the freeholders says as a judgment that since William of Tewenhall is of free condition he ought not contribute to the villeins or to their amercements for false presentation or concealment but [ought to be amerced] only for his own offence. And therefore it is deemed that said William recover his damages against the township of Ridgeacre, and the aforesaid township is in mercy for its false assessment (*ingistiamentum*).[6]

Clearly the custom at Halesowen was that the villeins were subject to a common fine if as a body they made concealments or false presentations in the manorial court. Freemen, on the other hand, were apparently amerced only for their private offences. William of Tewenhall was free; nevertheless the villeins of the township of Ridgeacre had assessed him for a share in a common fine which they had incurred. Therefore William received damages. Another point must be noticed here. The inquest was an inquest of all the freeholders. The freeholders themselves were the persons who determined whether a man was one of their number.

In spite of this decision, the status of William of Tewenhall, or of his son by the same name, was still in doubt in a case which came before the hallmote of Halesowen later in the same year. The case was recorded as follows:

William, son of William of Tewenhall, distrained by one heifer for taking the oath for the office of keeper of the assize (of ale), comes and replevies his distress and finds pledges to obey the right, to wit, Philip Belegaumbe and John o' the Hethe, and said William is arraigned to take the oath for the office of juror. He is present and says that he is not bound to take the oath or to be in that office by election of the villeins or to be in any other bailiwick by their election, and he puts himself on the judgment of his peers, and the villeins are asked whether they wish to maintain his election at their peril or choose another juror at their election. They say that those who are of better condition are not at that court but are in the service of the lord King, and therefore the parties have a day until the next court.[7]

Just as the villeins were subject as a body to common fines, which they assessed among themselves, so also, at Halesowen and elsewhere, they elected from among their number certain manorial officers and named the jurors of the manorial courts. That is, they named the villein jurors. If there were need, the freemen might form a jury of their own. William claimed to be a freeman and therefore to be discharged of these duties of the villein community, and in order to establish this fact he threw himself upon the judgment of those whom he claimed as his peers, the freemen. If the villeins had persisted in electing William to their jury, they would have done so at their peril. That is, they would have been fined if it were established that he was not one of their number. But William's alleged peers, the freemen, were away with King Edward the First's army in Wales, and therefore the decision in the case was postponed. The ale-tasters of a village had to determine whether the ale brewed for sale therein was up to the standard set by the royal assize of ale. If it was not, the lord of the manor took a fine from the offending brewer. Countless such fines were levied in manorial courts.

These Halesowen cases bring to the front an important matter concerning the classes of men in an English village. Some modern theorists of social organization have advocated the organization of society according to estates. They do not argue simply that society be divided into classes: most advanced societies are so divided. They do not argue simply that the classes be more sharply differentiated than they are in most of the western nations today. They argue that the classes be treated in some manner as corporative bodies, each with its collective duties and privileges.

The authors of this theory admit that it is based in part on their understanding of the social order of the Middle Ages. They are thinking of such things as the Estates General of France. But even in a much more humble part of medieval society, a village of England in the thirteenth century, the different classes behaved in some manner as estates. In the hallmote of Halesowen, the villeins as a body made presentations of matters which concerned the good order of the manor, and they were collectively responsible for any mistakes or concealments found in the presentations they had made. As a body they elected the villein jurors of the manorial courts and several of the other manorial officers. The freemen were not so closely organized as the villeins. A freeman was not only secure from the power of his lord but also free from certain duties which would have fallen upon him, if he had been a villein, as a member of a community. Nevertheless the freemen behaved in some degree as an estate, if only that one of their number had the right to demand that judgment be passed in his case not by the villein jurors but by the men of his own estate, his peers. It is doubtful whether the line between bond and free was drawn as strictly in the courts of other manors as it was at Halesowen, but there are hints, as we shall see, that in many parts of England a man was in some degree responsible to the body of men of his own class.

The first classification of the sorts and conditions of men is that of the law, according to tenure and status. The second is that according to the parts men played in the economy of a manor. Of course there were many landless men: undersettles, anilepimen, servants who lived at the manor house. But the important villagers were the landholders, the tenants. From the point of view of a man who was in charge of the management of a manor, there were two main kinds of tenants: those who for the most part paid rents, and those who rendered heavy services in tilling the demesne. Here at once there was a rough coincidence between the legal and the economic classification. Whatever the legal tests of villeinage may have been, the chief practical difference on most manors between the freeholders and the villeins was that the former rendered to their lord money rents with few work services or none, while the latter rendered heavy work services and usually some rents as well. But the body of freeholders might include men who occupied very different stations in the eyes of their neighbors. A freeholder might be a man who held a large amount of land, a hide or two. A freeholder might also be a man who held nothing but his cottage. The two were lumped together as freeholders only because both paid rents and did no work services. For this reason the line between bond and free cannot everywhere be admitted as a line between genuine social classes.

Furthermore, not all men who paid rents and were quit of work services were freeholders. On some manors there was a class of men who were bound to pay merchet, serve as reeves, and be tallaged at will — in short they were villeins — but who did few works or none at all. They were called *censuarii* in Latin, in English *molmen*, because they paid *mol*, rent. The molmen were created by the process of commutation. They or their ancestors had once done heavy work services, which the lord had commuted to money rents. Often he arranged that they should either work or pay rent, according to what seemed at the moment the more profitable practice.[8]

Finally, more men were villeins in the eyes of the law than were commonly called villeins. In many manorial custumals, for instance that of Spelsbury, the name of villein was given only to those tenants who held substantial tenements and did heavy work services for the lord of the manor. They were also called *consuetudinarii* or *custumarii*, "customers," because their services were customary services, or *werkmen*, because they did works, in contrast to the molmen. On some manors, the werkmen had to labor three or four days a week for their lord; on others their works were less and their rents correspondingly greater. In this respect manors varied greatly, according to the size of the demesne and the way it was tilled, whether by the services of villeins or by the work of hired hands.

Of lower degree than the men who held the substantial tenements, the yardlands and the oxgangs, was a class of cotters, each of whom held a cottage and perhaps a few acres of land. Many of the cotters were villeins in the legal sense of the word, but they were not commonly called villeins. In the cotters a real social class coincided with a group of men set apart in the manorial economy. A man who had a small tenement and maintained only a small household could not be required to do much work for the lord. Accordingly the cotters did fewer work services than the men who held comparatively large tenements. Indeed on some manors the cotters were called *lundinarii*, Mondaymen, because they were bound to work for the lord only one day in the week, Monday, whereas the villeins with larger holdings had to work for several days.

Outside of these main economic classes, men might be grouped under special names if they held some particular kind of land or performed some special service. Instead of being kept in the hands of the lord, some part of the demesne might be put out at rent. Then there would be a group of men called tenants of the demesne. Again, a few of the villeins might be designated to hold the lord's plows and tend his plow teams. For this special service, they would be given special privileges and discharged from part of the works they would otherwise have had to do for the lord. These men would be called in old English *akermen*. But commonly, according to the part he took in the economy of a manor, a man who held land would fall into one of four classes. He would be a freeholder, or a molman, or a villein, or a cotter. Of course on any given manor one or more of these classes might not be represented.[9]

Neither the division of villagers according to legal status nor that according to the parts they played in the economy of a manor will seem to a student of society as important as the division into classes which was determined by the company men kept and the degrees of consideration accorded them by their neighbors. In connection with the different classes of tenements, something has already been said about village social classes. Something has also been revealed by the legal and manorial classifications of the sorts and conditions of men, since these coincided at some points with the social classification. The custumals are especially helpful in this matter. They record the amount of land held by every tenant of a manor, and in a relatively stable community of subsistence farmers, the amount of land a man held was closely correlated with his social position.

Indeed in considering the main village social classes, the landless men — undersettles, anilepimen, and the rest — can be disregarded. Often the custumals record the old English names the villagers gave to the men of different classes, and these names are the surest evidence that such classes were in fact recognized.

In the thirteenth century there were three main social classes of villagers, which will here be called by the English names which seem to have been in commonest use at that time: franklins, husbonds, and cotters. It is convenient to begin by describing the middle and largest class of villagers. In the North of England and in the east Midlands they were called husbonds. In those days *husbond* meant a man of a certain class. He was a bond who had a house, in contrast to a cotter, who had only a dwelling of a poorer sort, a cote. But the middle-class villagers were called by many other names. In parts of Wessex and of the southern Midlands they were called *neats*. For instance, the custumal of the manors of the Bishop of Rochester, in the course of an account of the customs of Haddenham and Cuddington, Bucks., states that:

The lord can put to work whichever of his neats (*neti*) he wishes on St. Martin's Day. And be it known that the same neats are the same as *neiatmen* who are somewhat more free than cotmen. They all have yardlands or half-yardlands at least.[10]

The words *neat*, *neiatman*, *net*, and *neth* must come from the Anglo-Saxon word *geneat*, meaning a villein, and this *geneat* in turn seems to be related to the German *genosse*. The neats were, so to speak, the fellows of the village, those who partook in its commonwealth. In some parts of the West, men of the husbond class might be called by a still more obscure name, *enches*.[11] Or they were called simply yardlings or half-yardlings after their tenements. In Latin, of course, they were always the *villani*, the villeins proper. In the legal sense of the word, members of the cotter class might be villeins, but almost all the custumals, including Domesday Book, which use the term at all, group the more substantial villeins under the heading *villani* and the less substantial under the heading *cottarii*.

Whatever the differences in their names, the husbonds of Somersham, the neats of Haddenham and Cuddington, the villeins of Spelsbury were evidently men of the same rank. They were the men who held in their villages the tenements consisting each of a considerable number of strips scattered over the open fields, tenements equal in size class by class. In the South, they were the men who held the yardlands and half-yardlands. In the North, they were the men who held each one or two oxgangs. They were not all equals in wealth, but their holdings, compared with those of the other two classes of villagers, were of the same order of magnitude. Everyone who held, say, between ten and forty acres would have been recognized as a husbond.

Unless they were freemen or had been made molmen, the husbonds of a village were the men who had to labor on the lord's demesne for several days a week throughout the year. They had to wash and shear the lord's sheep, mow and make his hay, reap, shock, and carry his corn, then thresh and winnow it, and so forth. To say a man did works "with fork and flail" was to say he was a villein.[12] But the most important of the services performed by this solid middle class of villagers was plowing. Using their own teams or joining their yokes of oxen with those of their fellows to make up common teams, they were bound to plow the demesne of the lord and then harrow it with their horses, week after week at the great plowing seasons of autumn and spring. And at least once a season, when the lord saw need for haste, he might call upon them to appear with their teams at special boon-plowings. In 1336 the tenants of Darnhall and Over, Cheshire, revolted against their lord, the Abbot of Vale Royal, and went before King Edward III with their grievances. The old account says:

The bond-tenants aforesaid, on account of certain grievances which they were told the abbot made them suffer, went to complain to the king aforesaid, carrying with them their iron plowshares; and the king said to them: "As villeins you have come, and as villeins you shall return."[13]

The story of the revolt is absorbing but not now important. What is important is the symbolism. The plowshare was the villein's badge of office. When he appeared as a type in literature, he was called Piers Plowman. The plow was his life.

The villagers of the middle class were called by different names in different places. The villagers of the lower class were not. They were called cotters, cotmen, cotsetles. In every instance, the name given them referred to the kind of houses in which they lived. They lived in cotes or cottages, and in those days as in these, the word *cottage* meant a house which was smaller than other houses. In Domesday Book, many of the lower class of villagers were called *bordarii*, and bordars also appear, though very rarely, in documents of the thirteenth century. But the bordars can be distinguished from the cotters only in name, and their name, like that of the cotters, referred to their houses. They were the men who held bordels.

Their name distinguished the cotters from other villagers as having smaller houses; their tenements also were smaller than those of their neighbors. If a man held much more than five acres in the fields, besides his cote and the land around it, he would not have been recognized as a member of the cotter class, and many cotters held nothing but their cottages. In other respects the tenements of the cotters tended to follow the general pattern of village tenements. In any village the cotlands were likely to be equal in size, or rather, equal in size class by class, since sometimes there were sub-classes even among cotters — greater cotters as well as lesser cotters.

A man's being a cotter depended not on his status according to the law but on the amount of land he held and the degree of wealth and consideration which derived therefrom. The fact that he was free did not make him any less a cotter. We read of men who were specifically called free cotters.[14] Indeed, since their services in any case were few and light, men of the cotter class were more likely to be set free altogether than were men who held substantial tenements and did valuable week-work. Freemen were common at the bottom of society as well as at the top; they were less common among villagers of the middle class.

The cotters fell into two groups: those who held their land immediately of the lord of the manor, and those who were given cotes on the tenements of the more prosperous husbandmen of the village. If the villagers had been nice in their use of language, men of the second group should always have been called under-settles. As a matter of fact, they were commonly termed cotters, or better, coterells, with a hint in the last word that they were very humble cotters indeed.[15]

We have seen that the rents and services of a bondman were roughly proportional to the size of his holding. Whereas a yardling would be working for his lord for several days a week throughout the year, a cotter would be working only one day a week or less. This arrangement was in the nature of things. A man who held a yardland was able to support a large household and get his land tilled even when he himself was busy working on the lord's demesne, but a cotter would have to till his land without the help of serving-men. Furthermore, he probably was not able to support a family simply from the fruits of his own small holding, but had to add to his livelihood by getting wages in money or kind for labor done for his wealthier neighbors. For these reasons, a lord could demand only a few days of work from his cotter.[16]

Often the rents and services of cotters differed from those of husbonds in kind as well as in degree. The Ely Custumal of 1277 says of a cotter at Wilburton, Cambs., that:

He and his fellows ought to gather, prepare, pitch, and cock all the hay in the park of Dunham which all the aforesaid holders of full lands and half-lands have mown.[17]

So also among the services owed by the holder of a half-hide at Cakeham, Sussex, as they were recorded in the custumal of the manors of the Bishop of Chichester, was the following:

He shall cart the bishop's dung with his own wain and have the aid of the cotters in loading it.[18]

These entries are trivial in themselves, but they suggest that in the organization of manorial work the husbonds were treated as one body and the cotters as another. As in the hallmote of Halesowen, so on the demesnes of Wilburton and Cakeham, the classes behaved in some manner as estates, each taking a different part in the work. If these distinctions in the kinds of work owed to the lord were made between the two classes, can we doubt that in the other affairs of village life numberless other distinctions were made between them? One common distinction made between the husbonds and the cotters was in the manorial and village offices which they were eligible to hold. A yardling or half-yardling was bound to serve, if chosen, as reeve or hayward; a cotter had to serve as the lord's plowman, shepherd, or neatherd. In the custumals, no reasons are given for this distinction, but we can guess what they may have been. Probably no cotter had the wealth or the authority necessary to maintain himself in the important offices of reeve or hayward. Probably, on the other hand, the work of plowman, shepherd, or neatherd was beneath the dignity of yardlings. In some villages, there was even a physical separation of the lands of the two classes. We hear in a final concord of 1241 of "five perches of marsh . . . as they lie between the common marsh of the cotters and the common marsh of the villeins of Anwick." [19]

Of the differences in the services of the cotters and the husbonds, there is one which seems particularly important. On many manors, though not on all, a husbond did much of his work for his lord in the shape of plowing, either with his own team or with his oxen joined to those of his fellows to make a common team, whereas a cotter did only "hand works," that is, delving, threshing, winnowing, and the like. This arrangement again was in the nature of things: the holdings of the cotters were small, and there comes a point when a piece of land is too small to support an ox or a horse as well as a man and his family. So we infer, but beyond inference there is evidence that small holders were not likely to have plow oxen. The entry for the manor of Aldenham, Herts., in a custumal of the estates of Westminster Abbey, of the time of Henry III, makes the following statement:

Everyone having a plow, although he has only five acres, ought to plow three times a year without food. If indeed the lord wants to have the plows for a longer time, he ought to find food for them, and whoever does not have a plow owes one work. [20]

Clearly, the wording of the entry implies that a man who held only five acres was unlikely to have a plow team. But of course he might have one ox or a yoke of oxen to join with those of his fellows to make a common team. We must have grounds more firm than this for the statement that small holders were not likely to have beasts of the plow. A custumal of 1301 of Stoke Courcy, Somerset, speaks of nine "customers," each of whom held five acres of land. Each was bound to plow, with as many oxen as he yoked in the plow, for three days at winter seed and three at lenten seed. Each plow received a penny a day as "reprisal," and it was estimated that four tenants commonly could make up one plow between them. If a tenant had no oxen, he was bound neither to plow nor to make any other render in place of the plowing. Each of the nine customers was bound in theory to perform this service, but the custumal goes on to say:

Since it commonly happens that he has no oxen and that this custom is not worth more than the reprisal, therefore it is not extended.[21]

Here is a plain statement that, at least at Stoke Courcy, a man who held only five acres and was certainly a member of the cotter class did not commonly possess plow oxen.

Another suggestive circumstance is the following: on many manors the lord's plowman was chosen from among the cotters, and on these manors the plowman was commonly allowed, as one of his perquisites, to use the lord's plow team on Saturdays to plow his own land, Saturday being a day when bondmen were not usually bound to work for their lords.[22] If the plowman had had a plow team of his own or oxen of his own which he could have joined with those of his fellows to make a common team, the use of the lord's team would have done him no good. We must suppose that he did not have a team of his own. But no rule about village society in England in the thirteenth century holds true for every village, and there were villages where men of the cotter class were expected to possess plow oxen. At Wrington, Somerset, for example, a man who held five acres of land, in the year 1235 or thereabouts, was bound "to come twice to the boon plowings of the lord with one ox and with more if he has them." [23] Whether or not cotters possessed plow oxen probably depended on the amount of pasture and meadow pertaining to their village.

The reason for laboring the point that in England the husbonds possessed plow oxen, the most important single instrument of husbandry, whereas the cotters often did not, is that elsewhere in the peasant social order of Europe this economic distinction between men was linked with a social distinction. In France, as we have seen earlier, the two main classes of villagers were formed by the men who were able to keep teams and the men who had only their hands with which to work. The former were the *laboureurs*, the latter, the *manouvriers*. The *manouvriers* may have delved up their lands with their spades, by hand, but in most villages a man feels bound to help his neighbor, and the *manouvriers* could commonly borrow the plow teams of the wealthier villagers. If they did so, they were expected to give the *laboureurs* certain days of their hand work.[24] A similar cleavage may have divided the husbonds from the cotters in medieval England, and a similar coöperation may have bound the two classes together. Indeed we know that this pattern of behavior was followed in at least one case, when the lord of a manor chose one of the cotters to be his plowman, allowing the cotter in return the use of the plow team to plow his own land.

Besides the husbonds and the cotters, a third class of men might be found in a village of the thirteenth century, a small class but the highest of the three in rank and wealth. These were the franklins.[25] The word *franklin*, which comes from the Anglo-Norman dialect, means freeman, but not all freemen were franklins. There were men who were called free cotters. Presumably there were also free husbonds. Such men held tenements of the same order of magnitude as those of other cotters and husbonds, but differed from them in being free from the services and other incidents of villeinage. Such men would not have been called franklins, nor would members of the nobility and gentry, though they also were freemen. In the course of a hidage, dating from 1184–1189, of the knights of Ramsey Abbey, the cartulary of the abbey furnishes an early use of the word *franklin* and a description of the franklin's status. The hidage gives the names of the men who held land from the abbot by military service, the size of their fees, and the number of knights each was bound to furnish to make up the quota due from Ramsey when the king summoned his feudal array. Four hides of land made a knight's fee, but many of the knights held less than a full fee, though none less than one hide and a half. The hidage then goes on to state:

Besides these there are many franklins (*frankelanni*) some of whom hold a half-hide, some more, some less, and they ought and are accustomed to aid the knights to do service.[26]

This passage establishes the position of the franklins, at least on the Ramsey estates. Greater in consequence than the franklins were the knights, the least of whom held a hide and a half of land. Lesser than the franklins were the husbonds, none of whom was likely to hold more than a yardland. Since there were four yardlands in a hide, the franklins were freeholders who held tenements of the order of two yardlands in size. Such is the general statement concerning the franklins, and the thirteenth-century custumals of Ramsey manors, which are included in the cartulary, show that in many villages there was in fact a small but distinct body of men who held just the position which the hidage assigned to the franklins.

Furthermore, men who held a position just like that of the Ramsey franklins were to be found in many villages of the Midlands and southern England. They were freemen; they held tenements which were smaller than those of the feudal gentry, the lords of manors, and larger than those of the middle class of villagers. Almost all the persons who are recorded in the Hundred Rolls as bearing the last name of *Franklin* were of this station. Thus in Spelsbury, John the Frаunckelein was a freeholder who held two yardlands and six acres of assart, whereas the most substantial villein held no more than a single yardland. But names in the thirteenth century were unstable, and no solid argument can be based on them alone.

Most of the franklins held their land in what the lawyers came to call socage, the great residual class of free tenures. They did not owe military service for their holdings, nor were they sergeants. They paid their lord rents, and often not very heavy rents; they were not closely bound into the manorial economy. They were called franklins not simply because they were freeholders, but because they were freeholders in spite of being husbandmen and villagers. Most villagers were required to do labor services for their lords; the franklins were freemen and quit of all services or most of them. Even when they were accustomed to do services, these were special ones. In order that they might look out for the interests of the manors to which they belonged, many franklins were bound to do suit to the courts of the hundred and the shire and attend the king's justices in Eyre when they were sitting in the neighborhood. That is, they had to do what was called forinsec (foreign) service. These duties often involved the franklins in toilsome rides far from their villages; indeed they were sometimes called hundredors (*hundredarii*) after their duty of suit to the hundred court.[27]

More interesting were the services owed by the franklins at the lord's harvest bidreaps. At Denton, Sussex, in 1274, John

Partrich was a freeholder and held half a hide. The custumal of the manors of the Bishop of Chichester goes on to speak of his services:

He has to find at each harvest boonwork one man to reap, at the lord's food, and he, John, has to be at each harvest boonwork in the place of a sergeant, bearing a rod in his hands, faithfully and honestly to gather in the lord's corn, at the lord's food.[28]

Again, at Northleach, Glos., in 1267, Robert of the Hall held three yardlands:

And he himself will come in his own person with his rod, and will be among the reapers for three days, to see that they work well and faithfully, and then he will be at the lord's table.[29]

A service of this sort was common on many manors. There is even a drawing in one medieval manuscript which shows an overseer carrying his rod and supervising the reaping in harvest.[30] It is true that the overseers were sometimes chosen from among the villeins of the wealthier sort as well as from among the franklins, but they were always villagers of high rank. The organization of the lord's harvest work made use of the class alignments of village society.

In short, there is good evidence that in rural England in the thirteenth century a small class of freeholders existed, less wealthy than the gentry, more wealthy than the husbonds and cotters, and that these men were called franklins. In the century to come, if we can judge from Chaucer's franklin, members of this class throve and gained much wealth and power.

In no society is the composition of the classes of people static. Men do not hold just the same positions in the scale of rank and wealth as those their fathers and grandfathers held. Some men of ability, or often simply men with energy and without the scruples which interfere with success, rise to a station in life higher than the one in which they were born. Other men, without the qualities which sustained their forefathers in high place, sink and carry their children with them. The speed and the avenues of this circulation of men through the classes of society vary from society to society and from time to time in the history of any one society. In the western world in the last century the circulation has been rapid, and its importance has been impressed upon students of human affairs.

The speed of this circulation is greatest in times of disturbance or of economic expansion. The high Middle Ages were neither disturbed nor by our standard wealthy, and the circulation was correspondingly slow. A countryman in England in the thirteenth century, if he were thrifty and lived in a village where the restraints of the alienation of land were weak, might accumulate holdings and die the wealthiest husbandman of the village. That he or his children could achieve recognition as one of the landed gentlemen of the neighborhood is hard to conceive. If he wanted to make a great advance in the world, a man had to leave the community where he was born and brought up, where people had made up their minds about the standing of himself and of his family. He had to leave his village.

There were two main avenues for a young man's ambition, the boroughs and the Church. In the thirteenth century, London and the lesser boroughs were growing; there was money to be made in them. His father was probably a good customer of the tradesmen in the borough nearest his village and might bind the son apprentice to one of them. Whatever the circumstances of his seeking his fortune in a borough, a man who had luck, talent, and a willingness to work hard could make himself a man of means. Then perhaps his grand-daughter would be married, with a large dower, to one of the gentry, and in this manner the family would return to the land in a later generation and a higher station.

The other opening was in the Church. A villein had to pay a fee to the lord before his son was allowed to take the tonsure, but once the boy had gone to school and become a clerk, a great career was possible for him. Not only might he become a bishop or an abbot, but as a bishop or an abbot one of the men who ruled England. Most of the high prelates of England were younger sons of gentlemen, but not all were. Besides men bearing Norman names, such as St. Thomas de Cantilupe, Bishop of Hereford, there were bishops like St. Thomas Becket who were merchants' sons, and even one who had been born a villein. That was Robert Grosseteste, Bishop of Lincoln, the friend of the friars and of Simon de Montfort, one of the ablest and most liberal of the churchmen of medieval England. At least the rumor was that he was a man of low origin. In 1239 a quarrel arose between him and his cathedral chapter. Chapter priests, that is, canons, were especially likely to be of the gentry, and during the quarrel, Matthew Paris says, the canons of Lincoln "were deeply ashamed that such a bishop was created over them from such humble station, and this they protested publicly in the presence of the bishop himself." [31] If a man had ability, he could rise farther and faster in the Church than in any other career. The Church furnished the only means by which men of humble birth could come to exercise great gifts for administration or spiritual leadership.

CHAPTER XVIII

SERVICES

IN STUDYING the relations between the lord of a manor and his tenants, at least two factors have to be considered: the interests of the two parties and their sentiments. This point was made in an earlier chapter. Now we come to study these relations in greater detail, as they are revealed in the manorial rents and services. But we shall not understand the services unless we take into account still another factor: the intellectual scheme in terms of which both the lord and his men thought of their relations to one another.

This scheme is revealed by turns of speech and by ceremonies. If you asked a workman of the present day why he received wages from his employer, he would tell you that he received them in return for work done for his employer. In the same manner, if you had asked a medieval villein upon what terms he held his land, he would without question have replied that he held his land as a grant from the lord of the manor and in return rendered him certain rents and services. In both instances the relation between one man and the other, or, if you will, between master and man, was conceived to be reciprocal. It was thought of as being based upon an exchange.

Consider next what happened when a tenant died, particularly one who held land in villeinage. If no heir of the tenement was at once forthcoming, the order was given in the hallmote to take the tenement back into the lord's hands. When the heir according to the custom of the manor did appear, he came into the hallmote and paid his predecessor's heriot and his own fine or relief for having entry into the tenement. Then, as the court roll might put it, "he was given seisin of the tenement to have and to hold to himself and his, doing the due and accustomed services thereof." The doctrine was thus reasserted that the tenement was granted only on condition that the proper services be rendered.

Often the heir was given seisin "by the verge." That is, the lord's steward, who presided in the court, extended to the heir a rod, and when the heir took hold of it, he was then understood to have seisin, as if the seisin had flowed from the steward's hand to the tenant's along the rod. A amusing description of seisin being given by the rod is the following from the court rolls of 1275 of the manor of Wakefield:

William son of Soignyf had two oxgangs of land, and in open court he granted one oxgang to Thomas, his firstborn son, and the other to Richard, his younger son, with Thomas's consent. And after the death of William, their father, the said Thomas and Richard came in open court, and paid 16 s. as a relief for the said two oxgangs of land; and the Steward, holding a rod in his hand, of which one end was black and the other white, gave seisin to Richard with the white end, because he was fair in colour, and gave seisin to Thomas with the black end.[1]

This passage is interesting for more reasons than one. We must observe that it is an instance in which a holding was divided between two of the sons of the last holder, in spite of the fact that the custom of the Wakefield countryside was that a holding descended to only one son. But it is not an instance of thorough-going partible inheritance. In the first place the holding was a large one. In fact it was two holdings — two oxgangs. It was probably more common to divide large holdings than small ones. In the second place the eldest son, the son who would have inherited the whole if no division had been made, had to give his consent to the transaction. In this instance, as in so many others, the consent of the heir was required before land might be alienated in any way out of the customary line of descent. Villein tenants were often called tenants "by the verge" (*per virgam*) in contrast with free tenants, who were spoken of as tenants "by charter" (*per cartam*).

When a man had seisin he did fealty. So the court rolls testify, without saying in what form it was done. But in the fourteenth and later centuries many manuals for the holding of hallmotes were drawn up, and these manuals give formulas for doing fealty which cannot have been much unlike those actually used. For instance, the *Modus Tenendi Curias* (*c.* 1342) supposes a certain Roger W. to have given three pounds for entry into the messuage and yardland which his father had held and for which he would do the services which his father had done. Then, says the manual, "he shall do fealty thus: — 'Hear this my lord! I, Roger, will be faithful and loyal to thee, and faith to thee will bear of the tenement that I hold of thee in villeinage, and will be justiciable by thee in body and chattels. So help me God and his saints.' " [2] The oath of fealty may have been no more than an empty form, but at least it professed that the relation between lord and man was not to be one merely of economic advantage. The man was to bear faith and loyalty to his lord.

To sum up: when a man died who held a tenement in villeinage, his heir according to the custom of the manor at once succeeded him in possession, as a chain of heirs had done before him. But his succession was marked by a ceremony performed before the hallmote. This ceremony was elaborated around the fiction that, when the last holder died, the lord repossessed himself of the tenement and then regranted it to the heir. The tenement was sometimes said to have been taken back into the lord's hands; the heir always had to pay a fine for having entry, and he was given seisin in a manner which implied that seisin flowed from the hand of the lord's steward to his own. All the symbolism of language and of action reinforced the original fiction. The lord's repossessing himself of the tenement and his regranting it to the heir were accomplished only in ceremony, but this ceremony before the hallmote was enough to reassert the doctrine that the land was the lord's to bestow on whom he would and on what terms he would. And if it were thus established that the land was the lord's to bestow, then the rendering of services in return for its bestowal seemed only proper. The conception of an exchange of benefits between lord and man seemed that much less a pretence.

The relation between lord and tenant was conceived as being based on an exchange: rents and services were rendered in return for a grant of land. Another theory which was current in the Middle Ages envisaged the reciprocal relations between the class of gentlemen and the class of husbandmen as based on a much more general social compact. One form of the theory is developed in the ninth Passus of *Piers Plowman*. Piers has met a knight, who says that he does not know how he shall live since he has no understanding of husbandry. Piers answers him thus:

> 'Sykerliche, syre knyȝt' · seide peers þenne,
> 'Ich shal swynke and swete · and sowe for us boþe,
> And laboure for þe while þou lyuest · al þy lyf-tyme,
> In couenaunt þat þou kepe · holy kirke and my-selue
> Fro wastours and wyckede men · þat þis worlde struen.
> And go honte hardiliche · to hares and to foxes,
> To bores and to bockes · þat brekeþ a-doune menne hegges;
> And faite þy faucones · to culle wylde foules,
> For þei comen to my croft · my corn to defoule.' [3]

In short Piers was to grow enough corn to feed both of them, and in return the knight was to protect Piers against men and beasts. The tenants of a lord did in fact receive from him a large measure of protection. For one thing, his bailiffs defended them against damages done to them by the men or officers of another lord. Nevertheless we may doubt whether any such notion as this one of *Piers Plowman* were ever widely popular among plowmen in real life.

The relation between lord and tenant was conceived as being based on an exchange. We must now take leave of the theory and turn to the facts. The important point to be made is that the facts do give some justification for the theory. The lord and his tenants in many of their activities did in fact give aid and comfort to one another. To be sure, each party paid for the aid it got, but mutual help there was nevertheless. One of the chief circumstances in which the relation between employer and workman today differs from that between lord and man in the Middle Ages is the following: whereas a modern workman gives one thing, his work, in exchange for one thing, his wages, the exchanges of benefits, real or conceived, great or trivial, between lord and man were many and extended far beyond the main exchange which was a grant of land in return for the render of rents and services. Indeed we may classify the reciprocities and speak of them, outside the main exchange, as being special or ceremonial. Like all classifications, this one is simply a matter of convenience and is made only in order to bring out certain facts.

The rents and services which a villein was bound to give as a condition of holding his tenement — the rents and services *of*

the tenement — are described in the manorial custumals.[4] In
the best of the custumals they are described in elaborate detail.
If a well educated man, not a special student of the subject, is
asked to outline the organization of a manor, he will undoubtedly
begin by speaking of the labor services in tilling the demesne
performed for the lord by his villeins. As a matter of fact, on
most manors the labor services of the tenants were worth less
than the rents they paid in money. But the services have always
been emphasized, and the so-called week-work most of all. Many
villeins had to work on the lord's demesne for one, two, three,
or even more days a week throughout the year. In the autumn,
the villeins would be plowing, with the lord's teams or with their
own. Later they would be sowing, harrowing, and ditching, or
instead of working in the fields, they would be busy in the
manorial grange, threshing, winnowing, and doing the other
chores of a farmyard. In the spring they would be plowing again,
for the sowing of the spring corn, and in the early summer there
would be one or more fallow plowings. In June and July the lord's
sheep had to be washed and shorn and his hay made. And at
last in harvest, when the number of days a week on which the
villeins were bound to work for the lord commonly increased, his
corn had to be reaped and bound into sheaves, and the sheaves
shocked and carried to the grange.

Besides this work in tilling the soil, villeins were commonly
expected to perform other services. For one thing, they had to
carry the lord's goods between the manor and other places, using
their own horses. When a manor was part of a large ecclesiastical
estate which was managed as an economic unit, and at the same
time was some distance away from the abbey or cathedral which
was the head of the estate, the carrying services were especially
heavy. The villeins of Haddenham and Cuddington, Bucks.,
manors of the Bishop of Rochester, had to carry to Oxford,
Wallingford, and Wycombe. None of these towns was far away,
but they also had to go to Gloucester on the Severn and to
Rochester itself and fetch back fish, and these two places are
on opposite sides of England.[5] Even in fresh-water shires, salt
herring was often a part of the fare provided for workers at
the harvest boons and must always have been a common food.
These carrying services took men away from their manors for

several nights. They dispose of the notion which once was popular that a villager of the Middle Ages rarely passed the boundary of his own village and can have met only a few hundred persons during his lifetime. On the contrary, he saw a good deal of England and ought to have picked up some knowledge of the world.

So much for what has here been called the main exchange between the lord and his tenant — a grant of land on one part in return for the rendering of rents and services on the other. In economic terms this main exchange was by far the most important, but we are not interested here in giving its proper weight to each of the elements of the income derived from a manor. We are interested rather in bringing out the character of the social relations between the lord of the manor and his men. Here the special exchanges are revealing. They may be called special because they took place on special occasions and were often named by special names. In them we can see more fully an important trait of the reciprocity between the two parties. A body of benefits accorded by the lord was not met by a body of rents and services rendered by the tenant, but a series of particular benefits was given in return for a series of particular renders, and the memory was preserved of the association between each benefit and the corresponding render. These special exchanges may be divided into two classes: those in which the benefit was required in the first instance by the tenants, and those in which the benefit was required in the first instance by the lord.

The lady of Spelsbury — Spelsbury has been taken as a manor having many of the common features of manors — possessed in the nearby forest of Wychwood woodland appurtenant to the manor. "In return for having dead wood," presumably in this woodland, every yardling was bound to give the lady a hen "against Christmas." The hen was a special rent given in return for a special right conferred by the lady on her villeins, that of gathering wood in her woodland. This rent was a common one, and on some manors its reason for existence was preserved by its name. The hen was called the woodhen (*wodehen*). The possession of the woodland of a village was often an ambiguous matter. On the one hand, the law was inclined to say that the lord of a manor might deal as he would with all land within the boundary of his manor which he had not specifically granted to freeholders, and so might allow the villeins or refuse them, as he pleased, the use of the woodland. On the other hand, the villagers were likely to have made use of the wood for many generations and to consider it rightfully their own, however legally their lord's. On some manors, villeins in fact enjoyed the rights of *husbote* and *heybote* in the lord's wood, the rights of gathering wood for building their houses and making their hedges, without paying a rent in return. Perhaps the forefathers of the villeins of Spelsbury had always taken wood from Wychwood, and the lords of Spelsbury had been able to maintain their own full legal possession of it only to the extent of requiring the villeins to pay a rent for its use. Perhaps, indeed, they had secured no more than a rationalization of an existing rent — the circumstance that the woodhen was paid "against Christmas" makes it possible that the rent had once been a ceremonial gift made to the lord at that season, without any association with the right of gathering dead wood. But this is only a possibility. By the time the Hundred Rolls were drawn up, the accepted doctrine was that the villeins of Spelsbury paid their lady hens in return for her letting them take her wood.

Besides woodland, the lord of a manor often had more pasture than he could use, or perhaps there was some such ambiguity about the possession of the pasture of a village as there was about the possession of the woodland. In any event the lord allowed his tenants to put their cattle on this pasture, and in return he required a service from them. Usually the service which was given in return for the use of the pasture was a plowing or series of plowings, and it was commonly called *graserthe*. As in the case of the woodhen, the name of the service bore witness to the particular benefit for which it was given. Graserthe was given in return for having grass. *Erthe*, it seems, was the generic name given by countrymen to any plowing. At Stretham and Wilburton, Cambs., there were customary plowings called *wyntererthe*, *lentenerthe*, and *sumererthe* after the seasons of the year when they were done, also *benerthe* and *nederthe*, boon-plowings.[6] Furthermore, if the graserthe was commuted into a money rent, the money rent would still be called graserthe and probably would still be paid at the time when the original plowing service had been rendered. The old associations were preserved at all costs.

The fact that the service was done in return for a particular benefit was not kept alive in memory only. If the service was refused, the corresponding benefit was stopped. Thus in a court roll of 1290 of Elsworth, Cambs., a manor of Ramsey Abbey, the following event is recorded:

> The jurors say that [the names of various persons are given, tenants of lords other than Ramsey] did not come to a boonwork in harvest, which coming they were accustomed to make for having common of pasture. Therefore, if henceforward their beasts are found in the pasture, let them be impounded.[7]

In this case, the people who enjoyed the pasture were not the lord's own tenants but those of other lords. And they were accustomed to give a harvest boonwork instead of a plowing. But the principle of reciprocity was the same. What was true of woodhen and graserthe could be shown to have been true of a large number of other customary rents and services.

The use of the wood of the manor and its pasture were benefits which were needed by the tenants and granted by the lord. But there were occasions when the lord needed the help of the villagers and they gave it him. Chief among these were the crises of the farming year, when the lord's plowing, mowing, or reaping had to be done in a hurry to take advantage of good weather or avoid bad. Then the lord had the right to call upon his tenants to leave everything else and work for him for a certain number of days. More men labored for the lord at these times than labored for him in week-work, commonly, indeed, every villager who could be spared from household duties, and whereas most services were done at fixed times — a villein, for instance, might have to work for the lord on every Monday, Wednesday, and Friday — these other works were done when, in the judgment of the lord's bailiff, they seemed most needful.

These movable works were called in Latin *precarie*, in English boons, benes, or, to specify the kind of benes they were, *benerthe*, *benemawe*, or *bidripe*. There will be something to say later about the significance of these names. Besides the fact that they were movable, that they were done when the lord called for them, there was another characteristic common to the benes. On the day when a bene was performed, the lord gave his villagers food, or drink, or money, or all three together, by way of return for their labor. This was the "reprisal." Sometimes a custumal admitted that the value of the reprisal came to as much as or more than the value of the work done. But even if it was measured in the cost of hiring other men to do the same work, the money value of the benes must have been largely conventional. What was valuable was not so much the work in itself as the circumstance that it could be mobilized at once. The benes were in fact the longest preserved of all work services. Free-holders rendered them when they rendered no other services; villeins still rendered them when all their other services had been commuted.

Of all the benes the harvest bidreaps were the most important. The food and drink to be given to the tenants and their families at the bidreaps were fixed in custom and most carefully entered in the custumals. Indeed the different boon days were often called after the kind of food the tenants were given on each day. Thus with a grim humor that cuts through the centuries, some of the tenants of Ramsey Abbey called their three harvest benes the *alebedrep*, the *waterbedrep*, and the *hungerbedrep*, according as the lord gave them ale or water with their meals, or they had to find their own food.[8] But all the benes, those of plowing and of mowing as well as those of reaping, followed essentially the same pattern, as the following account of the plowing and harvesting benes at Bishopstone, Sussex, a manor of the Bishop of Chichester, will show:

All the plows of the customers of Bisshopeston, Norton and Denton shall come to the two plowing boonworks and have meat one day and fish the other and a fair amount of ale (*ceruisiam rationabilem*); and all who have oxen in the plow teams shall come to supper at the lord's house if they wish. All who have come to the wheat harvest boonwork shall have for dinner soup, wheaten bread, beef and cheese, and for supper bread, cheese and their fill (*ad sufficienciam*) of ale; the other day they shall have soup, wheaten bread, fish and cheese and their fill (*sufficient'*) of ale. At dinner each shall have as much bread as he wishes to eat and at supper a loaf apiece.[9]

At both the plowing and the reaping boonworks, all the customers were expected to come, and after the work was done the lord gave them their dinner.

When the victuals given were not up to the accustomed

standard, the villeins sometimes struck. According to the record of a court held on November 22, 1291, at Broughton, Hunts., a manor of Ramsey Abbey:

All the villeins of the township of Broughton, in contempt of the lord Abbot and moreover in his presence, went away from the great harvest bene, leaving their work from noon till night . . . giving the malicious and false cause that they did not have their loaves as large as they were accustomed formerly and ought to have them, and it is found in the Register of services and customs that said villeins ought not to have bread other than of purchase, if the lord wished, so that two men should have in common a loaf of three farthing's worth. And because said villeins, as is said above, were unwilling to receive such loaves, in contempt of the lord, but went away from the lord's work in harvest time to the grave damage of the same lord, they are in mercy, 40 s.[10]

The Ramsey Register, that is, the Ramsey custumal, has already been mentioned in these pages. Since the services recorded in a custumal were commonly attested as customary by a jury of the villagers themselves, the latter can have had no reason to complain of oppression if they were required to perform those services. From the rarity of records of strikes like this one at Broughton, we can perhaps infer that there were few attempts made by lords to cut down the amount or the quality of the food customarily given to their tenants at the harvest works.

The services which have just been described were called in Latin *precarie*. In English they were even called *lovebenes*. And at Rettendon, Essex, there was a boon service of reaping called *thanchalfaker*.[11] The emphasis in their names is all upon these services being boons, done by the tenants at the asking of the lord, out of love. The cynical will at once protest that whatever they were in theory, and whatever the names they bore, these services were in fact not freely given but exacted. The cynical will be confirmed by entries in manorial court rolls which show that tenants were amerced for not performing their benes properly. It was recorded at a court of Minchinhampton, Glos., of about the year 1290 that:

The workers of the village are distrained for a default in plowing the bene, since where each plow ought to plow three acres at the bene, whether it was of three yokes or of four, there it plowed only an acre and a half.[12]

Or at a court of Elton, Hunts., a Ramsey manor, in 1278:

From Henry Godswein, 6 d., because he was unwilling to work at the second bidreap of harvest and hindered said bidreap by ordering that everyone go home before the hour and without the permission of the bailiffs, to the lord's damage of a half mark, and because in other ways he reaped his béénes badly on the lord's tilth.[13]

But it is possible to be too cynical in these matters. The benes were a customary service. Though they might once have been given only out of love at the prayer of the lord, in course of time they had been given so often that the tenants felt obliged to give them. In the Middle Ages mere practices rapidly turned into customs, and as soon as they became recognized as customs they could be exacted as a right by those who benefited from them. No line could have been drawn between what was customary and what was exactable. Both the lord and his tenants may have been able to think of the benes with full sincerity as being given out of love even when they had to be given. Indeed in the field where a long course of repetitions had not hardened the work into custom, tenants still did services for the lord literally "out of special love." That at least is what is alleged in a court roll of Elton of the year 1300. Nineteen cotmen, the entry states:

were attached and accused because they did not come to load the lord's carts with hay to be carried from the meadow to the manor, as formerly they were accustomed to do in times past, as is witnessed by Hugh Prest, Claviger. They come and allege that they ought not do such a custom save only out of love at the instance of the sergeant or the reeve, and they beg that this be inquired into by the freemen and others. And the inquest comes and says that the abovesaid cotmen ought to stack the lord's hay in the meadows and likewise in the courtyard of the lord Abbot, but that they are not bound to load the carts in the meadows unless it were out of special love at the instance of the lord. And because the steward had not the Ramsey Register by which he could make sure about this matter, the aforesaid demand is placed in respite until etc. And let the said cotmen have speech and dealing with the lord Abbot about said demand.[14]

This entry has many points of interest beside the main one. The cotmen appear in it as doing, as an estate, a particular type of work, and they appeal to another estate, the freemen, to support their contentions. The reeve is shown as the man in charge of the manorial husbandry. This is his usual position. His duties will later be described in full. The steward is presiding in the hall-mote, and once more he looks to the Ramsey Register as the final authority for settling all questions about customary works. Lastly, the cotmen are to deal directly with their lord, the abbot, about the matter. The lowest and the highest orders of society are to meet face to face. But all this is incidental. The important point is that the cotmen had refused to do a certain work and made the assertion, in which they were confirmed by the inquest, that they were bound to do it only out of special love at the request of the lord or of his officers. The cotmen were bound to stack the lord's hay in the meadow and again in the manorial farmyard. These were exactable services. But if they chose they could refuse to load the hay into carts to carry it from one place to the other. Perhaps the services rendered by the villeins to their lord were built up and elaborated by a long process in which works done for the lord out of love, though there must always have been a large admixture of fear with the love, became customary and exactable in the course of many repetitions.

Let us review the characteristics of benes. They were works done for the lord by every villager who could be spared from other work, or at least by many more villagers than were working for the lord week by week. The number of the benes was fixed, but they were done when the lord's officers called for them, and not at fixed dates. They were done, in theory at least, out of love and not as a service binding on the different tenements. And they were rewarded by the lord's giving food and drink to the workers at the benes.

What is next to be established concerns those English villages which have been founded outside of England. When a body of men and women move to a new country, leaving the one in which they were born and bred, they do not try to adapt the system of customs to which they were used in the old country to the conditions obtaining in the new one. Instead they try to change the new conditions to fit the old customs. The new country may be too strong for the colonists and force them to give up many of their traditional ways, but they begin by doing their best to preserve them. In this manner, we must suppose, the people who in the Dark Ages came to England from Denmark and north-western Germany repeated so far as they could in England the customs they knew in the homeland.

When Englishmen came to make their next great migration, that from England across the Atlantic to what is now the United

SERVICES 265

States, they did what their ancestors had done when they moved across the North Sea. They took their village with them. They did not take it to the South, although Englishmen went to the South. In the South, except perhaps in Maryland, the convenience of organizing life and work in large plantations prevented the village from taking root. But they did take it to New England. New England was settled from the beginning in villages, or rather in towns — town is the proper Yankee name, as it is the proper old English name for a village. The earliest New England towns even had such champion institutions as "commons" and common herds.[15] These were abandoned when the vastness of the land grew upon people and the techniques of clearing the wilderness were perfected, but the town as a basic social unit remained. Two circumstances, indeed, gave it more coherence than ever. A town in the early days was also an independent Puritan congregation. And on the frontier the townsmen had to cling together for mutual defense against the attacks of Indians. There remained long after in the most anciently settled parts of New England a tendency for the houses of a town to be built close together at one center.

In one thing only did the New England towns differ sharply from their English ancestors. There were no lords of manors; there were no landed gentry. Instead the towns went back to a tradition of democratic self-government, which, as we shall see, was strong in the English villages of the thirteenth century. Outside the cities, New England is still organized in townships. Their affairs are administered by boards of selectmen, elected every spring by all the voters of the town in town meeting assembled, and the selectmen are governed in their actions by the votes of this town meeting.

One of the most famous of the institutions of New England towns was the *bee*.[16] If a man wanted to have his corn husked, or the frame of his new barn raised, or any other work done which had to be done in a hurry or required more hands than his own family was able to supply, he let it be known to his neighbors that he was going to hold on a certain day a husking-bee or a raising-bee, or a bee of some other kind. The neighbors would gather at his farm on the appointed day and all together would supply more than enough hands to do the work. The man who

held the bee was expected to supply them with food and drink
in plenty, and was of course expected to appear himself when
one of his neighbors held a bee. Bees were much enjoyed as
times of fun and neighborliness. In the life of a New England
town, which was often hard and without festivity, the bees
filled both an economic and a social need.

An institution like the bee became most elaborately developed
in a country like New England in the days of the frontier, when
there was much hard work to be done and few hands to do it.
It fell more and more out of use as the country became settled
and the dependence of people on one another less immediate.
But bees are still given in New England,[17] and indeed some such
custom of mutual aid is a feature of any community of poor
husbandmen. The bee itself, like the other institutions of New
England towns, was nothing more than a descendant of a custom
of English villagers. Among the usages of Yorkshire in old
times was that of holding *bean-days*. One observer wrote
as follows:

When a new-comer enters late upon the occupancy of a farm, the rest of the
farmers of the village will unite in doing him a good turn. If it is plowing
that requires to be done, they will go on the land with their teams, and plow
all in a day without unyoking, thus enabling the late-comer to 'overtake the
season.' The evening of such a day is spent in a festive manner; the neighbors,
generally, enjoying the farmer's hospitality. At times of push, as during rape
and mustard threshing, there are *bêan-days*, when neighbors assist each other,
by hand and implement, with a merry evening to follow. If a person allows a
footpath across any part of his land, this act of sufferance is recognized by a
bêan-day, when the farmers render suit and service for the concession.[18]

Evidently the bean-day corresponded to the New England
bee. It was given when a farmer had some pressing piece of
work to be done which he could not do with the labor of his own
family. It was given not at a fixed time, but when it was needed.
And the man for whom the bean-day was given rewarded his
neighbors with his hospitality. There is no record of the thirteenth
century yet discovered which refers to a bean-day given to a
villager by his neighbors. That was not the sort of matter with
which records were concerned. Only in recent years have people
been interested in the customs of peasants for their own sake;
in the past they were interested in these customs only so far

as they affected the income of some gentleman. But that mutual aid in some form such as the giving of bean-days was exchanged among villagers in the thirteenth and earlier centuries is most likely, since the conditions which made mutual aid needful were certainly present. And there was one institution of villages at that time — here at last we have reached the object of this long digression — which much resembled the later bean-days. That was the custom of villagers giving benes to the lord of the manor.

In the first place, the names of the two institutions are the same. *Bêan* of the nineteenth and *bene* of the thirteenth century are certainly the same word, and a reasonable guess is that the American word *bee* is also a derivative of *bene*. But for one letter the two words are the same, and already in the thirteenth century the word *bene* was being spelled, and presumably pronounced *bééne*. The dictionaries, it is true, do not give their authority to this identification; indeed they do not even discuss it as a hypothesis.[19] The important point is not that the words but that the institutions were alike. If we think of the lord, with willing suspension of disbelief, as just another one of the villagers, then we see that the benes which were done for him in the thirteenth century, in plowing, in mowing, in harvesting, were like those which in a later century might have been done for any needy villager by his fellows. In both cases the work was done not at a fixed time but when the needy villager asked for it. It was done not by one or two men but by all the neighbors in a body. It was rewarded by the villager for whom it was done by his finding the neighbors in food and drink. And the name sometimes given to the lord's benes — they were called *lovebenes* — shows that in theory they were done for him as they would have been done for any other one of the neighbors, as a favor. In some degree benes were done for the lord as if he were any villager in need of help. Perhaps at one time they were wholly of this nature and were given freely and only in the course of many repetitions became customary and therefore exactable. Perhaps, on the other hand, the benes which in later centuries the neighbors did for each other were modelled on those their fathers had once done for the lord. But these are questions of origin which can hardly be settled at this date. The important point is that the pattern of behavior was the same in the two cases, that the villager worked for his lord in somewhat the same way that he worked for one of his fellows.

There were three kinds of exchanges between lord and tenant. There was the main exchange, according to which a tenant held his land in return for his render of rents and services. There were the special exchanges, according to which a tenant might do a plowing in return for having the use of the lord's pasture, or might work at a bene and have in return a meal. And there was a third class of renders, which can only be called ceremonial. This class, like the second, may be divided into two subclasses, the first including renders made by the tenant to the lord and the second including renders made by the lord to the tenant.

Chief among the ceremonial renders made by a tenant to his lord were the rents in kind which he paid at the time of certain great church festivals. The custom was to give the lord hens at Christmas and eggs at Easter. Though these rents were often a considerable source of income to the lord, it is hard to believe that they had not at one time been ceremonial gifts and perhaps even in the high Middle Ages kept some tincture of ceremony. Eggs, however stylized, are still given ceremonially at Easter, and were so given in many parts of Europe in the Middle Ages. The impression which is left by many of the manorial rents, as by the benes, is that villagers extended to their lord the system of exchanges in use among themselves, and that in time these gifts became customary, exactable, and a source of profit to the lord. Sometimes the reason brought forward for the tenants' presentation of hens at Christmas was that they were given in return for the right to use the lord's wood. They were woodhens. But as often as not no such explanation was offered, so that it is reasonable to suppose that the gift of the hens was the primary phenomenon, and the assertion that it was made in return for having dead wood nothing more than a later rationalization. A ceremonial render of a different kind, which should here be called to mind, was the dinner which on some manors every tenant on his wedding-day was bound to give to the manorial servants.

Christmas was the time when the villagers drew most closely together in good feeling, and at this time the ceremonial exchanges between lord and tenant became especially elaborate. Against Christmas, the tenants would bring their hens or other food to the hall as a *lok*, a gift, in Latin, *exennium*. Or they would bring grain and brew it into ale for the lord.[20] For his part, the lord regularly gave on Christmas Day a feast for all or most of his tenants, and sometimes the kinds of food to be provided at this dinner were elaborately specified in the custumals. We must not think of a custumal as stating only a tenant's duty toward his lord; the lord's duty toward his tenant was also a part of the record. But any long account of the village Christmas festivities had better be put off until it is time to speak of the husbandman's year. Often the tenants must have eaten and drunk the food and ale they themselves had provided the lord against Christmas. Indeed a custumal will sometimes state that they came to the lord's Christmas dinner *because* they had earlier brought him a gift of food. Thus the inquest jury whose findings were recorded in an extent of 1301 of Siston, Glos., spoke as follows:

They say that there are there twelve customers, each of whom holds twenty acres of land and renders at Christmas one loaf, worth 1 d., and one hen, worth 2 d., for which he will come with his wife on Christmas Day and will have his food at a meal or will receive from the lord 3 d. for the same. And because said custom is not worth more than the reprisal, therefore it is not extended.[21]

Here the tenant at Christmas gave his lord food, and his lord in return gave him a meal worth just as much. The function of the lord would appear to have been nothing more than to organize the village Christmas dinner and get it cooked. But we must not think of this exchange in purely economic terms. The *lok* given by the tenant and the dinner given by the lord were ceremonial renders at least in the sense that they were given in preparation for and celebration of the greatest holiday of the husbandman's year. The relative economic value of the two is irrelevant in the eyes of a student of society. On some manors the *lok* was worth more than the dinner; on others it was not worth as much. But this chain of gifts between a lord and his tenants must have helped to soften the sentiments of the two parties toward one another and to symbolize the reciprocity which was conceived as the foundation of their relationship.

There is another feature of the reciprocity between a lord and his tenants which has been called the "sporting chance." [22]

The sporting chance was much more elaborately applied in parts of the continent than it was in England, but it was not unknown there, appearing especially in the customary gifts which a lord made to his hay-makers: the bundle of hay, as large as he could lift with his scythe, which was allowed every evening to each mower, and the sheep which was given to the mowers as a body when they had finished their job. At Wilburton, Cambs., according to the Ely custumal of 1277, the holder of a "full land" had the following customs in mowing:

He shall mow for one whole day, and shall scatter for one work until the meadow shall be cut, and at this he and the whole township shall have one mutton, or 12 d. and one cheese, or 2 d. And he shall have, on the day that he mows, as much grass as he can lift with his scythe, that is, in the evening, and if, in lifting the grass, he shall break the haft of his scythe, then he shall have no grass.[23]

The provision that if the scythe broke the villein lost his grass was calculated to prevent his being greedy about taking grass. But it may have had another effect besides. The extra risk involved may have given the villein the greater satisfaction when he succeeded in winning an especially large bundle of grass from his lord.

The sheep which was given to the mowers as a body after they had finished mowing the lord's meadow is mentioned in an inquest concerning the customs of Barton-in-the-Clay, Beds. The sheep must have been used to make a dinner for the hay-makers. Barton was a Ramsey manor, and the inquest, following the practice of most custumals, spoke as if the Abbot of Ramsey in person gave the sheep to his mowers. His bailiff, his reeve, or some other officer must in fact have acted in his place. The entry is this:

He himself will place a sheep at large in the meadow in the midst of the mowers, and if they can catch it, they shall have it, and if it can escape, in that year they shall lose it.[24]

Since we are unable to watch the villeins catching the sheep or to talk with them about it, we cannot tell what kind of satisfaction this game gave them. Although a series of exchanges of gifts and services disguised the fact that the interests of lord and tenant were divergent, they remained divergent none the less. Did the sporting chance resolve the anxieties and tensions of this conflict by turning it into a kind of gamble? We cannot tell. But whatever further function the custom had, it had at least the immediate one of making a villein's work somewhat more interesting. There are many skeptics who will not look further than this.

What have been described so far are the peculiarities of the different rents and services. From now on the characteristics common to all of them will be considered, and in the first place the standards according to which it was judged whether or not a rent had been paid in full, a service performed properly. There are few words which occur more commonly in English documents of the Middle Ages than custom, *consuetudo*. At an earlier stage of civilization people perhaps take for granted and do not notice the process by which acts which at first simply *are* repeated after a course of time *must be* repeated. But in the twelfth and thirteenth centuries, though the process by which simple practice crystallized into inviolable custom remained much what it had always been, Englishmen were preoccupied with it. Like their descendants today, they did not lightly set a precedent or break one.

Now the rents and services which a villein was bound to do for his lord were customs. It is true that the lawyers always spoke of them as "uncertain"; the lord might make them what he wished, and there is no doubt that in the beginning and middle of the thirteenth century many lords did in fact increase the services of their tenants. But if they did there was likely to be trouble. Whatever the theoretical rights one man has over others, he can never exercise them to the full because the human medium is stubborn. And in manorial documents, which were much closer to the realities of country life than the books of the law, the rents and services of villeins were spoken of not as being "uncertain" but as being "customary"— something a little different. Customer (*custumarius, consuetudinarius*) was a common synonym for villein; a custumal was a book in which his customs were registered. His rents and services were customs in the sense that his rules of inheritance were customs — as the rules of inheritance had been observed, so the rents and services had been paid from a time to which the memory of man ran not to the contrary. Before they could have been regarded as customs, the rents and services on some manors must in fact have been maintained unchanged for many years, and a tenant must have felt that after they had been rendered for so long, the lord had the right to require that they should continue being rendered. Even when services were commuted for money rents, the memory of the original custom was often preserved in the name of the rent.

In so far as rents and services were customs, the same procedure was followed, when there was a question of what in fact they were, as was followed in the case of other customs. They were "found" by the people who had the best right to know about them. Almost all the manorial custumals were drawn up from the findings of sworn juries of the villagers who actually performed the services and paid the rents. Without doubt if the members of an inquest had reached a finding which the lord of the manor considered to be false, they would get into trouble, just as a jury in a manorial court would be fined for false presentation. But certainly in no simple way were the manorial rents and services imposed on the tenants.

Anyone who has studied manorial custumals must have been struck by the extreme detail into which they go. For instance, they often do not say simply that a man must plow, sow, and harrow one acre of the lord's land. They say that he must plow it with as many oxen as he has in his plow, harrow with his own horse and harrow, and sow it with seed which he must fetch from the lord's granary with his own horse and sack. Services were remembered in minute detail, and when further details, even the most obvious and the most necessary, were not nominated in the custumal or attested by a long history of past performances, they were not custom and were not done. We must remember the cotmen of Elton who admitted that they were bound to stack the lord's hay in his meadow and again in his barnyard, but maintained that they were not bound in custom to load it into carts to be carried from the first place to the second.

In theory long continued failure by a tenant to render his customary rents and services ended in his forfeiting his holding. What happened in practice was that a tenant who was too poor or too feeble to maintain his holding and its services surrendered it to the lord in the hallmote, whereupon it was regranted to some other person, sometimes the son of the last tenant, who was able to "defend" it. The usual provision would perhaps be made for the support of the last tenant out of the profits of the holding. Single defaults in doing particular services were punished by amercements at the hallmote. Records of these defaults are to be found in almost all series of court rolls, but they are not very plentiful. The impression they leave is that there were few general refusals to do customary labor services unless there was a disagreement between the lord and his villeins as to what in fact the customs were. The amercements for obstructing the lord's work are sometimes amusing. There was Hugh Walter's son of Shillington, Beds., who was fined 6 d. at a hallmote held there in 1288:

because he lay at the head of a ridge in harvest and impeded the work of the lord.[25]

An early example, perhaps, of passive resistance. And there was Robert Crane of Broughton, Hunts., who in 1311 was fined 3 d.:

because he played alpenypricke during the lord's work.[26]

We are not told what this game was.

All that has gone before has told when and how works for the lord were done. There remains to tell when and why they were not done. Though the custumals usually speak of the number of days of work a villein owed his lord, the villein often did not work for his lord from dawn to dusk on these days. For instance, if he were threshing in the manor grange, the custom might be that he was free as soon as the lord's plows ceased plowing for the day, which was commonly in the early afternoon. For the rest of the day he was his own master. Another thing to be remembered is that, except at the boon days, a villein did not bring other members of his household with him to work for his lord. Therefore the tillage of his own tenement would not necessarily be neglected while he was busy on the demesne. Perhaps the tenant was not even bound to go in person to the lord's work but was held to have acquitted himself of his service if he sent an able-bodied person in his stead.[27] A condition which would stop some kinds of work, particularly plowing and sowing, was bad weather: rain or frost. Then the villein was let off his plowing or put at some other kind of work. And if a villein were sick he was released from his regular week-work, usually for thirty days, if he were sick so long. Nevertheless the custumals state that he was still bound to do his plowings, his carrying services, and the harvest benes.[28] He may in fact have been allowed to send other members of his household to take his place. In the same way, if a man died, his wife was commonly quit for thirty days of the services due from the holding, except again for plowing and harvest benes.[29]

No heavy week-work was done for the lord during holiday seasons. What happened on these holidays will be described under the subject of the husbandman's year. Enough to say here is that there were three of some length. Almost everywhere villeins did not labor during the twelve days of Christmas, nor during Easter and Whitsun weeks. Furthermore, they did no work on certain of the other great feast days of the Church. What these feasts were to be for a given manor was sometimes specified in the custumal; sometimes the question was left apparently indeterminate, as at Hartest, Suffolk, where, according to the Ely custumal of 1222, villeins were to be quit of work on "every day so solemn that the plows ought not plow." [30] When one of these feast days fell on a day of the week on which the villeins would otherwise have worked for the lord, this day, according to some arrangements, was a dead loss to the lord. According to others, one feast day was allocated to the villeins and the next to the lord. That is, on every other feast day that fell on a work day the villeins worked for the lord, or worked on some other day of the week to make up for it. In their exaction of services, the lords of manors do not seem to have disregarded the sentiments of their tenants.

Much has been said here about the services due from the villeins being fixed in the custom of the manor. But anyone who knows how people often behave who have power over others and economic interests opposed to theirs will have every right to suspect that some lords of manors tried to increase their tenants' rents and services. How some of these increases may have been made has already been suggested: the lord may have requested certain works as, literally, lovebenes, which in the course of time became customary and exactable. But lovebenes were special services; it is hard to believe that this process was followed when the number of days' work was increased which a villein had to do for his lord in every week of the year. Maitland found by comparing the two custumals of the Bishop of Ely, those of 1222 and 1277, that between those dates on four of the manors, Wilburton, Lyndon, Stretham, and Thriplow, an extra work-day every week had been put on between Michaelmas and Hocktide.[31] There is only the mute evidence of the custumals. How the increase was managed and what the villeins felt about it we do not know.

According to legal theory, villeins were at the economic mercy of their lords. When their services were increased, they had no remedy. The only exceptions were the villein sokemen, who held land in manors which had been part of the ancient demesne of the crown. If their lords exacted unaccustomed services, these villein sokemen could secure the royal writ *monstraverunt*, which was directed to the lord and required him to cease his exactions. If he did not do so, the case could be removed to a royal court. Two of the most interesting of the actions under the writ *monstraverunt* were those brought in 1275 by men of King's Ripton, Hunts., one of the Ramsey manors with which we have become so familiar, against their lord, the abbot. The men claimed that the abbot had forced them to do work services and pay merchet, when in the time of Henry II, a century earlier, they had only paid rents for their tenements. But those cases have been reported elsewhere.[32] The men lost at every point.

Again, when the royal inquests were made which now are called the Hundred Rolls, men who claimed to be villein sokemen asserted that their services had been increased. For instance, the men of Westoning, Beds., — Westoning certainly was ancient demesne and the men claimed to be villein sokemen — complained that the lords of the manor had increased their services. Formerly they had done three harvest works; now they were forced to do ten, plus one waterbedripe. Formerly they had conjointly given the lord two marks a year as tallage; now the lord absolved one or two people from the payment but continued to exact the whole sum from the rest.[33] There is plenty of evidence that some lords of manors pressed for an increase of services. But from the middle of the thirteenth century on, the trend, if not toward a decrease of the total burdens of villeins, was at least in the direction of commuting work services into money rents.

The most dramatic of recorded bondmen's revolts against what they felt to be the oppression of their lords, before the great revolt of 1381, was that of the year 1336 of the bondmen of Darnhall and Over, Cheshire, against their lord, the Abbot of Vale Royal. But that story too has been told elsewhere.[34] A less dramatic case of quarrelling between a lord and his men, but one even more interesting because it was chronic, was that of the manor of Halesowen.[35] It also involved a claim made by the tenants that they were privileged villeins of the ancient demesne. The dispute went on for more than a hundred years, and during all that time the differences between the lord and his tenants centered around their belief that he had exacted services other than those they were accustomed to perform. The case has a further interest because the court rolls of the manor of Hales are among the most complete and detailed of all surviving sets of manorial court rolls. They have been printed and they have often been cited here.

Halesowen was a large manor, including several member hamlets, on the border of Worcestershire and Shropshire. It took its name from David ap Owen, Prince of Wales, who married a sister of Henry II. He became lord of Hales in 1177. After his death in 1204, the manor reverted to King John, who regranted it in 1214 to Peter des Roches, Bishop of Winchester, in order that he might found a religious house there. An abbey of the White Canons of the Premonstratensian Order was in fact established,[36] and Henry III confirmed the manor to its abbot and convent. The first sign of trouble between the abbey and its tenants came in 1243. For the 27th of April of that year, in a plea roll of the court of King's Bench sitting at Westminster, it is recorded that the men of Hales acknowledged that they paid their lord merchet when their daughters married, whether they married in or out of the manor, that they had to have their corn ground at the lord's mill, that if they were amerced in the manor court, the amount of the fine ought to be according to the transgression, that they paid relief for entry into their tenements, that they were tallaged according to the custom of the manor whenever the king tallaged his manors, that every yardling ought

to do six plowings and six harrowings in Lent, and lesser holders
in proportion, and that they ought to perform all other customary
services. This list of services was not unusual or heavy, as
services went. We are told nothing about rents. On his part, the
abbot granted for himself and his successors that they would
not exact any other services, that the tenants did not have to buy
at the market of Hales, that if the abbot obstructed access to
the tenants' common of pasture, the default should be rectified
by the view of lawful men. Lastly the abbot remitted to the
men 12½ marks pledged to him as tallage.[37] This settlement
must have been made as the termination of some action at law,
but we are told neither how the action came before a royal
court nor what the issues were. From the terms of the settlement
we can infer what some of them must have been. There must
have been trouble between the abbot and his men about the
market and the common of pasture, but since the settlement
took the form of a statement of customs, the dispute must have
arisen chiefly over the abbot's exaction of services.

Nothing more is heard of the abbot and his men for some years.
Then in 1252 the abbot secured a royal writ close, ordering the
sheriff of Shropshire, since the king was tallaging his demesnes,
to see that the abbot had reasonable tallage of his tenants of
Hales, which once (so the writ ran) had been demesne of the
king's.[38] According to the settlement of 1243, the abbot had a
right to this tallage, but had the tenants acquiesced in the settlement with a good grace? Did the abbot secure the writ because
without the help of the sheriff he was unable to wring the tallage
from his tenants? Again we are not told. The fact that the
manor was said to have been royal demesne gives some clue
to the means by which the dispute of 1243 was brought before
the King's Bench. The men of Hales must have argued, as the
men of so many other manors had argued, that although they
were privileged villeins of the ancient demesne of the crown,
whose customs might not be changed at the will of the lord, the
abbot had nevertheless forced them to perform services other
than those which were customary. We must notice also, in view
of what was to happen later, that now in 1252 the abbot as well
as the villeins was claiming, or at least making use of a writ
which claimed, that Hales had once been royal demesne.

There is no further news of trouble until 1255. In that year a royal inquest found:

that the Abbot of Hales and his bailiffs often kept the beasts of the men of the manor of Hales against gage and pledge, and afterward those men sought writs of the lord King and presented the writs of the lord King in the county court, and they could not have right in the county court because of their [the abbot and convent's] charter.[39]

The charter which was cited in court was without question that by which King John granted the manor of Hales to Peter des Roches for the foundation of a religious house. That charter freed the abbot and convent from suit to the courts of hundred and of shire.[40] The abbot and his bailiffs may have taken the beasts in order to distrain the men to perform certain services, or they may have taken them in connection with some new dispute about the common of pasture. Unless the "men of the manor of Hales" were merely the freemen of Hales, the fact that once more they seem to have had no trouble in securing royal writs must mean that the royal courts were still prepared to countenance a claim that they were privileged villeins of the ancient demesne.

Not until twenty years later, at the beginning of the reign of the new king, Edward I, did the quarrel come to a head. Edward was energetic in his efforts to restore to the crown rights alienated without warrant, and in consequence, in November of 1275, in the fourth year of his reign, a royal inquest sat at Shrewsbury to report concerning the manor of Halesowen. According to the record, the jury found that:

the abbot and convent of the house of Hales Oweyn made increase in the customs and services on the manor of Hales Oweyn greater than they [their men] were accustomed to do in the time of King Henry, son of King John, but that the aforesaid abbot and convent made a pact with the aforesaid men of Hales Oweyn, that they would keep them in the customs and services in which they were in the time of said King Henry and would withdraw from them the increased customs, and they were thus withdrawn after the last advent of the king's justices in Eyre through a certain pact made between them before the advent of the justices.[41]

This statement seems to imply that the abbot and convent had made the pact because they feared what might happen if their men brought their grievances before the justices. The abbot had not kept the settlement of 1243, in which he had promised not to increase the services of his tenants, and his tenants evidently believed that he was not to be trusted to keep this new "pact."

In any event, in the next year of the reign, a writ was issued directed to the sheriff of Shropshire, "on the part of the tenants of the Abbot of Hales Oweyn," requiring the sheriff to make inquisition by a jury, composed partly of Shropshire and partly of Staffordshire men, concerning the wrongs complained of by the tenants. The inquest was held in June, 1276, and drew up a schedule of the customs of the tenants which was substantially the same as that of the settlement of 1243, except that it ended in the following way: "And they say that the said King John granted the manor subject to the same services by which the lands were held of him." [42] This must simply have been the belief of the jury, because in point of fact there is no such clause in the foundation charter.

Throughout these years, the tactics of the tenants had evidently been to insist that the manor of Halesowen was ancient demesne of the crown, and that they were accordingly privileged villeins, who might not be required to do more than their ancient services. They had tried to have these ancient services attested by solemn inquests. The royal courts must have accepted their claim at least at its face value, or royal writs would never have been issued to the tenants with such regularity. So far they had been wholly successful, but the abbot soon began the counter-attack and aimed it at the argument which the tenants had made the foundation of their claims.

Two years later, in 1278, probably when Parliament met at Easter, the abbot and convent went to the length of presenting a petition to the king and his council. The petition asserted that the men of Hales had recently impleaded the abbot and convent in the king's court concerning the customs and services which they were accustomed to do when the manor was in the hands of the kings of England, saying that they were of the ancient demesne of the crown. Domesday Book, however, showed that they were not. (At law, ancient demesne was not, of course, land which had been at any time in the hands of the kings of England. The test was whether it had been in the hands of King Edward the Confessor before the Conquest, and this was held to be determined by Domesday Book.) The petition went on to say that the men of the manor disseised the abbot and convent of services, without a judgment of the king's court, in accordance with a writ of the king, and that any distraints made by the abbot and convent, the case pending, were set free by the sheriff of Shropshire. Accordingly the abbot and convent begged for a remedy and seisin of the services until the case was heard. The king's answer to the petition was that the canons ought to defend themselves against their men by the law of the land or seek a writ for the recovery of services and customs — nothing further.[43]

The king, his justices, and the sheriff of Shropshire cannot be charged with having shown partiality to the Abbot of Hales, but when the quarrel finally came before the king's court for settlement, it was decided in favor of the abbot. The tenants certainly could not plead that they were freemen, because by one of the commonest tests, that of paying merchet, they were villeins. The question was whether they were privileged villeins of the ancient demesne or villeins pure and simple. If they were the former, the royal courts would protect them against any increase in their customary services. If they were the latter, they held their tenements at the will of the lord and he might change their services as he would. Land was held to be ancient demesne if Domesday Book showed it to have been before the Conquest in the hands of King Edward the Confessor, and Domesday showed that Halesowen was not ancient demesne. Whatever the arguments used, the suit brought by the tenants must have collapsed soon after the abbot and convent presented their petition. In the Plea Roll of the Easter term of the King's Bench in the same year, it is recorded that the abbot was allowed to go *sine die* because his tenants had not prosecuted their writ against him which they had secured on the claim that he was exacting services other than those which they ought to do.[44]

The case seems to have had one embarrassing sequel for the the abbot. Perhaps as a result of the lawsuit of the year before, the king in the Michaelmas term of 1279 required the Abbot of Halesowen to show by what warrant he held the manor. The abbot produced the charter by which King John had granted it to the Bishop of Winchester and the confirmation by King Henry III. His title was good.[45]

The battleground was now shifted from Westminster back to Worcestershire. The villeins must have been much embittered if they were ready to carry their quarrel to the king's court. Their defeat there in 1278 cannot have made them any less so. Worsted at law, they resorted to direct action. At least when we find that in December 1278 the Bishop of Worcester sent a mandate to the Deans of Warwick, Pershore, and Wick to excommunicate those who laid violent hands on the Abbot of Hales and his brethren at Beoley, it is hard to believe that this fight had no connection with the great quarrel.[46]

In these years, the surviving court rolls of Halesowen begin to yield news about the struggle between the abbot and his men as it took place at the manor itself. There had been no cooling during 1279. At a hallmote held on November 20 of that year, jurors were named:

to tell the truth about all those, whether they are men or women, who withdrew themselves from the lord's land with their chattels, where they are and who they are and where their chattels are.[47]

Here is a good measure of the tenants' discontent. A medieval villager could make no more desperate move than to leave his land, his only means of livelihood, and run away. But running away was common at Hales in 1279, and in the next few years there were several instances of individual fugitives.[48]

Having won his legal victory over his tenants, the abbot wanted revenge. At the very next meeting of the court, December 11, 1279, the following entry was made on the roll:

Roger Ketel made fine with the abbot for a hundred silver shillings, to be paid in five years, because he impleaded the abbot unjustly in the court of the lord King and was in aid and council with his other neighbors impleading the abbot. . . . And the abbot ceased the indignation which he had conceived towards Roger and granted that he should hold the land he held in that condition which is stated in the writ of judgment, namely servile at the will of the lord.[49]

Thus we learn that a writ of judgment in favor of the abbot had been issued by the King's Bench stating that the tenants were of service condition, villeins, holding at the will of the lord. The fine was a heavy one, and must have been designed to punish Roger Ketel as a ringleader of the rebels.

But the efforts of the tenants did not end here. They took their case to court once more. Unhappily we know nothing about this second lawsuit, save for one short and violent entry of the year 1286 in the Plea Roll of the court of King's Bench. The entry is: "Another judgment for the Abbot of Halesowen against the tenants, that they are villeins forever." [50] Nothing could be more eloquent.

For forty years after the abbot's victories, there were few outward signs of trouble between the convent and its tenants. Abbots died and new ones were installed during the course of this long story, but too little is known of them to allow us to guess how their traits of character influenced the controversy with the tenants. In 1311, to be sure, the Premonstratensian visitors to the abbey found the abbot incontinent and generally unfit to rule, and the conditions in the abbey wretched.[51] From the beginning we must suppose that the administration of the abbey had been brutal and tactless, or there would have been no bitter and prolonged struggle with the tenants. But the revelations of 1311 seem to have had no effect on the relations between the convent and its men.

The next important date is 1327. At a court held at Hales at the Annunciation in that year, the first of the reign of Edward III, the abbot, for a consideration of 100 s. sterling, commuted into money rents all the labor services of his men. He also agreed that none of the customers was to be distrained to act as beadle and that all other ancient customs were to be maintained without impediment or reclamation. On their part, the customers recognized that they were bound to elect a greater and a lesser reeve, who had to pay for holding the office. The terms of this agreement were enrolled on an indenture, of which the customers kept one part. For a consideration of 23 s., services were commuted on the same day at Romsley, a member of the manor.[52]

Thus commutation came to Halesowen. The thirteenth century saw the culmination of the manorial economy, the organization according to which large demesnes were tilled by the labor services of villeins. At the end of that century, and more frequently in the centuries which followed, labor services were being commuted into rents. Already in 1381 one of the demands of the rebellious peasants was the total abolition of villeinage; by the death of Queen Elizabeth there was no such thing in England as a villein. We do not know all the causes of the movement of commutation.

Some economists will speak of the development of a money economy. The fact is that men had decided, as a result of experiences about which we know little, that tilling their demesnes with labor services was not as efficient as tilling them by other means. Indeed both elements of the manorial economy disappeared, the demesnes themselves as well as the labor services: with the movement of commutation went a movement on the part of some landholders to abandon tilling their demesnes even with hired labor. They put the whole of their lands out at rent. The monks may have been particularly partial to this change. In giving over much of the direct management of the economy of the country, which they had held under the manorial organization, they lost many of the qualities which in the thirteenth century had made them leaders in their communities. They became ripe for spoliation by Henry VIII's low-born plunderers, the ancestors of a new ruling class.

One might have thought that commutation would have eliminated the most aggravating source of dispute between the Abbot of Halesowen and his men, but it did not. In the reign of Richard II, which saw also the great Peasants' Revolt of 1381, the old quarrel was revived on exactly the same terms as those on which it had begun almost a hundred and fifty years before. In fact all services cannot have been permanently commuted in 1327, because in 1387, the tenth year of the reign, a commission of oyer and terminer was issued to justices of the king:

on information that divers bondmen and bond tenants of the Abbot of Halesowen at Romsley, Co. Salop, have refused their customs and services for their holdings and confederated by oath to resist the abbot and his ministers.[53]

The inquest summoned according to the commission was held at Bridgnorth, Shropshire, before two of the king's justices. The jury found on oath that the abbot had summoned his villeins to be on a certain day at Romsley to do fealty and such other services as by their tenure they were bound to do. John atte Lythe and his wife and Thomas Putteway, with others, had failed to appear. Such was the finding of the inquest. Thereupon a writ was directed to the sheriff ordering him to have the bodies of these persons at Hales on a certain day. At Hales the abbot appeared before the sheriff, who declared that Putteway had died in prison at Shrewsbury Castle and that the Lythes were not to be found. At the four next county courts they were summoned to appear and were outlawed when they failed to do so.[54]

Thus ends the story of a century and a half of bad feeling between a lord and his villeins. It illustrates admirably many of the events of any such dispute: the effort made by the abbot to increase his customs, the resistance put up by his villeins, based on a claim that they were privileged villeins of the ancient demesne, their resort to force and flight when legal action failed, the use made by the abbot of his hallmote, the royal courts, and royal officers in order to punish his tenants and force them to render their services. We are able to see clearly the different parts played in the struggle by the tenants, the abbot himself, the Bishop of Worcester, the king and his council, the justices, and the sheriff. All these points are illustrated admirably, because the quarrel was a long one. But such quarrels were exceedingly rare. If they had been general, the fabric of society would have dissolved in anarchy or revolution. Lords and villeins may have distrusted one another, but active struggles between them were uncommon, if only because the villeins were so little likely to win.

CHAPTER XIX

TRADESMEN, SERVANTS, AND OFFICERS

IN ANY MANOR, in any village, there were men who were set apart from their fellows because they followed a calling which was useful to the village and required special skill, because they served the lord of the manor in some special way, or because they held some office of government in the manor or the village. Among this number were men of low and high degree, but many of them had one trait in common, that they were servants both of the lord and of the community of villagers. Because they served two masters they must often have served uneasily.

The miller was commonly one of the most considerable men of the village. Thus at our model manor of Spelsbury, the miller, William of Colthurn, was a freeholder and paid a large rent. The lord of a manor unusally enjoyed the monopoly of the village mill; that is, his villeins were bound to take their corn to his mill to be ground. The revenue of the mill came from the multure, the share of the flour which the miller kept in payment for his services. If the mill belonged to the lord, the multure went to him. But the lord seldom kept the management of his mill in his own hands. He put it out at farm to a miller or a group of millers. The miller was likely to be the village capitalist. Though he was responsible for the payment of his farm and had to maintain the mill, which was the largest, indeed the only piece of machinery in the village, he also had the chance of gaining more by his labor than most of the other villagers. He was always suspected of gaining by foul means. By the use of false measures and by other frauds, he was suspected of taking a larger part of the flour than was allowed him according to the customary multure. Chaucer's *Reeve's Tale* reflects the traditional opinion about millers. There was reason for it, as suits brought against millers show. When millers took more than was their due, they were injuring villagers where they were most sensitive, in their store of food. No wonder that many men were willing to grind their flour in hand-mills, querns, even at the risk of being amerced at the hallmote for this breach of the lord's monopoly.

The village smith was a man of less substance than the miller. At Spelsbury he was a freeholder, but a freeholder who held only one yardland. In many places he was a villein and held far less land than that. The account of the duties of the smith at Aldingbourne, Sussex, entered in the custumal of the Bishop of Chichester, is full and revealing and as nearly typical as any single entry can be. It runs as follows:

The smith's widow holds 4 acres and renders 100 horseshoes a year to the lord's chamber (*thalamum*), whereof 50 with 8 holes and 50 with 6, without nails, and she shall have therefor 25 d. She shall shoe the steward's hackney (*palfredum*) at all his comings if needed and have 1 d. for the four shoes. She shall find the iron and shoe the sergeant's horse and the carter's horse all the year at 1 d. for the four shoes. She shall make of the lord's iron and mend and sharpen the irons of two plows all the year and shall charge nothing; she shall mend the irons of (the other) two plows when needed and the lord shall pay her. She shall have her coals of the lord's wood at the three terms. She shall have her dinner while the lord stays here. The lord shall plow all her land till sowing is done. If she dies the lord shall have the best aver at her house.[1]

One difficulty must be faced at once. Blacksmithing is not one of the jobs which women can do as capably as men, but this entry speaks as if the smith's widow actually did the smith's work. What it means of course is that the duty of finding a smith fell upon a particular holding in the village. When the last smith died, another man who happened to know the trade was not arbitrarily chosen as the new smith. Instead the duty continued to fall where it had fallen in the past. Without doubt the smith's son was the man who usually succeeded: his father would have taught him the trade. Here at Aldingbourne, as elsewhere, the two chief jobs of a worker in iron were making the shares and coulters for the plows and making the horseshoes and shoeing horses. Frequently the blacksmith did not furnish the raw iron himself: it was supplied by his customers, and all he had to do was fashion it according to their orders. At least this arrangement was adopted when the blacksmith made the lord's plow-irons, and in this instance, as in many others, there is a presumption that the way work for the lord was managed, which we know, resembled the way work for common villagers was managed, which we do not know. The lord paid the blacksmith partly in money and partly in perquisites. The smith took his charcoal from the lord's wood; he had his dinner in the hall while the lord was at the manor (a common perquisite of manorial servants), and he had his land plowed in seed-time by the lord's plows. This last perquisite is the most interesting of all. The blacksmith was not wholly dependent on his smithy for his livelihood. He also held land and tilled it. But he was not likely to hold much land. At Aldingbourne he held only four acres and took rank as one of the cotters, as one of the men, that is, who were often unable to keep plow oxen of their own. It is significant that the smith had the use of the lord's plow team. Indeed we may find in this fact one more hint that in England, as in France, the villagers of the poorer sort supplied their wealthier neighbors with hand labor and in return had the use of the plow oxen of the latter. We are making the assumption that the villagers extended to their lord the kinds of exchanges to which they were used among themselves. But is this assumption justified? Was the blacksmith's work rewarded by the common villagers in the way in which it was rewarded by the lord? Did they pay him in money, or were there customary exchanges of wrought iron against food or farm work? We do not know, nor do we know whether smiths in England were believed to be workers in magic, as they were and are in other times and places.

These two, the miller and the smith, were the only men practicing particular mysteries who were given acknowledged special places in the village economy. There were men who bore the surname of Carpenter, but they were not given special perquisites and rewards by the lord of the manor for following their trade. Since carpentry in the Middle Ages was not elaborate — the only timbers in a villager's house were the posts and beams of its frame — it is likely that many men were their own carpenters.

Beside the tradesmen, another group set apart in the village life were the manorial servants, the *famuli*. Even when the lord's demesne was tilled almost wholly by the customary works of his villeins, there were a few such servants, living at the manor court: a dairymaid, a neatherd, a carter, farm laborers and house servants. Furthermore the custumals reveal that certain holdings were bound to furnish certain kinds of servants for the lord, when he chose to have them. People who held tenements of the lesser sort, whether half-yardlands or cotlands, often had to serve as the lord's plowmen to hold the lord's plows and tend his plow oxen, or as his shepherds to keep his sheep, or as his swineherds, and so forth. So long as they acted in these capacities, some or all of the other services due from their holdings were remitted, and they were allowed important perquisites besides.

The duties of the lord's plowman, or *akerman*, have been described earlier. Here the duties and perquisites of the lord's shepherd, as they were described in the very detailed custumal of Bleadon, Somerset, will stand as an example of those of the manorial servants in general. At Bleadon, Nicholas Monk held a ferdell of land, which ranked as a cotsetle. Among his services were the following:

He ought to keep the lord's sheep, if ordered to do so, and then be quit of all day-works. And he will carry or remove every day the lord's sheep-fold, and he will have the lord's fold on his own land from Christmas Eve until noon on the eve of Epiphany if the lord's sheep then lie in the fold. . . . And he will keep the ewes until they have thirty lambs; then the lord will find another shepherd to keep the ewes and the lambs which they have dropped; and the shepherd of the village will keep the other ewes until lambing; and after lambing he will give them to the lord's shepherd, and will help the lord's shepherd so that the lambs are given suck early and late. . . . And he will have at Christmas Eve a white loaf and a dish of meat, and on Christmas Day he will have a loaf for his dog.[2]

These were not all the shepherd's duties and perquisites at Bleadon, but they give us enough to consider. First there is the matter of the fold. England's mild winter climate, which made it an excellent country for sheep, gave Englishmen one of their best means of putting heart into lands which had been worn with cropping. Men folded sheep inside hurdles and then moved the folds from day to day, so that the land was systematically dunged with sheep-droppings. In some parts of England the sheep of villeins were bound to lie in the lord's fold on the lord's demesne, and in Norfolk the fold-courses were an important factor determining the character of husbandry and holdings. Here at Bleadon one of the main duties of the shepherd was moving the lord's fold from day to day over the lord's land. If the lord chose Nicholas Monk to keep his sheep, Nicholas was quit of the other works which as a villein he was bound to do for the lord, and besides this main reward, he was allowed as one of his special perquisites to have the fold on his own land from Christmas to the Epiphany. These were the twelve days of the great Christmas holiday, when every villager wanted to be making merry. Perhaps the lord felt that by giving his shepherd a personal interest in the sheep during this time, he could make sure that the shepherd would not neglect them. But it may be that the holiday season was chosen as the time of the shepherd's reward for the very reason that it was a time of good will, the suitable time for doing a favor. This one of the shepherd's customs was common to many manors. At Bleadon he also had his dinner from the lord at Christmas, and even his dog was remembered. When lambing came, the lord provided another shepherd to take care of the lambs and their mothers, and from this moment onwards Nicholas Monk is apparently called the shepherd of the village (*bercator ville*) to distinguish him from the shepherd provided by the lord. The men of many a village did in fact elect a common shepherd to keep the sheep of all the villagers, just as they elected a common neatherd to keep all the village cattle.[3] More often, perhaps, every family kept its own sheep.

The tradesmen formed one group of people who held special positions in the village, the manorial servants another, and the officers of local government a third. One important fact about these officers must be brought forward at once. The duties they performed were very diverse, but they had certain traits in common. In many cases, they were elected to office by their fellow villagers, and for their misdeeds the villagers as a body were responsible. But if the village was responsible for the actions of its officers, the officers were not responsible solely to the village. They were, as we shall see, officers of the lord as well as of the village, and even when they were elected by the villagers, the lord often exercised the right of accepting them or not, as he chose. He paid his officers just as he paid his smith or his plowman: he set them free in whole or in part from the services they would otherwise have done for him, and he gave them special perquisites besides.

Here we must take up again a theme which has been quiescent ever since the bylaw was described — the organization of a village as a community, a community in the sense in which the word was understood in the Middle Ages. The men of a champion village formed a community in that their husbandry was governed by a set of rules binding upon all the villagers. They formed a community in that these rules were set forth and emended by a deliberative assembly, the bylaw, in which every villager had a voice. And now we observe that they formed a community in this further respect that the rules of the champion husbandry were enforced and the other functions of government performed by officers elected by the body of the villagers. The fact that the lord shared many of these officers with the community can be explained on the assumption, which may or may not correspond to what actually happened, that the original lord of the manor took over for its management a set of officers who had previously been the executives of the village community. To do so would have been wholly natural. The lord would prefer to work through an existing organization rather than set up a new one of his own.

It is a mistake to suppose that the same set of officers was named in every village or that because two officers bore different titles their duties were necessarily different. On one manor a reapreeve might do the work which a hayward did on another; on one manor a sergeant might take the position a bailiff took on another. The surprising thing is that the duties of the different officers in different parts of England corresponded as closely as in fact they did. The list of the officers is long, and they were of many degrees. It is well to begin with the less important ones and move toward the more important. One of the lesser officers was the woodward. The election of the woodward in the hallmote is recorded as follows in a court roll of 1275 of Hallingbury, Essex:

Walter of Cowyk is made woodward by the election of all the tenants and is sworn to keep the lord's wood well and faithfully under pain of forfeiture of all his goods.[4]

The woodland appurtenant to a manor was likely to be a matter of dispute between the lord and his tenants. In the eyes of the law, it was viewed as the lord's private possession, but the village community had made use of it for unnumbered generations. In some places the tenants were conceded the rights of *husbote* and *heybote*, the rights of taking wood for house timber and for hedges. The woodward was the lord's servant, but he was also one of the villagers and was elected to office by his fellows. The conflict in the interests of the two parties fell heavily upon him, a fact which is well illustrated by an entry in a court roll of 1273 of Minchinhampton, Glos.:

William de la More is accused of this, that he felled to the ground one young oak in the defence of the lady. He admits that he did so and calls Henry of Burley, under-woodward, to warrant, and says that he was in such a business because the beam of his plow broke near the wood and that the tree was given him to repair this. And because he well knew that the woodward might not warrant such a gift, he remains in mercy.[5]

His amercement was one day's work of plowing. The phrase, "in the defence of the lady," must have meant within what the lady of Minchinhampton had announced as the boundaries of her private wood. Minchinhampton belonged, as its name implies, to the nuns of the Holy Trinity of Caen.

Harvest was the time when people were afraid of having that stolen from them which they valued most — their crops. No wonder, then, that certain villeins were bound "to watch in harvest and keep the lord's corn in the fields at night."[6] But the plain villager's corn had to be guarded as well as his lord's. In champion country many of his lands were far from his house and scattered all over the open fields of the village. The corn was ripe for cutting or was standing in sheaves which could easily be spirited away, and there were a large number of harvest laborers about, who had no ties in the neighborhood and were often with justice suspected of being evil-doers. On some manors it was the duty of the hayward to watch all the crops of the village during harvest, but on others the duty fell on the men who were especially elected for the purpose. *Custodes autumpni* were elected at the hallmotes of the Ramsey manors, whose duty was not only to keep the fields but also, by a natural extension of their work, to see that the harvest bylaws were observed.[7] At Halton, Bucks., also, there were "keepers of the harvest statutes." Such *custodes autumpni* seem to have been called in English reap-reeves (*ripereves*).[8] According to the finding of the hallmote of Littleport, Cambs., in 1316, the reap-reeve had taken from divers trespassers in harvest-time the gleanings they had wrongfully acquired. But he had at once appropriated the corn for himself. He had had it threshed and had gained a bushel of wheat, a bushel of barley, and two bushels of beans, worth 4. s. 4. d. That amount was ordered levied from him.[9]

The beadle was either chosen by the lord or elected by the homage, and was commonly one of the lesser men of the village. He was in the first instance an officer of the hallmote. As his name implies, his duty was to make all summonses ordered by the hallmote. He also levied distresses, made attachments, and collected fines. Sometimes he collected the rents of the tenants as well. His cannot have been a pleasant or popular undertaking. Furthermore he might be given other and quite different duties connected with the management of the lord's demesne farm. As usual, the Bishop of Chichester's custumal has a good description of the office of beadle. It is found in the entry for Preston, Sussex:

William Bedell holds three acres and a house and shall sow after the bishop's plows. After the plowing boonwork he with the other helpers shall have one seedlip (*semor*) full of wheat, barley and oats. He shall mind and water the bishop's oxen as long as they are at grass in the manor. He has to mind the bishop's corn and pasture, and shall answer for damages done. He shall carry out all distraints and summonses at Huue and at [the houses of] the men of Wyk. He and the reeve shall measure the lands before the plows and the crops in harvest. . . . He shall have his dinner in the bishop's manor house whenever the steward holds Halimot. . . .[10]

William was a poor man: he held only three acres of land. He was an officer of the hallmote: he carried out distraints and summonses. But he was also, under the reeve, one of those who managed the lord's husbandry. This curious mingling of the officer of the hallmote with the supervisor of farm work is typical of the rare accounts of the duties of a beadle. We must remember that the same kind of work was performed on different manors by men who bore different titles. Here at Preston, for instance, the beadle had to mind the lord's corn and pasture, work which would have been performed elsewhere by the hayward.

The two most important personages who were at once officers of the lord and officers of village government were the hayward and the reeve. One of the best single accounts of the duties of a hayward (in Latin, *messor*) is that of the thirteenth-century law book *Fleta*. Under the heading of *De Messore* the author of *Fleta* wrote:

The hayward ought to partake of the virtues of firmness, sharpness, health, and fidelity. Early and late he ought to go about and watch the court, woods, meadows, fields, and other things pertaining to the manor, impound cattle found in damages to the lord, and when quarrels arise and surety has been given for their prosecution, make summonses and attachments, fix a day for the parties at the next court, and openly present in court what he did in the matter. He is also bound to receive seed by measure and, after the lands have been sown therewith, to answer to the granger for the remainder. It is also his duty to oversee the plows and harrows in both seed-times, so that any defect (if there be any) may be made good properly. He ought also to collect the customary and boon plows in their places, and during the whole year the reeve ought to tally against him for seed received, sown, and returned, as well as for works, both customary and requested. For whatever arrears there be, let him answer to the reeve or the granger, and the reeve to the bailiff, who, if he have answered sufficiently, is not bound to account further.[11]

Before we turn to the duties of the hayward, there is one incidental point in this passage which is worth noting. A clear distinction is drawn between customary and boon works, and the latter are spoken of as if they were in fact "requested." *Fleta* is sometimes said to be an untrustworthy source, but in this instance everything it says about the duties of the hayward can be confirmed by other evidence. About some matters it has nothing to reveal. It tells us nothing about how the hayward was chosen or how he was paid for his work. In fact, like most of the other village officers, a hayward was sometimes chosen by the lord, but more often was elected by the homage, and he was allowed exemptions from many of the services he would otherwise have done, besides being given certain special perquisites.[12] Nevertheless, being a hayward can never have been an easy job, and many a man went into devious dealings in order to be quit of it.[13]

According to *Fleta*, the main duties of a hayward were three: to impound straying cattle, to serve under certain conditions as an officer of the hallmote, and to act as a subordinate member of the management of the lord's demesne farm. In his first duty, the hayward resembled the fence-viewer of a New England township of the old days: he was the warden of the hays, the hedges which in a champion village enclosed such of the open fields as were under crop. The hayward had to see that there were no gaps in the hays, through which the cattle of the village, which were ranging over the fallow field and other common pastures of the village, could break through into the meadow or corn. In some villages, indeed, the hayward may have taken over the duties of a village herdsman. *Fleta* and many of the other sources speak as if the hayward only protected the lord's crops; in fact he was chosen to protect the crops of all the villagers. His duty to his lord was only a part of his duty, though it was the most important part.

In the anxious time of harvest, the hayward's work as guardian of the crops of the village became especially hard. *Piers Plowman* says that among the offices which any villager might be called upon to fill, was the following, to

> . . . haue an horne and be haywarde · and liggen oute a nyghtes
> And kepe my corn in my croft · fro pykers and þeeues.[14]

Like so many others in *Piers Plowman*, this point is confirmed by the records. In the custumal of Brightwalton, Berks., a manor of Battle Abbey, the statement is made that the hayward was bound to watch by night around the lord's corn in harvest.[15] This duty was performed elsewhere by special reap-reeves. The hayward's horn, his badge of office, must have been used to give warning that cattle or other trespassers were in the corn. Little Boy Blue was a hayward.

If cattle, horses, sheep, or even geese did get into the corn or meadow, it was the hayward's business to impound them. Several entries in the court rolls reveal how he performed this part of his office. Was there in the thirteenth century a town pound into which the hayward drove straying cattle? In later centuries there were pounds in many towns of both old and New England, and often officials called punders. In some villages the hayward took a fee from every man whose beasts were found straying in the corn. This fee must have gone as damages to those whose corn had been injured. Thus one of the customs of Haddenham and Cuddington, Bucks., was the following:

If it happens that the lord's hayward impounds from the lord's corn any horse or animal from Martinmas to St. John's Day, he ought to have one loaf from the house of that man to whom the horse or animal belongs. Then from

St. John's Day until Michaelmas cornbote is given for all damages, such as he wishes to swear to according to custom.[16]

These dates are interesting. Martinmas (November 11) was the date on which the sowing of winter corn was expected to be over: a hayward's duties would begin then. St. John's Day (June 24) was recognized as the beginning of hay-harvest. By that time of year loaves would be scarce, so that the hayward would take the damages directly as *cornbote*, in the form of standing corn.

The hayward protected the corn not only against cattle but also against men. In comparing the way the king's messenger travelled with the way a common merchant did, *Piers Plowman* speaks as follows:

> Thauh þe messager make hus wey · a-mydde þe whete,
> Wole no wys man wroth be · ne hus wed take;
> Ys non haiwarde y-hote · hus wed for to take;
> *Necessitas non habet legem.*
> Ac if þe marchaunt make hus way · ouere menne corne,
> And þe haywarde happe · with hym for to mete,
> Oþer hus hatt oþer hus hode · oþere elles hus gloues
> The marchaunt mot for-go · oþere moneye of hus porse.[17]

We are not interested in the king's messenger, who could do what he liked, but in the merchant. If the merchant rode across standing corn, the hayward, if he caught him, would take from him a "wed," his hat, his hood, his gloves, or a sum of money, presumably as satisfaction for the damages.

From his primary duty as the warden of the corn and meadow, the hayward's duties as an officer of the hallmote followed naturally. He had to present in the hallmote all cases of straying animals, so that the injured villagers might have their damages and the lord his amercements for these trespasses. Furthermore, distresses levied in manorial courts were commonly levied in cattle, cattle being the only form of property which was both valuable and movable. Since the hayward impounded cattle as a part of his regular duty, he was often called upon to carry out these distraints. An example of what might happen when a hayward took a distress is recorded as follows on a court roll of 1298 of Newington, Oxon., a manor of Christchurch Priory:

Inasmuch as William Cloock, hayward of Berrick, took distresses on the fee of the prior, to wit, three of John Kybe's geese, and drove them into another fee so that a release could not be made, therefore it is ordered that he be distrained to come and answer concerning the foregoing, and the lord's tenants are forbidden to pay the same hayward his stipend until he clears himself.[18]

Both Newington and Berrick were of the fee of the prior. The most interesting point in this entry is its mention of the hayward's stipend. For the first part of his work, that of protecting the lord's corn, the hayward was released from some of the services he would otherwise have done; for the second part of his work, that of protecting the corn of the villagers, they paid him a stipend, just as they paid the common neatherd or the common shepherd. At least they paid him a stipend at Newington, and if at Newington, then probably elsewhere.

Fleta says that besides being an officer of the hallmote, the hayward, like the beadle, was one of the staff of the lord's demesne farm, but good independent evidence of this fact has been found only in the court rolls of Sevenhampton, Wilts. There, in the years 1290–1295, the haywards, first Stephen, then Robert, then Roger, all elected by the homage, were amerced in the hallmote on different occasions for not overseeing the plowmen, for allowing the lord's land to be badly plowed, for allowing his corn to be badly reaped, for failing to clean the grange of threshed corn, and for other slackness. Therefore we must assume that the hayward held some position of responsibility in the management of the manor. As a matter of fact, the reeve was associated with the hayward in some of these amercements, and the hayward seems to have been the reeve's lieutenant.[19]

We can best discover what a manorial officer ought to have done by looking at what he was punished for not doing. The most severe recorded indictment of a hayward was that of John Beucosin, hayward of Littleport, Cambs. At a court held there in 1325, an inquest concerning his behavior towards his lord and his neighbors was taken by twelve of the villagers. They said on their oath:

that the said John does not behave himself towards the lord as he ought, nor guard the fields and meadows of the lord as he ought. Likewise they say that the said John makes attachments upon the defendants in pleas at the instance of the plaintiffs without taking from the latter gages or pledges to prosecute their demands, to the deception and in fraud of the lord's court. . . . Likewise they say that the said John keeps to himself the forfeitures and amercements arising from the executions done by the lord's court, and makes use of and wastes and expends them to the damage and prejudice of the lord and his neighbors; and thus he did concerning a brazen dish taken by way of attachment from William at Whippe.[20]

And various lesser complaints were brought against him. The court ordered that the body of John be attached by the steward and that he be removed from the office of hayward. Afterwards the whole homage became manucaptors for John that he would satisfy the lord for his trespasses. They chose John Albin to be hayward in his place.

From one form or another of the Old English word *gerefa*, two words in later use were derived: grave and reeve. Grave was in use in the North Country,[21] reeve in most of the rest of England. Both were translated into Latin as *prepositus*, provost; both were names given to a personage who was only a little less important as one of the management of a manor than he was as the chief officer of a village. A study of the reeve might begin with one of the thirteenth-century manuals for the management of estates, with *Fleta* or the *Seneschaucie*.[22] Both of these books tell how a reeve ought to behave, but the telling is long, and in custumals and court rolls there are plenty of statements which are concerned with actual reeves rather than ideal ones. Although no single one of these statements brings out all the characteristics of a reeve, yet as a body the picture they leave is full and consistent. On these sources will be based the description of a reeve which is given here.

The reeve was commonly chosen at the end of September, about Michaelmas, when harvest was over and the new year of husbandry about to begin. His term was one year, and on some manors the understanding was that the men who were eligible for the office served in turn. This arrangement may have been designed to insure an even distribution of the burdens of serving as reeve, which were often so heavy that men paid fines in the hallmote in order to be released from being reeve or refused to serve when chosen, so that the lord was forced to distrain them to do so. On other manors, the reeve was returned to office year after year. When the lord had once secured an able man to be his reeve, he was naturally delighted to retain him as long as possible. But everything goes to show that the burdens of the position varied greatly from manor to manor. A reeve whose tasks were great and whose rewards were small would not be willing to serve for long.

The methods of choosing the reeve also differed greatly from manor to manor. Several custumals state that the lord had the right to choose as reeve any one of his villeins he wished. Elsewhere the villeins assembled in the hallmote elected a certain number of their fellows who were most suitable to serve as reeve, and then the lord through his bailiff chose the reeve from among this number. The villeins could thus express, within limits, their wishes in the matter. Another common custom was that the villeins elected the reeve, but that the lord had the right to accept or not, as he liked, the man they had chosen. Finally, on some manors, the villeins elected the reeve without any explicit inter-ference by the lord, though the lord must always have had means of making his will felt, and there is at least one instance, that of Staplegrove, Somerset, a manor of the Bishop of Winchester, in which the tenants bought from their lord the right to "elect their own reeve and have no reeve except by election." [23] Usually, in the thirteenth century, the reeve was in one manner or another elected by the tenants, just as they elected the hay-ward and other manorial officers, and they were responsible as a body for the shortcomings of the man they had chosen. A good statement of the case appears in a set of rules for the management of a manor which is included in the cartulary of Gloucester Abbey. It runs as follows:

Let the reeve be elected by the community of the hallmote, who ought to elect a man who is known and held to be suitable by merit in tilling his own land and managing his other goods discretely and circumspectly, for whose defects and omissions the whole hallmote ought to answer, save where urgent need or a probable cause may give the hallmote a reasonable excuse before the bailiff of the place.[24]

Not every tenant of a lord was required in custom to serve as reeve if chosen. In the first place, freeholders were exempted. Just as the reeve was commonly elected by the villeins, so he was elected from their number, that is, from the body of men who performed the customary services which it was the reeve's chief duty to supervise.[25] Indeed the duty of serving as reeve at the will of the lord came to be one of the recognized tests of villeinage.[26] Furthermore not every villein had to serve as reeve: the lesser villeins were exempted. In the tillage of the lord's demesne, a reeve was set in authority over his fellows. If he had not been a man of standing in the village, they would not have accepted his leadership. Whereas the lord's neatherds, shepherds, and beadles were drawn from the cotter class, his reeves and haywards usually came from among the more substantial villeins. Many a custumal states plainly that this arrangement was the accepted one. Thus at Spelsbury Thomas Reeve held a full yardland: his social position was like that of reeves everywhere.

A reeve's task was hard, and his rewards were correspondingly great, though they followed the pattern of the rewards given to other manorial officers. He was quit of all or a large part of the services he would have performed if he had not held the office of reeve. He was often paid a stipend as well, and given a number of perquisites. For instance, he was allowed to keep his horse in the lord's pasture or have the use of a special piece of land while he was in office. One of his commonest privileges was that of being at his lord's table in the manor hall from Lammas to Michaelmas, that is, during harvest, when the reeve had to give all his time to watching over the husbandry of the manor.

In spite of these rewards, the men of many villages were eager to avoid serving as reeve. The reeve's task was hard enough, in all conscience. Without doubt his duties varied somewhat from village to village, but entries in manorial custumals and treatises on the management of manors are in substantial agreement as to the common ones. In association with a bailiff or a sergeant, the reeve was responsible for the management of the lord's demesne farm and especially for getting out and overseeing the work services owed by the villeins. As in the case of the hayward, the reeve's shortcomings are the best evidence of his duties. In manorial court rolls we find that reeves were amerced for giving away the keys of the lord's barn, for not having the corn in the lord's barn properly cleaned, for allowing certain ridges to lie untilled. And villeins were fined for not obeying the reeve's orders.[27] The *Seneschaucie* asserts that the reeve:

ought to see that the keepers of all kinds of beasts do not go to fairs, or markets, or wrestling-matches, or taverns, whereby the beasts aforesaid may go astray without guard, or do harm to the lord or another, but they must ask leave and put keepers in their places that no harm may happen.[28]

But a reeve had duties besides those connected with husbandry. There were reeves who collected the lord's rents, who took over tenements which had escheated to the lord, who distrained men to do homage and fealty, who had the power of giving permission to villeins' daughters to marry outside the manor, who had to be present when a villein's will was made, who had custody of the rolls of the hallmote.[29] A reeve often had a principal part in the general administration of a manor.

In *Piers Plowman*, Sloth in the guise of a parish priest says:

I can holde loudedayes · and here a reues rekenynge.[30]

The best evidence of the position of the reeve is the fact that more often than not it was he and not the bailiff who accounted every year for the income and the outgo of a manor. The account was made about Michaelmas, when the farming year ended, and in it were reckoned on the one hand the rents, the profits of the court, the sales of corn and stock, and so forth, and on the other all expenditures incurred in the management and maintenance of the manor. At the same time an inventory of the live stock was taken and "an account of the produce of the manor and how it had been consumed," including the works owed by the villeins. The parish priest or some other clerk enrolled all this information on parchment: the reeve himself was commonly unlettered and in making his reckoning had to rely on a good memory for practical matters, the tallies he claimed when he was authorized to surrender his lord's goods, and without doubt a set of notches on the barn door, such as many a husbandman has used since.[31] On well managed estates, this *compotus* was afterwards audited, either by the lord's steward or by special auditors who went about from manor to manor for the purpose. Sometimes the reeve ended by owing his lord money and would have to account for his arrears at the beginning of the compotus of the next year. Reeves' and bailiffs' accounts of the thirteenth and later centuries survive in large numbers and are among the most important sources of English economic history.

The reeve was the manager of the lord's demesne farm; he was often in general charge of the administration of a manor;

furthermore, he was often a kind of village headman. As such he was perhaps more prominent in earlier centuries than he was in the thirteenth. Professor Stenton observes that in the twelfth century and in the Danelaw the reeve appears in the records sometimes as the headman of a village, sometimes as bailiff of an estate, never as a "serf overseer of serfs." [32] But even in the thirteenth century, and even when the reeve was a villein, he often acted as a village leader, who had to be consulted in everything. This fact will become plainer when we study the way the village was represented before the royal courts, but let us consider now the following verdict of one of the Suffolk juries whose findings have been preserved among the Hundred Rolls:

They say that Roger, reeve of Rattlesden, with the whole township of Rattlesden took away, from the coroner of the liberty of St. Edmund, Beatrice Cobbe and Beatrice, daughter of said Beatrice, and Elias Scallard, indicted for and guilty of the death of William Cobbe, husband of said Beatrice, and thus prevent the coroner from doing his duty.[33]

It would be delightful to know the events leading up to the situation revealed in a bald entry such as this, but we do not know them, and a historian has no right to imagine them. The important fact is that the reeve was the leader of his township even in the defiance of the law.

The account of the duties of the reeve of a village may well be summarized, as was the account of the duties of a hayward, by speaking of the misdeeds with which this officer might be charged. For this purpose, there is an amusing and illuminating case of slander recorded on the roll of a court held in 1278 at Elton, Hunts., one of the Ramsey manors:

Michael Reeve complains of Richer, Jocelin's son, Richard Reeve and his (Richard's) wife, for the reason that when he was in the churchyard of Elton on Sunday before the feast of All Saints in this year, there came the aforesaid Richer, Richard, and the wife of said Richard and insulted said Michael before the whole parish with foul words charging that the same Michael gathered his own hay with the works of the lord Abbot, and that by benes done by the customers of the abbot he reaped his corn in harvest, and that he plowed his land in Eversholmfield with the boon plows of the township, and that he released customers from their works and carrying-services on condition that these customers would grant and lease their lands to the same reeve at a cheap rate, and that he should have taken gifts from rich men that they might not be rent-payers and should have put poor men at rent.[34]

The *debuit* of the last clauses has been translated ambiguously as *should* because its own meaning is ambiguous. Was it wrong of the reeve that he should have taken, that is, did take gifts from rich men that they might not be rent-payers? Or should the reeve, that is, ought the reeve have taken gifts from rich men for this purpose but did not do so? It is hard to believe that the former was not the intention of the clerk, but he failed to make himself clear. The court found that the reeve was guilty of no article of the accusation, and the defendants paid him damages. But for our purposes this fact makes no difference. If the charges were not true of this particular reeve, they must have been true of others. Otherwise the slanderers would not have thought of making them. Plainly the manorial court furnished the lord with an excellent check upon the actions of the reeve. Even his misdeeds confirm what has been said about his duties. That he was the boss of the customary works of the villeins is shown by the fact that he might be accused of using them to till his own land. That he was in charge of the general management of a manor is shown by the fact that he might be accused of taking bribes for allowing men to render works instead of rent. Elton seems to have been one of those manors where villeins were bound either to do works or to pay rent according to the convenience of the lord. Why the men were, if our interpretation is correct, unwilling to pay rents, be made *censuarii*, we are not told. Perhaps, like husbandmen of a later century, they had plenty of spare labor but little cash. But this entry is not interesting solely for what it has to reveal about a reeve. It also describes what must have been a characteristic scene of the Middle Ages. All the people of a parish are gathered in the churchyard on Sunday, presumably after the celebration of the mass. They are gossiping before going home, and some of their number are taking the opportunity of slandering a neighbor as an unfaithful officer and a receiver of bribes.

Students of society will compare the reeve with the man who holds a corresponding position today — the first-line supervisor of workmen in a factory.[35] If modern industrial management cannot conceive of a supervisor who is elected, like the reeve, by the very men he supervises, the reason must lie in a difference between the conditions under which a reeve worked and those under which a supervisor works. This difference has two aspects: the nature of the work to be done, and the nature of the groups of men who do it. In amount and kind, the work done by villeins for their lord was customary. It was customary in the sense that all work in husbandry was customary in the Middle Ages: men did not seek to improve upon the methods their fathers used. It was customary also in the sense that many villeins, from a time to which the memory of man ran not to the contrary, had done certain services for their lord and expected to continue to do the same ones. Often the villeins themselves were the men who had to say what the services were, and their findings, made under oath, were enregistered in custumals. Even if the lord had the legal right, as he did, to exact what works he pleased, there was in fact a strong tendency for the works to remain what they had been in the past. From the customary nature of the services and the permanence of the bond linking lord to man, certain methods of enforcing the performance of work followed. The rules of rendering the services were, so to speak, established ordinances. Their violation was punished as the violation of any other ordinance would be punished — by a fine levied in the hallmote. In short, the standards of work were customary, and the villeins themselves participated to some extent in setting the standards.

If you told one of the management of a modern factory that his methods were customary, he would be likely to take your remark as a reproach. Change is assumed. Management is preoccupied with changing the methods of production so as to make them more efficient. So far as the relations between the management and the workmen are concerned, change in itself is not as important as the manner in which change is effected, and management has paid too little attention to this question. When an efficiency expert has reached the conclusion that an operation could be more efficiently performed if performed in a new way, management through the grades of its hierarchy is apt to order the workmen to change their methods forthwith. Change is forever being imposed on the workers from above by a power mysterious to them. Often the intentions of the mysterious power are in fact benevolent. Often the object of the management is to make work easier or to offer more inducements to work, but for one reason or another, the workmen are irritated, and say that the object is to make them do more work for less money.

In the nature of the work he supervised the reeve differed from the modern supervisor; he differed also in the nature of the group of men under his charge. These men were members of an organized and recognized community. They formed a community not only because they obeyed in common the rules of the champion husbandry, but also because they were together as fellow villagers in all the other labors and activities of life. The reeve was himself a member of this community; he was elected to office by the community; the community was responsible for his shortcomings. He was first only among peers and only, in many cases, for a limited term.

The management of a modern factory takes cognizance of the fact that its workmen fall into groups, but does so in only a few respects. Men form groups in that they are engaged in the same operation, in the same room, under the same supervisor. Sometimes men are divided into groups for payment according to some scheme of group piece-work. These are the only groups management recognizes, but in point of fact in all factories groups of men have formed and are forming all the time which have more important characteristics than those recognized by the management, characteristics which are comparable with those of communities of villagers. Their members behave as a group, not only in the immediate business of work, but in conversation and recreation, in the appearance of rules of conduct binding on all the members of the group, in the punishment of members who will not conform to the rules, and in the presentation by the group of a united front towards outsiders, including both other groups and management.

If the management finds that its men fall into groups in these respects, it is usually suspicious, and probably will not explicitly recognize the groups, though it may in fact take them into consideration. A characteristic situation is the following. The management decrees some change in the method of doing work or of payment. Management may be sincerely trying to improve conditions of work, but a group of workmen who are ordered to carry out the change may conceive it to be a threat to the existence of the group or the welfare of its members. The group, as far as it can, will try to make sure that none of its members put the change into effect. Even if the change is such that thereafter the increased output of any workman will yield increased pay not only for himself but for all the other members of his group, the group will often act so as to prevent any one of its members from taking advantage of the change, will threaten him with trouble if he raises his output above a certain level, although it is to the direct economic advantage of the group that he do so.

Consider now the position of a first-line supervisor. The supervisor is always in one sense a member of the group working under his charge and often is felt to be a member. He is with the group all day. Yet he is appointed by management; his duty is to see that the work is done as management wants it done and that the workmen carry out all changes in their methods of work decided on by management. If he does not do so to his full ability, he is disloyal to management, but many of the plans made by management are irritating to the members of his group. If he insists on carrying them out, he may lose any satisfactory personal relations with his men which he may have built up. Furthermore the men are in a position to make his life actively unpleasant.

Plainly the conditions under which a reeve worked differed at many points from those under which a supervisor works in a modern factory. The reeve had to call out and supervise services which in amount and kind were fixed in ancient custom. The supervisor is in charge of work the methods 'of which are not only being changed continually in the interests of efficiency but also being changed by fiat from above. The men whose work the reeve supervised were members of a recognized community, men who worked together not only in performing the lord's services but also in many of the other activities of the village. The men under the supervisor's authority form a group in something the same way the villagers formed a group, but the group is not recognized by the factory management. If then the reeve was a member of his community and elected to office by his fellows, whereas the supervisor is with his workmen but not of them, and is appointed by management, there is no reason for surprise. The other differences in the positions of the two men are enough to explain this final one.

Of the two other important officers of a manor, the bailiff and the steward, little need be said here. Being appointed by the lord, they were wholly his servants and in no sense the elected officers of a village. Any treatise on the management of estates in the Middle Ages must speak of them at length, but they are not of the first interest to a student of the village social order. Up to this point, the reeve has been described as if he were the man who was in active charge of the management of a manor. On some manors he was that, but more commonly, perhaps, he was subordinate to a resident bailiff. In this case the bailiff would probably take general charge of the manor, and the reeve's duty would be confined to the husbandry of the demesne, especially in overseeing the work-services of the villeins. The bailiff and the reeve may have resembled the plenipotentiaries of two nations: the bailiff represented the lord's interests; the reeve, those of the men.

When a lord had many manors, the man who was put in charge of the administration of all or a group of them, over both the bailiffs and the reeves, was the lord's steward or seneschal, often a man of birth and position. His office forced the steward to ride hard. For one thing, he went from manor to manor holding the hallmotes and presiding in them. *Piers Plowman* bears witness to this fact:

> Somme aren as seneschals · and seruen oþere lordes,
> And ben in stede of stywardes · and sitten & demen.[36]

For another thing, he had to go with the auditors from manor to manor, especially after the end of the farming year at Michaelmas, to hear and audit the accounts of the reeves and bailiffs.[37] The instructions which Thomas de Cantilupe, Bishop of Hereford (1275–1282), gave to his steward spoke of both these duties:

Let the view of the accounts of the reeves be made from one quarter of the year to another, by the steward or at least by the bailiff of the place with the steward's clerk.

Then, addressing the steward in person, he went on:

We order that you be not so solicitous or assiduous about holding courts and hearing pleas that you fail to have an open heart and a watchful spirit for the tillage, the issues of the granges, and the other profits of the manors.[38]

We know more about the great estates of England in the Middle Ages than we do about the small ones, because only the great estates had resources available for the making of elaborate records and only on the great estates were such records necessary for administration. And it is likely that only the great estates had a full complement of manorial officers: a steward, with general supervision over all the manors; bailiffs, each in charge of the administration of a particular manor; reeves, each in charge of the husbandry of a particular demesne; and other lesser officers: haywards, beadles, and the like. But we must not be too sure that even on the smaller estates the administrative hierarchy did not have a number of members. Experience shows that when men are working together supervision of some sort is necessary and that the number of men whose work can be overseen effectively by any one supervisor is small.

Here, to close the account of the village officers, it is proper to quote a great passage in *Piers Plowman*. It is the following:

> Romynge in remembraunce · thus reson me aratede.
> "Canstow seruen," he seide · "oþer syngen in a churche,
> Oþer coke for my cokers · oþer to þe cart picche,
> Mówe oþer mowen · oþer make bond to sheues,
> Repe oþer be a repereyue · and a-ryse erliche,
> Oþer haúe an horne and be haywarde · and liggen oute a nyghtes,
> And kepe my corn in my croft · fro pykers and þeeues?
> Oþer shappe shon oþer cloþes · oþer shep oþer kyn kepe,
> Héggen oþer harwen · oþer swyn oþer gees dryue,
> Oþer eny oþer kyns craft · þat to the comune nedeþ,
> Hém þat bedreden be · by-lyue to fynde?" [39]

William Langland, if it was he who wrote *Piers Plowman*, here lumps together, as work which was needful for the village, for the *commune*, work of the most different kinds, from singing in church to reaping and making bonds for sheaves, from serving as hayward or reap-reeve to keeping sheep and kine and making shoes or cloth. He speaks of these works as done not for private profit but for the common good and for the support of the poor and old. Langland was a sentimentalist. He wrote of Piers Plowman as a left-wing novelist writes of the worker, and for the same reason. His sympathies were with the common man at a time when the conflict between the classes of society was bitter. At such a time the members of the same class call for solidarity among themselves, as Langland called in this passage for solidarity among the husbandmen. But some of his inspiration may have come from sources more ancient than sympathy for the common man — from attitudes of English villagers who felt that they were bound to help their neighbors and to do what they could, each man in his office, to further the common good of their village.

CHAPTER XX

THE HALLMOTE

THE CHIEF SOURCES of what has been said in these pages have been the rolls of manorial courts. Each citation which has been made from them has something to tell about the organization of the courts and the procedure followed in them, but this something has so far been treated as incidental information. In studying the record of a plea of land, we have been interested in such things as the customs of inheritance which it disclosed and not in the manner in which the plea came before the hallmote and was decided there. Yet the hallmote was one of the characteristic institutions of a manor. In the hallmote the lord furnished justice for his tenants, and he himself was, in a measure, subject to the decisions of his court. No investigation of the relations between villagers or between villagers and their lord can be complete without some account of the way justice was done in the hallmote. The great historian Maitland has been first in this field,[1] and a man who is not trained in the law can do little more than restate Maitland's findings in some straightforward fashion.

Any freeman had the right to hold a court for his tenants and take the profits of the court. That is, the right was not denied in legal theory. In practice it was exercised much less widely than theory allowed. Between any landholder and the king there might be a long chain of mesne lords, and if all these lords had held courts for all their tenants, great and small, a complicated hierarchy of seigniorial courts would have existed, inconvenient for litigants, for the suitors of the courts, and even for the lords who held them. Accordingly there were few private courts above the manorial courts. Sometimes a great landholder, an abbot, a bishop, an earl, would hold a special court for his free tenants, a court of his honor. And on a manor which included several villages within its bounds, arrangements were sometimes made for holding courts for the subordinate villages as well as a court for the manor as a whole. This practice was adopted at the manors of Wakefield and Halesowen, from which good sets of court rolls survive.[2] But manors as large as these were rare, and commonly only one court was held for each manor. This was the court called the hallmote (*halimote*, etc.). Though the derivation of the word is uncertain, its first element is probably the word *hall*. The lord's hall (*aula*) would be a common feature of a manor. The hallmote was, we must suppose, the moot that met at the hall, but manorial courts met at many other places, in the parish church or even in the open air. In theory, hallmotes were held every three weeks, or to use the medieval expression, from three weeks to three weeks. In practice they met much less regularly. A meeting of the hallmote was called a law-day.

The profits of the hallmote went to the lord and were entered in the accounts of his bailiff or reeve. Hallmotes were profitable because offenders were regularly punished by fines. Sometimes men and women were put in the stocks (*in compedibus*) for their misdeeds, but not often. The offences within the competence of manorial courts were not important enough to be punished by imprisonment, and in any case public officials in the Middle Ages were reluctant to imprison, because prisons were expensive to keep and troublesome to guard. When a court roll states that so-and-so was "in mercy" for such and such an amount, it means simply that he was fined that amount, that is, "amerced." Amercements were sometimes levied in days of work instead of coin. Besides amercements for offences against the lord or the community, there were amercements connected with the conduct of the court itself. Men were amerced for failure to prosecute a plea, for false complaint, for improper pleading, and so forth. Even when there was no particular business to come before it — and some court rolls reveal a remarkable lack of business — a hallmote could make money. The tenants as a body, or at least the villein tenants, were bound to attend the court. If any one of these suitors of the court failed to attend or send a suitable excuse, he was amerced. We may suspect that, simply because they were profitable, courts were held on some manors more often than there was any need to hold them.

Besides the amercements, the hallmote brought money into the lord's purse in two other ways. A man could offer money to the lord, through his representative presiding in the court, for the privilege of having an inquest made by the court. This trait of medieval justice was universal: even the king sold his writs. And when men inherited land they came into the hallmote to pay their reliefs and heriots. Hallmotes were a source of profit to the lord, but the fact that they were profitable to him did not make them useless to his tenants.

There were two kinds of meeting of a manorial court: the ordinary customary courts, the hallmotes, which were held every three weeks, and the courts of the View of Frankpledge, which were held twice a year. There will be something to say about the View in another place. The person who called the hallmote, presided in it, and went from one of his lord's manors to another holding hallmotes was the steward. Sometimes he sent a substitute in his place. *Fleta* says that it was the office of a steward:

to hold the courts of manors, and even if he does this often by a substitute, nevertheless at the View of Frankpledge, or, if the lord does not enjoy that liberty, then at least two or three times a year, if he cannot be at leisure for this purpose more often, he ought to hold the court in person.[3]

Though the steward presided in the hallmote, we shall see that he was in no sense a judge, except perhaps in the case of offences against the lord. He gave effect to the judgment of the court; the men who reached that judgment were the jury of the court or the body of its suitors.

The body of the court was formed by its suitors, those who owed suit to the court. The lesser courts of medieval England, those of the shire, the hundred, and the manor, were not attended simply by the men who had business before the court. They were attended by all persons who by reason of their tenure, their status, or their office owed suit there. The suitors of a hallmote were, first of all, the tenants in villeinage. On some manors many of the freeholders were bound to attend or, at least, were bound to attend twice a year at the courts of the View of Frankpledge. Thus the miller, William of Colthurn, was bound to attend the court of Spelsbury twice a year. The rule of law was that a freeholder did not owe suit to a hallmote unless his ancestors had done suit from of old or unless such suit was expressly stipulated in the charter by which he held his land.[4] All suitors who did not attend and did not send another man with an excuse, an *essoin*, were amerced, especially when they were parties to suits which were coming before the court. The usual manorial court roll begins with a list of the jurors; a list of the essoins comes next.

Out of the suitors, out of the persons who formed the *curia*, a number of men, usually twelve, were chosen to be jurors (*iurati*). In some villages the jurors were drawn from the bondmen alone. In 1278 at Elton, Hunts., one of the Ramsey manors, certain men refused to serve on the jury, giving the reason that they were free, and we have seen that something of the same sort happened at Halesowen.[5] Without doubt on such manors a special jury of freemen would be formed when a case concerning a freeman came before the court: a freeman would demand trial by his peers. The usual manorial jury was a jury of bondmen because the usual cases were cases concerning bondmen. In some villages, a tendency can be observed for the names of the jurors to repeat themselves on the rolls of court after court:[6] there was an aristocracy of jurymen, and in fact in some villages the jury was always made up of the heads of the frankpledge groups. But no general uniformity can be found in the composition of manorial juries. The jury was of course sworn in, and its duties were twofold: to make presentation of offences (at least it had this duty at the court of the View of Frankpledge), and to give judgment in the different pleas both as to the facts and as to the custom of the manor.

Besides the steward and the jurymen, there were other persons who had special parts to play in a manorial court. The beadle or the hayward made the summonses or attachments ordered by the court. The different manorial officers might be called upon to make presentation of such offences as concerned their offices. If the lord held from the crown the privilege of holding the royal assize of ale, that is, the right to determine whether the ale brewed on the manor and offered for sale was up to a standard set by statute, then ale-tasters would be chosen, who would present all breaches of the assize. In many instances, most of the brewsters of a manor — brewers were usually women — had brewed contrary to the assize and were amerced small sums. The assize of ale came to be nothing more than a means of levying a small tax or licence fee. Finally, at the hallmotes of some manors, special affeerors (*taxatores*) were chosen whose duty was to assess the amounts of the amercements to be paid for the different offences.

Certain matters were not within the competence of hallmotes, above all the so-called pleas of the crown. A number of the lesser regalities, such as the right to hold the assize of ale or the View of Frankpledge, had been assumed by lords or specifically granted them by charter. Sometimes a manor had a gallows where thieves were hung if they were caught on the lordship. But few seigniorial courts, if any, could hold the greater pleas of the crown, such pleas as those of murder and other felonies. Hallmotes were also restricted in regard to freemen. For minor misdeeds a free-man could be amerced by a manorial court, but the suit of one freeman against another, especially a plea of land, was a different matter. It might conceivably originate in a hallmote and even be settled there, but the action of either party could easily remove it into a royal court.[7] Hallmotes, then, were chiefly concerned with villeins, with suits of villeins against villeins, with offences committed by villeins against the lord or the community.

Even so limited, the business of a hallmote was varied. It has been well illustrated by the entries from court rolls which have been cited here. First, there were the matters to which the lord was a party. If he had the right to do so, he held the assize of ale and the View of Frankpledge and took their profits. Here in the hallmote were punished all trespasses against the lord, including all withdrawals of rents and services. Here were paid the fines for incontinence, for permission to marry, for per-mission to enter religion. Here, when a tenant died, his heir came to pay the heriot and the relief, to have seisin and do fealty. Here the manorial officers were elected and took their oaths. Sometimes the jury even chose a man to take over a tenement which had fallen vacant.[8]

Second, there were the matters in which the whole community of a village was concerned. Villagers were amerced for allowing their cattle to stray into the corn, for harboring malefactors in harvest time, for breaking the rules of the champion husbandry, and for other petty offences. Bylaws were made for the benefit of the community, and in the fourteenth and later centuries they were entered upon the court roll.

Lastly, there were the matters in dispute between two or more villagers: slanders, trespasses, pleas of transgression, of debt, of covenant, and especially all the pleas of land, which have been so largely used in illustrating the customs of family law. In all of these cases, the hallmote offered an orderly means of settlement.

We must now consider the procedure in manorial courts, which was not informal and haphazard but well ordered and established in the custom of every hallmote. In any doubtful case there were manuals to tell a steward how he ought to hold a hallmote. Procedures varied somewhat from manor to manor but everywhere kept a common likeness. In at least one important respect all hallmotes differed from the royal courts: professional pleaders were not admitted. There is no reason to linger over the procedure in criminal cases, except to remark that when a man was charged with an offence, the steward might allow him to wage his law six- or twelve-handed. That is, he might order the accused to find, if he could, five other men or eleven other men who would swear as a body, the accused the sixth or the twelfth, that he had not committed the misdeed with which he was charged. If he could find the necessary oath-helpers, he went free. The wager of law was an ancient legal institution of the northern peoples of Europe. It could have been a satisfactory one only when men lived in communities where everyone knew his neighbors and his neighbors' business.

But let us follow the procedure before the hallmote in what we should now call a civil plea. Let us suppose that a man brought action against one of his neighbors who, he believed, had deforced him of a tenement unjustly. Actions of this sort, as they were recorded on court rolls, have yielded much information about the customs of inheritance of villagers. The procedure was by complaint. The demandant appeared before the hallmote and complained that such and such a man unjustly deforced him of such and such a tenement which was his by hereditary right. He brought suit: that is, he brought men with him who were ready to support the truth of his complaint, and he was ordered to find pledges that he would prosecute his suit. The finding of pledges, sureties, was a feature of medieval justice. When a court wished to make sure that a man would prosecute an action, appear in an action to which he was a party, pay an amercement, keep good behavior, or anything of the sort, it could order him to find a certain number of men willing to become his pledges. If the man defaulted, his pledges were distrained or amerced. Like the wager of law, this institution was characteristic of a society where the bonds between person and person in the local community were strong.

The defendant was allowed a certain delay before he was forced to make his defence or lose the case by default. The usual custom was that he was allowed three summonses, three distraints, and three essoins. That is, at three different courts orders to summons him to appear were issued; at three other courts orders to distrain him to appear were issued, and he had the opportunity to replevy the distresses; and at three further courts he could send essoins, excuses, for his failure to appear. The court had to find the essoins lawful. Only after the defendant had exhausted his summonses, his distraints, and his essoins would the court set a day for the pleading, and on that day the defendant was bound to appear or run the danger of having judgment given against him by default. In the usual case, of course, issue was joined much earlier, but the manorial court rolls show that many demandants were forced to appear in court after court before ever their suits came to trial.

The case, of course, might never be tried. The demandant might think better of it and pay the lord's steward a fine for leave to withdraw. Or he might fail to prosecute his suit; in this case he would be amerced. If the manner in which cases are recorded in the better court rolls is any sign of the sequence of the actual proceedings in the hallmote, the demandant opened with a statement of his plea; the defendant followed, making his defence, and perhaps each party had a rebuttal. Great stress was laid upon strict verbal accuracy in pleading: the demandant had to make his plea according to the customary form, and the defendant had to deny the plea word for word. This is another trait of the ancient law of the northern peoples, most highly developed in the lawsuits at the Thing in Iceland as they are described in the sagas. The pleadings were treated as if they were charms which would lose their virtue if changed in the least

particular. Even in England in the Middle Ages, before these
lowly hallmotes, many a plea was lost because a man did not
repeat the formulas correctly. Indeed, in their insistence on
strict verbal propriety, the hallmotes were more archaic than the
royal courts.

For instance, at a hallmote of King's Ripton, Hunts., held on
Lammas Day (August 1), 1303, William, son of Reginald le
Stalkere, appeared against John le Stalkere in a plea of land.
He made his demand, saying that the land and messuage was
his through the right of his father. The entry continues:

> And the aforesaid John comes and denies the force and tort and the right of
> said William, when, and so forth. And he says that he is not bound to answer
> to his (William's) pleading because in pleading he does not say that the same
> John deforces him of the aforesaid tenement with appurtenances, nor says in
> pleading in what township the aforesaid tenements are, nor which ancestor
> of his was seised, nor how the right ought to descend to him, nor in the time
> of what king his ancestor was seised thereof, nor what esplees he took, and
> he brought no suit, all of which are necessary to the pleading. And therefore
> he begs judgment whether he ought to answer to such pleading. And in this
> matter he puts himself upon the consideration of the court. And the aforesaid
> William likewise. And therefore by consideration of the whole court it is
> deemed that the aforesaid William take nothing by his writ but be in mercy
> for false claim. And the aforesaid John goes *sine die*.[9]

Let us consider this entry point by point, because it illustrates
not only the insistence on observance of the customary forms
of pleading but also the nature of the forms themselves. The
defendant began by denying word for word the complaint of the
demandant, denying the wrong done and the force used in
maintaining the wrong. This statement was simply the customary
preamble of the defence. When they made their entries in the
court rolls, some clerks made no mention of these words or,
as in this instance, used "etc." liberally. Then the defendant
advanced the claim that he was not bound to answer the demandant, since the latter's pleading had not been technically
correct, and he stated several respects in which it had not been
correct. That each of the statements which he asserted the
demandant had failed to make was in fact required in pleas
of land before hallmotes can be confirmed in court rolls from
all parts of England. Incidentally, the *esplees* of the land were
the profits of the land. Taking esplees was evidence of having

seisin. The defendant made the further claim that the demandant had not brought suit, that is, that he had not brought men with him into court to support the truth of his complaint. These men were the suit; their production in court by a plaintiff is the origin of our expression "to bring suit." They cannot have been important as witnesses. The court rolls do not mention that the suitors testified to anything as individuals or as a group, but say only that suit was brought. Bringing suit was part of the customary form and therefore strictly to be followed.

At this point both parties put themselves upon the court, and the whole court, that is, all the suitors of the court who were present, gave judgment for the defendant, apparently in agreement with his contention that his adversary's pleading had been faulty. The next thing to be explained is the writ. King's Ripton, as we know from its name and from another famous suit, had once been a manor of the king's; it was ancient demesne, and presumably William ranked as a privileged villein of the ancient demesne, a villein sokeman. Therefore he could secure at a royal court the little writ of right close addressed to the bailiffs of the manor, requiring them to see that right was done to the plaintiff according to the custom of the manor. Such a writ was William's. These royal writs of right are sometimes found stitched to the margin of court rolls of manors of the ancient demesne.

The later history of this case is interesting. After the failure of his first suit, William seems to have secured another writ and sued again through several courts. According to the custom of the manor, the defendant could take three summonses, three distraints, and three essoins before losing the case by default, and John took as many as he could. At last, at a court held in 1307, nearly four years later, the case came to trial, and it was found that Reginald, William's father, had lost the tenement to John at an earlier court "by a like writ," (*per consimile breue*).[10]

This case of King's Ripton, illustrating the insistence on strict verbal accuracy in pleading, has led far away from the story of the progress of a plea of land through the hallmote. When the demand and the defence had been heard, one of a number of things might happen. One or both of the parties might beg the steward for the grant of a special inquest, offering a sum of money for the privilege. The members of the inquest would be chosen and sworn in and then would give judgment. Or judgment would be given by the regular jury of the hallmote. Or, as in the case just cited, the parties might put themselves upon the consideration of the whole court. Whatever body was charged with giving judgment in the case had to decide both as to the facts and as to the law. It had to decide from its own knowledge whether the story told by the demandant or that told by the defendant was correct, and then it had to apply the custom of the manor. It had to give judgment according to the custom of the manor, the custom of the township — these are the phrases which appear again and again in the court rolls. If the custom of the manor was that a tenement descended to the youngest son of the last holder, and this custom determined who was the rightful holder of the land in dispute, the jury or the whole court gave judgment accordingly. The jurymen and the other suitors of the court were well equipped to decide both as to the facts of the case and as to the relevant custom. They dwelt in a community where nearly everything that happened was a matter of common knowledge; they had been born to the custom of the manor and had lived under it all their lives. Therefore they were the persons who gave judgment in the hallmote: the office of the steward was merely to give effect to their judgment.

Even after judgment had been given in an action between two villagers, the lord had something to gain. If the demandant lost, he could be amerced "for false claim." Of course, the case might never come to judgment. The parties would pay a fine for licence to agree out of court, or if, in the opinion of the court, a suit was nothing more than an expression of long-standing bad feeling between two villagers, the steward would order the parties to hold a love-day (*dies amoris*) at some time before a stated meeting of the hallmote. In the love-day, the two parties were to settle their differences by agreement and be reconciled. Perhaps the parish priest or mutual friends would intervene to bring them together. The line of *Piers Plowman* has already been cited in which Sloth in the guise of a parish priest says:

I can holde louedays · and here a reues rekenynge.

Sometimes the terms of these settlements were entered in the court rolls. One such entry is to be found in the rolls of Halton, Bucks., under the year 1286. It runs as follows:

When a quarrel had been moved between Sir Robert, rector of the church of Halton, on one part and Thomas of Merden on the other, by friends intervening they were made friends under the following form, that the aforesaid rector, and Thomas likewise, grant that if either one of them be justly convicted of any misdeed toward the other he will give the lord 4 s. without the admission of any plea.[11]

Other such settlements are recorded in which the first offender was to pay his fine to the fabric of the parish church or was to remain in a room and repent for one day while market lasted. Keeping a villager away from the interest and society of the market may have been a heavy punishment.[12]

It is plain that a hallmote could be impartial when an action in which both parties were tenants of the lord was to be terminated by a jury or the whole body of suitors of the court giving judgment according to the custom of the manor, but its impartiality was at once in jeopardy whenever the lord's interests were concerned. The court was the lord's court. It was held and presided over by his steward or another of his officers. The villeins, the largest part of the suitors of the court, were tenants at his will. He could, in theory, deprive them of all their lands and goods and drive them from the manor. He could make their rents and services what he wished. Unless they were privileged villeins of the ancient demesne, they had no remedy against him at law. Under these conditions, the arbitrary power of the lord appeared to be limited only by his good will.

In one way the lord's interest was involved in every case which came before the hallmote. The profits of the court were his; it was his interest to increase the amount and number of amercements. In some hallmotes affeerors were chosen to assess the amercements for the different offences. In others, perhaps, this duty was assumed by the jury or the court as a whole, but there is no doubt that the steward could overthrow the assessments of the affeerors and on some manors set the amercements himself. When in 1329 the bondmen of Darnhall rose in revolt against what they felt to be the oppression of their lord, the Abbot of Vale Royal, one of the charges they made was that:

It was not lawful for the abbot to punish them for any offence, except by the assessment of their neighbors.[13]

Robert Mannyng of Brunne complained bitterly of the arbitrary dooms handed down by stewards in manorial courts:

> Among hem, stywards mow be tolde,
> Þat lordynges courtys holde,
> For nyrhand euery a styward,
> Þe dome þat þey ʒeue, ys ouer hard;
> And namely to þe pore man,
> Þey greue hym alle þat þey kan.
>
> .   .   .   .   .
>
> Ʒyf þou haue be so coueytous
> To mercs men ouer outraious,
> And pore men, specyaly,
> Þat ferde þe wers for þat mercy,
> Sykyr mote þou be, syre styward,
> Þy mercyment shal be ful hard.[14]

Besides the matter of amercements, the lord's interests were at stake in the hallmote whenever a dispute between himself and his tenants was brought up there. The striking fact is that many such disputes were settled in the hallmote just as they would have been if the parties had both been simple villagers. They were settled in the usual way by judgments given according to the custom of the manor, and some of the judgments went against the lord. For instance, at a hallmote held at Cakeham, Sussex, in 1315, certain tenants claimed that they were not bound to cart the dung of their lord, the Bishop of Chichester. An inquest of three hallmotes was taken and the contention of the tenants was confirmed.[15] Since it was entered in his official custumal, we can only suppose that the lord reconciled himself to the adverse judgment. The lord's arbitrary will was bounded, or rather he allowed it to be bounded, by custom as found by the tenants. Without doubt the tenants felt strong sentiments, confirmed by a long tradition, that matters at issue between their lord and themselves, like any other dispute between villagers, ought to be decided according to custom declared in the hallmote. And the bishop had come to the conclusion that it was not the part of a man of sense to incur the hatred of his tenants for the sake of asserting his legal right to arbitrary power over them.

To take another instance, on the margin of a court roll of 1295 of Bromham, Wilts., there is the word *inquisicio*, and beside it is the following entry:

They say on their oath that all men, as well free tenants as others, give the lord for entry after the death of their predecessors what they were accustomed to give according to the size of their tenements. The villeins do not appease the lord at his will.[16]

From this entry we can only infer that the lord had claimed the right to fix at his will the fines men paid for having entry into tenements which they had inherited, that the tenants had denied his right, saying that the fines must be of the customary amount and assessed in proportion to the size of the tenements, that an inquest on this matter had been named at the hallmote, and that the inquest had found for the tenants. Once again, the lord's will was bounded or was suffered to be bounded by the custom of the manor as declared in the hallmote.

An interesting case of a dispute between tenants and one of their lord's officials, which perhaps reveals characteristic behavior on both sides, appears in a court roll of 1300 of Elton, Hunts., one of the Ramsey manors:

William James' son, Richard Blakeman, William Chyld, Reginald the Wise, Henry in the Lane, Richard Carter, John Trune, Ralph of Washingley, and Geoffrey at the Cross were attached by Hugh Prest, the claviger, and accused of this, that they drove their beasts through the way which is called Greenway when the cultures of the lord Abbot abutting thereon were sown. And the aforesaid men say that they and all of the village of Elton ought of right to have said chace at all times of the year just as all outsiders going by that way with all manner of their cattle can have their free chace without blame or hindrance. And the aforesaid Hugh says that although outsiders have their chace there, nevertheless said customers and their parceners occasionally paid 4 s. to the use of the lord in order to have their chace there when the cultures of the lord were there sown. And the aforesaid customers and all others of the village, as well freemen as others, and likewise the twelve jurors whose names are contained at the beginning of the roll say and swear that if any money was given by the customers of the village in order to have their chace there, said claviger by distress and extortion wilfully took that money and unjustly levied it of the same. Whereupon the said steward, seeing the dissension and discord between the claviger demanding and the said men gainsaying him, was unwilling to pronounced judgment against said claviger, but left this judgment wholly to the disposition of the lord Abbot, that the same lord, having scrutinized the register concerning the custom in the matter of this demand, should do and ordain as seems best to be done. . . ."[17]

Like many others in manorial court rolls, this entry tells us several things besides those with which we are immediately concerned. The claviger seems to have been identical with the monastic officer called the cellarer, and Elton must have been assigned to him for the maintenance of his office. At St. Albans Abbey, the cellarer was one of the most important administrative officers. At this hallmote of Elton, the steward was present in person and presiding, and before him came these tenants and Hugh Prest, the then claviger, as the two parties to a dispute. The matter at issue is not stated with perfect clarity. The claviger's argument seems to have been that in the past the tenants had paid the lord for the right of driving their cattle in the Greenway, that they had not paid on the present occasion, and that therefore they were to be refused the right. The tenants denied that they had ever paid for their free chace, unless it had been through extortion, and they claimed that they had always enjoyed the right, just as outsiders enjoyed it. Furthermore, not only the villein tenants in question, but all others of the village, free and unfree, and the jury of the hallmote swore that this statement was true. Therefore the steward was expected to pronounce judgment for the villeins. The part he had to play in the hallmote is here shown clearly: the jury and all the men of the manor having declared their verdict, his office was to give it effect. It is noteworthy also that the clerk who was present in the court and drew up the court roll made the steward's action perfectly plain in his record. He seems to have been without bias in his statement of the case, in spite of his being, as we must suppose, in the pay of the Abbot of Ramsey. This trait seems to have been universal among the clerks who drew up the court rolls: their entries do not give the impression of being colored in favor of the lord. But to return to the case — as we might have expected, officials hung together. The steward of Ramsey was unwilling to pronounce judgment against the claviger, but passed the responsibility on to the highest source of authority, the abbot himself. Even here the villeins were to have some safeguard against an arbitrary decision. As in other cases which have been cited, the register of the customs of the tenants of Ramsey was to be consulted, and this register was compiled from the findings of sworn inquests of the tenants themselves.

The lord of a manor was recognized at law as holding arbitrary power over his villein tenants. But cases at issue between the lord and any of his men were not ended by the arbitrary action of the lord. They were supposed to be settled, and often in fact were settled, by a jury of the hallmote declaring the custom of the manor in the matter. The lord, in his own court and in a case in which his interest was involved, was treated much like any other villager. This ambiguity in the position of the lord in the hallmote is only one of a number of such ambiguities. The lord's wood in a manor was treated at law as his to deal with as he would; in fact his tenants had enjoyed immemorially and continued to enjoy certain rights of using the wood, and a number of rationalizations were devised to reconcile the law with the practice. By law the lord was allowed to require of his villeins what services he pleased: the services they actually performed were likely to be those they had performed in the past. This fact was recognized in the speech of the time: the services were said to be customs. The lord exacted from his villeins the performance of benes, but the benes were spoken of as being done for him out of love, and in fact the villeins' behavior at the benes done for the lord was something like what it would have been at benes done for any needy neighbor. Again, the reeve, the hayward, and the rest were the elected officers of a village community and at the same time members of the managing staff of the lord's manor. We can account for these facts if we suppose that at some time in the past the lord's predecessor imposed his overlordship upon a village community hitherto independent. But he was far from being able to do what he pleased with the community, since its members kept their ancient sentiments and traditions. Indeed in exploiting the community for his maintenance, he had to make use of the customs of collaboration which were already in use among the villagers. It is a striking fact that the manorial system grew to its fullest development only in the champion country, the country of the big villages, the country, that is, in which large-scale coöperation in community agriculture was a fact.

When it came to making a working description of this situation, the law assigned to the lord powers over his villagers which in fact he was unable to exercise. The law was developed by men of the class of lords of manors under the influence of Roman concepts. But to argue in this way is to argue about origins of which we know little. The ambiguous relationship between the lord and the community of his villagers is a fact of the thirteenth century, the most important that is revealed by a study of the hallmote. In later centuries it was replaced by something more like the modern relationship between a landlord and his tenants.

There were two kinds of manorial courts: the common hallmotes and the courts of the View of Frankpledge. After the Norman Conquest, and perhaps in earlier times, a standing order of the kings of England was that all men twelve years of age or older were to be in frankpledge.[18] But Bracton, writing in the thirteenth century, considered that the numbers were more limited and that, at least in the country districts, freemen did not have to be in frankpledge.[19] In its commonest form, the arrangement was the following: men were divided into groups of ten or a dozen persons called frankpledges or tithings. One member of each tithing was its head and was called variously the headborough, dozener, chief pledge, or tithingman. He was commonly elected for a year's term but often served for many years on end. These chief pledges were the men who, on some manors, particularly in the East of England, formed the juries of the hallmotes. The frankpledge system was a police measure. The tithing as a whole was responsible for producing in court any one of its members accused of a misdeed, and it could be amerced for not doing so. By this means, the rulers of England made full use, as they did in other instances, of the principle of collective responsibility.

Frankpledge was not found everywhere in England, but only in the counties to the south of Yorkshire and to the east of Cheshire, Shropshire, and Herefordshire. In the other shires, those of the northern and western borders, it was not in general force.[20] Nor did it everywhere take the same form. In the ancient kingdom of Wessex, that is, in Hampshire and the other south-western counties, the tithing was territorial. There the court rolls speak of the tithingmen of such and such a place. For example, Bromham in Wiltshire had three tithingmen, the tithingmen of Hethestret, Hauckestret, and Westebroke, and their tithings must have consisted of the men who lived in the three parts of the village which were called by these names and not simply of even groups of ten or a dozen persons.[21] A smaller village would be a tithing in itself. In Wessex, also, the tithingman took over many of the duties which belonged elsewhere to the reeve, particularly those duties which concerned local police and the representation of the village at the courts of hundred and shire.

Kent, which differed from the rest of England in many respects, differed also in this one. There, as in Wessex, the tithings were territorial, but they were called *borghs*, and the heads of the tithings, who had duties like those of the tithingmen of Wessex, were called *borgesaldres*, later *borsholders*.[22]

Originally one of the duties of the sheriff, the chief officer of the king in a shire, was making sure, in the course of his tourn, his circuit, about the shire, that all men were in tithing who ought to be in tithing. He amerced all men and all tithings in default in this matter. The tithings were to be kept full. This inspection was called the View of Frankpledge and was held twice a year. On some manors in the thirteenth century the sheriff still did his ancient duty. In the Hundred Rolls, for instance, it is recorded that whereas Kettleby and Sysonby, Leics., were accustomed to appear at the sheriff's tourn with four frankpledges they then appeared with only three.[23] But as a result of long usurpation or specific royal grants, a great many lords of manors had taken over from the sheriff the right to hold the View. When the lord of a manor exercised the right to hold the View of Frankpledge, he held it twice a year as the sheriff had done, commonly once near Hocktide and once again near Michaelmas.

But the business of the View was not limited to seeing that all men were in frankpledge who ought to be in frankpledge. The Views were also courts — "Courts of the View," as any good set of court rolls will reveal. In fact they were the most important manorial courts of the year. To use another expression of the time, they were "Great Courts," great not only because certain freeholders exempted from attendance at ordinary hallmotes were bound to come to the View, but also because matters came before the View which did not come before ordinary hallmotes.

At these courts the chief pledges and their tithings made presentations concerning all matters of local police, especially the lesser pleas of the crown. They presented purprestures, encroachments on the king's highway, breaches of the assize of ale, raisings of the hue and cry, and so forth. A man was bound to raise the hue (*huthesium*), that is, cry out, whenever he believed a felony had been committed. When the hue was raised, the neighbors had to turn out with their weapons and pursue the malefactor. But raising the hue wrongfully was a punishable offence. For all these misdeeds men were amerced at the View, and the tithings were amerced if they failed to present known offences and produce the offenders.

One word about the court rolls, the records of the hallmote. The entries were made on long strips of parchment, less than a foot wide, which were rolled up and kept as rolls. Sometimes two or more membranes were stitched end to end to form a roll; sometimes a number of membranes were stitched together at the head and then rolled. The entries were made in Latin in a cursive hand by a clerk who was probably present in the court and wrote out his record either while the court was sitting or soon after it had finished its work. The rolls bear many signs of haste, although, it is fair to say, fewer than might have been expected. The writing is often wretched, the entries full of abbreviations, the constructions ungrammatical and ambiguous. On the left margin of the roll note was made of the kind of entry to be found opposite, the kind of judgment rendered, the amount of the amercement. And at the foot of the entries for a given court, the sum of the amercements of that court was recorded.

Some court rolls look as if they had been drawn up yesterday, while others are so stained and torn as to be illegible. But aside from these differences due to the accidents of three hundred years, court rolls vary greatly in their interest. Some, for instance, are full of amercements for straying cattle; others have few entries of this sort but many concerning all kinds of dealing in land. These differences must reflect differences in the activities of villagers. Some court rolls contain little more than notes of the amercements made in court; others contain detailed accounts

in elaborate legal language of the pleadings, findings, and judgments. The joy of the investigator can be imagined when he first
comes upon rolls of this last sort, rolls such as those of the
Ramsey manors or of Newington and Halton. Another kind of
court record should be mentioned once more. Some lords of
manors considered that it was worth their while to employ
clerks to go over their court rolls and copy out the more important
entries carefully in court books. The most notable surviving
court books are those of the manors of St. Albans Abbey, from
which much has been cited in illustration of the customs of family
law. Since court rolls contained the records of public pro-
nouncements concerning the customs of manors, rents and
services, the tenure of land, they were considered of the greatest
importance, for good and evil, both by the lord and by the
tenants. That the lords took good care to preserve their court
rolls is shown by the fact that so many of them have survived
to this day. On the other hand, one of the first acts of rebellious
villeins in the Peasants' Revolt was seizing and burning court
rolls, because in them was the evidence of their bondage.

CHAPTER XXI

THE VILLAGE AND THE WORLD BEYOND

HERE AND IN OTHER BOOKS much has been written about the villages of medieval England as "village communities," that is, as bodies of men with traditions and customs of acting in concert. The basis of the common action of the men of a village was the champion husbandry. Its rules allowed the villagers to make joint use of the resources of the village. When the rules were to be changed or put in force anew, action was taken with the consent of the neighbors gathered as a bylaw. Furthermore, the lord of a manor did not deal with each of his men singly so much as deal with the body of them as a community. This fact became plain in the way the manorial officers were elected and in the way the hallmote treated matters at issue between the lord and his men. But the villagers acted as a community not only in the champion husbandry and in dealing with the lord of the manor; they acted as a community in many of their relations with the great world beyond the village bounds. Here there remains much to be considered.

The measure of the cohesion of community is its distrust of outsiders. A village acted as one body most simply and directly when it fought with the men of another village who were suspected of having done evil. Thus the men of the manor of Halesowen had a quarrel of long standing with the men of the neighboring township of Clent in Worcestershire. The quarrel may have arisen over the use of the commons, which still exist or existed a few years ago, between the manor of Hales and the manor of Clent. On Saturday, July 7, 1274, according to presentation made in the Halesowen hallmote three days later, the men of Clent had thrown down the hedge of a certain Lovecoc at Hayley, whereupon the hue had been raised.[1] A few years later a much more serious struggle occurred. According to the roll of the assizes held at Shrewsbury in 1292 before the king's justices in Eyre, another dispute had arisen between the men of Clent and the men of Hales. A man of Clent had shot a man of Hales with three arrows, and from these wounds he died on the fourth day afterwards. The fact that Thomas, chaplain of Dudley, and Simon, the priest of Clent, were in the gang hailed before the justices, tells us much about the position and character of priests in the Middle Ages.[2]

The greatest demand a nation can make upon its citizens is that they fight in its defence. In the thirteenth century, as today, war brought villagers into the life of the larger community of which they were members. Some of the feudal lords chose to serve in person with their retainers rather than pay scutage in commutation of the military service they owed for their fees. For the rest, the English armies of the thirteenth century were made up of levies from the armed men of the shires. The various Assizes of Arms stated what kinds of weapons every man, according to his wealth, ought to keep in readiness, and made provision that there should be "views of arms." At the head of the armed men of the shire was the sheriff, and in the early campaigns of Edward I the sheriff sometimes led the levies to war in person, but as the king grew in experience he came to appoint special officers, later called Commissioners of Array, with authority given them by writ to raise a specified number of men. The crown paid the wages of its soldiers, but only from the date of their first march to the war.[3]

Unlike the next century, the thirteenth century was a time of peace. After King John's defeats, there were no serious wars on the continent, and the struggle between Henry III and Simon de Montfort, Earl of Leicester, was civil war and was short. Only on the Welsh Marches and the Scottish Border did the energy of Edward I and his talent for war express themselves in important and frequent campaigns, and his practice was to raise levies for these wars only from the shires near the scene of the campaign. But two of these shires were Yorkshire and Shropshire, and the court rolls of Wakefield in the one and Halesowen in the other have something to tell about the way the levies were made.

The court rolls seem to show that a village was ordered to produce a certain number of men, and that these men were elected by their fellow villagers, just as the officers of a village were elected, though in neither case do we know the manner in which the election was held. Thus an entry for January 19, 1295 in the Halesowen rolls speaks of a number of men as "elected" to go to Shrewsbury for the king's army in Wales. A certain Thomas Hill, who must have been a clever fellow, had gone to each of the men elected, and each had paid Hill to go as substitute to the army in Wales. Hill had then disappeared with the money. He kept out of the way for some time after this coup, but returned at last and made amends. There was probably nothing wrong in taking a man's money for going to the wars as his substitute: Hill's only fault was to have played the game too well. At the next court it was found that Thomas in le Putte had gotten 9 d. from the community for his expenses in Wales but had not gone.[4] For the king's officers the inefficiency of this method of levying recruits must have been galling. Desertions also were common.

The way in which the village dealt with the lord in the hall-mote has already been described. But in this matter there is more to be said. Sometimes the community of a village entered into negotiations with the lord as if it were a corporation which could hold property. To a court of 1296, for instance, came the community of the villeins of Brightwalton, Berks., and surrendered to the lord, who was the Abbot of Battle, all the right of common which they claimed in the lord's wood called Hemele, and in return the lord surrendered to the community his common in the Eastfield and in the villeins' wood called Trendale, making other concessions as well.[5] The lord and the community of the villeins exchanged their rights as if the villeins were the lord's equals at law and not tenants at his will.

And just as the corporation of a borough held the borough at farm from the king or from a mesne lord, so village after village in the thirteenth century was held by its inhabitants at farm from their lord.[6] They assessed and levied from among themselves the amount of the farm: the political constitution of the community was strong enough for this purpose. The only difference between a borough and such a village was that the borough remained permanently at farm, the village simply for a term of years. A good example of an agreement whereby a village was put at farm to its inhabitants is found in the Ramsey cartulary.[7] The abbot granted the manor of Hemingford, Hunts., to the men of Hemingford for seven years beginning at Michaelmas, 1280. They were to pay forty pounds sterling a year for all rents and services. They were also to have the demesne farm and the issue of all actions before the hallmote except those which could not be terminated without the abbot or his bailiffs. The abbot was to have half the issues of actions of the latter sort. They were not to have the advowson of the church, nor the profits of the fish-pond, the mill, and the View of Frankpledge. And so forth: there were a number of lesser provisions. The men were not to transfer their lands to outsiders without the abbot's permission. Finally, a description was given of the state in which the manor was turned over to the men and the state in which it was to be turned back. In short, the men of the village were to govern the village themselves. The rules by which under these conditions political and administrative power was delegated and exercised, the means by which the villagers managed their affairs when free of the influence of the lord are matters on which scholars are still ignorant. One hint is given by the bylaw and another by the reeve, elected by his fellows to manage the demesne farm, and there are others. But they do not come near to revealing the whole constitution of village self-government.

Sometimes a lord who had granted a manor at farm to his villeins found fault with the way they managed it. Thus in a court roll of 5 Edward II of Elton, a Ramsey manor, the following entry appears:

All the customers of Elton, who have the aforesaid village at farm, are hereafter forbidden by Sir J. (John de Sautre), the Abbot, to suffer that any man or woman of the lord's villeins leave the lord's fee in order to dwell upon another fee, or to receive any outsider to dwell within the aforesaid village without the lord's special permission, fine being made before the aforesaid lord, and it is also forbidden them that gersums or fines hereafter be made except before the said lord Abbot. And if the aforesaid customers be convicted of acting against the aforesaid form, to wit, in part or in whole, they shall be in heavy mercy, taxed at the will of the lord.[8]

It appears that the villeins had been prepared to say what persons were to leave the manor or take land in it. They had been prepared to take complete control of the manor. But the lord was not willing to let them do so. Though the manor was at farm, he insisted on maintaining his power over certain matters. Indeed the character of the court rolls of Elton did not change conspicuously in the time when the villagers had the manor at farm.

When communities of villagers exercised, and were ready to exercise, authority in all matters of local self-government, we cannot be surprised to find entries such as the following, from a court roll of 1295 of Bromham, Wilts.:

All the customers made fine because they made a common seal in contempt of the lord.[9]

A note on the margin of the roll informs us that the fine was one hundred shillings. Besides exercising an authority like that of the corporations of boroughs, some bodies of villagers, in this case of villeins, wanted the outward signs of incorporation. Naturally the lord felt that the signs of incorporation were also the signs of independence, and objected. The entry is all the more interesting because Bromham does not seem to have been a village which was in any way out of the ordinary.

Some hint of the methods by which villagers assessed and levied by common consent among themselves the amount of the farm they owed to their lord is given by what they did when they had to meet certain other charges. In a plea before the hallmote of Sutton, Lincs., in 1306, Robert Galardon complained of three men that they had unjustly taken seven of his sheep in the king's highway in Sutton, had driven them to a pound, and had kept them until they were freed by the bailiff of the court, wherein Galardon said that he suffered damages of one half-mark. The entry continues:

And William Bridde and the others in the quarrel defend force etc. and they argue the seizure good and just in the aforesaid place because they say that Robert Galardon was assesed at a half quarter of oats on Thursday next after mid-Lent in the year past, by the common agreement of the whole village, and this by order of the sheriff to the use of the lord King, and because the aforesaid Robert was unwilling to pay over the aforesaid corn, therefore they took his beasts, as well they might. And Robert says that he was not assessed by agreement of the village nor had beasts beyond his sustenance, and that etc. Therefore let an inquest come. And it is accepted by the inquest that Robert Galardon was assessed at a half-quarter of oats by the community of the village as one having more than his sustenance; therefore he is in mercy for false claim.[10]

The sheriff, the king's chief officer in a shire, had the right to make requisitions for the service of the king. In theory payment ought to have been made for these requisitions. But lesser folk were likely to have trouble about getting back the value of their goods. In any case, such seizures were dreaded. The sheriff of Lincoln seems to have ordered Sutton as a township to produce a certain store of corn, and the *communitas* of the township had assessed various of its members to pay parts of this store. One of the rules according to which the assessment was made was evidently the natural one, that only such men were bound to pay as had more goods than they needed for their own sustenance. The assessment was made according to the ability to pay. Robert Galardon had been assessed to pay a half-quarter of oats, and had refused to do so, whereupon the community had proceeded to enforce its will upon him, by levying a distress. Seven of his sheep had been impounded. And when he brought a complaint of damages into the hallmote, the inquest of the hallmote supported the actions of the community. A record of the proceedings of the community of a village in making an assessment of this sort would be of the greatest interest. But if any such records were kept, they do not seem to have survived.

A village appeared in the guise of an independent, self-governing body most prominently when it came into contact with the organs of local and national administration. Before the courts of hundred and shire, before the king's justices in Eyre, at the sheriff's tourn, at a royal inquest, villagers appeared not as individuals but as representatives of their communities. This statement is a first approximation and must be qualified at once. Let us consider then the composition of a county court, such as was assembled when the king sent a mandate to the sheriff of the county to call the county to meet the justices in Eyre. The sheriff summoned all prelates and all laymen holding by feudal tenure. (These magnates might send their stewards or attorneys in their place.) He summoned all freeholders. He summoned each hundred of the county to be represented in court by twelve freemen, each borough to be represented by twelve burgesses, and each village to be represented by the reeve and four other men of the village.[11] This last fact is the important one for the present purposes. Once more we have to do with the reeve, this time with the reeve as the head of a delegation representing his village.

The early history of the reeve and four as the standard delegation representing a village is interesting. The commissioners appointed by William the Conqueror to make the inquests which were compiled in Domesday Book made inquiry of the priest, reeve, and six *villani* of every village.[12] Again, the twelfth-century compilation which bears the name of *Leges Henrici Primi* stated that a village was to be represented at a hundred court by the reeve, priest, and four of the best men of the village.[13] And the compilation of still more questionable origin which was piously called *Leges Edwardi Confessoris* stated that when valuable goods had been found, the finder had to go to the church of the village into which he brought the goods and show the priest, the reeve, and the best men of the village what he had found. The reeve then summoned the priest, reeve, and four best men of each of the neighboring villages, and they in their turn were shown the goods.[14] Whether or not the two sets of *Leges* describe what was actually the practice makes little difference: they describe at least a tradition of the practice. The important point about all these early instances is that they show that the reeve was not alone at the head of the delegation representing the village; he was always accompanied by the priest. But in the thirteenth century the priest wholly disappeared from the village delegation. It would be good to know the reason for his disappearance. One guess is that the movement of appropriating the revenues of parishes for the support of religious houses, a movement which became powerful in the thirteenth century, had something to do with it. The new beneficiaries put the cure of souls into the hands of poor vicars, who can no longer have been, as the old priests had been, the foremost men of their parishes. On the other hand, the result may have been due to the degradation of the reeve to the position of a "serf overseer of serfs."

As usual, the representation of a village by the reeve and four was not a practice uniform over all England. A village of Wessex was represented by the tithingman and four men, a village of

Kent by the borgesaldre and four men of every borgh. In Shrop-shire the village sometimes sent six men and the reeve,[15] and in the North it sent four men, without any mention of the reeve at all.[16] The cost of sending this delegation to the courts or elsewhere was sometimes divided between the lord and the village,[17] and sometimes, as was to be expected, the duty of attending the courts was made one of the services of certain tenements. Since all freeholders were summoned in any case to attend the hundred and county courts, the rule was that the reeve and four men who attended from every village were villeins, but the custumals of the estates of several of the greater religious houses show that on these estates each village was represented only by a small number, often four, of the wealthier freeholders, men of the franklin class.[18] They were called hundredors after their service. No one else was bound to attend.

In this scheme of representation, no cognizance was taken of manors. The officers of the crown realistically dealt with the natural units of the population, the villages, rather than with the tenurial units, the manors. But many a village was divided into two or more manors, so that the lords of the manors and their tenants had to distribute the membership of the village delegation among the men of the different manors. Again, where villages were small, two or more of them were grouped together as a *villa integra*, and this became the unit which sent the delegation.[19]

The hundred and county courts were not the only places where the reeve and four men of every village appeared. They appeared also at the sheriff's tourn and before the justices in Eyre when they were in the neighborhood. But the communal and royal courts were courts of freemen. The reeve and his companions were commonly villeins, and villeins, save in matters of life and limb, were justiciable only by their lords. Therefore they appeared in these courts only in order to make presentations of matters concerning the king's peace which had arisen within their village. They appeared also before all royal inquests, and were even among the men who made the assessments of royal taxes.[20]

There would be no reason to dwell upon the fact that in all important matters of local justice and administration the reeve and four men were summoned to represent their village, if these men did not sometimes appear in a much more important and interesting position, as a responsible board administering the affairs of a village. For instance, when in 1203 the Norman lords revolted against King John, the lands which they held in England escheated to the crown. Inquests were held before the king's justices concerning the value of these lands, and at these inquests appeared the reeve and four men of each of the escheated villages. So far the procedure is familiar. What is new is that the reeve and four men of one of these villages, Kirtlington, Oxon., were spoken of as "those to whom the village has been handed over." And elsewhere the reeve and four men were called *custodes ville*.[21] They were not only making reports of the value of each village, but also in fact administering the affairs of the village. Again, the register of the Dean and Chapter of Lincoln contains two charters in which four villagers and the whole community of the village of Wellow, Notts., undertook for themselves, their heirs and successors, who for the time being should be of the same community, to maintain a chaplain in the chapel of Wellow which belonged to the mother church of Edwinstowe, and they, as a community (*communiter*), bound themselves by an oath and affixed to the charters the seal of their community (*sigillum communitatis nostre*).[22] Wellow, then, unlike Bromham, was allowed to have a seal of the community. It could bind itself by charter and affix its seal to the charter. Furthermore four villagers of Wellow were evidently in some leading position in the administration of the village. Again, according to a court roll of 1290 of Oxnead, Norfolk, all the lands and holdings of the village were given into the custody of the reeve and six other men; they were to answer to the amount of two shillings for every acre that became damaged and for all other matters pertaining to the manor.[23] Evidence of this sort is excessively rare, but what we have seems to show that a board of villagers, with or without the reeve, could be and was empowered to administer the affairs of a village and speak in its name. The reeve, of course, was already the manager of the lord's demesne farm. To become the first among his peers in the general administration of his village cannot have been a great extension of his responsibility. When the men who founded the townships of New England put their government into the hands of elected boards of selectmen, where it still remains, they were following the ancient traditions of the villages of the mother country.

The men of boroughs were engaged chiefly in the crafts and in trade, the men of villages in husbandry. But many boroughs, especially the smaller ones, had common fields, and most villages had their fairs, even if they were nothing more than the yearly wakes, and their crafts, even if they were practiced by only a few poor cotters. A shift in trade routes, an increase in general prosperity, might make a village a center of trade; the renown of one of its cottage industries might make it a center of manufactures. Then the villagers would be on their way to losing their predominant concern with husbandry. Many boroughs had once been villages. Nevertheless, borough and village were clearly set apart in the minds of men. A borough was a center of exchange for the surrounding villages. In the borough the country people sold as large a surplus of their corn and cheese as they could; in the borough they bought what they were not able to make for themselves; to the borough they sent their sons to be bound apprentices. On their part, the townspeople, like townspeople always and everywhere, must have been inclined to laugh at their country cousins.

Borough and village were two different worlds. But from all that has gone before, the fact should be plain that in form the organization of boroughs in the Middle Ages much resembled that of villages. Even when practices differed in the two places, the sentiments and traditions to which these practices gave effect were akin. This observation has often been made and it is an important one.[24] Thus in borough as well as village the regulation of economic activities was dominated by what can only have been a desire to maintain the equality of the members of the community in economic opportunity. The minds of the men who put into force the ordinances against forestalling, regrating, and all other practices which prevented the enjoyment by all burgesses of a fair and cheap market, who devised the ancient right of lot, according to which a burgess had the right to buy a share of any goods offered for sale in the borough at the same price as any other burgess had paid — the minds of such men were dominated by sentiments like those which maintained the elaborate arrangements of the champion husbandry. In the early days, the burgage tenements even tended to be equal in size, like oxgangs and yardlands, and the rules of family law which applied to tenements in the boroughs were the same in kind as those of the neighboring villages, though the burgesses were commonly more free than the villagers from customary restraints on alienation.

Some of the customs of a community of villagers were exactly the same as those of a community of burgesses. Just as merchants of a borough could be distrained for the debts of a fellow citizen, so could villagers be distrained. One of the Northamptonshire inquests which have survived in the Hundred Rolls records that:

William Strake, Roger Crowe, and many others, by order of William Passeleu, steward of the Earl of Gloucester, of Rothwell, took outside of the bounds of his bailiwick sixty beasts of the township of Orlingbury for a certain debt in which Ralph, father of Robert of Orlingbury, was bound to a certain merchant of Rothwell and kept them until the same Robert satisfied said merchant to the extent of twenty marks, and a half-mark for keeping the beasts.[25]

The men of a village were collectively responsible for all fines and other charges laid upon the community, as were the burgesses for all charges laid upon the borough. Fellow villagers were even spoken of as being at scot and lot with one another, the phrase which was always used of fellow burgesses.[26]

Finally, in their government borough and village were akin. The communities of the boroughs held the boroughs at farm from the king or mesne lords; the communities of many villages held the villages at farm from their lords, if not permanently, then at least for a term of years. The affairs of a borough were administered by a mayor and aldermen; the affairs of a village might well be administered by a reeve and four other men. The community of a village might even have a seal. In fact in their form of government some villages were boroughs in every respect except the possession of a charter. They were not boroughs only because they were not recognized as such.

Strong walls may have divided the borough from the village, and a difference in callings, but in the sentiments and traditions which gave them their form the two were social organisms of the same kind.

CHAPTER XXII

LORD AND MAN

IN EVERY SOCIETY there are men who control more of the food, clothing, and other forms of wealth produced in the society than do other men. The word *control* is used deliberately: from many points of view the control of wealth is more important than its mere possession, but this assertion raises questions which cannot be answered here. The ways in which the distribution of wealth takes place are various. Nevertheless in all societies, or better, nearly all societies, people will admit that there are rich men and poor men. In English villages of the thirteenth century, the only important source of wealth was land as used in husbandry. Accordingly, when villeins worked for several days a week tilling their lord's demesne, no Karl Marx was needed to explain to them that their lord was richer than any one of them because they yielded him a surplus of their labor. On his part the lord made certain gifts of money and food to his men — we must remember the Christmas dinner and the meals given at the harvest benes — but the value of the things he gave them was clearly less than the value of the rents, services, heriots, fines, and amercements they rendered to the lord.

The distribution of wealth between the lord and any one of his men was not only unequal, but was unequal because the man spent a part of his time working, without return, for his lord. Yet the minds of men did not dwell upon this inequality, except in times of disorder. Men usually look at the distribution of wealth not as it really is, that is, as it would appear to a skeptical outsider, but only as it is conceived to be according to a traditional mythology. Perhaps it is better to say that in every society a few men have been able to see the distribution of wealth and other such institutions as they really are, but if a few men have penetrated that far, they have usually penetrated far enough to know better than to give the reality away. They know that the reality in this sense is a matter of no importance. We recall the remark of Waldershare in Disraeli's *Endymion*. He said that sensible men were all of the same religion. And when asked what that was, he replied: "Sensible men never tell." That the distribution of wealth is never described as it really is but only as it is conceived to be according to a traditional mythology is as much true of our own times as it was of the Middle Ages, though most of us, very properly, will be irritated if we are asked to admit this fact. The only myths are the myths of other people.

One thing the mythology of the Middle Ages had in common with the mythology of our own times was that the relation between lord and man then, as between employer and workman now, was described as based upon an exchange. If a workman today, or any one of us for that matter, is asked why he receives pay from his employer, he will answer that he receives it in return for work done for his employer. In the same way, if a villager of the Middle Ages was asked by what right he held his tenement, he would have answered that he held it in return for rendering to the lord the due and customary rents and services of the tenement.

A mythology is a matter of language. Let us inspect the language used in the Middle Ages in speaking of landholding. This inspection, more than anything else, will reveal the schemes according to which the men of the time envisaged the distribution of wealth, and it will reveal the assumptions concealed in these schemes. Men said — that is, lawyers said it most elaborately, but the main terms were common to all men — that a lord held a fee, an estate in land. The use of the word *hold* made the lord's possession of his fee resemble his possession of such an object as his sword. If this fee was a manor, the lord was said to keep part of the land in his own hands. Observe the metaphor again. The rest was divided up into holdings or tenements, which the lord was said to grant to his tenants, the men who in fact occupied and tilled the land. And just as the lord held his fee of another lord above him in return for rendering him certain services, such as the furnishing of a knight in time of war, so these tenants held their tenements of the lord in return for rendering him due and accustomed services, which in this case were money rents and services in husbandry. We now call this system the feudal system. Or rather, we mean many things when we speak of the feudal system, but we mean at least the particular verbal scheme according to which the men of the Middle Ages described the distribution of wealth and certain other relations between man and man. The feudal system has often been described as if it applied only to the landed aristocracy: in the sense in which the expression is used here, it applied to all men.

Let us now consider the influence this way of looking at things had on the sentiments of men. In most societies the things a man owns most intimately, the things that he holds — his sword, his plow, his money — are felt to be his to deal with nearly as he wishes. By the legal mythology of the Middle Ages, the possession of land was likened to the possession of such objects. And another one of the commonest and strongest sentiments of men might be expressed in the following way: if one man gives another something he owns, the other man owes him a return. The legal mythology of the Middle Ages likened the grant of land to a tenant by a lord, followed by the render of services and rents to the lord by the tenant, to a simple exchange, as if it were something like a render of money in a market by one man to another in exchange for goods. But the two transactions were not the same. In a market a man gives another man something substantial, money, in exchange for something substantial, goods. In the exchange between lord and man nothing of the sort occurred. Whereas the man rendered to the lord something substantial enough, namely rents and services, the return the lord made, namely the grant of land, was purely verbal. The lord said he granted the land to the tenant, and there was even a ceremony in the hallmote symbolizing the grant — one of the important functions of courts, and one which is often forgotten by men who are concerned with reforming them so as to make them more efficient, is giving ceremonial representation to many of the vital myths of a society. But in point of fact the tenant's forefathers had usually held and tilled the land for generations. They had been in continuous possession. The larger share of the wealth produced in the society which went to the lord was made up by the rents paid by his tenants and the work they did in tilling his demesne, but they were said to pay these rents, render these services in return for a grant of land which was not real but a fiction.

Of course, the legal language of landholding, for many men in the thirteenth century, may have come to be nothing more than a set of formulas. But even formulas, if they are in habitual use, may keep our thinking within certain channels. For instance, at the present day, the law in the United States treats a corporation as a person which, like other persons, has rights which can be taken from it only by due process of law. We recognize that a fiction has been created, even if the fiction is an inevitable and useful one. But who shall say that in some corner of our minds we do not in fact think of a corporation as another human being?

Yet to suppose that there was not something real involved on the lord's side would be absurd. Let us consider what would happen if a tenant refused to pay his rents and render his services. The lord would declare his land forfeit, grant it to someone else, and eject the old holder with force if necessary. And if any large number of tenants joined together in refusing their rents and services, the matter would be treated as rebellion and once more would be put down by armed force. Something of this sort actually happened in the Peasants' Revolt of 1381. Then the gentlemen of England showed that they had the qualities necessary to maintain their position at the top of the social system. If they had not used as much force as was necessary, the form of society would have rapidly changed until a new position of equilibrium was reached, marked by a new grouping of men in classes, a new distribution of wealth, and even, perhaps, a new mythology in which the new situation was interpreted. In short, there would have been a revolution. A cynic will say that the land law of the Middle Ages came down to something very simple. In effect, a lord said to his men: If you do not render me rents and services, I shall punish you with force of arms to the utmost extent of my power. But men did not in fact speak of the distribution of wealth in this way, and there is no sense in saying that they were hypocrites. History and anthropology show that men describe their social institutions not in realistic terms but in mythologies, and, what is more, the mythologies of a stable and successful society are not those which set men against one another but those which help them work together with good will.

In any case, our experience of our own times tells us that the language of the law can describe the relations between people only very inadequately. More was involved in the relationship between lord and tenant than economic interest on one side, fear of coercion on the other, and a mythology common to both parties in which this conflict of interests was rationalized. That more was involved was recognized in the very ceremony by which a man entered into possession of a tenement. He was given seisin but he also did fealty. He swore to bear truth and loyalty to his lord. The lord controlled a larger share of the total wealth produced in his society than any of his men, and he did so for the very reason that they either paid him rents or rendered him services in tilling his demesne. All these facts are admitted. But in medieval society, as in other societies, the economic form of the production and distribution of wealth was often less important, in determining whether men were to be discontented and irritated with one another or contented and collaborating successfully with one another, than certain of the other conditions under which production and distribution took place. The theme of much that has gone before has been that certain features of the traditions according to which the men of a village worked for their lord were favorable to successful human relations between lord and men. These features can perhaps be brought out and summarized by comparing them with the conditions under which a man works for his employer in many a modern, particularly an American, factory. There is plainly something about the conditions of work in modern factories which leads some workmen to ask why they have to be working for their boss at all, and this something may be a good deal more than the reason they commonly give, which is that the boss pays his men low wages and works them long hours.

The best evidence of the nature of the relations between a lord and his men is to be found in the work services they did for him in tilling his demesne, as these are described in the manorial custumals. The first thing to be said about the services is that they were customary. The villeins themselves were often called customers, because they performed customary services, and in the same way a detailed statement of the number and nature of the services was called a custumal. The services were customary in the first instance because in those days all the methods of husbandry were customary. Gervase Markham, writing in the seventeenth century, observed:

This labour of Husbandry consisteth not for the most part in the knowing and understanding breast, but in the rude, simple, and ignorant Clowne, who onely knoweth how to doe his labour, but cannot give a reason why he doth such labour, more than the instruction of his parents, or the custome of the Country. . . .[1]

Markham's statement holds true for most husbandmen at most times in history and certainly for English husbandmen four centuries before the time when Markham wrote. But the services of villeins were customary also in that they were rendered in the amount and in the manner in which they had been rendered from a time to which the memory of man ran not to the contrary. In theory a lord had the right to make the services of his villeins what he would. They were tenants at his will. And in fact there are several well attested instances of lords who deliberately increased the amount of the services of their villeins. But no matter what abstract rights one man has over others, he is often unable to insist upon them in practice, because the human medium is stubborn. If villeins had strong sentiments that their services ought to remain what they had been in ancient custom, a lord would find great practical difficulties in the way of increasing the services. In drawing up a statement of what the services were, that is, in drawing up a custumal, the same procedure was followed as was followed in recording any other custom for legal purposes. The custom was "found" by those best qualified to know what it was — the villeins themselves. The services were affirmed by sworn juries of the villeins, by the very people, that is, who were to perform the services. And there is evidence, especially in the case of the Ramsey register, that when the amount or manner of performance of a service was in dispute between a lord and his men, the appeal to the custumal was recognized by both parties as final.

Today, in the organization of work in a large factory, a distinction between men is made which would not have been made in the past, or at least not systematically as it is now. On the one hand there are the technical experts, and on the other the men who actually tend the machines. The technical expert, as such, is of relatively recent appearance. His labor consists precisely in the knowing and understanding breast, to use Gervase Markham's words. He must continually apply observation and reasoning to the methods of doing work. If you told him that any of the methods followed in his factory were customary, he would probably take the remark as a reproach. His business is to change them so as to make them more efficient, or at least to think about changing them. Wherever he sees that an improvement is possible, he reports to the operating management, and the management orders the men who tend the machines to make the change forthwith.

Unlike the technical expert, the man who tends the machine remains much what workmen have always been. Perhaps he is not so much bound by custom as was Gervase Markham's husbandman, but if he has worked out a method which he feels is satisfactory for doing his job, he is reluctant to change it, especially when changing it means changing his relations with his fellow workmen. He may himself devise technical improvements, but he adopts them with sentiments quite unlike those with which he adopts the changes planned by the technicians and ordered by management. Indeed he may act so as to nullify many changes of the latter sort, even when they are in his own interest. They are imposed, not developed by the workman himself. They are imposed, often without his understanding why. They are imposed by a power whose intentions are looked upon with suspicion, however benevolent they may be in fact. In contrast with the work done by the villeins on the lord's demesne, the work in a modern factory not only does not remain fixed in custom but is frequently changed in the way most irritating to the men who do the work. If there is a solution of the problem, it is not to do away with the technical experts but rather to extend the scope of their studies to include the behavior of the human beings who must put technical changes into effect.

If the first condition of work on the lord's demesne was that it was customary, the second was that the men who did the work were members of an organized community and were recognized as that. To a high degree, the actual social organization and the recognized social organization coincided. The men were members of the community not only in work but in all the other activities of life. They were villagers, and a village was a physical, economic, and political unit. We have seen that a great ambiguity appeared between the powers which the lord was allowed by law to exercise over his villeins and the treatment he actually accorded them and was accorded by them in turn. The ambiguity had two aspects. In the first place, the lord was treated in some manner as if he was a member of the village community, even if a peculiarly respectable one. The boon services which he required his tenants to perform, they spoke of as being done out of love, as if they were done for any other one of their fellows who needed help, and there are hints that in a much wider sense the villagers extended to the lord the forms of activity which they followed among themselves. Again, the lord took the profits of his manorial court; his steward presided in it; in legal theory his villeins had no remedy against his arbitrary actions, but in point of fact cases at issue between the lord and any of his men were often settled by a jury of the court declaring the custom of the manor in the matter, just as if the parties were fellow villagers.

In the second place, the lord often dealt with his men less as individuals than as members of a community. The officers they elected for governing the community: the reeve, the hayward, and the rest, became also the officers in charge of the management of the lord's demesne farm. A lord might put his manor out at farm to a community of villagers and even treat the community as a corporation which could hold and dispose of land.

A modern factory is not a community in the sense that a medieval village was. For one thing, the workmen usually do not live together as well as work together, or if they do live in a single neighborhood, their common employment at the factory is not emphasized as a principle binding them in one body. Nevertheless, within a factory, groups of workmen are continually forming which have some of the characteristics of communities of villagers. But these groups are not recognized by management, although management may act as if in fact it was taking them into account. We have seen how this and other contrasts between work on the lord's demesne in the thirteenth century and work in a large modern factory are related to the further contrast between the position of a reeve and the position of a first-line supervisor.

A third characteristic of the conditions under which tenants worked for their lord has already been considered at length. The lord and his men thought of their relationship as a reciprocal one. Not only were the rents and services rendered by the men to their lord conceived as being rendered in return for his granting them their tenements, but also, outside of this main exchange, there was a series of exchanges of benefits between the lord and his men. If the men used the lord's wood or pasture, they each paid him a hen in return for the privilege or plowed a half-acre of land, and the name of the rent or service, *wood-hen* or *grass-earth*, reminded men that these special services were rendered in return for special benefits. On the other hand, if at one of the crises of the farming year, at seedtime or harvest, the lord need to get his demesne land plowed or his corn reaped, he had the right to call out all his men to work for him. Although in fact a man might be amerced for not performing these services, they were spoken of as being done as a favor, out of good feeling. They were called love-boons. And they were rewarded by food and drink given by the lord to his men. But for an understanding of the relationship between the lord and his men, the fact of payment is no more important than the fact of mutual aid.

The point to be emphasized is that the lord's affairs and those of his men came into contact in all the activities of the neighborhood, in husbandry, in government, in festivity. Of course the actual economic exchange of benefits was strongly in favor of the lord, in the sense that his income was larger than the income of any of his men, but the circumstances under which his income was gained must be considered as well as its actual amount. We have inherited from the Middle Ages the notion that the relationship between employer and workman is a reciprocal one, that the employer pays his workmen wages in return for their labor. What makes this relationship different from the relationship between lord and men in the Middle Ages is that this single exchange of pay for work is often the only link between the employer and his workmen. Nothing in the other activities of life binds them together. This fact is what we are talking about when we say that the employers do not have or do not take the "social responsibility" which ought to go with economic power.

A final characteristic of work done by tenants for their lord was the following: besides fulfilling an immediate economic end, it was also an occasion for a pleasant social gathering. Sometimes indeed the economic end in view may have been almost incidental to the company to be enjoyed. When in an old-time New England town a family held a bee, calling in the neighbors to help in some special piece of work, the party was by all accounts among the most enjoyable of the farmer's year. The work to be done was little more than an excuse for holding the bee. In any backward farming community much of the work has these characteristics. It must be done in coöperation and is enjoyable as a gathering of company. So it was in English villages of the thirteenth century. The benes of harvest must have come near to New England bees as occasions for society. Then a whole village, young men and old, freemen and villeins, was called out to reap the lord's corn and was rewarded by a dinner given by the lord. But in a modern factory, work and pleasurable social life are conceived to be two different things. There is a proper time for the one and a proper time for the other. Workmen are supposed to go to the factory to work, not to enjoy the society of their fellows. Sometimes they are not even allowed to talk. Conviviality is for after hours.

Villagers can never have been pleased to have to work for the lord, and when the lord was such a one as the Abbot of Halesowen their services became intolerable. But under favorable circumstances, and the present interpretation perhaps has dwelt too much on the favorable circumstances, a villager's work for his lord was customary, was done by him as a member of a strong and recognized community, was often an occasion for pleasant social intercourse, and was accompanied by the sentiment that if the men were doing something for their lord, he was doing something for their advantage as well. In so far as the work was done in this manner, it was well adapted to the sentiments of men, at least in the sense that it was not actively irritating and perhaps also in a much more positive sense. In many modern factories, many of these conditions of work do not exist, and even if they do, management sometimes does not recognize them or thinks it must disapprove of them. To say that the one system is good and the other bad is absurd. Both are at fault, but in different ways. The ancient system was in economic terms inefficient and unproductive. On the other hand, the disregard, under the modern system, of satisfactory social conditions of work may induce irritations and disorders which are dangerous to the stability of society. It is fair to say that nothing has so far been discovered which leads students of human affairs to believe that the good features of the two systems cannot be combined: the high economic flexibility and rationality characteristic of the modern system with the high morale characteristic of the medieval as of other primitive systems. Today, as in the thirteenth century, there is in force a regime of unequal distribution of wealth, accompanied by a particular mythology in terms of which it is described. The system of distribution and its mythology are not independent of the social conditions under which productive work is done, but rather the two are in a state of mutual dependence such that a maladjustment in the social conditions will be one of the causes of an attack on the system of distribution and its mythology.

BOOK IV

FEASTS

CHAPTER XXIII

THE HUSBANDMAN'S YEAR

THE HUSBANDMAN'S YEAR of work and play, as it was in the thirteenth century, can be reconstructed only by piecing together two kinds of information from two different sources.[1] The manorial custumals tell in some detail what the labors of the year were and when they were accomplished. We must assume that at the season when a villein was doing a certain kind of work for his lord, which the custumals relate, he was doing much the same kind of work for himself, which they do not relate. Incidentally they tell the names of the holidays which marked when the different working seasons began and ended. But if we relied only on thirteenth-century records, we should know little about what the husbandman did on these holidays, except in so far as they were feasts of the Church, and this of course is a great exception. We should know much about how he worked, little about how he played. We should know, for instance, that Mayday, under that name, was kept in the thirteenth century; we should not know how it was kept. On such matters our only means of making a guess are the customs now called folklore, and these were first collected and recorded long after the Middle Ages were at an end. One of the first of the folklorists was Thomas Tusser, who included in his *Five Hundred Pointes of Good Husbandrie* a passage describing the plowman's feasting-days, as they were kept in Tusser's time in the middle of the sixteenth century. But most of the work was done no earlier than the nineteenth century, when many of the old customs were falling into decay. If any sort of reconstruction is to be made of the husbandman's year in the thirteenth century, a traditional cycle of holidays, which is known in detail only from collections of the nineteenth century, must be projected upon a traditional cycle of working seasons which is known from contemporary records. This form of reconstruction has obvious weaknesses and is tolerable only for lack of a better. For one thing we are forced to make the assumption that the observance of the different holidays in the nineteenth century was, to a first approximation, the same as the observance of these holidays in the thirteenth. This assumption is hazardous, but it has this justification that, from the rare medieval descriptions which have come down to us, we know that a few of the holidays were kept in the Middle Ages in much the way they were kept several centuries later. What was true of a few is likely to have been true of others.

The husbandman's year, in the thirteenth century as now, was considered to be divided into four seasons, but these did not begin and end at the times they do now. Winter (*yems*) was then the name given to the working season from Michaelmas to Christmas. This was the season of the sowing of wheat and rye; therefore these grains were called winter seed (*semen yemale*). The forty days before Easter were kept in much the way they are now, but the name Lent was loosely given to the whole time from the end of the Christmas holidays to Holy Week. The grains sown in this season — oats, barley, vetches, peas, and beans — were the lenten seed (*semen quadragesimale*). The seasons were divided as the great planting seasons were divided. The time from Hocktide, after Easter Week, to Lammas (August 1) was summer (*estas*). Accordingly a May Queen was also a "summer queen." And the time from Lammas back to Michaelmas again was harvest (*autumpnus*).[2]

Michaelmas (September 29), the feast of St. Michael and all Angels, marked the beginning and ending of the husbandman's year. At that time harvest was over, and the bailiff or reeve of the manor would be making out the accounts for the year. At that time also in a champion village the gaps in the hays would have been opened, and the cattle of the village would be wandering over the stubbles of the crop. But at once after Michaelmas, if not before, the planting of the new field of rye and wheat would begin, the field which had lain fallow during the year past.

During October men would be out on the lands with their oxen and plows, their horses and harrows. In later centuries the custom was to make a feast when the winter sowing was over. Thomas Tusser has his husbandman say to his wife:

> Wife, some time this weeke, if the wether hold cleere,
> an end of wheat sowing we make for this yeere.

Remember you therefore though I doo it not:
  the seede Cake, the Pasties, and Furmentie pot.[3]

Furmentie was a dish made of boiled unground grains of wheat,
with milk, currants, raisins, spices — a favorite at all the plowman's feasts. Tusser speaks of this custom as one of Essex and
Suffolk. In Lincolnshire, too, the custom was for farmers to give
a supper at the end of seedtime, a supper which was there called
hopper-cakes.[4] Hopper-cakes were spiced cakes steeped in ale,
and plainly were named after the hopper or seedlip, hanging
from the husbandman's shoulders, from which he scattered seed
when he sowed.

The sowing of the winter corn field was expected to be done
by All Hallows (November 1) or at least by Martinmas (November 11). Thomas Tusser advised:

> The rye in the ground, while September doth last:
>   October for wheate sowing, calleth as fast.
> What euer it cost thee, what euer thou geue,
>   have done sowing wheate, before halowmas eve.[5]

Or, in the Rochester custumal, there is the following statement
of the services of the tenants of Southfleet, Kent:

They will plow, sow, and harrow twenty-five acres, and will bring seed into
the field at the summons of the reeve at the time when wheat is sown, so that
if anyone is found who has not accomplished this, so much as pertains to his
land, before St. Martin's Eve, he will be in the lord's mercy.[6]

At some time before this date the lord would have called for
the boon plowings of his tenants in order to get his seed into the
ground in good season. And in a champion village, as soon as the
fall sowing was done, the gaps in the hays around the winter
corn field would be closed, and the duty of the hayward, in
guarding them, would begin.

Hallowmas, the feast of All Saints (November 1), was one of
a cycle of four feasts which were ancient in northern Europe.
They were evenly spaced in the year: the other three came at the
beginnings of February, of May, and of August, and all were still
celebrated in the thirteenth century in holidays either of the
Church or of the folk. In an age when men lived by their herds
even more than they did in the Middle Ages, the first of November
was a crucial season, since the cattle would then be driven in from
the summer pastures to winter in the byre. At that time, above

others, the work of evil spirits was to be feared: at Hallowmas
and especially on Halloween witches were abroad and they
had to be propitiated. In primitive society evil spirits are re-
cruited chiefly from the ranks of the dead. Accordingly the
great feast of the beginning of November, when the year entered
its *morte saison*, was a feast in honor of the dead. Such it remained
in spite of the Church, which as a part of its campaign against
heathen practices turned November 1 into a feast in honor
of All Saints, and even the Church did not wholly disregard
the origin of the feast, ascribing the next day, November 2,
to All Souls. All Hallows, and especially Halloween, the night
before, were celebrated, as the other feasts of the ancient cycle
were celebrated, with fires, which have now become merged with
those of Guy Fawkes Day.

By the Anglo-Saxons, November was called the blood-month,
and still in the thirteenth century this was the traditional time
for the slaughtering of cattle.

> At Hallontide, slaughter time entereth in,
>   and then doth the husbandmans feasting begin,

says Tusser.[7] Especially was this work associated with Martinmas
(November 11), which was also the beginning of Advent. People
spoke of Martinmas beef. The catttle had fattened on the pastures all summer. Now the grass was no longer lush, and the
frosts were coming on. Since he did not have a large store of
hay, the husbandman could keep only a certain number of his
beasts in the byre through the winter. The rest he would have
to slaughter. For these reasons November was the proper time
for slaughtering and for salting meat.

After the sowing of the winter corn field, the husbandman
would be likely to turn from the land to the barn, where he would
busy himself with the sheaves of the last harvest. First he
would thresh, that is, separate the ears from the straw, either
beating the corn with the old-fashioned flail which consisted of
two stout sticks bound together with a thong[8] or driving his
oxen over the corn on the threshing floor. Then he would winnow,
that is, separate the grain from the chaff, using a winnowing fan,
or a sheet, or a shovel, or a sieve to cast the corn up into the
air so that the grain would fall apart from the lighter chaff. Such

were the ancient methods of processing grain. Until the ground became stiff with frost, the husbandman might also spend his time giving a preparatory plowing to land which in the spring would be plowed again and sown.

Christmas, with the twelve days that followed through the Epiphany (January 6), was the greatest holiday of the husbandman's year. A husbandman could not take his vacation in the summer, as we do, because summer was the time when he was busiest. He could take it only in the middle of winter, when the fields were drowned with rain or bound with frost, and there was perforce a stoppage of outdoor work. Christmas also came between two distinct farming seasons. The season which had been dominated by the sowing of the winter corn field was over, and the sowing of the spring corn field had not yet begun. Almost everywhere the works which villeins had to do for their lords ceased for the twelve days, and some of the manorial servants were given special perquisites, as that the lord's shepherd was allowed to have the lord's fold on his own land during this time. Men gathered to keep the ancient feast of Yule, which had once marked the turning of the sun to the north and now celebrated the birth of Christ.

Christmas was the time of greatest community good feeling. Cattle, sheep, and swine had just been slaughtered. The harvest was in. Of this plenty the husbandman feasted, without giving a thought to the lean times which might be to come. And the height of this feasting was the dinner which on any proper manor on Christmas Day the lord gave in his hall to all his tenants. "At Christmas," says Tusser, "we banket, the rich with the poor." [9] Perhaps it is better to say that the lord did no more than organize the dinner. Villeins were bound to bear their lord a *look* (gift) against Christmas. They had to brew ale for him, to find for him a customary number of loaves or fowls. These gifts must have furnished the substance of the dinner which the lord gave his men. Indeed a custumal sometimes stated in so many words that the workmen received their *lookmete* only in return for their *look*.[10] In primitive societies such ceremonial exchanges take a much more prominent part in the distribution of wealth than they do in modern civilized societies. One of the best accounts of the Christmas dinner is that which appears in a custumal of 1314 of North Curry, Somerset, a manor of the Dean and Chapter of Wells. There John de Cnappe, with a partner and tenants, held two and a half yardlands. Among the privileges he was to enjoy was the following:

> . . . his *gestum* at Christmas with two others, namely two white loaves, as much beer as they will drink in the day, a mess of beef and of bacon with mustard, one of browis of hen, and a cheese, fuel to cook his food and that of the other tenants of the king's ancient demesne, and to burn from dinner time till even and afterwards, and two candles of assize to burn out while they sit and drink one after the other if they will sit so long, and if he come not he may send three men in his stead, or send for the bread, beef and bacon and two gallons of beer; and the next day immediately after noon his medale with one man, as much beer as he will drink till even. . . .[11]

A browis was a soup or broth of juice of boiled meat, with thickening ingredients. The *medale*, as its name suggests, must have been given by the lord to those of his tenants who had come in summer to mow his meadow. On the same manor, Roger Bat held a fardel of land. He too was entitled to a dinner at Christmas, although, as befitted his lower station, no such respect was paid to him as was paid to John de Cnappe. In the words of the custumal, he was to have:

> . . . *gestum* and medale as before, but he must bring with him to the *gestum* his own cloth, cup and trencher, and take away all that is left on his cloth, and shall have for himself and his neighbors one wastel cut in three for the ancient Christmas game to be played with the same wastel. . . .

What exactly this ancient Christmas game was we do not know, but we do know that games which must have been akin to this one were still being played at Christmas dinners hundreds of years later, for instance the game of King of the Bean.

In many primitive societies, unlike our modern ones, there are definite periods set aside by custom when the rules which ordinarily govern men's behavior become by common consent no longer binding. Whether the licence men enjoy in these periods allows them to obey more whole-heartedly during the rest of the year the conventions of their society we do not know. It may have some such function. In the Middle Ages Christmas was a time of licence. There was plenty to eat and drink, and men partook of it heartily, without another thought for the days before harvest when food might be hard to come by. But Christmas was more than a matter of gluttony. It was the time of the election of the Lords of Misrule, of the Feast of Fools: everyday rules no longer applied. Christmas was an orgy. People seem to have anticipated riots then: some villeins were bound in the twelve nights to serve as waits, to watch about the lord's hall. At Wickham, Essex, a manor of St. Paul's, London, "John Aldred, a customary tenant, was bound with the other tenants of the same rank to provide that one of them should keep watch at the court from Christmas to Twelfthday, and have a good fire in the Hall, one white loaf, one cooked dish (*ferculum coquinae*) and a gallon of ale; and if any damage were done, he that watched was to make it good, unless he had raised the hue and cry for the village to go in pursuit." [12] Evidently trouble was expected to break out at any time. Chaucer, in his description in the *Franklin's Tale* of Janus, the god who faces both to the old year and to the new, gives the tone of the old English Christmas in the most wholesome of old English speech:

> The bittre frostes, with the sleet and reyn,
> Destroyed hath the grene in every yerd.
> Janus sit by the fyr, with double berd,
> And drynketh of his bugle horn the wyn;
> Biforn hym stant brawen of the tusked swyn,
> And "Nowel" crieth every lusty man.

More mysterious, the twelve days of Christmas were the time of the performance of the mummers' play. Whether the play was associated with the sword dance, as it was north of the Humber, or with the celebration of Plow Monday, as it was in parts of the Midlands, or took the special form of the St. George play, as it did in Wessex, one of its constant themes was the killing of one of the actors and his later revival.[13] The mummers' plays, in the forms in which they have come down to us, probably are not older than the sixteenth century, but it is hard to believe that they are not descendants of plays which were performed long centuries earlier, and that the death and revival did not symbolize the message of the season at which they were performed: the death and the coming to life again of all growing things. How far the husbandmen who saw the mummers' plays were aware of this symbolism we cannot tell.

New Year's Day of course was celebrated. In the West Country in the last century, a blackthorn "bush" was lighted and carried across the ridges of newly planted wheat, "the number which can be traversed while the bush remains alight being considered an omen or forecast of the number of successful (farming) months in the year." [14] But much more interesting were the ceremonies which marked the resumption of work after the Christmas holidays. Man's work in the Middle Ages was work in the fields and woman's work was work in the household. Adam was always represented with a spade in his hand and Eve with a distaff, called also in old English a *rock*, and what was true of the father and mother of mankind, that the one delved and the other spun, we must suppose to have been true of most medieval fathers and mothers. The plow or the spade was the badge of man's condition, the rock of woman's.

When men and women took up work again after the greatest holiday of the year, they honored the plow and the rock. January 7, the day after the Epiphany, was called in some places St. Distaff's Day, as Robert Herrick tells us, and *Dives and Pauper*, a fifteenth-century treatise on piety, condemns as men who forsake Holy Church those who practised:

ledyng of the plough about the fire, as for good beginninge of the yere, that they shoulde fare the better all the yere folowynge.[15]

Here the plow, the symbol and most important instrument of husbandry, was joined with the hearth, the symbol and center of family life, to form a powerful magical rite. But more common, perhaps, than these practices were those which in many parts of England marked the first Monday after the Epiphany, called by women Rock Monday and by men Plow Monday.

Plow Monday was kept in the nineteenth century in most of the shires of the North and East.[16] On that day it was the custom for a body of young plowmen, who called themselves the plow-bullocks, to drag about from house to house in the village a plow called the fool plow or white plow. At each house they asked for pennies, and if anyone refused to contribute, they plowed up the land before his door. The plow-bullocks made themselves gay with ribbons, and perhaps cut plows, horses, cats, and dogs out of cloth and sewed them onto their shirts and smocks. Since it was called the white plow, the plow itself must have been decorated. The leader of the plow-bullocks was dressed up as a brazen old woman, who was called Bessy. In the old days she wore a bullock's tail under her gown behind, cut capers, and went about with the money box. In connection with the Plow Monday procession, one form of the mummers' play was sometimes performed, and then Bessy became one of its characters. Another one of the traditional figures was a man who wore a fox's skin as a hood, with the tail hanging down his back. Another was of course the Fool, with his stick and bladder. If the winter was a hard one, threshers carrying their flails, reapers with their sickles, and carters with their gad-whips would go about with the fool plow, and sometimes even the smith, who made the plow irons, and the miller, who ground the corn.

In the nineteenth century, the money gathered by the fool plow went to pay for the entertainment of the bullocks and their band at the tavern. In earlier times in many villages there was a gild of those who were husbandmen. They had a feast on Plow Monday and went about with the white plow. The money they collected went to keep a plow-light burning at the shrine of the gild in the parish church. Sometimes, it seems, the plow itself stood or was hung near the shrine.[17] But aside from all practices of conviviality and Christianity, it is hard not to see Plow Monday as a ceremonial first striking of the ground, such as the Chinese emperors had to perform at the beginning of every year.

No record has so far appeared which proves that Plow Monday, in the form its observance took from Tusser's time on, was kept in the thirteenth century. But there is no reason to believe that it was not: folklore is not commonly the stuff of medieval records, and the practice looks old, so to speak. Among the interesting matters which are revealed by a curious lawsuit concerning Carlton in Lindrick, Notts., is the fact that the men of that village held a plow race on the morrow of the Epiphany.[18] Before the King's Bench in the Easter Term of 1292 came Thomas de Evesham, the parson of Carlton, and complained of Richard de Furneys, lord of the village, and six other men, that on July 22, 1291, they reaped his rye in a field called Persones Breck and depastured his oats by their cattle for a whole week. The lord pleaded that the land was his, and the others said that it was their common pasture. The plaintiff replied that it was the soil and dower of his church. The issue went to an inquest jury of men of the countryside. They found that:

the land is not the several land of Richard, nor of Thomas, nor of the others, but is the common of the whole community of the said vill, and from of old the custom of the vill was and still is that the lord of the vill and the parson and every free man of the vill may come to the said place on the morrow of the Epiphany after sunrise with his plow, and as many ridges as he can cut, with one furrow in each ridge (*et quot seliones trahere poterit unico sulco in quolibet selione*), so many (ridges) may he sow in the year, if he pleases, without asking for licence, provided that he applies no compost; and if he applies compost he may not sow the composted land without the licence of the community of the said vill; and if without licence he sows the composted land, the community may depasture with its beasts the land so sown at whatever time it pleases.

The jury went on to find that the parson had sown both composted and uncomposted land, without licence, and had therefore suffered the penalty: the beasts of the defendants had depastured the land.

The position of the jury was perfectly clear. They regarded the land as common of the whole community of the village. Richard de Furneys' claim that the land was his because he was lord of the manor they brushed aside. They regarded the land also as a kind of *intake* or *innam*, and the fact that it was called a *breck* supports their view. As the common of the village, it would ordinarily be depastured by the beasts of the men of the village, but under certain conditions, which were fixed in the custom of the village, it might be brought under crop. These conditions were that at once after the Christmas holidays, at sunrise on the morrow of the Epiphany — this date links the custom with the practices of Plow Monday — all freemen who wished to take part in the intake gathered there with their plows and raced to see in how many different ridges each could draw a furrow. The ridges which each man had thus marked were those which he might sow in that year. As Maitland, who reported the case, put it: "The custom which would prevent a man from composting the land that he had seized, looks like an attempt to prevent the establishment by an individual of the right to have the same strip year after year." As an intake, the land was outside the part of the village which was regularly tilled. It was to be cropped temporarily and then returned to pasture. Therefore the villagers tried to take care that no one by squatting on the land for a number of years acquired a prescriptive right to it.

But this is just what had happened at Carlton. The jurors had to admit that the parson had sown the land, with or without licence of the village, for fifteen years, in fact ever since he became parson of Carlton. He had found his church seised of it; it was called Persones Breck. Therefore the court gave judgment for the plaintiff, saying that the act of the defendants was a manifest injury and not to be upheld by any bylaw (*quod quidem factum manifeste est iniuriosum et non per aliquod birlawe sustinendum*), and damages were awarded. The tilled land of many a village may have been gradually extended by such a process of bringing intakes permanently under crop.

Though men kept Plow Monday, it is not likely that they did much actual plowing in the cold weather of January. Candlemas (February 2), the feast of the Purification of the Virgin Mary, seems to have been the customary time for the resumption of tillage. Let us recall the state of the fields at this time in a champion village. The field which had lain fallow in the year before had been sown in the fall with winter corn. The field which had been in spring corn was going to lie fallow all the next year. The third field of a three-field village, the field which had been in winter corn in the year before, was going to be sown in the spring with oats, barley, peas, and beans. From the last harvest it had been depastured by the cattle of the village: this had been its "open time." But now, at Candlemas, in any proper village, the cattle would be driven from this field. It would be put "in defence," and the spring plowing would begin. Candlemas was also the customary time for putting meadows in defence, and thereafter cattle would not be suffered on them until hay harvest was over, at Lammas (August 1).[19] Candlemas itself took the place of one of the ancient heathen quarterly feasts, of which the others were Hallowmas, Mayday, and Lammas. Its name came from the custom of carrying candles, which had been blessed, in procession on this day. Women carried candles with them when they went to be churched after childbirth; therefore people carried them in honor of the Purification of the Virgin.

From the great penitential season of the forty days before

Easter, the whole period from the Epiphany to Easter came to be called Lent. Shrove Tuesday — so called because people came to be shriven on the last day before Lent proper; it was also called Fastens E'en — was a time famous throughout England for traditional games and sports. Tusser mentions it, together with Plow Monday, Sheep Shearing, Wake Day, Harvest Home, and the Seed Cake, as one of the holidays especially honored by plowmen. The spring corn sowed in this season was always called *semen quadragesimale*. It was the lenten tilth. Husbandmen expected to have the seed in the ground by Lady Day (March 25), the feast of the Annunciation,[20] or at least by Easter itself.

Lent and Easter were then celebrated with more outward show than they are now in reformed England. During Lent a veil was hung before the sanctuary of the parish church or on the rood screen between the chancel and the nave and kept up until, on the Wednesday of Holy Week, the words of the Passion were read: "And the veil of the Temple was rent in twain." Or it was suffered to fall at a similar point in the service of Good Friday. Crosses and other images were also shrouded, save on Sundays. On Palm Sunday, instead of palms, the parishioneers carried yew or willow twigs in procession after the Host and the Cross around the churchyard. On Good Friday the Cross was unveiled and set down on the steps of the altar, where people came to kiss it, approaching it kneeling and bowing low — the "creeping to the Cross." After this, the Cross and Host were buried, in some temporary receptacle, in a special "Easter Sepulchre" built into the walls of the church, or in a chapel, and candles were set round about. On Easter morning the sepulchre was opened and the Cross and Host carried about the church to the altar. This "visitation of the sepulchre" grew in some places into an elaborate dramatic performance. On Easter Eve, as on the two evenings before, all fires and candles were extinguished in the service of the tenebrae. Then a new fire was ceremonially kindled, and from this the great Paschal candle was lit, which gave light during the watching of the church on Easter Eve.[21] Every rite led the hearts of men with mounting excitement to the mass of Easter morning, the most solemn ceremony of the Catholic Church.

Easter, like Christmas, was a day of exchanges between the lord and his men. As they brought him hens at Christmas, so they brought him eggs at Easter. On large estates, the villeins' eggs came to have economic importance, but it is hard to believe that they had not once been simply a ceremonial present, like the Easter eggs which are given now and were given throughout the Middle Ages. On his part, many a lord gave his men, or at least his manorial servants, a dinner on Easter Day. Easter Week, that is, the week after Easter, together with Whitsun Week and the twelve days of Christmas, were the villein's three long holidays. We must suppose that they were real holidays, that the villein then ceased work on his own lands as well as on the lord's demesne. Easter Week was ended by Hocktide, the second Monday and Tuesday after Easter. What the element *hock* means here is unknown. In the nineteenth century the custom was that on the Monday the women of a village held up and bound all the men they could lay their hands on and kept them captive until they paid a fine to be set free, and on the Tuesday, Hockday proper, the men held up the women in like manner. Hockday was certainly kept in the thirteenth century. It was an important term day, and therefore its name appeared often in the documents of the time, but how it was kept we do not know. We do not know whether its customs in later times were but rudimentary survivals of what Hockday once had been. Comparing Easter with Christmas reveals that the celebration of these great feasts of the husbandman's year fell into a single pattern. They began with a feast of the Church. There followed a week or more in which a villein was set free from working for his lord, and probably in fact all men rested from their labors. Then the end of the vacation and the resumption of work was marked by another festival, which this time was not a feast of the Church but a feast of the folk. This pattern is clear in the celebration of Christmas. It began with the feast of Christmas itself. There followed the twelve days of holiday, and then work began again after Plow Monday. The same pattern was followed at Easter. First came the great feast itself. There followed a week of holiday, and then the resumption of work was marked by a festival of the folk — Hocktide.

Hocktide marked also the beginning of what in the Middle Ages was called summer. In winter, in Lent, and in harvest, there was pressing farm work to be done, but in summer, though there were many different jobs which kept the husbandman busy, none of them were as important as those of the rest of the year and none had to be done under pressure of time. The field which was lying fallow throughout the year would be given a fallow plowing after Easter, and perhaps another, a *rebinatio*, before Midsummer. The growing corn had to be weeded, the sheep sheared, but not until hay harvest did the husbandman's greater worries return. Perhaps this was the reason, together with the joyousness that men feel in summer time, why summer was the season when there were more holidays than at any other time of the year.

As Hallowmas or Martinmas may once have marked the time when the cattle were driven in from the pastures to be kept through the winter in the byres, so Mayday may have marked the time when they were put out to pasture again. There are hints that this was still the tradition in the thirteenth century, at least in Lincolnshire.[22] Such was the economic importance of Mayday. As for Mayday as a holiday, we know that it was kept in the thirteenth century, because the name of the feast appears in documents of that time. And Robert Grosseteste, Bishop of Lincoln, in a letter he wrote in 1244 to his archdeacons, complained of clerks who made "games which they call the Bringing-in of May or of autumn." [23] But just how Mayday was kept in the thirteenth century we do not know. English literature has made familiar to everyone the customs of its observance in later times: how on Mayday the young folk went out early in the morning and brought in sprays of the blossoming hawthorn, with which they dressed their houses, how the handsomest girl of the village was crowned with flowers as the May Queen, the summer queen, how the maypole was set up and garlanded with flowers and the girls and boys danced around it.

In the later Middle Ages, May was the time of the performance of the Morris Dance and the Robin Hood Games, but again we know little of the "somour games" of the thirteenth century. Clearly they resembled in part those of later times. In his constitutions of 1240, Walter de Cantilupe, Bishop of Worcester, forbade "games to be made of a king and a queen" [24] — there must have been a lord and lady of the May in those days as afterward. The very games of the folk imitated the aristocratic organization of society. Again, Robert Mannyng of Brunne condemned the following method of breaking the Sabbath:

> ȝf þou euer yn felde, eyþer in toune,
> Dedyst floure-gerland or coroune
> To make wommen to gadyr þere,
> To se whych þat feyrer were;
> Þys ys aȝens þe commaundement,
> And þe halyday for þe ys shent;
> Hyt ys a gaderyng for lecherye,
> And ful grete pryde, & herte hye.[25]

Such a game must have been very like the May game of later centuries. Sometimes a scene of happy riot appears for a moment in the midst of a sober legal document. The record of one of the Gloucestershire inquests which is included among the Hundred Rolls tells the story of certain men who:

came where boys and girls were carolling for doves, and one boy said that one of the girls carolled well, and he gave her doves, but this being heard by Nicholas Calf and Thomas le Prute, who put up (*posuerunt*) the doves, they said that he lied and that she should not have the doves, and beat said boy over the head with a certain cudgel.[26]

Carolling was one of the sins which the more puritanical clergy-men denounced throughout the Middle Ages, and setting a prize for competition between the girls was a part of other "somour games," but we are told nothing about this particular game of carolling for doves.

The clergy spoke of the dances and carollings as "gatherings for lechery," but the specific charges they made about what happened at these games are harmless enough. Perhaps such men were too respectable to state the facts which would make their insinuations good. Mayday was a festival of the boys and girls of a village. There are many hints that it was the traditional time of love-making, when every Jill chose her Jack, and, as we know, a young couple in those days were likely to be bedded before they were wedded. Sometimes the boys and girls would go out of the village to bring in the May not on the morning of Mayday but on the evening before, and would spend the night afield.

> Between the acres of the rye,
>> With a hey, and a ho, and a hey nonino,
> These pretty country folks would lie,
>> In the spring time . . .

This is the most interesting thing about Mayday, and of course the one about which pious people had least to say.

The second of the feasts of the Maytime consisted of the Rogation Days, the Monday, Tuesday, and Wednesday before Ascension (Holy Thursday). Under the name of the Gangdays, they were kept in the days before the Norman Conquest,[27] and they were kept under the same name a thousand years later.[28] They were called Gangdays because people went a-ganging then. Led by the priest and carrying the Cross, banners, bells, and lights, the men of a village went in perambulation about the boundaries of the village. They beat its bounds. The small boys who went with the procession were thrown into the brooks and ponds or had their buttocks bumped against the trees and rocks which marked the bounds, so that they should remember them the better. And at certain customary points in the ganging, at every "Holy Oak or Gospel Tree" the procession stopped, and the priest offered up prayers and blessed the growing crops. The Rogation Days were devoted to special supplications for the forgiveness of sin and for the protection of the fruits of the earth: primitive people do not expect their economic activities to be successful unless they themselves have observed the morality of the community. The Gangdays were peculiarly a festival of the champion country. There, no one held his land in one compact plot, but every villager had a bundle of strips scattered over all the fields of the village and used its woods and wastes in common with his neighbors. The bounds of his village were the most important bounds he knew.

The third of the feasts of the Maytime was Whitsunday, the feast of the Pentecost. With Christmas and Easter, it was one of the three great feasts of the church year, and on most manors villeins did not have to work for their lords in Whitsun week.

In June, at some time before St. John's Day, the husbandman

would drive his sheep to the nearest pond or stream, wash them, and then shear them. After the sheep-shearing, he would hold a supper for the men who had worked for him. Thomas Tusser's husbandman orders his wife thus:

> Wife make vs a dinner, spare flesh neither corne,
> make wafers and cakes, for our sheepe must be shorne.
> At sheepe shearing neighbours none other thing craue,
> but good cheere and welcome like neighbours to haue.[29]

The fullest, most famous, and most charming of the descriptions of English sheep-shearing feasts is the fourth act of Shakespeare's *Winter's Tale*.

The summer counterpart of Christmas was Midsummer, the feast of the Nativity of St. John the Baptist, June 24. A book of sermons on the different feast days, written in the thirteenth century by a monk of Winchcomb, describes how St. John's Day was kept in that time. Or better, it describes how the even of St. John's was kept. The exciting part of this festival, like so many of the festivals of the folk, took place on the night before. The monk wrote as follows of St. John's Eve:

Let us speak of the revels which are accustomed to be made on St. John's Eve, of which there are three kinds. On St. John's Eve in certain regions the boys collect bones and certain other rubbish, and burn them, and therefrom a smoke is produced on the air. They also make brands and go about the fields with the brands. Thirdly, the wheel which they roll.[30]

The monk explained the fires as designed to drive away the dragons which were believed to be abroad on St. John's Eve, poisoning the springs and other waters. Each of these observances was maintained in much later times: the fact that in a few instances like this of St. John's Eve the practices of the festivals of the husbandman's year can be proved to have been the same in the thirteenth as they were in the nineteenth century gives us the better reason to assume that there was a similar continuity in the larger number of instances in which it cannot be proved. Bonfires are still lit on Midsummer Eve on hilltops in many parts of the British Isles, and not long ago brands were carried around the fields on that night. There is independent evidence that the latter custom was observed in the thirteenth century. One of the services which Geoffrey Salferloc, a cotsetle of Longbridge,

Wilts., owed his lord, the Abbot of Glastonbury, was the following:

Whether this Geoffrey be plowman or harrower, he ought, together with the other holders of such tenements, to watch with the hayward on St. John's Eve at the end of the lord's tilth and to partake with them of one wether and to have one branch of the lord's wood for fire on that night.[31]

The wether must have been for the watchers' supper. The wheel which the monk of Winchcomb said was rolled on Midsummer Eve must have been like those wheels which later observers of the customs of the folk in many parts of Europe reported as being set afire on that night and sent rolling down the hills. And his explanation of the custom is the one which is always given. He said:

The wheel is rolled to signify that the sun then rises to the highest point of its circle and at once turns back; thence it comes that the wheel is rolled.

St. John's Day, like Christmas, was a feast of the solstice.[32]
    At St. John's Day, farm work again became pressing, and thereafter until the end of harvest on many manors the number of days a week a villein had to work for his lord increased. St. John's Day was the traditional time to begin hay harvest. Says Tusser:

> At Midsommer, downe with the brembles and brakes,
>   and after, abrode with thy forks and thy rakes:
> Set mowers a mowing, where meadow is growne,
>   the longer now standing the worse to be mowne.[33]

From St. John's until nearly Lammas the husbandmen must have been busy making hay: mowing, tossing, cocking, and stacking. At the end of hay-making, the game would be held in which a sheep was put out in the field among the mowers for them to have if they could catch it. Or the lord would allow the men who had mowed his meadow to have a *sithale*. At Lammas (August 1) hay harvest was expected to be over, and at that time the meadows were thrown open for the cattle of the village to crop what was left after mowing. On such meadows, which were called Lammas meadows, there can have been no rowen.
    As Lammas marked the end of hay harvest, so it marked the beginning of corn harvest. According to the church calendar,

Lammas was the feast of St. Peter *ad Vincula*, but its importance was clearly derived not from this circumstance but from its being a turning point in the year of husbandry. In the time before Lammas many a poor cotter must have run through his store of flour and must have been eagerly awaiting the harvest. In *Piers Plowman*, Piers speaks of how little food he has, and then says:

> By þis lyflode we mote lyue · tyl lammasse tyme;
> And by þat, ich hope to haue · heruest in my crofte.[34]

And after that he was going to live well. Lammas, if the harvest was a good one, must have been a joyful time indeed. Lammas was a feast of first fruits. It derived its name from the Anglo-Saxon *hlaf-mass*, that is, loaf-mass. On that day, in the time before the Conquest, bread, which must have been made from the new wheat, was brought into the churches and blessed, and this hallowed bread was used afterwards in magic.[35]

Though harvest was the season of the year when everyone, young or old, man or woman, had to work hardest, yet the very circumstance that everyone who could be spared from other work was in the fields must have made it a time of company, and the many traditional sports and gifts of harvest helped the work to go forward cheerfully. From the manorial custumals we know something about the harvest benes, the bidreaps. At these bidreaps all the villagers were called out to reap the lord's corn, except, as the custumals sometimes specify, the housewife, the shepherd, or the nurse of each household. The workers were given their dinner of herrings or flesh, with bread and cheese and perhaps ale. And over the workers at the harvest benes were set the substantial freeholders, the franklins, with rods in their hands, to see that the work was done well and properly. Of the other customs of harvest in the thirteenth century we know little or nothing. In later centuries and in large households, a harvest lord was named to lead the reapers and perhaps also a harvest lady to be second sickle. The reapers worked in teams along the ridges, some to reap and others behind them to bind and shock the sheaves. On the last day of reaping the teams liked to race to see which should be the first to finish a ridge. The last patch of corn would be left standing to be cut with some ceremony. Perhaps the handsomest girl would cut it, or the reapers would throw their sickles at it until all had fallen. The last sheaf would be decorated and placed on top of the hock-cart, the last wain that carried corn to the barn. Then the hock-cart would be brought in with music and merriment, and in the evening afterward the harvest home supper would be held.[36] Says Tusser:

> In haruest time, haruest folke, seruants and all
> should make all togither good cheere in the hall:
> And fill out the black boule of bleith to their song,
> and let them be merie all haruest time long.[37]

Thus, at the end of the thirteenth century, the men of Headington, Oxon., were bound to come to the lord's court between Michaelmas and Martinmas "with a full dittany, as they hitherto were accustomed to do." They must have come to sing harvest home.[38] But after feasting his men, the master still was not free. To quote Tusser again:

> For all this good feasting, yet art thou not loose,
> till ploughman thou giuest his haruest home goose.
> Though goose go in stubble, I passe not for that,
> let goose haue a goose, be she leane, be she fat.[39]

The goose was a stubble goose because it had battened on the stubbles of the harvest. It was a descendant of the *repegos* which in the thirteenth century was either given in fact or commuted for a money payment. After harvest had been carried, the poor people who wished to glean would be allowed on the stubbles, which would afterwards be opened to the village herds. With Michaelmas, the cycle of the year began again.

Only one of the plowman's feasting days remains, the one which was commonly called the wake day. Most of the holidays were wakes, in the sense that men kept the night before the feast. To farmers as to children, since both are used to going to bed early, staying up late is a special treat. But the feast now considered was the wake specially so-called. In theory, the wake was the feast of the saint to whom the parish church was dedicated. On this day, any congregations which had been formed by separation from an older parish went in procession to honor the mother church. Robert Grosseteste, Bishop of Lincoln, in 1236 ordered his archdeacons to forbid:

that in the processions in the yearly visit and honoring of the mother church any parish fight to go before another parish with its banners, since thereof are accustomed to arise not brawls only, but cruel bloodshed.[40]

If wake days had always been kept on the days of the saints to whom the parish churches were dedicated, they would have been scattered all over the year. In fact most wakes came in the late summer and early fall. Bishop White Kennett spoke of this fact in his *Parochial Antiquities* (1695). He said:

For among the injunctions of King Henry VIII, An. 1536, it was order'd, that the dedication of Churches should in all places be celebrated on the first Sunday of the month October for ever. Yet this order was not inforc'd, or not obey'd; but however most of those Jubilees are now celebrated near the time of Michaelmas, when a vacation from the labours of harvest and the plough, does afford the best opportunity for visits and sports; so at Pidington and other places in this county (Oxfordshire). . . . But as to those Wakes which are precedent to Michaelmas, or distant from that time: these we may believe have continued in their primitive relation to their proper Saint, and no farther remov'd than to the immediate Sunday following.[41]

We know that wakes were held in the thirteenth century, because in *La Court de Baron*, a manual of that period on the manner of holding hallmotes, a model case is included in which a man who was charged with slaying his lord's pig was unable to wage his law because his oath-helpers were at the feast of another village.[42] But how the wake was kept in the thirteenth century we do not know, and we must be content with the customs recorded for later times. Then, as on the other *vigilyes*, people stayed up the night before, and on the morning of the wake day went to a mass in honor of the patron saint of the parish church. After mass the day was eminently given up to sports, which were commonly held in the churchyard of the parish church, in spite of the execrations which bishops throughout the Middle Ages addressed to those who made the churchyard a place of games and markets. Less often they were held on hilltops, by the sides of wells, or near some large tree or stone.[43] We may suppose that the wake went back to some heathen festival, and that the Church had tried to make it respectable, if it could not be destroyed, by linking it to one of her own rites. But in some places the wakes were still held in the holy places of the heathen.

Thomas Tusser has his husbandman say to his daughter:

> Fill ouen full of flawnes, Ginnie passe not for sleepe,
>   to morow thy father his wake day will keepe.
> Then euerie wanton may daunce at hir will,
>   both Tomkin with Tomlin, and Jankin with Gill.[44]

A flawn was a kind of pancake. A wake day was filled with dances, games, and drunkenness; in later days there was much of the favorite sports of wrestling and grinning through a horse-collar for a prize. On wake days, too, a village entertained its neighbors. The dates of the wakes were so arranged that the wake of one village did not conflict with that of another village nearby.[45] And since the countryside gathered to wakes, some of them in the course of time became important fairs. A wake seems also to have been an occasion when people who had left a village came back to visit their kinsmen and friends. William Warner, in *Albion's England*, speaks of "our wakes twixt Eames and Sibbes." The English wakes corresponded to the *kermesse* of the continent: in this respect as in so many others the holidays of the folk throughout Europe were more alike than we might guess from the present differences of the European nations. The wake must have been peculiarly a feast of the big villages of the champion country. It presupposed a certain amount of village consciousness. At a wake, a village celebrated its identity, so to speak, and invited the neighboring villages to join in the celebration.

William Warner's charming description of the countryman's year as it was in the sixteenth century may properly bring this long account to a close. He supposes a northern man to be speaking:

> At Ewle we wonten gambole, daunce, to carrole, and to sing,
> To haue gud spiced Sewe, and Roste, and plum-pies for a King,
> At Fasts-eue pan-puffes, Gang tide gaites did alie masses bring,
> At Paske began our Morrisse, and ere Penticost our May,
> Tho Roben Hood, liell Iohn, Frier Tucke, and Marian deftly play,
> And Lard and Ladie gang till Kirke with Lads and Lasses gay:
> Fra Masse and Eensong so gud cheere and glee on ery Greene,
> As, saue our wakes twixt Eames and Sibbes, like gam was neuer seene:

At Baptis-day with Ale and cakes bout bon-fires neighbours stood,
At Martlemass wa turnd a crabbe, thilke told of Roben hood,
Till after long time myrke, when blest were windowes, dares & lights,
And pails were fild, & hathes were swept, gainst Fairie-elues & sprits:
Rock, & plow Mondaies gams sal gang, with saint-feasts & kirk-sights."[46]

Polybius and Machiavelli — the one after personal observation
and the other after a study of history — have expressed their
opinion that the Roman religion was valuable in giving rise to
well regulated conduct.[47] But many other religions which have
existed and still exist are more like the Roman religion than a
set of camp-meetings, and it is probable that they have had in
greater or lesser degree a like good effect on the behavior of men.
Indeed, this statement is proved by what happens when such a
religion is destroyed. Many observers have testified that when
contact with white men has undermined the system of magical
and other ceremonies which once accompanied the daily work
of a primitive people, the primitives become lazy and shiftless.
They seem to lose the interest they once took in work. The old
Roman religion was what may be called a religion of ritual.
That is, it consisted of a set of acts, to be carried out in a particular way on particular occasions, and little attempt was made
to explain in a theology why these acts were performed. Of the
religious practices of the Middle Ages, those which conformed
most closely to this model were the ceremonies of the folklore
year. People maintained them through many centuries and do
not seem to have offered any reason for doing so other than
custom. More important, though not from the present point
of view more religious than the folklore practices, were the
ceremonies of the Christian year. Catholic worship in the Middle
Ages was made up of many elements, but it consisted at least,
like the Roman religion and the rites of folklore, of sets of acts
to be carried out in a particular way on particular occasions.
True, unlike the other two cults, the liturgy was given meaning
by an elaborate theology. Only a few educated men, however,
were familiar with theology in detail: the common people
venerated the mass and the other ceremonies of the church to a
certain extent as magic, especially as they were conducted in an
unknown language.

Husbandry has always been full of uncertainties. When a

farmer has done the best he can to see that his fields are properly tilled and his cattle properly tended, he is still not sure of a crop or of the increase of his herds. Bad weather or a murrain may overwhelm him. His technique of work is not such that he can count upon getting the results he desires. In this situation he feels a sentiment which we call anxiety. This statement will have to be qualified later, but it remains true in any case that people like ourselves who live in a civilization which has achieved an extraordinary power of control over its environment have little appreciation of the anxiety, fear, even terror which often possesses the mind of primitive peoples. Of course the fear becomes generalized beyond the actual dangers of famine, disease, or warfare, and the world becomes populated with evil spirits. *Primus in orbe deos fecit timor*. And over against the evil spirits, men cling with a fiercer intensity to everything protective and sustaining — the society they live in, its customs, its rituals. A dualism of good and evil is native to the primitive mind. The men of the thirteenth century in England were not primitives but they kept something of the emotional attitudes of primitives.

Men have a tendency to express their sentiments in actions. The word *sentiment* is used here in its most general sense of any psychological state.[48] What we actually observe is, of course, the overt behavior of men. That they have certain sentiments which lead them to behave as they do is no more than a hypothesis, but it is a hypothesis which is very old and has probably never got anyone into trouble. The tendency to express sentiments in actions is one of the traits men share with the other animals. Dogs express their sentiments in actions — by wagging their tails. The actions in which men express their sentiments of anxiety are often called magic. Such actions take the place of the logical, practical actions, unknown to men or beyond their powers, which would have insured their getting the results they desire. The truth of this statement is shown by the fact that men do not perform magical actions if their techniques are such that they are sure of getting these results. In one island of Melanesia, there is a lagoon within the arms of the island, and beyond the lagoon the open sea. The technique the natives use of fishing in the shallow waters of the lagoon is such that they are practically sure of making a catch, and they perform no magic in connection with this fishing. But when they fish in the open sea they are far from sure of making a catch, and with this fishing there is associated an elaborate magic.[49] Magic is not performed unless there is some anxiety about securing a desired practical result.

The expression *logical actions* has been used. By logical actions are meant those actions which appear both to the men who perform them and to a detached observer efficacious means to the end in view. The actions may not be the most efficient means, but they are means of some sort. The agricultural experts of the eighteenth century condemned the techniques of medieval husbandry as inefficient; they never claimed that these techniques would not do for lack of better ones. Non-logical actions are all other actions. Clearly many of the practices of the husbandman's year were non-logical in this sense. They were magic. We need only recall the customs of the New Year and the Gang Days. It is true that, besides behaving in certain ways, men like to talk about their behavior, and they may say that the non-logical actions they perform are in fact efficacious means to the end in view and may even explain why they are efficacious. In the Middle Ages a man who led his plow about the fire on New Year's Day may have said that this action insured his being lucky all the year following. He may even have believed it, though we probably do not know what we are talking about when we talk of belief. But the verbal explanations of non-logical actions, if only because they are so much more variable than the actions themselves, are more usefully considered as phenomena of the second order, as rationalizations.

Since the forms of non-logical actions are not determined, as are the forms of logical actions, by the nature of a practical result which must be accomplished, these actions can take forms which are determined only by the sentiments and fancies of men. They may be spells: we must include this use of words within non-logical action. They may be rites, and several common intellectual motives of rites are recognized, sympathies and antipathies, for instance. Another common motif is the following: men employ in magic objects which are of great importance to them in their day-by-day lives. In the Middle Ages men used the plow in this way, setting it up in a shrine in the parish church or dragging it about the fire for a good beginning of the year.

The performance of magic both arises out of the sentiments of men and reacts upon them. The mere execution of a magical action eases the anxiety of a husbandman or, as we might say, works it off. He feels that he must "do something"; he does something — no matter what — and he feels better. But the effect of the performance of magic is seldom as simple as this. The husbandman not only performs the magic but while he performs it he believes that it will help him win a good crop. The performance reassures him, gives him confidence in his work. But at this point a qualification must be introduced. What has gone before is a theory of the origin and function of magical rites, not a description of the behavior of men as they are observed to perform the rites. If at one time husbandmen felt anxious because their techniques were not certain to produce the results they desired, and performed magical rites which had the function of working off the anxiety, what is now in fact observed is that they feel anxiety only when the customary rites themselves are not duly performed. And their anxiety is extended far beyond the rites: they feel that unless all the moralities of the society are observed, husbandry will suffer. God will visit their sins upon his people. Rites of purification may be performed to allay the secondary anxiety which arises from a breach of custom. Instead of saying that the husbandman does worry, it is better to say that he would worry and the worry might hamper his work, if there were not some regular way, preferably in the reassuring company of his fellows, by which he might accomplish magical rites. The fact that he had a recognized method of manifesting in actions of this sort his sentiments of uncertainty may have been one ingredient in the well known fatalism of the tiller of the soil. One observer has said of the Polish peasant: "The fact is that when the peasant has been working steadily, and has fulfilled the religious and magical ceremonies which tradition requires, he 'leaves the rest to God,' and waits for the ultimate results to come; the question of more or less skill and efficiency of work has very little importance." [50]

The sentiments of anxiety to which men give expression in the rites of magic would have led them, if their techniques had been well enough developed, to logical actions having a practical effect on the environment. But there are some sentiments which cannot in any case lead to such practical action. Among them are the sentiments connected with the changing seasons, with hard work well done, with the winning of a good harvest. To all these sentiments the sports and revels of the husbandman's year gave expression. The form of their expression, to be sure, was not like that of the sentiments of anxiety. It was rather convivial than magical.

The rites of magic and the festivities of the seasons are not observed to be performed at random. They are a matter of custom; they have a calendar. By the thirteenth century the sequence of the husbandman's feast days had become well adapted to the sequence of the works of the year. The greater feasts fell in the interstices between the farming seasons, when one kind of work had been finished and another not yet begun. Thus Christmas came after a season dominated by the sowing of the winter corn field had ended and before the sowing of the spring field had begun, Easter at the end of the spring sowing, and the wake commonly between harvest and the fall plowing. This arrangement is the natural one, if only for the reason that men must have leisure for sport and ceremony. As for the lesser feasts, many of them had become linked with a particular kind of farm work. Thus Martinmas was the traditional time for slaughtering, and Candlemas the traditional time for putting meadows in defence. The works of the year and its festivals intermeshed to make a single and stable cycle.

Since husbandmen formed at least nine-tenths of the population, this traditional year governed the behavior of most men and was represented as common to all. A part of the scheme of decoration of many a cathedral was a series of capitals or other sculptures picturing the works of the months and sometimes the pleasures as well. For January, for instance, Janus would be shown sitting by the fire with double beard and drinking of his horn, for May, a woman offering to a man a spray of foliage, for July, a scene of mowers, and for September, a man holding a sickle in his right hand and a handful of corn in his left.[51]

The year of work and play remained a single and customary

cycle for centuries after 1300 and had been that for centuries before. Of the process by which this stable adaptation was reached we know little but can infer much. We must assume that, when the people of western Europe were converted to Christianity, the cycle of heathen festivals was already well geared to the traditional farming year. Such of these festivals as the Church felt were incompatible with her teachings or her supremacy and was able to suppress, she did suppress. These, it is likely, were few. The larger number she took over for her own uses and gave them at least a veneer of Christianity. Often this process was only a matter of words. A feast which had once been kept in honor of some heathen god was now said to be kept in honor of a Christian saint or anniversary, while the practices of the feast remained very much what they had always been. Christmas must have taken the place of a much more ancient feast of the solstice, and many of the customs of Christmas remained scandalously heathen. Other holidays may have seemed more important in the eyes of a plowman than they did in the eyes of a member of a cathedral chapter — Lammas, for example, the feast of St. Peter *ad Vincula*. Others, such as Mayday, were never rationalized as feasts of the Church, and a few others may have been wholly feasts of the Church in origin — Easter, perhaps, but even Easter bears the name of an Anglo-Saxon goddess.

A set of rites, like those of the husbandman's year in the thirteenth century, which were to be performed in a particular way at particular times, has then a further function. The tyranny of the weather forces a husbandman to get certain pieces of work done on time if he is to survive. Fall planting must be finished before the ground freezes. Hay must be harvested with dispatch for fear of rain. The customary calendar of festivals helped insure that such things were accomplished, because the proper times of beginning or ending many kinds of farm work were linked with the neighborhood of definite Christian feasts or saints' days. Such associations made it perfectly plain to a man and to his neighbors when he was late with his work, and gave the neighbors an excuse for laughing at him for it. They also allowed a man to get through the routines of the year to some extent without taking thought, simply by doing the customary things at the customary times. Of course, since the weather varies somewhat from year to year, such dates fixed in the religious calendar may never be perfectly adapted to economic conditions. Indeed the mild climate of England allows husbandmen considerable latitude in choosing when the labors of the year are to be performed. The important point is that the adaptation was good enough, and the work got done.[52]

A religion of ritual, like that of the Catholic Church in the Middle Ages, gives rise to well regulated conduct in at least two ways. It gives men's feelings of helplessness and those linked with the changing seasons adequate and orderly social expression. And it helps insure that the routines of life are carried on in the usual manner, since these routines are tied to the festival calendar.

CHAPTER XXIV

THE PARISH CHURCH

WHEN A MAN DESCRIBES a society which is not his own, he often leaves out those features which the society has in common with his own society. He takes them for granted, and so his description is distorted. For instance, few anthropologists make anything of the fact that something like the ten commandments is established in every society, though experience shows that such constant factors in phenomena are important factors: if the temperature of your body varies so little as one degree from normal you are probably sick. The Church is one of the features which our own society has in common with the Middle Ages. The functions she performed then were in part the same as those she performs now and those other churches have performed in other times and places. They were of great importance and cannot be disregarded. But the organs of the Church were many: the hierarchy, the monasteries, the friars, and the rest, and only one of them was intimately related to village life. That was the parish.

Indeed the parish was the village. Especially in champion country, the parish commonly coincided with the village and not with any of the manors which might divide the village between them. The boundaries of the parish were the boundaries of the village, so that today, when the villages in their old form have disappeared, the parish boundaries are held to be good evidence of the former village boundaries. But common bounds were only the outward sign of something much more important which parish and village had in common: the congregation of the parish church was the body of all the villagers. The men who worked together worshipped together.

The French have a phrase "the spirit of the steeple" which they use when they speak of a man whose interests and sentiments do not run beyond his local community. They mean that the heart of a village has always been the parish church, if only for the reason that the houses of the villagers cluster around it. According to the ancient custom of England, part of the fabric and furniture of the church was maintained by the parishioners. They were bound to keep the nave in good repair, while the rector's province was the chancel. As priest and people stood in different parts of the church during services, so they divided the responsibility of its care. A decree of Robert Winchelsea, Archbishop of Canterbury, specified what objects of church furniture the parishioners were bound to provide. Among these objects were:

a bell to be borne with the Body of Christ in visiting the sick, a pyx for the Body of Christ, a proper Lenten veil, a banner for the Rogation Days, bells with ropes, a bier for the dead, a vessel for holy water, a pax, a candelabrum for the Easter candle, a font with a lock, images in the church, a principal image in the chancel.[1]

A word of comment on these articles of church furniture: the bells in the church tower were an important part of the equipment of any church, because they told the villagers scattered far about in the open fields not only when the different rites were being celebrated but also when any alarm had been raised or news had arrived. The bells were even used to regulate the observance of harvest bylaws: villagers might be allowed in the pease field only "between bell and bell." The font had to be kept locked for fear that the holy water would be stolen for use in witchcraft.[2] The principal image in the chancel was the image of the saint to whom the church was dedicated.[3] It probably stood at the side of the altar. Another important feature of the furnishing of a church was a light to be kept lit while divine service was celebrated. Plots of land were given by pious people for the endowment of the light in the church, or the parishioners paid a small tax to support it.[4] In later centuries the business of raising and spending funds for the maintenance of the fabric of the parish church was in the hands of elected churchwardens, who came to have other functions in local government besides, but nothing is heard of churchwardens before the end of the thirteenth century.[5]

Today, in most English villages, the parish church is the only building that has come down from medieval times. Being built of stone and solidly put together, it was on occasion many things besides the House of God. It was a storehouse, a courthouse, a prison, a fort. It was the strong place of the village. For instance, the Hundred Rolls tell of one Shropshire inquest jury which found as follows:

that Alice of Haughmond, dwelling at Burton, was indicted in the great Hundred of Condover because she broke into Burton church and carried off the cloths of Richard of Bath.[6]

And a Lincolnshire inquest found as follows:

that a certain felon was in Fosdyke church, by whose stay the township was much burdened, so that the township went to said Simon, the coroner, and offered him a half-mark to come and take said felon from the church, and he would not come unless they would give him one mark, and thus he (the felon) stayed in the church for forty days by the fault of the coroner.[7]

Or we read how in 1293 a violent attack, with injuries amounting to bloodshed, was made in the church of Easton on Master H. de Rowadon, the rector there, as he was about to celebrate divine service. He had been besieged in the church for more than four days, the besiegers refusing him food. As usual, the record leaves out the most interesting part of the story by giving no reason why the attack was made.[8]

Around the church lay the churchyard. In spite of the prohibitions of bishop after bishop, the churchyard throughout the Middle Ages was used for many purposes besides that of a burying-ground. Here was the common gathering place of all the villagers, whether they stayed to gossip after mass on Sundays or came to learn any news of general importance. According to a Northamptonshire inquest of 1246, a certain M. de Meht had found a flayed doe in the king's forest, together with a snare. This was good evidence of poaching, and the record says:

He went to the church of Sudborough and let the whole township know what had happened.[9]

Here in the churchyard, in summer after evensong, the girls of the village gathered to dance and carol. Here fairs and markets were held and even the sports of the wake. Here, too, the villagers were united in death as life. On the sunny south side of the churchyard lay the villagers who had died in the bosom of the Church; on the dark north, the suicides.

The ordinary revenues of a parish in the Middle Ages derived from several sources. The most important source was that of the tithes. In theory the rector had the right to take one tenth of the whole yearly income of every man in the village: one tenth of his corn harvest, one tenth of the increase of his cattle, one tenth of the produce of his garden, one tenth even of his wages, if he were a laborer. If his hens had produced ten chickens in the course of a year, one of them should have gone to the parson. And so on. In practice certain kinds of tithes were not easily collected and certain kinds brought in much more revenue than others. The "great tithes" were the tithes of crops and cattle; the "lesser tithes" were the others. In some villages, the rector took every tenth sheaf of the harvest; in others he still took his tithes in the thirteenth century as his predecessors had taken them in the tenth, "as the plow traversed the tenth acre." [10] That is, he took the crop of every tenth acre of a man's tilth. Another important source of the revenue of a parish was the land in the village which belonged to the church — the glebe. The amount of the glebe varied considerably from village to village: on the Glastonbury manors, the glebe lands varied in size from a half-hide to three acres, for which the parsons rendered rents and services to the lord.[11] We read of parsons who had tenants under them, and even of one, the parson of Aylesbury, Bucks., who held the View of Frankpledge and the assizes of bread and ale,[12] but many a parson must have tilled his glebe with the sweat of his own brow. He was deep in the husbandry of the village. The third source of the revenue of a parish was the altarage, that is, the customary oblations parishoners made on important occasions, for instance, when they buried their kinsmen or communicated on one of the great feast days. Many a bishop declared roundly that priests compelled poor people to make oblations, a practice which came perilously close to the crime of selling the sacraments.[13] Lastly, in many parts of England, the rector of the parish took as a mortuary the second best beast of every deceased villein. The best beast, of course, went to the lord of the manor. The assumption was that the dead man during his lifetime must have avoided paying some of his tithes. The mortuary made good his default.

Besides supporting himself, the rector had several obligations to meet out of the revenues of his parish. He had the duty of giving alms and hospitality to the poor. According to tradition, one third of his income ought to have gone for this purpose; actually he must have spent much less. He also had the duty of maintaining in good repair the chancel of the church, the part which was peculiarly his domain. Then, too, if the parish was a populous one, the rector would have to pay the wages of a number of lesser clergymen, usually in minor orders but sometimes priests. One of them might be a chaplain, who assisted in the parish church or served the chapels attached to it. Another might be a holy-water clerk, who took care of the church, read the epistle and the responses, carried holy water. He might serve at the same time as the parish clerk, and in some villages his wages were found by the body of the parishioners.[14] The *beneficium aquae benedictae* was a means of providing for a poor student who was going to take orders.[15] These clerks may all have lived together at the rectory.

If they had not been diverted in some part to other ends, the revenues of most parishes would have been large enough to meet these demands and provide the rectors with good livings as well. But the rector might go off to a university, to court, or to some other congenial dwelling place, instead of residing in his parish and doing its work himself. Then he would hire a vicar to take his place: the word *vicarius* means literally a substitute. Or he would put the parish out at farm to a religious house or a single clerk. The rest of the revenues he would keep for his own support. Before he left his parish, the rector had to secure the permission of his bishop, but permission was easily given to those younger sons, men of gentle birth, who held so many of the rich livings of England. If this practice was one means of endowing university education — and many of the ablest clergymen of the Middle Ages were supported in this way while they were studying or teaching — it was also a means of maintaining wastrels in a soft life.

Or the benefice might have become appropriated to a religious house.[16] The twelfth and thirteenth centuries, particularly the former, were the time of the great enthusiasm for founding religious houses, and there were two common ways in which a rich layman could contribute to the endowment of his favorite house. He could make it a grant of land to be held in frankalmoin. According to this tenure, the only feudal duty which the grantee owed the grantor in return for holding the land was the duty of giving alms to the poor. Or he could give the house a benefice. Most people know that the advowson of a parish in England was the right to name a priest as rector whenever the living fell vacant. To use the customary phrase, it was the right to present a priest to the living. And the patron of the church, the man who held the advowson, was commonly the chief landholder of the parish, the lord of the manor. Some patrons made their advowsons a source of profit to themselves by accepting gifts from priests who hoped for preferment. But let us suppose that as an act of piety the lord who held the advowson of a church decided to give this benefice to an abbey. Thereupon, the bishop granted the abbot and convent the right to convert the church "to their own uses"— *ad proprios usus* in the words of the charters — at the same time naming the abbot and convent rector of the church without the duty of personal residence. Since the abbot and convent formed a juridical person and did not die, they remained rector of the church forever and, as rector, enjoyed its revenues. By such an act, the benefice was said to be appropriated to the abbey. Out of the revenues of the appropriated church, the abbey would maintain a vicar. Thus the rector of the church was the abbot and convent as a corporation; the vicar was the real priest who took the place of this fictional rector and had the cure of souls. Here we must distinguish between two kinds of vicars. Any priest who acted as substitute for the rector of a church was a vicar. But some vicars were appointed for the time being and were paid wages, while others were appointed permanently and were supported by a definite part of the revenues of their parishes set aside forever for this purpose. When a church was appropriated to an abbey or other religious house, the bishop often ordered that a *congrua portio* of the revenues be perpetually allocated for the support of a vicar. He instituted what is called a perpetual vicarage. Of course, the vicar might have to provide not only for his own sustenance but also for that of one or two lesser clerks.[17] The surplus, often the larger part, of the revenues of the church went toward the maintenance of the abbey.

The first perpetual vicar to be mentioned in English records seems to have been one at Pershore in 1147,[18] and many others were instituted in the second half of the twelfth and in the thirteenth century. According to the so-called *Taxatio* of Pope Nicholas, there were 8085 churches in England and Wales in 1291. Of these churches 2711 had revenues of less than ten marks yearly each. In these churches were instituted 1487 vicarages, and 1125 of these vicarages had revenues of less than ten marks yearly each.[19] A constant concern of bishops was that the value of a vicarage should not be so low that the vicar was not decently supported. The sum they usually set as a minimum was five marks (66s. 8d.). Immediately after the Black Death, when the cost of living increased, the minimum was raised to six marks by Archbishop Islip and, in 1378, to eight marks by Archbishop Sudbury.[20] If we remember that the estimate has been made that the income, reckoned in money, of a yardling in a village such as Crawley, Hants., amounted to something like 55s. 7d. in a good year, in the thirteenth century and the beginning of the fourteenth, and 36s. 8d. in a bad year,[21] we can form some judgment as to the economic position of the poorest parsons. It was somewhat, but not much, better than that of the middle sort of villagers.[22]

In the societies of Europe, men have commonly been unwilling to enter an office which will not support them in the manner to which they feel they have a right by birth and station. Thus the value of the benefice held by a clerk in the Middle Ages corresponded roughly with his social origin. It corresponded only roughly: the avenues of advancement in the Church were not wholly closed to men of low degree. Grosseteste, the great Bishop of Lincoln, was reputed to have been born a villein. But a poor boy was not likely to get a good living. Indeed, the Church in England has always been one of those careers which are suitable for the younger sons of gentlemen. In the Middle Ages their fathers were the sort of men who held the advowsons of parishes, their uncles the sort of men who were bishops or abbots, men who were glad to present a kinsman to a benefice or admit him to one of the aristocratic monasteries. Some parsons "had been presented with livings not only before they had taken holy orders, but even in their youth and boyhood."[23] And as soon as they were beneficed, they were likely to go away to a university and perhaps remained away as permanent absentees. Such clergymen were lords by birth and many of them lived like lords on the revenues of their benefices, to the scandal of many puritans.

An interesting proof of the fact that the rich benefices were held by gentlemen's sons, and that these benefices had to be rich enough to support their incumbents in the proper style, comes from the events which followed the Black Death. At that time, the relative value of benefices decreased, since wages and prices both had risen. *Piers Plowman* describes the temper of the parish clergy in those days. It describes how:

> Persones and parisch prestes · playneþ to heore Bisschops,
> Þat heore Parisch haþ ben pore · seþþe þe Pestilence tyme.[24]

And in some parts of England, as soon as the value of the parishes decreased, their aristocratic rectors disappeared. Augustus Jessopp describes this change taking place in one village of Norfolk. He writes: "The great family of the Bardolfs were lords of the manor of Cantley, on the river Yare, from Norman times down to the reign of Henry the Fourth. As lords of the manor, they were patrons of the rectory, and resided in the parish. The rectors for nearly two centuries were either Bardolfs or bore the names of the great county families. The last of these aristocratic parsons of Cantley . . . was presented in 1372. After that date the rectors are evidently plebeians, of whose origin we know nothing." [25]

The men who were rectors of the parish churches of England and the men who did the actual parish work formed two groups which overlapped but were not identical. When the incumbent of a rich living was an absentee, the parish work must have been done by a vicar who came of low station and had to be satisfied with a low wage. Indeed, many a poor vicar had been born a villein. His father had paid the fine which the lord required of any one of his bondmen who took the tonsure. The young man then acquired such learning as the parson of his church could give him and picked up some knowledge of the duties of a parish priest from years of service as holy-water clerk or chaplain. Such a candidate for preferment cannot have been well schooled. According to the records of a visitation of

1222, there were priests serving dean and chapter livings of the cathedral of Salisbury who were found "unable to construe even the first sentence of the first collect in the canon of the mass." [26]

No one considering their origin, their training, and their surroundings could expect cultivated behavior from the poor priests. Although all clerks were freemen, the rector of Brightwalton was spoken of in a court roll of that manor as a villein, so closely had he become associated with the body of the villagers.[27] There were priests who were huntsmen, taverners, robbers. There were priests who took part in fights between villages, men like Thomas, chaplain of Dudley, and Simon, the priest of Clent, who were haled before the king's justices because they had taken part in a fight against the men of Halesowen in which a man had been killed. Many priests kept women. In fact, the decision of the reformed Church of England to allow the marriage of the clergy did little more than make legal a condition which had existed throughout the Middle Ages. We are often told of the sons of priests, and there is a letter from Innocent IV to the Bishop of Worcester in which the Pope complains that he has heard that in that diocese clerks renounced their benefices "on condition that these may be conferred upon their sons, nephews, or other kinsmen." [28] There were priests who used their churches as their barns and were as much concerned with husbandry as any of their neighbors. Such was the vicar of St. Mary Church in Devon, of whom his parishioners reported during a visitation of the year 1301:

that the same vicar keeps all manner of his beasts in the churchyard, by which it is badly trampled and vilely fouled. . . . The same vicar also has his malt prepared in the church and keeps his corn and other things therein, by reason of which his servants, going in and out, leave the door open, and the wind getting into the church in bad weather is wont to unroof it.[29]

But there must have been many poor parsons of towns of whom their parishioners could testify as the parishioners of Staverton, Devon, testified of their vicar in the same visitation. Their testimony was recorded as follows:

The parishioners say, when charged, that Master Walter, the vicar, behaves himself well and honestly, and informs them excellently in spiritual matters, nor, as they say, is he at fault in that. They know nothing of any hidden mortal sin. And his vicarage is worth, as they say, ten marks.[30]

The religion of the Catholic Church in the Middle Ages was eminently a religion of ritual. It consisted of a series of actions to be performed in a particular way on particular occasions. Much importance was attached to the performance of the cere- monial in precisely the manner prescribed by tradition. The liturgy was treated as if it were an incantation of magic which would lose its virtue if it departed from the proper form in the slightest particular. Perhaps villagers were able to forgive a good deal of scandalous behavior on the part of their parson, so long as he was able to celebrate the mass and the other rites of the Church as they had always been celebrated. To say that the religion of the Church was eminently a religion of ritual is to say that in the Middle Ages there was relatively little of another element which is important in some religions at some times — the element of exhortation, of prophecy. There was little preaching. According to the Constitutions of John Peckham, Archbishop of Canterbury, a parish priest was required to preach at least four times in the year. The fact that his minimum re- quirements were set so low must show that at best he cannot have preached often. In preaching, he was ordered to:

expound to the people in the vulgar tongue, without any fantastic texture of subtlety, the fourteen articles of faith, the ten commandments, the two pre- cepts of the gospel, namely, those of the twofold charity, the seven works of mercy, the seven deadly sins with their progeny, the seven chief virtues, and the seven sacraments of grace.[31]

The friars were the only churchmen who preached often, and one reason why they took this duty upon themselves was that it was being neglected by the parish priests.

Men who live in a great modern city have difficulty in con- ceiving how much the life of a villager in the Middle Ages was pervaded by the rites of the Catholic faith. Even when he was not in church, the bells in the steeple reminded him that the mass was being celebrated. The festivals which marked the turning points of the year have already been described. Almost every one of them was kept with some religious observance, more or less solemn. Even more important were the rites which marked the beginning and ending of every stage of a man's passage through life.[32] His baptism at the font of the parish church marked his becoming a member of society. If he died without having been baptized, even though without having sinned, he would inherit only "the easiest room in hell." His marriage at the church door marked his becoming a man of full standing in the community, a householder. The last rites of the Church prepared him and his family for his departing this life. The procession of those going to visit the desperately sick, the priest bearing the Host, accompanied by his chaplains or clerks carrying bell and candle, must have been one of the daily spectacles which put a villager most in mind of his mortality and of his dependence on the Church for his salvation. His burial in the churchyard finally ushered a man out of the society of the living, but even in death he remained a villager. The villagers clustered about the church in death as in life.

Only one of the rites which marked the passage of a man from one stage of existence to another escaped being made a a ceremony of the Church. That was the *lychwake*, the ceremony of watching the body of a dead man. This feast seems to have been kept in England in the thirteenth century in much the same manner as it is kept in Ireland today. A court roll of 1301 of Upwood with Great Raveley, Hunts., manors of Ramsey Abbey, has something to tell of the way men behaved after a wake. The entry runs as follows:

And they (the jurors) say that John Willem, John Ryngedele, William, servant of Robert Godhosebonde, John le Taillur, Robert, son of John Olyner, Hugh Curteys, Thomas le Akerman, Robert, son of Thomas Manger, and two shepherds of the abbot, all of Wistow, came to Great Raveley to watch the body of Simon of Sutbyr' through the night, and in returning they threw stones at the neighbors' doors and behaved themselves badly, for which the neighbors justly raised the hue upon them. Therefore the reeve and beadle are ordered to sue them in the court of Wistow.[33]

They must have been drunk, and in that state many a good man has come home from a wake since that time. We have seen from other instances that Robert Grosseteste, the great Bishop of Lincoln, had a good deal of the puritan about him. In the letter which he wrote in 1236 to the archdeacons of his diocese, he warned against many abuses in popular custom and ordered among other things that the people be admonished:

lest in the exequies of the dead, from a house of sorrow and remembrance, for the prevention of new sins, they make a house of laughter and play, to the multiplication of sins.[34]

All these hints tally with what is known of wakes in other times and places. When a villager died, his body must have been laid out in the best room in the house, the fire lit, candles set about the corpse, and perhaps (this was one ancient usage) a plate of salt put upon its breast. The dead man's neighbors and friends would gather. The greybeards would tell tales of his deeds and of old times in the countryside. The young would play games. And all would pray for the soul of the departed and partake of cakes and ale. The lychwake was a feast in which all the traditional virtues of neighborliness were reaffirmed.

The central ceremony of the Catholic Church, in the Middle Ages as today, was the ceremony of the mass.[35] Until we have a much better understanding of the function of ritual than we have now, no one who attempts to describe either the behavior of men witnessing a celebration of the mass or the effect of their having witnessed it on their behavior outside church will be able to point out all the important matters involved. Here, in any case, a long discussion of theory is out of place. In every church in England in the Middle Ages, mass should have been celebrated at least once every day and more often on Christmas and Easter. Christians were expected to communicate three times a year, at the great feasts of Christmas, Easter, and Whitsun, but many men felt that it was necessary to do so only just before death. When parish priests were reduced to curse for their tithes, that is, to excommunicate those who had not paid the arrears of their tithes, many of the defaulters were so little disturbed that they still refused to pay.[36] But let no one be deceived by the fact that men did not communicate often. They at least witnessed the celebration of the mass in the parish church on Sundays, and the amount of money and goods laid aside to endow the performance of masses for the dead bears witness to the virtue men found in the rite. The mere celebration of the mass in the manner and at the times it had been celebrated of old was the thing men felt to be essential, not the communication of any individual.

Let us consider the behavior of the men and women of a village gathered together on some common Sunday in the parish church for the celebration of the mass. So they would have gathered in an English village of the Middle Ages; so they still gather in many a village of Europe. Indeed, the best evidence we have of the way people behaved at mass in medieval times is the way they behave at mass today. The congregation was united in time and place and purpose, and, more important, the people who were together thus in worship were the people who were together in their daily work and shared a common body of sentiments and beliefs. Of course, villagers were not all of a kind, and some of the distinctions which were made without the church were maintained within. In England, in the thirteenth and later centuries, the gentry, and particularly the patron of the church, might sit in the chancel.[37] The common people remained in the nave, and even in the nave distinctions of place may well have been made between the more and the less substantial villagers. The priest stood at the altar, and all eyes were or should have been directed at him.

The sight of the different gestures performed by the priest in the celebration of the mass and the hearing of his words act upon the sentiments and thoughts of the members of the congregation. Everyone is not affected in the same way: in all congregations at all times, there are persons who are distraught, bored, skeptical, who, to use the words of *Piers Plowman*, take no tale of other heaven than here. Perhaps no one responds to the mass with conscious emotion. The number of persons who are in this sense indifferent to its ceremonies is a measure of the hold a religion has over a people. A nation in which religion is a matter of strong emotion for many people is often a nation religiously divided. But even the indifferent get the same satisfaction out of going to church that they get out of doing any of the other things society expects of them. They go to church as they would take off their hats to a lady. At the least, it is safe to say that few persons leave church in the frame of mind in which they entered. Some change takes place.

The action of the ceremony upon the members of the congregation is twofold: direct, as they are individuals witnessing the ceremony, indirect, as they are members of an audience. Men do not behave in a crowd — listening to an orator, seeing a play, attending a ceremony — in the way they behave when they are in a small group talking together on equal terms, or when only two persons are present and one is interviewing the other.

Certain kinds of reactions can probably be obtained from human beings only in certain social situations. For the most part, the members of the congregation are passive witnesses of the ceremony, but at certain points in the ceremony they themselves perform minor ritual actions: they bow their heads, they kneel, they cross themselves. These actions, like those of the ceremony itself, must have an effect upon their sentiments. What we mean by this statement is not, of course, that we can observe the sentiments and the way they change, but that we receive certain impressions, often very diverse and very slight, which we choose to interpret as manifestations of a change in the sentiments of the congregation. We may say, to express the total of these impressions, that the ceremony has an emotional tone of its own, with a rise of intensity reaching a climax at the Elevation of the Host and a resolution of intensity thereafter.

If society is to exist and not dissolve in anarchy, the great majority of the members of society must act, in general and approximately, in certain ways toward their fellow members and fail to behave in certain other ways. The means by which men are brought to adopt such behavior are many: fear of coercion, training in childhood ending in the acceptance of rules of conduct, appreciation, gained as a result of associating with other people, of the reciprocal relations existing between men. But such behavior in any case there must be. For Christian societies the basic content of these modes of behavior is summed up in the ten commandments: thou shalt honor thy father and thy mother, thou shalt do no murder, thou shalt not commit adultery, thou shalt not covet, and so forth. Strong sentiments exist in support of these rules. That is to say, if any of the rules are broken, or better if any of them are broken flagrantly and often, men will show signs of an irritation out of all proportion with any damage which may have been done to them personally by the transgression. They will also act to punish the transgressor, not so much in order to deter him and others from repeating the offence as to reassert the absolute value of the rules.

Clearly it is better to speak of the commandments as ideals than as rules. Christian teaching sets a standard of behavior which few men of this world can attain or are expected to attain by the other members of the community. Christian teaching also lays great emphasis on the contrast, which it calls sin, between the standard of behavior and the way men actually behave. Faced with this contrast, all but hardened sinners experience at some time or other a psychological state akin to anxiety, or better, would experience such a state if there were not acts by the performance of which they might manifest their sentiments of guilt and by manifesting them work them off, as we say describing our intuition of a phenomenon we do not well understand. The foregoing, once again, is no more than a hypothesis. What is actually observed is that men perform rites which they say will absolve them, purify them from sin. Rites such as these allow the men of a Christian society to demand a high standard of behavior while tolerating in practice considerable departures from the standard.

All societies possess traditional and accepted codes of behavior. That is, the men of any one of these societies, in what they say, are commonly in substantial agreement about the way they ought to behave, and their actual behavior approaches this standard more or less closely. In some respects, as in forbidding under most circumstances the killing of one member of the society by another, the different standards are much alike. And the men of many societies perform rites of absolution or purification following breaches of their codes of behavior. But men do not simply act in certain ways and assert that they ought to act in these ways. They produce stories about the origins of the codes of behavior, and the stories at the same time authorize obedience to the codes. To say that God revealed the ten commandments to Moses on Mount Sinai is sufficient warrant for obeying the commandments. They also produce statements of what will happen to those who observe the codes and those who disobey them, theories of why the rites of absolution and purification do absolve and do purify. In any society, these verbal constructions are observed to be traditional and common to most members of the society. A large number of them are likely to be linked together logically or pseudologically to form a system of beliefs, a mythology, an ideology.

Codes of behavior and systems of beliefs will be found in all societies, but the forms the systems take are much more variable than many of the rules of the codes of behavior. In most societies men are taught that they must not in ordinary circumstances kill another member of society, but the reasons they give why they must not kill vary greatly. They may say quite simply that it is wrong to do so; they may say that it is contrary to the will of some deity; they may say that it is not in accordance with the principle of the categorical imperative. Therefore, we say that the behavior is the more important element in the phenomenon because it is the constant one, and the verbal interpretation of the behavior the less important element in the phenomenon because it is the variable one. By the more important element in the phenomenon, we mean the element which must probably be first considered in constructing a workable theory of the phenomenon.

In most Christian societies, until recent times, some of the central beliefs have been the following. A man who is righteous, who lives in accordance with the commandments, will enjoy when he dies the delights of heaven, while a sinner will suffer torments in hell. Adam, the ancestor of mankind, by breaking God's commandment and eating the fruit of the tree of the knowledge of good and evil, made all his descendants sinners from their births. But God, out of His infinite goodness, sent His only Son as a man into the world, who by His death on Calvary redeemed men from sin. And so forth: there is no need to go into details about what is still a matter of common knowledge, and we still feel uncomfortable when these subjects are discussed outside of a book of devotion.

Clearly these beliefs are associated with sentiments about how men ought to behave. For one thing, sin is a breach of an accepted moral code. But, as we all know, Christian beliefs were not simply concerned with a code of behavior. They formed a cosmology, in which the questions of men could find answers; their actions, justification; their fears, reassurance; their wishes, fulfillment. If a man wanted to know why mass was celebrated, there was the story of the Last Supper and Christ's command-ment: "This do in remembrance of Me." If he wanted to know how this world came to be what it is, there was the story of the creation and the garden of Eden. If he was afraid that his mis-deeds would have their just reward, there was the assurance of God's grace and mercy. If he was afraid that the misdeeds of others would not, there was the assurance of a hell to come.

Perhaps it is better to say that the cosmology answered such questions before ever they were asked. What is more, the beliefs tended to form a closed system, so that any one of them implied all the others, and the system was common to all men.[38] Indeed it still is, even in such an irreligious society as our own, in the sense that even men who do not believe in it are familiar with it and sometimes in spite of themselves speak in its terms. In the Middle Ages their common faith united men, helped them to work successfully with one another, just as the possession of a common language unites men today.

There are a few other points to be made. The chief personages in the Christian system of beliefs were a Father, who was viewed as just rather than kindly, a Son obeying His Father's commands, and a suffering and compassionate Mother. The family relationships of the Christian earth were repeated in the symbols of the Christian heaven. And the relations between God and men were conceived to be like those between a father and his children, or, less often, like those between a king and his subjects. The actual social order of the earth was the model for the conceived social order of the supernatural.

The beliefs of the men of a society are seldom brought within one single closed system. Besides the system of beliefs of the Christian religion, men in the Middle Ages in England and other countries of Europe were familiar with another mythology, less highly developed than the Christian, but perhaps much older. That was the mythology of the elves and the fairies. Countrymen performed certain ancient rites, especially about their hearth-stones, and said that the rites brought good success in housekeeping. They declared further that the reason the rites brought good success was that they gained the good will of the elves, of Robin Goodfellow. In the words of William Warner:

Pails were fild, & hathes were swept, gainst Fairie-elues & sprits.

But we know so little of the mythology of the elves, and what we know is of so late a date, that there is no good reason to talk about it in a description of countrymen in the thirteenth century.

We must now return to the ceremony of the mass, where we began. Since neither the actions performed nor the words used in the mass are determined by the nature of a practical result to be accomplished, they can be, and are, determined by other factors. We say that they are symbolic, meaning that the ceremony of the mass makes reference to the body of Christian beliefs. In so far as these references were made in speech, a villager who witnessed the celebration of the mass in a parish church in the Middle Ages could not have understood them, since he commonly had no Latin. No more can most Christians who attend mass. But there is more in the mass than words: it is celebrated with much outward show, and in any case there is a traditional understanding even among the unlearned of the references the different rites make, of the reasons why they are performed. In the Middle Ages a parish priest was expected to expound to his congregation the meaning of the sacraments. The reference which the ceremony of the mass as a whole makes to the body of Christian beliefs is commonly well understood. The mass is, as we say, performed in commemoration of Christ's sacrifice on Calvary, which He suffered for the redemption of men's sins. At the least, in the sentiments of the most ignorant villager, the mass must have been associated with everything he called holy. That main association, rather than the association of a series of particular words or acts of the mass with a series of particular beliefs, is probably the important one. Another thing to be noticed in passing is that the rites of the mass make use of materials which were of the greatest importance in the daily life of the countrymen of Europe. Bread was the staff of life everywhere, and wine was the drink of all but the men of the northern countries.

We all assume, more or less explicitly, and it is convenient to assume as a working hypothesis, that the sentiments of men exist in two main states, which may be called a latent state and an excited state. When, for instance, we hear a military band go by and see the flag of our country borne in parade, many of us feel that the sentiments we call patriotic have been aroused. We do not in the least doubt that, when the excitement has passed, the patriotic sentiments continue to be part of our psychological constitution and will be aroused again at other times by a military band and a flag or by other means. The music, the flag have become associated with certain sentiments;

they have become symbols, so that the sound of the music, the sight of the flag will make us aware that we possess these sentiments. It is possible that unless the sentiments are brought from time to time from the latent state to the excited state, their strength will decrease, and the sentiments in some strength are useful to the survival of the society in time of war. It may be important also that, when the sentiments have been brought to the excited state, there should be customs according to which these sentiments may manifest themselves in actions, however slight these actions may be. We must take our hats off as the flag goes by.

This example will seem trivial only to those who disregard its implications. We are forced to make the same kind of account of the functions of the mass in a society such as that of England in the thirteenth century. We must consider in fact the interactions of the following four elements: 1. the behavior of men outside church in their everyday affairs; 2. the behavior of men in church when witnessing or taking part in the celebration of the mass; 3. the statements they make about their behavior, both their behavior within church and their behavior without; 4. their sentiments. The first three elements are observable; the fourth is not observable but is part of the conceptual scheme in terms of which what is observable is described. All four elements are in a state of mutual dependence. That is, each element acts upon each of the other elements and is acted upon by them. Such a state of affairs can be adequately described only by mathematics. Since we cannot yet use mathematics in describing the mass, account can be taken of the state of mutual dependence only by the poor method of describing first the action of one of the elements upon the others and then the reaction of the other elements upon the first.

The rites of the mass (2) are in a state of mutual dependence with the system of Christian beliefs (3). In particular, and most important, the ceremony of the mass as a whole has reference to the central doctrine of Christianity, the doctrine of the Redemption. This doctrine is in turn in a state of mutual dependence with the sentiments of Christians about sin and righteousness (4), that is, with the sentiments they manifest by acting commonly and approximately in accordance with certain modes of behavior

(1). Unless they behaved in accordance with such modes, society would dissolve. Besides the indirect relation between the ceremony of the mass and the sentiments of men by way of the body of Christian beliefs, there is a direct relation. The celebration of the mass (2) is associated with everything men feel is good, righteous, holy (4).

When the people of the congregation witness and take part in the celebration of the mass, they are placing under powerful influences those of their sentiments which manifest themselves in everyday life in behavior which is viable in Christian society, behavior which allows the men of that society to live together successfully with one another. We assume that the celebration of the mass brings these sentiments out of the latent state into the excited state: the ceremony has a rising intensity of emotional tone, and when they have left church the people of the congregation feel righteous. Unless the sentiments were brought from time to time out of the latent state into the excited state, the strength of the sentiments would weaken, and on these sentiments depends the well regulated behavior of men in society. The function of the mass in medieval society, like the great ceremonies of any society, is that of helping to maintain the sentiments on which the survival of the society depends.

CHAPTER XXV

THE ANATOMY OF SOCIETY

IN MANY SCIENCES the men who have to deal with the facts in detail are also the men who construct the theories about the facts. This circumstance is probably useful: no theory is likely to endure which does not arise directly out of long-continued, intuitive familiarity with the welter of facts which it attempts to order. Useful or not, it is a fact of sociology and social anthropology — to take one science — that after a man has been studying a particular human society, he often tries to construct a conceptual scheme which he hopes can be used to describe not only that society but many other societies besides. He tries to make statements of uniformities in the organization of social systems in general.

In this book, the life of English villagers of the thirteenth century has been described in the usual literary manner and in the language of common sense. An attempt to do anything else would have lengthened the book and might have interfered with a consideration of the facts themselves. Nevertheless, this literary description can be translated, so to speak, into another and more abstract language and must be so translated if we are to develop a scheme which can be used to specify the elements which societies of different kinds have in common. This last chapter will be devoted, not to elaborating such a scheme in detail, but to suggesting what material the scheme ought to take into consideration.[1]

Two warnings are in order here. In the first place, a scheme which can be used to describe the elements which different societies have in common is necessarily an abstract scheme. However much it may arise out of familiarity with the phenomena in full, concrete detail, it can describe only certain aspects of the phenomena. In particular, the present scheme, like the book as a whole, considers a society as if it persisted without significant change. It is an anatomy of society rather than a physiology. In the second place, many things will have to be stated as simply as Bismarck spoke of blood and iron. People may say that they are commonplaces, and so they are. But the things we take for granted about a social system are apt to be among its most important features. When we say: "People do not often commit murder," our statement is a commonplace, but it is of the first importance.

If a definition is to be anything more than a means of linking one group of words to another, it must in effect point to certain facts. We teach a child the meaning of the word *dog* not by reading him its definition in the dictionary but by saying "dog" and pointing to the animal. We say of a number of human beings that they form a society. If we return from the word *society* to the facts we had in mind when we used it, we find that these human beings are acting, behaving, that they are acting in response to the actions of one another, and that the interactions are more frequent between fellow members of the society than they are between the members and other men whom we choose to consider outsiders. The most important thing we mean when we say that a village was a society is that the men of the village had upon the whole more contacts with one another than they had with outsiders, entirely aside from the question of what these contacts were.

What brought human beings to come together in societies we do not know, any more than we know what brought ants to come together in ant-hills or fish to come together in schools. But the fact is that they have come together and still do. We see every day groups of men forming — groups of friends, for instance, or fellow workmen — which have some of the characteristics of the older human societies. For some purposes it is convenient to consider those societies which are politically independent of other societies: nations and tribes. For others, it is convenient to study the societies which are formed within these larger societies. The most important societies which have been considered in these pages are families, classes, villages, and manors.

If we observe men who are interacting with one another in a society, we soon recognize elements in their behavior which, from one point of view or another, are recurrent. To use the word which has come down to us from the Middle Ages, the members of the society have developed customs, in which their activities are coördinated. Even if a man does not punish his fellow for a breach of custom, he will always feel uneasy whenever the actions of someone else with whom he is dealing do not in some measure fit into an expected pattern. And he will feel uneasy whenever he himself does not know how he is expected to act. In short, there is no greater mistake than to think of custom as a compulsion laid upon men. If they are not able to act in accordance with custom, most of them will feel actively distressed. They will try to return as soon as possible to their former routines. They may not be able to do so, but for a time they will try. And if for a long enough time, over a wide enough field of activity, they find themselves unable to follow custom, men will simply become bewildered, and will be unable to perform any sensible actions at all. In the continued performance of customs, of great number and variety, the stability of society consists.

To say that much behavior is customary, that it is a matter of routine, is not, of course, to say that it is impractical. In old and stable societies, men perform many of the most practical works not because they understand why these works are practical but to some extent simply because they have always performed them. In the Middle Ages a man would plow his field as he would woo his wife — in the manner expected in the community. Some early anthropologists noticed that the customs of the blackfellows of Australia helped insure the survival of the blackfellows in the hard conditions of the bush, and comparing the wisdom of the customs with the manifestly low intelligence of the blackfellows, they assumed that a far more intelligent race had once existed, had imposed the customs on the ancestors of the present blackfellows, and had later died out. This assumption was gratuitous. In point of fact no origin of the customs in the pure exercise of human intelligence, even at this remove, has ever been found. They must have been developed in the course of a long-continued process of interaction among many factors, including the sentiments of men and the external conditions of their lives, a process such as that which produced parliamentary government in England. No group of Englishmen, however intelligent, could by taking thought have devised and then imposed on their fellows a scheme of government which would have worked as well as parliamentary government has worked.

We have here been concerned with customs of many sorts: the customs of the champion husbandry, the customs of inheritance, the custom of the manor, the customary festivals. We have also been concerned with the peculiar form of custom which consists of customary statements about society and the world in general. A society in which the activities of the members is coördinated by custom is spoken of as an *organization*. But all organizations except the smallest are made up of sub-organizations. Therefore the word *institution* will be used when we are thinking of an organization as a part of a larger organization, and the word *organization* when we are thinking of an organization as an independent entity.

We have not progressed very far in studying organizations if we simply say that the behavior of men is customary. We must break custom down into its elements, the definitions of the elements being those of the operations used to isolate the elements. Furthermore, we may suppose that each of the elements will exhibit those features of recurrence, of regularity characteristic of custom as a whole. The elements which will be considered here are three: (1) interaction; (2) sentiment; (3) function. A word may be said about each of them.

Interaction. We speak of this element as communication when we are thinking of its relations to the other two elements. But in abstraction from the concrete things people are doing and the sentiments they are feeling, it is possible to observe that the action of one man is a stimulus for the action of a second, and that this action of the second is in turn a stimulus for the action of the first. Or the action of the second becomes a stimulus for the action of a third, and so forth. We have seen that a society can be defined as any group of people interacting in this way. Within the society so defined, the chains of interaction are infinitely complex and cover the society in a number of different ways. Nevertheless the chains of interaction tend to become permanent in some respects, and in particular a society builds up hierarchical organizations marked by the fact that certain members of the organization are centers of communication, so that they are in a position to act as stimuli for the actions of a relatively large number of other members. Accordingly they are able to coördinate the activities of these others, in so far as this coördination is not a matter of custom. We call these persons leaders or executives, and we have been concerned with many such persons in the course of the present study: fathers of families, reeves, lords of manors, priests, and so forth. Some of these hierarchies are formally recognized: in fact in some modern organizations elaborate "organization" charts are made. A very much larger number exist which are not formally recognized. This element of organization is relatively easily isolated. It is possible to watch a number of persons interacting with one another and not only record with a high precision the order in which interaction takes place but also measure in various ways the rate of the interaction.[2]

Sentiment. Purposive interaction, that is, collaboration between men, is impossible unless they are willing to collaborate. But in making a description of any concrete society, other sentiments must be taken into consideration besides willingness to collaborate. The sentiments of the members are in a complicated state of balance, some favoring collaboration and other hindering it. In discussing the element of sentiment we are on dangerous ground. Sentiment is always a question of individuals, though we may speak of the sentiment of a group to mean the sentiments of the members of the group. And at some time in the future, we may possess a good classification of sentiments based on the physiological states of individuals. But at the present time no such classification exists, and we are driven back upon an interpretation of the things men say. When they talk about friendship or hatred, awe or inferiority, constraint or ease, they are talking about the sentiments engendered in them as a result of their interaction with other men in society. Admittedly the interpretation of these expressions is not a matter of precision. Nevertheless a large amount of successful human action has been founded on such interpretation, and mere lack of methods of precision — precision is a relative matter in any case — should not inhibit our studying an essential element of human organization. We must do what we can.

Function. When we are thinking of the intentions of individuals we speak of purpose. The word *function* is used here to indicate not the purposes of individuals but the purpose of the organization to which they belong. There is little passive association among men. When they come together, they come together to do something, even if the thing to be done is trivial and what is important is the social contact incidental to its accomplishment. In short, if men do not have a common purpose, they invent one. In some organizations purposes are carefully formulated, but for the most part when we are studying function we are studying what organizations actually do, what changes they make in the environment upon which they are operating. An important part of the environment of a village is the soil, and we study the changes which the village organization makes in the soil: we study how the villagers collaborate to raise crops. An important part of the environment of an army is the opposing army, and we study the changes the army brings about in its opponent. When function is something concrete and tangible, or when it is the subject of definite specialization, it is rather easily recognized. Under other circumstances we are likely to be on unstable ground when speaking of this element. We have been concerned with function when studying the relation between the social organization of a village, its technology, and its geographical environment. We have also been concerned with function when studying religion.

Analysis is followed by synthesis. After we have identified the elements of the anatomy of society, we may proceed to consider systematically the relations between these elements in order to approach more and more closely to a description of the concrete reality. The method used here will be to indicate, by pairs, the mutual dependence of the elements. By mutual dependence we mean a situation such that the state of one element is determined to some extent by the state of a second, and that the state of the second is determined to some extent by the state of the first. The functions of an organization determine in part the state of the communication hierarchy, but the state of the hierarchy determines in part the functions. The elements of the anatomy of society, under the present scheme, being three, there are obviously three pairs whose mutual dependence must be considered, namely: interaction and sentiment, sentiment and function, function and interaction. The pairs may be taken up in this order.

Mutual dependence of interaction and sentiment. The most obvious statement which can be made on this point is that people who interact with one another develop common sentiments. People who are thrown together are likely to become friends, even if they have never known one another before. The girl you fall in love with is likely to be a girl you have met socially. These remarks are none the less important for being commonplaces. Furthermore, by the network of interaction (communication) extending over a large society, sentiments are spread so that they constitute "states of mind" and "public opinion." At this point a complication must be introduced. People share certain sentiments as members of what is for the moment treated as an independent organization. We share certain sentiments as Americans or Englishmen. But people also take definite attitudes towards persons who are in any way differentiated within the organization. They take definite attitudes towards men, women, whites, negroes, upper-class persons, middle-class persons, and so forth. Especially important are the sentiments taken towards persons who are differentiated not by what may be called natural causes, such as sex or color, but by position in the communication hierarchy, the sentiments, for instance, towards superiors, equals, inferiors. Indeed the so-called natural differences are ultimately important in society only if they are reflected in organizational differences. In their relations these sentiments may form a complicated system.

We have been concerned in these pages with the mutual dependence of interaction and sentiment. We have been concerned with the sentiments men felt as fellow villagers, for instance the sentiment they spoke of as neighborhood (*vicinitas*). We have been concerned with the sentiments which lord and tenant felt towards one another. But upon the whole we have not had much to do, at least explicity, with elaborate systems of sentiment, the sentiments, for instance, which every member of a family takes towards every other. In some primitive societies, these sentiments become highly standardized and specific.[3] For the thirteenth century the necessary factual material has simply not been available.

The mutual dependence of interaction and sentiment can be illustrated by a brief discussion of social classes. From the point of view of interaction, a class may be defined as a group of persons who hold similar positions in the institutions which make up society and at the same time interact with one another to a considerable degree. An upper class, for instance, is made up of persons who take the leading organization positions in a society and are in close social relation with one another. To carry the analysis one step further, there may be two sorts of persons who are felt to be not fully members of the upper class. On the one hand, there are the *nouveaux riches*. They hold high organization positions but do not yet have close social relations with other persons in similar positions. They are trying to build up these relations. On the other hand, there are the impoverished artistocrats. They continue to maintain social relations with other aristocrats but have lost the high organization positions of their ancestors. Incidentally, both these classes are described in terms of their wealth, but analysis will show that the decisive factor is not wealth but the high organization position which generally, though not always, is accompanied by wealth.

Around social classes as thus defined by the scheme of interaction, a series of sentiments clusters. Members of a social class share certain sentiments; the social classes fall into a definite rank; members of each of the classes take a definite attitude towards each of the other classes. For instance, an upper class and a lower class sometimes have more "sympathy" for each other than either of them have for the middle class, especially when the middle class is aggressive and is increasing in size and in importance. Something of this sort was an element in the division in England which led to the Civil War.[4] It has been observed in other societies.[5] The material has not been available to describe the relations between the classes: franklins, husbonds, cotters, in an English village.

Mutual dependence of sentiment and function. Rather obviously, the sentiments of individuals give rise to the functions of organizations. Such diverse sentiments as hunger, hatred, pity, and religious exaltation may do so. On the other hand, the members of an organization must believe in the real existence of a common purpose and the likelihood of attaining it, or their willingness to coöperate will be destroyed. This fact, for instance, explains much of the behavior of political and military leaders in time of war. Finally, coöperation is destroyed if men recognize a divergence between the function of an organization as they understand it and the function it is actually fulfilling. Such divergence is easily recognized when functions are concrete and tangible, less easily when they are intangible and sentimental as in religion. But even in this field, recognition of a divergence has often led to antagonism and cynicism.

Mutual dependence of function and interaction. Perhaps the most explicit discussion of this relationship appears in modern books on industrial organization, with their elaborate arguments about "line," "function," and "staff." As a matter of fact, the phenomena they talk about appear in all societies, For some collaborative purposes, only small organizations are necessary, for instance, families. For others, much larger ones are required, for instance, manors. Again, any large organization may be made up of several smaller institutions, each with its special function. Even in a medieval village, where the specialization on the whole was not elaborate, there were persons who performed special functions: the smith, the hayward, the priest, to say nothing of the division of functions between men and women. The history of mankind has been a history of increased specialization, and the specialization has been more and more a matter of organization. Whereas a primitive tribe will, in effect, resolve itself from time to time into a religious congregation or into a court, but have no specialized religious or legal institutions, a more advanced society will have a permanent priesthood, judiciary, and police. This point is the one which is important here, since each such specialization entails a further complication of the scheme of communication.

One distinction of particular importance must be made in the functions of an organization. This is the distinction between the functions which are concerned with whatever is the external environment of the organization and those which are concerned with its internal constitution. We have studied functions of the first sort when we studied the relation between the social organization of a village, its technical equipment, and its geographical environment. We have studied functions of the second sort when we studied the rites of the parish church, though religion is not the only function of an organization which is concerned with its internal constitution.

There was a time when men of letters looked at the rites of magic and religion, observed that their function was not what it was said to be, especially that they had no useful effect on the external environment of an organization, and therefore dismissed them as superstitions, the only purpose of which was to support a parasitical clergy. This attitude has been changing. To say that an action does not have an observable effect on the external environment is not to say that it has no function. Its function is concerned with the internal constitution of the organization. We have seen how the rites of the Church in the Middle Ages probably helped maintain the sentiments on which the effective collaboration of men in society depended.

The study of the rites of religion required that special attention be given to a particular part of the customs of men, that is, the customary statements they made describing the world in which they lived and especially their own behavior in society. These statements had at least two characteristics, one or the other of which might be the more important in any given instance. In the first place, some of these statements had elements in common which formed a scheme of interpretation in every way comparable to the conceptual schemes of science, though for some purposes less useful. They formed a cosmology, a mythology, a language for describing the world, and it is obvious that such a language must exist. All facts are stated in terms of a conceptual scheme: if you do not possess an elegant scheme, you use one more crude. Some of these schemes of interpretation were used to describe the external environment of society. The statement: "The sun rises," is a statement of fact made in terms of the Ptolemaic conceptual scheme of medieval astronomy. Some of them were used to describe the internal constitution of society. We have seen that what is called the feudal system was, in part at least, a verbal scheme describing some aspects of the relation between man and man in the more important organizations of society. The statement "X holds his land of Y," is a statement of fact made in terms of the feudal conceptual scheme of medieval sociology. In the second place, the customary statements men made about their behavior provided justification, or to use the modern expression, rationalization of this behavior. The feudal scheme provided a rationalization of the different positions men took in society. Most important of all in this respect were the dogmas of the Christian Church, which gave expression to the fundamental collaborative sentiment of society — what is love but that? — and to the sentiments men felt towards any breach of collaboration — what is sin but such a breach?

The study of the rites of religion required that particular attention be given to mythology, because the first statement which could be made about any set of rites — actions functionally specialized in relation to the internal constitution of society — was that they made symbolic reference to the mythology. Note should be taken that this statement is general: it speaks of any set of rites. The relation between rite and mythology was just as clear in the ceremony of giving seisin before the hallmote as it was in the mass of the parish church. Where one rite made reference to the feudal mythology, the other made reference to the Christian.

A more general statement about society can now be made. We speak of a society as a social system because it has certain characteristics in common with other systems. The elements of society, however they are defined, are in a state of mutual dependence with one another, not only directly but also indirectly in that all are members of a whole, a system of elements, which can for convenience be considered as isolated. If one element of the social system changes, all the other elements change and also the system as a whole. The system has the further characteristic of equilibrium. That is, if a change which would not otherwise have occurred is impressed upon the system, the system as a whole will react so as to lessen or eliminate the change. Thus after a flood, a pestilence, a war, a society tends to return to the state it would have reached if the disaster had not occurred.

One of the social sciences in which the problem of describing systems has become most pressing is anthropology. The typical anthropologist of the present generation has been studying a primitive society, that is, one which is small enough in numbers and little enough complex in institutions so that he can effectively consider all the elements of the social order. The very conditions of work in the field compel him to face the problem of describing a system as a whole. But the problem is new only to anthropology. It has arisen again and again in the physical and biological sciences when they have reached a certain stage of development.[6] As Newton constructed his solar system and Willard Gibbs his physicochemical system, so anthropologists and sociologists are now beginning the construction of the conceptual scheme of the social system. There is little doubt that the social scientists were led to attempt this work because the struggle to deal with the facts of human societies forced them to do so and not because they were familiar with the history of the more advanced sciences. Indeed if they had been familiar with this history they would have understood better what they were doing and would have avoided much bewilderment. At one time, for instance, there was talk about society being an entity *sui generis*.[7] This statement expressed a sound intuition but led in fact to much fruitless controversy over words. Only after the social scientists had themselves begun work on the facts could they appreciate the difficulties other sciences had encountered earlier. Only then could they apply to the phenomena they themselves observed some of the logical methods which had been developed in the more advanced sciences.

Let us return once more from the general statement to the particular instance. The anatomy of society has been described in terms of the mutual dependence of the elements of interaction, sentiment, and function. In illustrating the theory of the social system from what we know about English villages of the thirteenth century, the factor of mutual dependence will be considered at another and more obvious level, that is, the mutual dependence of the institutions which make up a society. For one thing, each of the dispositions of the champion husbandry was intricately dependent on all the others. If we are describing the common herd, we are at once forced to speak of the hayward elected by the community of the village, of the hedges set up around the common fields, of the common fields themselves, of the rotation of crops practiced on them, and so forth. In the same way each of the customs of a village family: the descent of land to one son, the marriage of that son, the fate of the children not inheriting, and the provision made for widows and widowers — each was adapted to all the others so as to form a consistent whole. What is more important, the constitution of the family and the constitution of village husbandry were themselves adapted to one another. How this adaptation took place nobody knows, but adaptation there certainly was. Any rule which maintained tenements undivided from generation to generation maintained also the ancient distribution of lands in the open fields and the ancient equality of tenements, class by class. Again, the organization of a manor was in mutual dependence with the organization of a village in other respects. The way the villagers worked for the lord was in some part determined by the way they worked for one another. That the arrangements should have been of this sort was only natural. The lord of a manor was not dealing with a mass of laborers who had never known one another before but with an ancient community and established ways. He had to make use of the institutions already existing, for instance, the customs of joint plowing, of holding benes, of electing village officers. It is significant that in Kent, where the forms of settlement were not what they were in the champion country, the typical manorial arrangements were also lacking. By 1300 there were said to be no villeins in Kent.

Examined in this way, the mutual adaptation of the institutions of society is obvious. It is hard to imagine some such articulation not existing. That the total articulation forms a social system appears clearly in the geographical distribution of custom in England. In the Middle Ages, as you moved from the part of England where one kind of field system was in force to the parts where others were in force, the forms of settlement, the customs of inheritance, even the organization of manors tended to change also. This statement cannot be pressed far, for there were many border districts where custom was mixed. But it is correct to a first approximation. The customs of inheritance: descent of land to one son, and the type of settlement: big villages, in such a county as Oxfordshire differed in many ways from the customs of inheritance and the types of settlement in Kent or in Cornwall. There was a tendency for the elements of society to vary in unison. Or to put the matter in another way, the elements of society were mutually dependent in such a way as to form a social system, and the social system of one district differed as a whole from the social system of another. This fact is the only justification for the statement with which this book began: By studying any state of affairs as a whole, as the sum of its parts and something more, we are often able to understand it in a way we could not otherwise have done.

NOTES

NOTES

CHAPTER I

1. Brit. Mus., Cotton MSS. Tiberius, B, II and Claudius, C, XI.
2. See A. E. Levett, *Studies in Manorial History*, 79–96. A court book of the 14th century has recently been edited and published:— E. Toms, ed., *Chertsey Abbey Court Rolls Abstract* (Surrey Record Soc.).
3. In W. O. Ault, *Court Rolls of the Abbey of Ramsey and of the Honor of Clare* and in Maitland, *Manorial Courts*.
4. Brit. Mus., Add. Roll 34333; cf. *Ramsey Cartulary*, I, 281 ff.

CHAPTER II

1. The distinction between champion and woodland is prominent in Tusser. In an entry of the year 1310 in a court roll of Duffield in Belper, Derbyshire, there is an interesting use of the word *champaynelond*: PRO, DL 30, Bundle 32, no. 287, m. 1: Villata presentat quod Radulphus Swan liber diem clausit extremum qui tenuit duo messuagia .j. acram et .j. rodam terre libere et per cartam domini reddendo per annum pro acra .iij. d. et tallagium. Item tenuit .iij. acras terre ad voluntatem del Champaynelond reddendo pro acra .viij. d. Item tenuit .ij. acras terre de dominicis reddendo pro acra .viij. d. Other entries use *campania*, the Latin form.
2. M. Bloch, *Les caractères originaux de l'histoire rurale française*, 58.
3. For descriptions and photographs of Cornish field walls, see O. G. S. Crawford, "The Work of Giants," *Antiquity*, X, (1936), 162–174.
4. In Tusser, 62, the following lines appear:

> In tempest (the wind being northly or east)
> warme barth under hedge is a sucker to beast.

And in the margin is printed "Woodland countrie."
5. E. Lamond, ed., *A Discourse of the Common Weal of this Realm of England*, 49.
6. Tusser, 141–142.
7. G. J. Turner, *A Calendar of the Feet of Fines relating to the County of Huntingdon* (Cambridge Antiquarian Soc.), cxviii.
8. Messrs. Griggs, *General View of the Agriculture of the County of Essex* (1794), 8.
9. P. Morant, *The History and Antiquities of the County of Essex* (1816), I, i. For other references to enclosures in Essex see *Victoria County History: Essex*, II, 322.
10. A. E. Levett, *Studies in Manorial History*, 185 ff.
11. The map of villages enclosed by act of Parliament should be compared with maps showing the proportion of land without common field in different parts of England at different periods. Such maps, redrawn from maps in E. C. K. Gonner, *Common Land and Inclosure*, are printed in H. C. Darby, ed., *An Historical Geography of England before A. D. 1800*, 400, 401.
12. H. L. Gray, *English Field Systems*, 305.
13. W. Harrison, *Description of England*, ed. F. J. Furnivall, (The New Shakspere Soc.), I, 259. See also I, 237.
14. A. Young, *Travels in France* (1794), I, 321. For the characteristics and distribution of ancient agricultural regimes in France, see M. Bloch, *Les caractères originaux de l'histoire rurale française*; R. Dion, *Essai sur la formation du paysage rural français*, and G. Roupnel, *Histoire de la campagne française*.

15. An excellent discussion appears in Dion, *Essai*, 24–30.

16. See the references in G. Slater, *The English Peasantry and the Enclosure of Common Fields*, 183–186.

17. In A. Meitzen, *Siedelung und Agrarwesen*.

18. For the customs of Kent and their history, see J. E. A. Jolliffe, *Pre-Feudal England: The Jutes*.

19. A. Owen, *Ancient Laws of Wales*, 743. See also H. Lewis, *The Ancient Laws of Wales*, 92, and F. Seebohm, *Tribal Custom in Anglo-Saxon Law*, 36.

CHAPTER III

1. The interpretation of medieval history presented in this chapter is largely that of the late Henri Pirenne, especially as stated in his *Economic and Social History of Medieval Europe*.

2. See A. Dopsch, *Wirtschaftliche und soziale Grundlagen der europäischen Kulturentwicklung, aus der Zeit von Caesar bis auf Karl den Grossen*.

3. See W. Sombart, *Der moderne Kapitalismus* (4th ed.), I, 124–179.

4. See N. S. B. Gras, *The Evolution of the English Corn Market from the Twelfth to the Eighteenth Century*.

5. M. Postan, "Revisions in Economic History: The Fifteenth Century," *Economic History Review*, IX, 160–7 (May, 1939).

6. See in J. Huizinga, *The Waning of the Middle Ages*, the suggestive chapter on the violent tenor of life in the fourteenth and fifteenth centuries.

CHAPTER IV

1. W. W. Skeat, ed., *Pierce the Ploughmans Crede* (EETS), ll. 421–440.

2. The best description of the champion husbandry as a matter of practical farming is that of C. S. and C. S. Orwin, *The Open Fields*.

3. See Sir W. Ashley, *The Bread of our Forefathers*.

4. See V. G. Simkhovitch, "Hay and History," *Political Science Quarterly*, XXVIII (1913), 385–403.

5. See M. Bloch, *Les caractères originaux de l'histoire rurale française*, 52.

6. *Statistical Account of Scotland* (1791), I, 391; V, 192; VII, 585. For methods of agriculture in the Shetlands, see Scott, *The Pirate*, chs. xiv, xv, xviii, xxx. That forms of the *araire* were used in medieval England is indicated by a drawing from Trin. Coll. Camb. MS. R. 17.1, of about 1150, reproduced in D. Hartley and M. M. Eliot, *Life and Work of the People of England, 1000–1300*, Plate 7.

7. *Hist. Nat.*, xviii, 18. Text emended by G. Baist, in *Archiv für lateinische Lexikographie* (1886), 285.

8. For methods of plowing ridges, see A. Dickson, *A Treatise of Agriculture* (1785), I, 308–312; Gervase Markham, *The English Husbandman* (1635), 38; C. S. and C. S. Orwin, *The Open Fields*, 33.

9. See *Rural Economy in Yorkshire in 1641 (Best's Farming Book)* (Surtees Soc.), 44; also *Finchale Priory Rolls* (Surtees Soc.), ccccxxxvii.

10. W. W. Skeat, ed., *The Book of Husbandry, by Master Fitzherbert* (English Dialect Soc.), 132.

11. *Gloucester Cartulary*, III, 218. The *selliginum* of the text I assume to be the same word as *sellionum*.

12. Tusser, 45.

13. *Rural Economy in Yorkshire in 1641 (Best's Farming Book)*, 128n: "In Northumberland, the plough was certainly drawn by 4 oxen, and from a purely blade diet and from other circumstances the teams worked alternately. Here were 8 oxen to each plow." For evidence that in the 16th century 8 oxen were felt to constitute "a whole draught," see O. Baker, *In Shakespeare's Warwickshire and the Unknown Years*, 80–81.

14. Quoted from *Orbis Sensualium Pictus* in J. Strutt, *A Compleat View of the Manners, Customs, Arms, Habits, etc.* . . . (1775), II, 12.

15. *Havelok* (EETS, E. Ser., no. 4), ll. 1017–1018.

> Bondemen with here gaddes,
> Als he comen fro þe plow.

16. Trans. in R. Steele, *Mediaeval Lore from Bartholomaeus Anglicus*, 143. *Mediaeval Lore* is included in the Medieval Library published in England by Messrs. Chatto and Windus and in the United States of America by the Oxford University Press. This passage is printed by kind permission of the publishers. Bartholomaeus Anglicus wrote before 1260. *Langhaldes* and *spanells* are ropes to hobble cattle.

17. *Fleta*, II, 78.2.

18. *Bleadon Custumal*, 205. This custumal dates from the 13th century, after 1221.

19. C. Pass. IX, ll. 112 ff.

20. See I. Taylor, "Domesday Survivals," in P. E. Dove, ed., *Domesday Studies*, I, 143–188.

21. Text in F. Tupper, *Riddles of the Exeter Book*. Trans. in R. K. Gordon, ed., *Anglo-Saxon Poetry*, 327. *Anglo-Saxon Poetry* is published in the Everyman's Library by E. P. Dutton & Co., Inc., New York. This passage is printed by kind permission of the publisher.

Chapter V

1. See *infra* pp. 155, 367.

2. J. O. Chambers, *Nottinghamshire in the Eighteenth Century*, 156, quoting from Lowe, *Agricultural Survey of Nottinghamshire* (1798), 21. On p. 155 Chambers prints a map showing the brecks of Carberton, in Sherwood Forest, in 1615. For similar arrangements in the Forest of Dean, see *Gloucester Cartulary*, III, 227.

3. J. Saltmarsh and H. C. Darby, "The Infield-Outfield System of a Norfolk Manor," *Economic History* (*A Supplement of the Economic Journal*), III, (1935), 30–44.

4. See J. C. Atkinson, ed., *Cartularium Abbathiae de Whiteby* (Surtees Soc.), II, 440. For a general description of the infield-outfield system, see H. L. Gray, *English Field Systems*. A late twelfth-century charter relating to Morton, Notts., printed in Stenton, *Danelaw Documents*, no. 372, speaks of totam terram in Mortona in Holm . ex parte aquilonali eiusdem ville que fuit Henrici clerici in campo interiori et exteriori.

5. This may be inferred from a convention of 1288 in *Oseney Cartulary*, IV, 235.

6. H. E. Strikland, *Agriculture of the East Riding* (1812), 114: "In most of the open-field townships on the Wolds, two crops and a bare fallow have been from time immemorial the constant course: the tillage-field . . . was then divided into six, nine, or twelve falls or fields, so that there might be at least one of the divisions under each kind of grain, and fallow, every year. The course pursued, was, generally, as follows: 1. Fallow. 2. Wheat. 3. Oats. 4. Fallow. 5. Barley. 6. Peas, or Beans."

7. Gray, *English Field Systems*, 73.

8. Brit. Mus., Add. MS. 40,010 (Rentals and Extracts from Court Records of Fountains Abbey, 1305–1435), f. 20r: Ricardus de Pobthorp (or Polithorp), Ricardus de Eskilby, Iohannes Ward ex parte liberior', Iohannes Robynson, Robertus Hardyng, Petrus Libi ex parte domini Ricardi Crope, Robertus Thomson, Robertus Dyconson, et Willelmus Ysacson ex parte Abbatis ordinati sunt ex eorum assensu et omnium tenentium ad faciendum et ordinandum meliori modo quo poterunt iactare campum in tribus partibus ita quod vna pars quolibet anno sit falgh'.

9. Gray, *English Field Systems*, 76 ff.

10. Brit. Mus., Add. Roll 39,754, m. 1d. Nomina eorum qui seminauerunt in warecto vbi liberi et custumarii habere deberent communem pasturam suam, videlicet . . . et quia testatur per liberos et per totam villatam quod terre predicte fuerant seminate quando ille campus fuit warectus et hoc viginti annis elapsis et amplius, ideo concessum est dictis hominibus quod citra proximam curiam querantur inde voluntatem domini Abbatis, quod si non fecerint, remaneant in misericordia.

11. For instance, in a court roll of 1305 of Halton, Bucks., PRO, Eccl. I, Bundle 16, no. 43, m. 27d: Item presentant (i. e., capitales decenarii) quod Willelmus de Merwelle fecit quandam paruam hechengam apud Merwelle de quantitate vnius dimidie acre de terra pertinente ad warectum . . . et dictus Willelmus dat domino .xij. d. pro illa terra seminanda quando pertinet ad warectum.

12. *Calendar of Inquisitions (Miscellaneous)*, I, 613.

13. For other interesting printed references to this custom, see W. O. Massingberd, ed., *Lincolnshire Records: Final Concords*, I, 298; *Oseney Cartulary*, IV, 235; *Gloucester Cartulary*, III, 36; *Lincolnshire Notes and Queries*, XII (1912–1913), 150–152; J. T. Fowler, ed., *The Coucher Book of Selby* (Yorks. Arch. Assn., Record Series), II, 220, 376; *Halesowen Court Rolls*, II, 453; E. Gutch, *Examples of Printed Folk-lore concerning Lincolnshire*, 295; W. Kennett, *Parochial Antiquities* (1695), Glossary, *s. v. inhoc.*

14. Sometimes, it seems, two neighboring townships arranged that their herds should pasture in common on the fields of both towns. Before the justices in Eyre at Bedford, 14 November, 1240, upon a complaint of loss of pasture, it was found that "according to the customs of the townships of Stanbridge and Tilsworth, when a field of Tilsworth lies out of tillage and to fallow, then likewise a field of Stanbridge ought to lie out of tillage and to fallow, so that they ought to common horn under horn."— *Publications of the Bedfordshire Historical Record Soc.*, IX, 83.

15. *Parson's Tale*, ll. 897–899.

16. *Rotuli Hundredorum*, II, 848.

17. F. Blomefield, *An Essay towards a Topographical History of the County of Norfolk*, IX, 294.

18. F. W. Maitland, *Bracton's Note Book*, no. 881.

19. J. G. Rokewode, ed., *Cronica Jocelini de Brakelonda* (Camden Soc.), 76.

20. *Estate Book of Henry de Bray*, 12–14. See also p. 93.

21. See G. L. Gomme, *The Village Community*, 163; F. Seebohm, *English Village Community*, 11; *Rotuli Hundredorum*, II, 402, 487, 862, 864; *Ramsey Cartulary*, I, 283, 295, 308, 321, 332; E. Powell, *A Suffolk Hundred in 1283*, *passim*: (in almost every township in this hundred one of the chief lords has free bull); Brit. Mus., Cotton. MS. Claudius, C. XI, *passim*. (This is the Ely custumal of 1277. On nearly every Ely manor the bishop has free bull and boar.)

22. Tusser, 141.

23. G. J. Turner, ed., *Select Pleas of the Forest* (Selden Soc.), 97.

24. *Oseney Cartulary*, VI, 83.

25. PRO, SC 2, Port. 179, no. 10, m. 10: Et dicunt (iurati) quod Iuo in Angulo habet vnam aperturam versus campum ad dampnum et nocumentum vicinorum. Ideo Iuo in misericordia .iij. d.

26. *Halesowen Court Rolls*, I, 129. See also I, 126; III, 92.

27. PRO, SC 2, Port. 175, no. 79, m. 4: Alanus de Forwude inculpatur de hoc quod fecit asportare hayas suas circa campum de Westfeld infra terminum, qui respondens dicit quod metentes et alii asportauerunt partem hayarum, ita quod in pluribus locis fuit introitus in pluribus locis (sic) ita quod aueria compmunem introitum habebant antequam aliquid asportauit. This entry is badly written, and its reconstruction is doubtful in several details.

28. Brit. Mus., Add. MS. 36237 (Extent and Custumal of Tittenhanger, Herts., manor of St. Albans Abbey, 5 Edw. III), f. 2r: Mensuratio terrarum dominicarum

de Tydenhangre per dominum abbatem. In Stertefeld' terre arabilis sunt .vj.ˣˣ
xiij acre et .xviij. pertice. . . . In sepibus et fossatis circumdantibus dictum campum
.v. acre .iij. rode .xviij. pertice et dim. In the same way, all other fields in which
the demesne lies are enclosed with hedges and ditches. But these fields are grouped
in three *seisone* of approximately equal size.

CHAPTER VI

1. PRO, SC 2, Port. 209, no. 55, m. 3: Omnes carucarii in misericordia quia
sinuerunt (sic) carucas stare contra mensuram.

2. Brit. Mus., Add. Roll 34324, m. 1: De Galfrido Lacy quia sine licencia
domini et balliui mensurauit terram domini Attebedesolewes cum virga sua .iij. d.
The phrase *attebedesolewes* shows that at Houghton some form of the Old English
word *sulh*, meaning *plow*, was in use.

3. C, Pass. VII, ll. 267–271. See also Robert Mannyng of Brunne, *Handlyng
Synne*, ll. 2443–2448.

4. PRO, SC 2, Port. 202, no. 56, m. 2: Inquisicio dicit quod Radulphus
Quintin amputauit duas quercus Galfridi filii Hugonis iniuste et remouebat metam
inter eos et occupauit duos sulcos iniuste de terra sua, et ideo in misericordia, et
dictus Galfridus quia occupauit sibi dimidium pedem ideo in misericordia.

5. Brit. Mus., Add. Roll 34803, m. 1: Et preceptum est balliuo et preposito
quod capiant secum totum homagium domini tam de magna Rauel' quam de
Upwod et adeant ibidem. Et videant quousque [*quisquis*] predictorum habeat
terras suas prout de iure habere debent et tunc ponant inter eos certas metas
et bundas, ita quod inde clamor non fiat amodo nec querela.

6. M. Bloch, *Les caractères originaux de l'histoire rurale française*, 194–200. See
also R. Dion, *Essai sur la formation du paysage rural française*, 52–3.

7. See S. R. Scargill-Bird, ed., *Custumals of Battle Abbey* (Camden Soc.),
53, for use of word *yherdlinges*.

8. J. E. A. Jolliffe, "A Survey of Fiscal Tenements," in *Economic History
Review*, VI (1936), 171.

9. E. Lamond, ed., *Walter of Henley's Husbandry*, 7–9.

10. W. Brown, ed., *Yorkshire Inquisitions*, Vol. I (Yorks. Arch. Assn., Record
Series), 249, 250. There is some evidence that when a man became a tenant of
a yardland his lord would provide him with a yoke of oxen, and that when he
became a tenant of an oxgang his lord would provide him with one ox. In this
case each hide or plowland would be able to make up a team of just eight oxen.
See the *gebur's* customs in *Rectitudines Singularum Personarum*: F. Liebermann,
Die Gesetze der Angelsachsen, I, 447: In ipsa terra, ubi hec consuetudo stat,
moris est, ut ad terram assidendam dentur ei duo boues et una uacca et VI
oues et VII acre seminate in sua uirgata terre. See also an entry concerning
Great Broughton, Yorks., in a series of extents of the lands of the Earl of Albemarle
in Cumberland and Yorks., 44 Henry III: PRO, Rentals and Surveys, General
Series, Roll 730, m. 15d: Memorandum quod predicti Bondi tenentes terras de
dominicis habent ad quamlibet bouatam terre .j. bouem de bobus Comi'e quem
debent vna cum terra quando eam reddunt.

11. An entry in the *Ramsey Cartulary*, I, 346, concerning services at Upwood,
Hunts., in 1252, is the following: Ad semen frumenti arabit unam sellionem
solus sine socio pro virgata sua. See also I, 310, for services of a yardling at
Caldecot, Hunts., in 1251: In secunda septimana post festum Sancti Michaelis
arabit dimidiam acram, quae appelatur Wodebene, sive propriam et integram
habeat carucam, vel iunctam cum aliis, pro uno opere.

12. See S. J. Madge, ed., *Abstracts of Inquisitiones Post Mortem for Gloucestershire* (The Index Library), Part IV, 137, for services of yardlings at Southam,
1286: "They ought to plow the land of the lord, as the plow is sometimes with
two virgators and sometimes with more . . . ;" *Glastonbury Rentalia*, 136,

for services of a yardling at Longbridge: Et debet arare ad preces domini unam acram semel in acra [? anno] si habet carucam per se; si duo vel tres participant secum in caruca non amplius debent arare nisi unam solam acram; *Rotuli Hundredorum*, II, 485, for services of free sokemen at Swaffham, Cambs.: Item si duo vel tres vel quatuor unam carucam coniunxerint semel ad semen hiemale et semel ad semen quadragesimale Priorem adiuuabunt ad arandum. The following entry concerning services at Siston, Glos., appears in a series of inquests of 29 Edw. I concerning the lands of Robert Walrand: PRO, Ancient Extents (Exchequer), no. 8, m. 1: Et estimatur quod communiter tres customarii possunt facere vnam carucam; see also m. 9 for services at Radway, Warwicks.: Et estimatur quod .iiij. custumarii facient .j. carucam que potest arare per .j. diem dimidiam acram; see *Chichester Custumals*, 95, for services at Bishopstone: "Note that if 4 men [bring] 1 plough to the Bishop's ploughing boonwork the four shall follow their plough and see that the lord's land is well ploughed, harrowed, and sown."

13. Brit. Mus., Add. Roll 34333, m. 1 (cf. *Ramsey Cartulary*, I, 474–486): Quolibet autem die Veneris predicti temporis, si propriam carucam habeat, dimidiam acram arabit et cum fuerit seminatum herciabit. Si autem propriam carucam non habeat, tot aueriis terram domini arabit quot arat propriam. Licet vero bene quatuor hominibus vel octo si cogat necessitas inuicem associari ad carucam si sue facultates vlterius non extendant, et quieti erunt pro arura dimidie acre ac si dicta caruca comunis solius esset.

14. Brit. Mus., Cotton MS. Claudius C. XI, f. 116r: Rogerus Holdeye tenet quindecim acras que faciunt dimidiam virgatam terre. . . . Et preterea arabit infra idem tempus qualibet die Lune usque ad horam nonam pro una operacione. Ita quod iste et tres alii pares sui faciant unam carucam cum octo bestiis. See also *Rotuli Hundredorum* II, 440, 442.

15. *Ramsey Cartulary*, I, 346. See also I, 310, for services of half-yardling at Warboys, Cambs., 1251: Ad omnes precarias carucarum venit cum caruca sua sicut iungitur; et non possunt plures in hyeme iungi quam tres, in aestate quatuor.

16. Brit. Mus., Add. Roll 27765 m. 3: Nicholaus Vpechepyng summonitus fuit ad respondendum Henrico Astil in placito conuencionis. Et vnde idem Henricus queritur quod dictus Nicholaus non tenet ei conuencionem de hoc quod conuenit sibi die Lune proxima post festum Omnium Sanctorum anno regni regis Edwardi nunc .xj.° in villa de Aulton quod inueniret pro caruca sua .iij. equos a die Lune predicto vsque festum Natiuitatis Domini proximum sequens eodem anno quam quidem conuencionem fregit ad dampnum ipsius Henrici .xx. s. et inde etc. Et predictus Nicholaus defendit, etc., et predictam conuencionem omnino dedicit et inde vadit legem se vj^a manu.

17. *Wakefield Court Rolls*, III, 161.

18. *Rotuli Hundredorum*, I, 341.

19. Maitland, *Manorial Courts*, 111.

20. Brit. Mus., Add. Roll 24681, m. 11: Robertus le Coc venit et queritur de predicto Fillipo, [et] dicit quod predictus Filepus recepit quendam ecum ab ipso in codam pacto, videlicet quod predictus Filipus debet custodire predictum ecum et pasterare et tractare in carucam. Preterea dicit [quod] verberauit predictum ecum et liguait petram in auriculam ipsius equi et debet predicto Roberto soluere arruram vnius diete.

21. PRO, Eccl. I, Bundle 26, no. 7, m. 1: Item dicunt quod Iohannes Grug et Galfridus frater eius ceperunt sine licencia bestias bonorum hominum de nocte in vigilia sancti Michaelis et arrauerunt .ij. acras et dimidiam videlicet cum tribus carucis. Inquisicio facta si Ricardus de Berewyc accomodauit ipsis duobus suam carucam aut non, et dicit inquisicio quod non in illo tempore. See also *Wakefield Court Rolls*, III, 72.

22. Brit. Mus., Cotton MS. Tiberius, B. II, f. 112v: Et sciendum quod si forsitan aliquis tenens vnam virgatam terre pro paupertate sua nichil habuerit in carucam, tenetur arare cum denariis suis per annum nouem acras.

23. In a court roll of 1297 of Bury, Hunts., a Ramsey manor: Brit. Mus., Add. Roll 39562: . . . ipsi arant super terram propriam vel etiam super terram alienam pro qua quidem arura terre aliene capiunt pecuniam.

24. H. C. M. Lambert, *History of Banstead in Surrey*, I, 321 (Extent of Banstead, 1325).

25. The following entry appears in an extent (*c.* 1295) of Bugthorpe near Pocklington, Yorks., printed in T. A. M. Bishop, ed., "Extents of the Prebends of York," *Miscellanea*, Vol. IV (Yorks. Arch. Soc., Record Series), 11: "William son of Thomas holds two bovates. . . . If he has not a plough of his own he himself with his partner (*cum suo maru*) shall do a boon service on those two days [once at the winter and once at the spring sowing], and the lord shall give them one meal a day." See also H. S. Bennett, *Life on the English Manor*, 45.

26. *Durham Hallmotes*, 56.

Chapter VII

1. G. J. Turner, ed., *Select Pleas of the Forest* (Selden Soc.), lxxviii: "Usually the same piece of land seems to have been sown alternately with winter and spring corn, and to have remained fallow for a year after a certain number of crops had been sown." For rotation of crops in assarts see also *Collections for a History of Staffordshire* (Wm. Salt Arch. Soc.), V, Part 1 (1884), 149.

2. *Estate Book of Henry de Bray*, 87.

3. See for example *Rotuli Hundredorum*, II, 873.

4. F. M. Stenton, ed., *Transcripts of Charters Relating to Gilbertine Houses* (Lincoln Record Soc.), 62. See also J. Parker, ed., *Yorkshire Fines (1232–1246)*, 162; a charter dating from the end of the thirteenth century, printed in R. P. Littledale, ed., *Pudsay Deeds* (Yorks. Arch. Soc. Record Ser.), 168, shows William de Roucestre granting to John son of John de Bolton all his lordship in Rimington except eight oxgangs, with the following provision: "And if it shall happen that the said John and his heirs shall make any improvements within the boundaries of the town of Rimington, then the said William de Roucestre shall take a part of that profit according to the proportion belonging to eight oxgangs."

5. See T. A. M. Bishop, "Assarting and the Growth of the Open Fields," *Economic History Review*, VI, (1935), 13–29.

6. For instance, in *Oseney Cartulary*, IV, 223, a charter of *c.* 1260 relating to Little Tew speaks of dimidia acra prati que iacet in decem acris uersus occidentem que prime sortite sunt.

7. G. J. Turner, ed., *Select Pleas of the Forest*, cxxiii: "It may be observed that the public had a right of hunting beasts *ferae naturae* in all unenclosed lands, unless the lands were subject to the forest laws or to some restriction upon hunting arising out of a royal grant." *Rotuli Hundredorum*, I, 317: Dicimus quod comes de Warenne appropriat sibi warennam ad manerium suum de Gretwell (Greetwell, Lincs.) juxta Lincoln' ubi omnes patrie solebant habere liberam chaciam in prejudicium Regis et dampnum patrie.

8. C. Deedes, *Register or Memorial of Ewell, Surrey*, xxii.

9. N. Neilson, ed., *A Terrier of Fleet, Lincolnshire*, (British Academy: Records of the Social and Economic History of England and Wales, Vol. IV), 214. See also C. S. and C. S. Orwin, *The Open Fields*, 24–6.

10. But such expressions by men of other countries have been recorded. See H. L. Gray, *English Field Systems*, 164, 191.

11. *Wakefield Court Rolls*, I. 261. Another indication that oxgangs were laid out so that they contained equal shares of good and bad land is found in a charter describing an oxgang of 17 acres in Normanton on the Wolds, Notts. This charter is cited in Stenton, *Danelaw Documents*, xxvii, note 10, and the significant words are: sex acras in meliori loco totius terre sue et quinque et dimidiam in mediocri loco et quinque et dimidiam in deteriori loco.

12. F. Seebohm, *The English Village Community*, 24–7.

13. *Estate Book of Henry de Bray*, 33.

14. *Ibid.*, 23, three yardlands in the manor of Upton, Northants., early in the fourteenth century are described as follows: quarum duae virgatae jacent per dimidias acras per hidam totius campi de Herleston (Harleston, Northants.) et una dimidia virgata jacet per totum campum per rodam et dimidiam quam Willelmus Pewere tenuit et alia dimidia virgata jacet per rodas quas Thomas le Bray tenet.

15. R. P. Littledale, ed., *Pudsay Deeds* (Yorks. Arch. Soc.), 296. The last clause is: que jacet versus solem in omnibus locis totius campi.

16. W. O. Massingberd, ed., *Lincolnshire Records: Abstracts of Final Concords*, Vol. I, 262. A Final Concord, or Foot of Fine is the record kept by a royal court of the settlement of a case before the court. A fine in settlement of a fictitious case was used as a means of conveying land.

17. *Estate Book of Henry de Bray*, 74-5. Even the half-yardlands which were not *in communibus campis* must have been in scattered strips, since one of them is described in a document on p. 76 as dimidiam virgatam terre quae jacet per particulas in dominicis suis (i. e., Hamonis de Vieleston).

18. *Ibid.*, 89. Pp. 89-90 show that the moiety of the tenement consisted of at least 7 yardlands.

19. W. O. Massingberd, ed., *Lincolnshire Records: Abstracts of Final Concords*, Vol. I, 89.

20. C. Pass. II, ll. 112 ff.

21. C. Pass. I, ll. 14-19.

22. For a concrete instance, inspect the map of Thorsjö in Sweden in A. Meitzen, *Siedelung und Agrarwesen*, III, Atlas, *Anl.* 143.

23. C. Hardwick, *Traditions, Superstitions, and Folk-lore*, 28.

24. *Tompt aer akers mopir*. See L. Beauchet, ed., *Loi de Vestrogothie*, 227, *Loi d'Upland*, 217; J. Grimm, *Deutsche Rechtsalterthümer* (1854), 539.

25. S. Aakjaer, "Villages, cadastres et plans parcellaires au Danemark," *Annales d'histoire économique et sociale*, I (1929), 564. See also J. Frodin, "Plans cadastraux et repartition du sol en Suède," *Annales*, VI, (1934), 51-61.

26. W. Brown, ed., *Cartularium Prioratus de Gyseburne* (Surtees Soc.), II, 42.

27. See K. Rhamm, *Die Grosshufen der Nordgermanen*, 38; L. Beauchet, ed., *Loi de Vestrogothie*, 214, 223.

28. F. M. Stenton, ed., *Transcripts of Charters Relating ot Gilbertine Houses*, 7; see also *Danelaw Documents*, lx, note 7: "The phrase *quicquid habui infra villam et quatuor divisas de X* is repeatedly used in charters of the twelfth and thirteenth centuries to describe an estate which would naturally have been written down as a manor in other parts of England."

29. *Transcripts of Charters Relating to Gilbertine Houses*, 62.

30. Vinogradoff, *The Growth of the Manor*, 178, cites a redivision of 8 hides in Segheho, but this redivision was made to correct usurpations made in time of war. It was not part of a periodic redivision of all the lands of a village.

31. Burton Agnes, Yorks. See the map printed in P. E. Dove, ed., *Domesday Studies*, I, 55. I believe this point is an important one. There is much to be discovered about the field systems of the North of England. The following entry from the rental of 1479 printed in J. Raine, ed., *The Priory of Hexham, Its Title Deeds, Black Book, etc.* (Surtees Soc.), II, 72, applies to the Manor of Salton, Yorks.: Sunt etiam ibidem xvj bovatae terrae dominicae arabilis; quarum quaelibet cont. ix acras terrae: unde octo bovatae jacent in quatuor flattes . . . . Istae praedictae flattae . . . sunt seperales. Et caeterae viij bovatae terrae jacent discontinue per diversas partes inter terras tenentium ibidem.

32. For a more detailed study of the evidence for some form of English *solskift*, see G. C. Homans, "Terroirs ordonnés et champs orientés: une hypothèse sur le village anglais," *Annales d'histoire économique et sociale*, VIII (1936), 438-448.

33. Trans. from W. O. Ault, "Some Early Village By-laws," *English Historical Review*, XLV (1930), 212. This paper is of great interest.

34. PRO, SC 2, Port. 179, no. 4, m. 3: De Editha Ordinar quia cariauit bladum suum de nocte contra statuta autumpni, et quia non venit ad arruram domini sicut debuit, ideo in misericordia .xij. d.

35. Brit. Mus., Cotton MS. Tiberius. B. II, f. 106r: Item sciendum quod de forisfactura de Belawe et de venditione iuncorum dominus habebit medietatem denariorum. See *Cambridge Antiquarian Soc. Communications*, VI (1884–1888), 168.

36. See T. W. Hall, ed., *A Descriptive Catalogue of Land-charters and Court Rolls from the Bosville and the Lindsay Collections, etc.* A map facing p. 77 shows the boundaries of the four byrlaws of the chapelry of Bradfield, near Sheffield.

37. Brit. Mus., Add. MS. 40010, f. 51v. This MS. is a compilation of entries from court rolls and other documents relating to Fountains Abbey in the 14th and 15th centuries. There are several interesting entries concerning byrlaws.

38. *Wakefield Court Rolls*, I, 278. The original of "by the community of the byrlaw" is *per communitatem plebiceti*. See also II, 48.

39. For further printed material on bylaws, see J. C. Atkinson, ed., *Coucher Book of Furness Abbey* (Chetham Soc.), I, 458; *Archaeologia*, XLVI, Part 2 (1881), 371 ff.; *Archaeological Journal*, XLIV (1887), 278 ff.; *Historical MSS. Comm., Report on the MSS. of Lord Middleton preserved at Wollaton Hall, Notts.*, 106–109; R. Twysden, *Historiae Anglicanae Scriptores* (1652), X (*Chronica W. Thorn De Rebus Gestis Abbatum S. Augustini Cantuariae*), 1936 (entry for 1283); see also the entry for 1303; *Abbreviatio Placitorum*, 286b; *Yearbook, 44 Edw. III*, 19; *North Riding Record Soc. Publications*, VIII, xi.

CHAPTER VIII

1. *Victoria County History of Kent*, III, 325.

2. F. W. Maitland, ed., *Bracton's Note Book*, no. 1770.

3. PRO, SC 2, Port. 181, no. 48, m. 4: Walterus, Robertus, Ricardus, et Iohannes filii et vnus heres Gerardi Ate Pirie vadiauerunt misericordiam pro contemptu etc. Predicti Walterus, Robertus, Ricardus, et Iohannes vadiauerunt releuium, quod est ij d. Et iurauerunt facere quicquid facere debent pro tenemento quod tenent de domino.

4. *Ibid.*, m. 3: Ricardus et Ricardus et Willelmus fratres et vnus heres Henrici le Lung optulerunt se ad faciendum post predictum Henricum quicquid de iure facere debent. Et vadiauerunt releuium. Et fecerunt feoditatem.

5. J. E. A. Jolliffe, *Pre-Feudal England: The Jutes*, 26.

6. F. LePlay, *Les Ouvriers Européens*, V, 188–191, 297–303.

7. T. Robinson, *The Common Law of Kent* (1741), 62–63.

8. Brit. Mus., Add. Roll 9158, m. 1d: Robertus Kempe, Willelmus Kempe, et Alanus filius Galfridi molendinarii petunt versus Alanum filium Willelmi Scholer vnum mesuagium cum pertinenciis in West Neuton vt ius ipsorum Roberti, Willelmi, et Alani. Et dicunt quod quidem Robertus Spondrift antecessor suus fuit seisitus de predicta terra cum pertinenciis vt de iure. Et post decessum dicti Roberti decendit ius et debuit decendere Ricardo Kempe et Galfrido Hauche vt .ij. filii et vnus heres. Et de predictis Ricardo et Galfrido decendit ius et debuit decendere Roberto Kempe, Willelmo Kempe, et Alano filio Galfridi molendinarii qui nunc petunt. Et quod talis sit ius suum petunt quod inquiratur. For further details about this family, see Add. Roll 9162, m. 1.

9. PRO, DL 30, Bundle 85, no. 1157, m. 4d: Robertus filius Simonis Horman qui tenuit de domino vnum mesuagium et duas acras terre natiue mortuus sine herede de se et super hoc venerunt Galfridus, Petrus, et Thomas filii Willelmi Horman fratres predicti Simonis et petunt acceptari ad dictam terram herietandam et dant domino pro ingressu x. s.

10. PRO, DL 30, Bundle 85, no. 1159, m. 12d: Nicholaus filius Galfridi Dod qui tenuit de domino vnum mesuagium dimidiam acram et octodecim

perticatas terre natiue vnde dimidia acra et nouem perticate tenentur nomine dotis mortuus est. Et super hoc veniunt Iohannes filius Willelmi Dod et Willelmus frater eius et Iohannes filius Fulconis Dod tanquam propinquiores heredes et petunt acceptari ad dictam terram heriettandam secundum consuetudinem manerii.

11. Brit. Mus. Cotton MS. Tiberius, B. II, f. 167v: Ricardus filius Hildebrond' et Adam frater suus et Ricardus nepos eorum tenent sexaginta acras pro decem solidis.

12. Brit. Mus. Cotton MS. Claudius, C. XI, f. 76v: Maynerus filius Iohannis Gocelin et Adam et Petrus nepotes eius tenent vnum mesuagium.

13. PRO, DL 30, Bundle 85, no. 1159, m. 2d: Robertus Denyel dat domino xij. d. pro racionabili parte terre patris sui habenda secundum consuetudinem manerii. Et quod mensuretur per bonos et legales vicinos. Et preceptum est quod mensuretur et diuidatur inter ipsum et fratres suos citra proximam curiam.

14. Such small holdings, as they were extended in the survey of 1291 of the lands of the Prior of Norwich in Martham, Norfolk, and the process of partition by which they were formed have been ably discussed in the papers of W. Hudson: *History Teachers' Miscellany*, I, 161; *Trans. of the Royal Hist. Soc.*, 4th Series, I, 28.

15. Sir F. Pollock and F. W. Maitland, *The History of English Law* (2d Ed.), II, 270: "A great deal of Norfolk seems to have been partible, and partibility reigned in several of the great 'sokes' of the Danelaw"; H. L. Gray, *English Field Systems*, 337: "That socage and villein holdings in East Anglia were ever subject to partible inheritance seems to have escaped the notice of legal historians." It had not escaped Pollock and Maitland, who wrote before Gray.

16. My present list, with abbreviated reference to the evidence, is: *Lincs.*: Fleet (N. Neilson, *Terrier of Fleet*), Sutton (PRO, DL 30, Bundle 85, no. 1159, etc.): *Cambs.*: Wisbech (Ely Custumals, see above), Tydd (Ely Custumals); *Norfolk*: Walpole (Ely Custumals), Walton (Ely Custumals), Terrington (Ely Custumals), Tilney (*Select Civil Pleas* (Selden Soc.), 6), Holme, (*Ramsey Cartulary*, I, 401–3), Brancaster (*ibid.*, I, 427), Castle Rising (F. W. Maitland, *Bracton's Note Book*, no. 1663), Smallburgh (*ibid.*, no. 154), Carbrook, Cranworth, Letton (*ibid.*, no. 1009), Heacham (*ibid.*, no. 1074), Roudham (*ibid.*, no. 1252), Eccles (*ibid.*, no. 1933), West Newton (Brit. Mus., Add. Rolls 9143, 9152, 9158), Whissonsett (Add. Roll 55591), Horningtoft (PRO, SC 2, Port. 193, no. 6), Martham (*History Teachers' Miscellany*, I, 161), Tivetshall (Add. MS. 40,063); *Suffolk*: Monks Eleigh (*Bracton's Note Book*, nos. 703, 1023), Sproughton (*ibid.*, no. 795), Ipswich (*ibid.*, no. 1023), Wykes in Bardwell (*Norfolk Archaeology*, XIV, 46), Rickinghall (Add. MS. 40,063), Westwood (PRO, SC 2, Port. 204, no. 22), Hadleigh (PRO, Eccl. I, Bundle 16, no. 1); *Essex*: Hatfield Broad Oak (Add. Roll 28519), Waltham (PRO, DL 30, Bundle 750, no. 62); *Herts.*: Stevenage (PRO, Eccl. I, Bundle 211, no. 1).

17. See the map above, p. 22.

18. G. Slater, *The English Peasantry and the Enclosure of Common Fields*, 78–86; H. L. Gray, *English Field Systems*, 305–354; D. C. Douglas, *The Social Structure of Medieval East Anglia* (Oxford Studies in Social and Legal History, Vol. IX).

19. See G. T. Clark, "The Custumary of the Manor and Soke of Rothley," *Archaeologia*, XLVII, Part I, 125: Item si aliquis de soka habens uxorem habeat de ea filios plures vel filias et ipse obierit, terra est partibilis inter ipsos vel ipsas sed inter filium et filiam nequaquam; et si sit unicus filius et plures filie filius habebit totum. See also Sir F. Pollock and F. W. Maitland, *The History of English Law* (2d Ed.), II, 270.

20. Pollock and Maitland (2d Ed.), II, 270.

21. For instances, see pp. 142, 254.

22. Brit. Mus., Add. Roll 26,876, m. 8: Iohannes filius eiusdem Roberti iunior est proximus heres eiusdem Roberti secundum consuetudinem manerii.

23. I have encountered the following other villages where descent to one son was probably the custom, east of the eastern boundary of the champion husbandry: *Suffolk*: Barking, Rattlesden, Bramford, Chilton, Pakenham, Polstead; *Essex*: Leyton. Without doubt there are others. See G. R. Corner, "On the Custom of Borough English," *Proc. of the Suffolk Institute of Arch., Statistics, and Natural Hist.*, II, 227–241, for a list of Suffolk manors in which Borough English was the custom in the 19th century.

24. J. E. A. Jolliffe, *Pre-Feudal England: The Jutes*, 79, shows that in eastern Sussex there existed forms of tenure intermediate between gavelkind and Borough English.

25. M. Olsen, *Farms and Fanes of Ancient Norway*, 29–60.

26. This chapter is based on G. C. Homans, "Partible Inheritance of Villagers' Holdings," *Economic History Review*, VIII (1937), 48–56.

CHAPTER IX

1. An example from the court rolls of Newington, Oxon., 28 Edw. I, PRO, Eccl. I, Bundle 26, no. 41, m. 1: Adhuc Symon de Berewyck venit in plena curia et dicit se kendam habere in illo tenemento quod Matilda de Berewyck tenuit et optulit se facere domino pro eodem tenemento ea que de iure facere debet.

2. PRO, SC 2, Port. 179, no. 6, m. 23: Tota villata dicit quod post mortem Thome Arnold clerici qui perquisiuit vnum mesuagium et .xiiij. acras terre in villa de Ripton Regis obiit seisitus de toto predicto tenemento. Et dicunt quod quidam Radulphus Arnold frater suus propinquior heres est de sanguine, set dicunt quod per consuetudinem manerii Nicholaus filius Iohannis in Angulo propinquior heres est dicti Thome ad predictum tenementum secundum consuetudinem manerii habendum, eo quod dictus Iohannes in Angulo pater dicti Nicholai qui fuit de consanguinitate ville disponsauit Margaretam sororem dicti Thome natam apud Bury iuxta Rameseiam de qua genuit [Nicholaum] qui modo petit. I have translated Iohannes in Angulo as John in Le Hyrne because he is in fact called by this name in m. 24. This case is cited in Maitland, *Manorial Courts*, 106.

3. PRO, SC 2, Port. 179, no. 6, m. 24.

4. For example, an entry for 21 Feb., 1278, in *Halesowen Court Rolls*, I, 101: Curia consideravit quod senior soror habeat principale mesuagium cum suis pertinentiis infra portam et extra, salva viduis sua portione dum vivunt, et alie singule sorores tantam placiam terre ubi voluerint eligere, et quod singule sorores habeant equalem portionem de utensilibus.

5. The application of the name was an accident. To repeat an old story: "In the Norman days a new French borough grew up beside the old English borough of Nottingham. A famous case of 1327 drew the attention of lawyers to the fact that while burgages of the 'burgh Francoys' descended to the eldest son, those of the 'burgh Engloys' descended to the youngest. It was natural for the lawyers to find a name for the custom in the circumstances of this case, to call it the custom of the borough English, or the custom of borough English, for such a custom came before them but rarely."— Sir F. Pollock and F. W. Maitland, *The History of English Law* (2d Ed.), II, 279.

6. An example appears in a custumal of Gringley, Notts., 25 Edw. I: PRO, Rentals and Surveys, Gen. Series, Roll 534, m. 3d: Item dicunt iurati quod iunior filius prime marite habebit terram patris sui sicut heres propinquior.

7. *Collections for a History of Staffordshire* (Wm. Salt Arch. Soc.), 1910 vol., 136.

8. Brit. Mus. Add. Roll 31,309, m. 9: Helewysa que fuit vxor Roberti le Capel venit in plena curia et reddit sursum domino .ij. partes tocius tenementi quod quondam tenuit dictus Robertus natiue et dicte .ij. partes dicti tenementi traduntur per dominum Philippo filio dicti Roberti ad faciendum inde domino

omnia seruicia inde debita et consueta vt predictus Robertus facere consueuit et dat domino pro ingressu habendo .vj. s. et soluit domine [?] et venit Stephanus filius dicti Roberti Capel iunior et concessit dicto Philippo fratri suo totum ius quod habuit vel potuit habere in dicto tenemento pro .v. s. .vj. d. et sic tradita est eidem Philippo seisina et dat domino pro releuio .viij. d. Add. Roll 31,310, mm. 1, 2 shows Adam, younger son of Philip, inheriting his father's land twenty-three years later. See below, p. 181 for a statement of the custom of Bucksteep. For another example of setting aside the proper heir, see *Chertsey Abstract*, 33.

9. Brit. Mus. Lansdowne MS. 434, f. 122v: Ab antiquo vsitatum fuerit in manerio ibidem quod post decessum cuiuscumque tenentis natus filius eorundem iunior inde consuetudine manerii predicti antecessores suos succedere solebant ad grave dampnum et detrimentum tocius homagii et tenementorum suorum. This MS. is an abstract of the court rolls of Chertsey Abbey, 1–21 Edw. III. The passage is cited in E. Toms, "Chertsey Abbey and Its Manors under Abbot John de Rutherwyk, 1307–1347," MS. Thesis for the degree of Ph D. in the University of London, 80. See also *Chertsey Abstract*, xiii.

10. PRO, SC 2, Port. 179, no. 18, m. 7: Walterus filius Gerardi Le [*Koc qui*] se per multum tempus elapsum subtraxit de feodo domini sine licencia venit et petit se admitti ad illam *[dimidiam vir]*gatam terre quam Willelmus Koc primogenitus frater eius tenet de domino pro gersuma inde prius facta racione quod ipse Walterus est postnatus filius dicti Gerardi; quare dicit se maius ius habere in dicta terra quam dictus Willelmus qui modo eam tenet. Et predictus Willelmus dicit quod iniuste illam terram petit pro eo quod ipse quadraginta annis elapsis tempore Willelmi de Gomecestr' tunc Abbatis Rameseie illam gersumauit secundum vsum et consuetudinem manerii; quia dicit quod tunc talis fuit consuetudo quod primogenitus frater gersumaret, haberet, et teneret terram seruilem post decessum antecessorum suorum, [*set quod*] Willelmus de Wassingle tempore quo fuit senescallus domini illam consuetudinem mutauit. Et quod tale sit ius [*suum*] petit quod inquiratur. The first two gaps in the text are due to holes in the MS., the last two to bad rubbing, but the reconstruction of the missing letters is fairly obvious.

11. Brit. Mus., Add. MS. 40,167, f. 31v (Court Book of Barnet, Herts.): Thomas filius et heres Walteri filii et heredis Walteri Bartholomei de la Barnet venit et petit versus Robertum filium Walteri Bartholomei vnum tenementum quod Iohannes Bartholomeu filius dicti Walteri Bartholomei iunior tenuit cum pertinentiis in la Barnet quod clamat esse ius et hereditatem suam, quia dicit quod predictus Walterus Bartholomeu senior fuit seisitus de dicto tenemento et quod idem Walterus dedit de licencia domini dictum tenementum cum pertinentiis dicto Iohanni Bartholom' filio suo iuniori tenedum sibi et heredibus suis, qui quidem Iohannes obiit sine herede de corpore suo procreato, post cuius decessum dictus Robertus ingressus est dictum tenementum cum pertinentiis et iniuste detinet ac ipsum Thomam de iure et hereditate sua deforciat, vt dicit, eo quod dictus Walterus pater dicti Thome fuit filius et heres dicti Walteri Bartholem' qui dictum tenementum dedit dicto Iohanni filio suo iuniori, post cuius decessum ad predictum Thomam filium et heredem dicti Walteri filii Walteri Bartholom' competit reuersio ratione hereditatis quia ius respicere debet ad exitum fratris senioris, et hoc petit quod inquiratur per inquistionem bonam. Venit dictus Robertus et dicit quod de consuetudine ville de la Barnet iuste ingressus est dictum tenementum post mortem dicti Iohannis fratris sui iunioris propter propinquitatem sanguinis in ascendendo et hoc petit quod inquiratur, et dictus Thomas similiter. Inquisitio capta per . . . qui dicunt super sacramentum suum quod de consuetudine ville de Barnet et halimoti ibidem tenementa sic data vt supradictum est alicui filio iuniori si plures fuerunt fratres semper proximo fratri secundum partum propter propinquitatem sanguinis reuerti debent et non ad fratrem seniorem nec ad eius exitum. Et hoc habent et vtuntur secundum consuetudinem halimoti eorundem et non secundum legem communem. Ideo

adiudicatum est quod dictus Robertus habeat seisinam dicti tenementi de domino et dat pro seisina habenda .xl. d.

12. Brit. Mus., Add. MS. 40,625, f. 15v: Iohannes de Eywode reddidit sursum in manus domini totam terram que vocatur terram Iulian' ad opus Iohannis filii sui et dominus seisiuit eundem de terra predicta cum tota vestura tenenda secundum consuetudinem halimoti faciendo etc. et dat pro seisina dimidiam marcam. Postea venit dictus Iohannes filius predicti Iohannis et concessit terram predictam cum pertinenciis dicto Iohanni patri suo tenendam ad totam vitam suam.

13. Brit. Mus., Add. MS. 40,167, f. 31r: Thomas Freysmouth reddidit sursum vnum mesuagium cum curtilagio et aliis pertinentiis sicut iacet inter tenementum Henrici Geffrey ex parte vna et Gunnildewelle ex altera abbuttant' iuxta cimiterium Sancti Iohannis in le Barnet. Et dominus seisiuit Willelmum filium dicti Thome de principali dicte domus et mesuagii cum vno solario et vna camera tenendo sibi et suis faciendo inde etc. Et etiam dominus seisiuit Galfridum filium dicti Thome de duabus cameris et vno solario dicte domus et mesuagii tenendis sibi et suis faciendo annuatim dicto Willelmo fratri suo .j. d. et domino alia seruicia inde debita et consueta, nec faciet vastum. Et dat domino pro seisina .ij. s., plegii etc. Et est forma seisine talis quod dictus Thomas et Agnes vxor eius tenebunt dictum mesuagium ad terminum vite eorundem. Another example of a settlement on two sons is to be found in Brit. Mus., Stowe MS. 849, f. 14v.

14. PRO, Eccl. I, Bundle 16, no. 43, m. 19: Ricardus Hycheman dat domino .xij. d. pro inquisicione habenda si Galfridus Leuwyne fecerit ipsum Ricardum heredem suum de tenemento quod idem Galfridus tenet in Halton post mortem ipsius Galfridi . . . . Inquisicio venit et dicit quod idem Galfridus venit in plena curia et duxit dictum Ricardum in manum suam et dixit in plena curia: Quia heredem de corpore meo non habeo et predictus Ricardus est filius sororis mee, ipsum facio et constituo heredem meum post vitam meam de eodem tenemento.

15. See an entry for 36 Henry III in the Court Book of Barnet: Brit. Mus., Add. MS. 40,167, f. 3v: Simon Godesdyng dedit domino .xij. d. pro licencia dandi iiij^or acras terre cum pertinentiis duobus pueris suis de secunda vxore sua quas cepit de domino de nouo assarto, quas videlicet cepit ad halimotum post festum Sancti Michaelis, et vnam acram alii puero quam tenuit de Iohanne le Bor et vnam acram alii puero quam tenuit de Willelmo Toby. See also an entry of 2 Edw. II in a court roll of King's Ripton, Hunts., Brit. Mus., Add. Roll 34,770, m. 1d: Rogerus Dyke qui mortuus est legauit Mariote filie Hugonis Russel vnam placiam de perquisito suo continentem vnam rodam, que dat domino etc. .j. d. There are other entries like this, all referring to land *de perquisito*.

CHAPTER X

1. The following entry appears in a court roll of Newington, Oxon., of 33 Edw. I: PRO, Eccl. I, Bundle 26, no. 47, m. 1d: Iohannes West qui tenuit de domino duas virgatas terre custumarie viam vniuerse carnis est ingressus . . . . Et Alicia vxor dicti Iohannis venit et habebit liberum bancum suum ad totam vitam suam et fecit feoditatem. Et inuenit plegios . . . ad sustentandum predictum tenementum in domibus et aliis sicut decet et ad custodienda principalia que ad heredem pertinent.

2. Henry E. Huntington Library, San Marino, California, Court Rolls of Wotton Underwood, m. 4. For other examples, see A. E. Levett, *Studies in Manorial History*, 191.

3. Sometimes nothing was left to the dead man, because the lord took his share, as, for instance, at Cardington and other towns of Shropshire, *c.* 1185; see B. A. Lees, *Records of the Templars* (British Academy: Records of the Social and Economic History of England and Wales), 41: Ius illud in obitu est tercia pars de catallis in omnibus, post debitis redditis. Secunda pars uxori et tercia

pueris. See also, J. Brownbill, ed., *The Ledger-Book of Vale Royal Abbey* (The Lancs. and Cheshire Record Soc.), 118, and R. Holmes, ed., *Chartulary of St. John of Pontefract* (Yorks. Arch. Soc., Record Ser.), II, 674.

4. Thus in a court roll of Wistow, Hunts., 22 Edw. I, Brit. Mus., Add. Roll 39,597, m. 3: Preceptum est balliuis capere in manum domini omnia bona infirmorum legata ad quorum testamenta facienda non vocantur.

5. Wilkins, *Concilia*, II, 156.

6. See, for instance, an entry of 9 Edw. I in the court book of Park in St. Stephen's, Herts.: Brit. Mus. Add. MS. 40,625, f. 22v: Iurati presentant quod Adam Amfelis manet London' et credunt quod est ibi apprenticius cuiusdam candelatoris.

7. F. W. Maitland, ed., *Bracton's Note Book*, no. 794.

8. See an entry for Feltwell, Norfolk, in the Ely custumal of 1277, Brit. Mus., Cotton MS. Claudius, C. XI, f. 257v: Item sciendum quod vnusquisque anilepimannus qui habuerit bestias in villa dabit pro qualibet vacca vnum denarium et pro quolibet bulloquio vnum denarium de cupany vt supra et omnes alie bestie sue iacebunt in falda domini.

9. See an entry for Brandon, Suffolk, *ibid.*, f. 312v: Et sciendum quod vnusquisque vndersetle vel anilepiman vel anilepiwyman domum vel bordam tenens de quocumque illam teneat inueniet vnum hominem ad quamlibet trium precariarum autumpni ad cibum domini vt supra.

Item sciendum quod vnusquisque anilepiman non habens aliquam mansionem in villa siue sit in seruitudo siue non inueniet vnum hominem ad vnam precariam autumpni tantum vel dabit vnum denarium.

10. *Ibid.*, f. 88v: Summa precariarum in autumpno duodecies viginti et octo cum prepositis preter coterellos vndersetles et anilepimans que (sic) innumerabiles sunt quia quandoque accrescunt quandoque decrescunt. The coterells and undersettles will be spoken of later.

11. Another is the Old German *hagestolz* (Old English, *hagustald*), which meant a celibate, and also a man who held only a small piece of land enclosed with a hedge. See J. Hoops, *Reallexikon der Germanischen Altertumskunde*, s. v. *hagestolz*.

12. PRO, SC 2, Port. 209, no. 55, m. 8: De Reginaldo Damemalde vt supra pro fine vnius virgate terre quondam Matilde matris sue de tenemento Iohannis de Sancta Elena; et idem Reginaldus concedit Waltero fratri suo vnam domum et quolibet anno ad festum Sancti Michaelis vnum quarterium frumenti dum ipse sine vxore et in dominio isto extiterit et hoc concessit coram plena curia. In margin: .vj. li. The fine seems large. John *de Sancta Elena* seems to have held a sub-manor in Sevenhampton.

13. F. M. Page, "The Customary Poor Law of Three Cambridgeshire Manors," *Cambridge Historical Journal*, III (1930), 128.

14. I have found entries in the court rolls of other Cambridgeshire manors which probably refer to a custom like these others, but only probably, for instance an entry of 1312 for Graveley, Cambs.: PRO, SC 2, Port. 179, no. 16, m. 6d: Iohannes Hughloc et Thomas Hughloc, Robertus Hughloc, fratres eiusdem Iohannis, et Alicia soror eorundem dant domino .xij. d. pro consideracione ville habenda de porcione terre quondam matris eorum que eos contingit secundum consuetudinem ville post mortem matris eorum. Et ideo preceptum est predictis iuratis similiter et toti ville quod facerent eis habere porcionem suam quam secundum consuetudinem predictam de terra matris eorum habere debent. Et postea consideratum est quod habeant hospicium et sex bussellos bladi de omnimodo blado. My interpretation of this passage is this: One of the sons of the woman who last held the tenement inherited it. Three of his brothers and one of his sisters now demanded a portion of the tenement as of custom. This portion cannot have been large, and must have been of the order of the grants to landless brothers at Oakington, Cottenham, and Drayton, because what the brothers and sisters finally

got was only lodging and six bushels of corn. And I guess that they would have lost this if they had married or left the manor. Again, an entry of 29 Edw. I for Over, Cambs.: PRO, SC 2, Port. 179, no. 11, m. 7: Rogerus Iue dat domino .vj. d. pro consideracione curie habenda vtrum habebit mansionem in mesuagio Roberti Iue fratris sui secundum consuetudinem ville nec ne. Ideo preceptum est iuratis quod adeant ibidem ad videndum et faciendum secundum quod viderit de iure expedire. Roger is to have a dependance on the holding of Robert his brother, who presumably is the heir. I suspect that he would have lost it if he had married. Again, an entry of 6 Edw. II for Chilton, Suffolk. PRO, SC 2, Port. 203, no. 23, m. 4 records that John, son of Gilbert Sheldrake, gave his brothers, Gilbert and William, and his sisters, Christiana and Avis, each one acre of land. Descent of tenements to a single heir was the rule at Chilton.

15. R. W. Darré, *Das Bauerntum*, 113.

16. Brit. Mus. Add. Roll 39597, m. 2d: Henricus filius Iohannis recognouit se teneri Willelmo Aleyn ex promissione cum filia sua mar' in vna roba precii dimidie marce et vna patella continente duas lagenas precii .xvj. d. et vno vrtiol' continente dimidiam lagenam precii .xvj. d. et .ij. tapetis precii duorum solidorum et in quinque solidis argenti ad vnam carectam ferro emendandam et in .vj. s. de argento dato eisdem ecclesie, summa .xxij. s. iiij. d. Ex quibus dictus Willelmus relaxauit .ix. s. Et pro iniusta detencione dictus Henricus in misericordia .xij. d. This is printed also in W. O. Ault, *Court Rolls of the Abbey of Ramsey and of the Honor of Clare*, 208.

17. PRO, DL 30, Bundle 32, no. 288, m. 2d: Ricardus filius Matillde summonitus fuit ad respondendum Iohanni Wade in placito detencionis catallorum. Et vnde idem Iohannes queritur quod dictus Ricardus ei iniuste detinet vnam vaccam precii .x. s. et vnam robam precii .j. marce que quidem bona dare sibi concessit cum filia sua eo tempore quando ipse Iohannes eam duxit in vxorem ad dampnum suum .xx. s. etc. . . . Ricardus filius Matillde summonitus fuit ad respondendum Iohanni Wade in placito conuencionis. Et vnde idem Iohannes queritur quod dictus Ricardus iniuste venit contra conuencionem et ideo iniuste eo quod conuenit inter eos die Veneris proxima post festum Inuencionis Sancte Crucis anno [   ] in villa de Duff' quod predictus Ricardus eidem Iohanni edificaret infra annum a die conuencionis predicte quamdam domum super placeam predicti Iohannis et Auicie vxoris eius in villa de Holebrok precii .xl. s. quam quidem domum dictus Ricardus nondum adhuc edificauit vnde dictus Iohannes deterioratus est et dampnum habet ad valenciam .lx. s. et inde producit sectam. . . . Per licenciam curie predicti Iohannes et Ricardus concordati sunt ita quod pro omnibus querelis accionibus et rebus preteritis dictus Ricardus filius Matillde concessit se dare incontinentim eidem Iohanni vnam vaccam cum vno vitulo precii .xiij. s. Item vnam supertunicam precii .v. s. vel .v. s. Item .iij. bidentes precii .iiij. s. vel. .iiij. s.

18. At times there is a hint that the lord and the custom of the manor did not allow the granting of land with a girl in marriage. Thus in a court roll of Hemingford Abbots, Hunts., of 22 Edw. I: Brit. Mus., Add. Roll 39597, m. 7d: De Simone Kok natiuo quia in preiudicium domini concessit Iohanni le Sachere vnam domum cum sorore sua quam duxit in vxorem .xij. d. . . .; m. 8: De tota villa et iuratis . . . quia in preiudicium domini et contra consuetudinem ville permiserunt Simonem Cok dare vnam domum cum sorore in liberum maritagium.

19. PRO, SC 2, Port. 171, no. 63, m. 6: Iohannes Russel de la Penne et Hanys' [perhaps Hanysia] vxor eius filia Roberti Osbern veniunt et dicunt quod dicta Hanis' est filia et heres propinquior predicti Roberti custumarii domini qui obiit seisitus in vno mesuagio et .xx. acris terre custumarie. Dant domino prout inquiratur. . . . Super quo tota curia carcata est et iurata vtrum dicta Hanis' sit filia et heres dicti Roberti secundum consuetudinem manerii propinquior vel si nunquam fuit extra homagium domini alleniata aut cum bonis et catallis dicti

patris sui maritata, quia plures habet sorores; que dicit vnanimiter quod dicta Hanys' est heres propinquior et quod nunquam fuit aleniata nec de bonis ipsius Roberti maritata per quod non debeat admitti ad dictam hereditatem obtinendam. Et concessa est eis seisina saluo iuris cuiuslibet. See also A. E. Levett, *Studies in Manorial History*, 241.

20. F. W. Maitland, ed., *Bracton's Note Book*, no. 988.

21. PRO, SC 2, Port. 179, no. 10, m. 14d: Rogerus Syward et Alanus Syward sunt plegii Margerie Syward de .ij. solidis soluendis domino Celerario vt habeat consideracionem Curie de porcione quam ei pertinet dum vixerit sine marito de vna virgata terre seruilis quondam patris sui modo mortui. Et villa venit et dicit quod dicta Margeria et Auicia soror eius secundum consuetudinem manerii habebunt hospicium et vnam ringam bladi videlicet medietatem de frumento et aliam medietatem de pisis vnde Rogerus Syward frater earum satisfaciet eis de medietate et Alanus alius frater earum de alia medietate ratione quod terra participata est modo inter dictos fratres.

CHAPTER XI

1. Brit. Mus., Add. Roll 39597, m. 16: Elyas de Britendon reddidit sursum in plena curia vnum mesuagium et dimidiam virgatam terre censuarie in Crangfeld cum bosco adiacente et cum omnibus aliis pertinenciis suis et tres acras terre de forlond in eadem ad opus Iohannis filii sui, qui quidem Iohannes venit per Willelmum le Moyne de Bernewell atornatum suum et fecit finem cum domino Abbate per tres marcas argenti pro eadem terra habenda. . . . Et prefatus Elyas vsque ad festum Sancti Michaelis proximum futurum colere faciet et seminare competentur totam dictam terram sumptibus suis propriis de qua terra recipiet plenarie sibi et Christiane vxori sue in proximo autumpno medietatem tocius vesture. Et predictus Iohannes de residuo inueniet eidem Elye et Christiane vxori sue honorabilem sustentacionem suam in cibis et potibus quamdiu vixerint et remanebunt cum predicto Iohanne in hospicio in capitali mesuagio. Et si contingat quod absit quod contenciones et discordie futuris temporibus oriantur inter partes quod insimul in vna domo pacifice stare non possunt, prefatus Iohannes inueniet eisdem Elye et Christiane vel cuicuique eorum diucius alterum eorum superuixerit vnam domum in curia sua cum vno curtilagio vbi possunt honorabiliter habitare et dabit singulis annis eisdem Elye et Christiane vel eorum alteri qui diucius vixerit sex quarteria duri bladi ad festum Sancti Michaelis, videlicet .iij. quarteria frumenti .j. quarterium et dimidium ordei .j. quarterium et dimidium fabarum et pisorum et .j. quarterium auene. Et insuper dicti Elyas et Christiana per conuencionem inter partes confectam integro habebunt penes se omnia bona et catalla dicte domus mobilia et inmobilia que sua fuerant illo die quando dictus Elyas soluit sursum in manibus domini terram suam predictam.

2. Among the printed court rolls, these transactions are common in the *Halesowen Court Rolls*; see I, 159, 165; II, 264, 293, 399, 481, 513, 557; III, 55, and in *Wakefield Court Rolls*: I, 86, 87, 286.

3. PRO, SC 2, Port. 171, no. 63, m. 17: Quia preceptum fuit ad vltimam curiam seisire in manum domini dimidiam virgatam terre custumarie quam Petronilla de Teye dimisit Iohanni filio suo sine licencia domini prout confertum fuit ad vltimam curiam et ad istam curiam concordatum est inter predictos Petronillam et Iohannem quod predicta Petronilla sursum reddat in manus domini totam predictam dimidiam virgatam terre ad opus predicti Iohannis cui tradita est seisina habenda et tenenda dicto Iohanni et suis de domino in vilinagio ad voluntatem eiusdem per seruicia et consuetudines debitas et consuetas, videlicet in forma subscripta, videlicet quod dictus Iohannes inueniet dicte Petronille ad totam vitam ipsius Petronille rationabilem victum vt in cibo et potu prout tali decet mulieri et preter hoc dicta Petronilla habebit vnam cameram cum garderoba ad orientale caput dicti mesuagii ad infra hospitandum ad totam

vitam ipsius Petronille et vnam vaccam, quatuor oves, et vnum porcum euntes et sustentatos super dictum dimidiam virgatam terre tam in yeme quam estate ad totam vitam ipsius Petronille pro vestu et calciatura sua.

4. As in the court book of Codicote, Herts., under 34 Edw. I, Brit. Mus., Stowe MS. 849, f. 28r: Et est forma talis quod dictus Galfridus habebit vnam cameram ad vnum caput de capitali domo in qua hospitari poterit ad terminum vite ipsius Galfridi. . . .

5. Brit. Mus., Add. MS. 40,167, f. 50v: Iohannes in the Hale reddidit sursum in manus domini vnum mesuagium et totam terram quam tenuit in le Estbarnet cum omnibus suis pertinenciis. Et Iohannes ate Barre venit et fecit finem cum domino tenendo dictum mesuagium et terram sibi et suis faciendo inde seruicia debita et consueta sub hac forma quod idem Iohannes ate Barre cognouit quod inueniet predicto Iohanni in the Hale annuatim quamdiu idem Iohannes in the Hale vixerit vnum nouum garmamentum cum capucio, precii .iij. s. .iij. d., duo paria lineorum, tria paria sotularium noua, vnum par caligarum nouum, precii .xij. d. et victum in esculentis et potulentis honeste prout decet. Et predictus Iohannes in le Hale laborabit et deseruiet eidem Iohanni ate Barre in honestis seruiciis pro posse suo. Et predictus Iohannes ate Barre satisfecit domino pro herietto dicti Iohannis in the Hale per vnum iumentum vnde balliuus oneratur. Et dat de fine pro ingressu habendo .ij. s.

6. PRO, SC 2, Port. 179, no. 17, m. 1d: Henricus Edmond et Simon filius suus queruntur de Ada Hog de hoc quod ad festum Purificationis duobus annis elapsis conveneant inter se et predictum Adam scilicet quod predictus Simon commoraret cum predicto Ada in domo sua a predicto festo Purificationis vsque ad terminum vite dicti Ade et post mortem predicte Ade predictus Simon haberet vnam virgatam terre eiusdem Ade, et ad istam conuentionem et huius rei maiorem securitatem plenius et firmius obseruandam predictus Adam reddidit sursum predictam terram suam in manus firmarii ville ad opus predicti Simonis tenendam post mortem suam sicut predictum est et predictus Henricus pater ipsius Simonis dedit dimidiam marcam pro gersuma pro dicta terra tenenda in forma predicta etc. Postea vero dictus Adam fugauit predictum Simonem extra domum suam ad festum Sancti Petri ad Inuincula proximum sequens et conuentionem ei fregit ad dampnum etc. Et predictus Adam predictam conuentionem bene cognouit in forma predicta set dicit quod predictus Simon commoraret secum in hospitio suo et ei deseruiret bene et honeste vt filius suus et quando cum ipso steterat a festo Purificationis vsque ad Gulam Augusti venit prefatus Henricus et attraxit predictum Simonem filium suum de eo per consilium et incitamentum suum proprium. Et quod ita sit petit quod inquiratur et alii similiter. Capta inde inquisitio per .xij. iuratos predictos qui dicunt quod predictus Adam non fregit conuentionem predictis Henrico et Simoni sicut questi sunt desicut idem Adam paratus fuit ad sustentandum eundem Simonem in domo sua et ad conuentionem tenendam si predictus Simon non recessisset contra voluntatem dicti Ade et adhuc paratus fuit postquam recesserat si redidisse voluerat. Quare consideratum est quod predictus Simon nichil habeat de dicta terra post mortem dicti Ade et quod ipse et pater suus pro falso clamore sunt in misericordia .vj. d. Et dictus Adam inde sine die sine calumpnia dictorum Henrici et Simonis.

7. J. Brownbill, ed., *Ledger Book of Vale Royal Abbey* (The Lancs. and Cheshire Record Soc.), 117.

8. PRO, Eccl. 1, Bundle 40, no. 1, m. 2: Mabilia de Middeton' que tenuit de domino quoddam tenementum seruile mortua est. Et dominus habet de herietto .j. iumentum. Et venit Ricardus filius et heres dicte Mabilie et dat pro ingressu et habet seisinam et fecit feoditatem et inuenit plegios de tenemento et seruiciis sustentandis. Et idem dat domino .xij. d. pro licencia habenda maritandi se.

9. Brit. Mus., Add. Roll 19069, m. 1: Caterina Leman reddit sursum in manus domini vnam acram et tres partes vnius rode terre cum vno mesuagio desuper

et vnam rodam herbagii ad opus Rogeri Grilling et Agnetis filie ipsius Katerine et heredum de corpore ipsius Agnetis exeuntium. Et si dicta Agnes obierit sine herede de corpore suo exeunte dicta terra heredibus ipsius Caterine reuertatur. Et pro ista reddicione dicti Rogerus et Agnes concedunt quod dicta Caterina teneat totam dictam terram dum vixerit. Et post eius decessum remaneat dictis Rogero et Agnete in forma predicta. Et in tali forma seisina eis liberatur tenenda in villenagio ad voluntate domini prioris etc., saluo etc. et dant etc. Et dicti Rogerus et Agnes dant pro seisina habenda et pro licencia se simul maritandi, plegius Bedell. In margin: fin' .v. s.

10. Brit. Mus., Add. Roll 9145, m. 3: Adam Waryn reddit sursum in manus domini vnum mesuagium et septem acras terre cum omnibus terris et tenementis que et quas habet in Scnytirtone ad opus Roberti Waryn et heredum suis (*sic*) habenda et tenenda predicto Roberto et heredibus suis in villenagio per seruicia inde debita et consueta saluo iure etc. et dat pro ingressu . . . . Et predictus Robertus concedit et obligat se et heredes suos et omnia tenementa predicta ad inueniendum et ad custodiendum dictum Adam ad terminum vite sue in victu et vestitu et omnia alia necessaria.

Et idem Robertus fecit finem pro licencia se maritandi. In margin: fin' .xiij. s. .iiij. d.

11. Of these court books, I have consulted those at the British Museum. They are: Stowe MS. 849 (Codicote), Add. MS. 6057 (Croxley in Rickmansworth), Add. MS. 40,167 (Barnet), Add. MS. 40,625 (Park in St. Stephens), Add. MS. 40,626 (Cashio in Watford). These places are all in Hertfordshire. The books consist of important entries extracted from the court rolls of these manors and written out in hands of the late fourteenth and fifteenth centuries. They include the earliest entries from English manorial court rolls now known, dating from 1236, and continue for two hundred years. So far as I know, there are no sources for English social history of such scope or interest, and some or all of them should be included in any program for printing English manuscripts of the Middle Ages. I have already drawn upon them, and shall continue to do so. They have been described in A. E. Levett, *Studies in Manorial History*, 79–96. See also *Hist. MSS. Com. Report on Various Collections*, VII, 304, 306. Luckily extents of some of the St. Albans manors have also survived and are in the British Museum. These are Lansdowne MS. 404, ff. 46–48 (Caldecote, 14 Edw. II), Add. MS. 36,237, ff. 1–12 (Tittenhanger, 5 Edw. III), Add. MS. 40,734 (Codicote, 1331).

12. Brit. Mus., Add. MS. 40,626, f. 2v: Walterus le King dat domino in gersummam .x. s. pro terra patris sui et pro vxore ducenda.

13. Brit. Mus., Add. MS. 40,625, f. 62r: Gilbertus Hendigome reddidit sursum in manus domini vnam ferthlingatam terre quam Iohannes Hugh aliquando tenuit quam quidem terram dictus Gilbertus habuit de dimissione domini. Et Willelmus filius dicti Gilberti fecit finem cum domino tenendi dictam terram sibi et suis faciendo inde seruicia debita et consueta, nec faciet vastum. Et dat de fine pro ingressu habendo et pro licencia se maritandi. .ij. s. For the whole subject of marriage custom on the St. Albans manors see A. E. Levett, *Studies in Manorial History*, 235–247.

14. PRO, Eccl. I, Bundle 26, no. 48, m. 1: Agnes ate Touneshende relicta Stephani ate Touneshene venit in plena curia et dicebat se esse inpotentem ad tenendum vnum mesuagium et vnam virgatam terre seruilis condicionis quam prius tenuit secundum vsum manerii de Newenton' post mortem dicti Stephani. Et de kinda iste terre inquisicio facta est per totam curiam que dicit quod Agnes que fuit filia Nicholai ate Touneshende kendam habet propinquiorem eiusdem terre secundum consuetudinem manerii faciendo domino quod de iure facere debet pro ingressu, et discessu eiusdem Agnetis dominus habebit pro herietto .v. s. quia nullum habet viuum auerium. Et postea venit dicta Agnes et finem fecit pro ingressu ad dimidiam marcam. Et postea venit Henricus filius Iohannis Aleyn et finem fecit

NOTES TO CHAPTER XII

437

vt ducere possit in vxorem dictam Agnetem ad dimidiam marcam, plegii vtriusque omnes tenentes domini. Et quia supradicta Agnes dictam terram reddidit in manus domini vt Agnes filia filii sui intrare posset, ideo dictus Henricus et Agnes concesserunt ad terminum vite eiusdem Agnetis ad inueniendum eidem Agneti victum et vestitum secundum quod status exigit, et si non placuerit eidem Agneti dabunt annuatim dicte Agneti tria quarteria bladi videlicet duo frumenti et siliginis et vnum ordei videlicet ad quatuor terminos [terms stated]. Et si defecerint in solucione ad dictos terminos in parte vel in toto, concedunt quod teneantur domino in dimidia marca et dicte Agneti similiter in dimidia marca pro suis dampnis.

15. F. W. Maitland, ed., *Bracton's Note Book*, no. 1922. This has *Anselinus*; it is possible that the original was *Anselmus*.

16. Robert Mannyng of Brunne, *Handlyng Synne*, ed., F. J. Furnivall (EETS), ll. 1121–1132.

17. W. A. Wright, ed., *The Metrical Chronicle of Robert of Gloucester* (Rolls Series), I, ll. 819–822.

18. See C. M. Arensberg, *The Irish Countryman*.

19. R. H. Tawney, *The Agrarian Problem in the Sixteenth Centry*, 101, 104n.

CHAPTER XII

1. B. Pass. IX, ll. 113–116.

2. This account of matchmaking is based on C. B. Robinson, ed., *Rural Economy in Yorkshire in 1641, Being the Farming and Account Books of Henry Best* (Surtees Soc.), 116: "Concerninge our Fashions att our Country Weddinges." Customs in the 13th century may have been much unlike these, but we have no account of them.

3. PRO, Eccl. I, Bundle 26, no. 20, m. 2d: Ita conuentum est inter Willelmum le Toter' de Warebry (?) ex parte vna et Iacobum West ex altera, videlicet quod dictus Iacobus ducet Aliciam filiam dicti Willelmi in vxorem et dictus Willelmus acquietabit dictum Iacobum de .xj. marcis versus dominum de fine et dabit ei Iacobo alia catalla sicut inter eos conuentum est, propterea dictus Iacobus concessit eidem Willelmo totum proficuum terre sue a festo Sancti Michaelis hoc anno vsque ad finem quatuor annorum proximorum sequentium et nulla bona extra feodum domini amouebit et domos sustinebit et emendabit et dictum Iacobum per dictum tempus detentionis sustinebit, et in quinto anno inueniet eidem Iacobo ad Gulam Autumpni inbladatam terram suam cum feno et omnibus aliis fructibus illius anni.

4. PRO, SC 2, Port. 179, no. 15, m. 6: Conuictum est per iuratos quod Stephanus prepositus fregit Andree preposito conuentionem eo quod conuenit inter eos quod prefatus Stephanus deberet sustinuisse Agnetem filiam dicti Andree et hospitasse in domo sua vel quod competens hospitium infra curiam suam ei inueniet cum omnibus suis necessariis ratione quod Stephanus filius prefati Stephani predictam Agnetem duxit in vxorem. Qui quidem Stephanus postea predictam Agnetem contra conuentionem predictam extra domum suam expulsit. Ideo predictus Stephanus in misericordia xl. d., plegii Iohannes Mareschal, Alexander prepositus, Robertus le Hyrde, Iohannes le Porter. Et pro eisdem plegiis prefatus Stephanus prepositus sustinebit predictam Agnetem cum viro suo in domo sua vel competens hospitium ei inueniet cum omnibus suis necessariis infra curiam suam, etc.

5. Brit. Mus., Add. MS. 40,626, f. 24v: Walterus filius Ailrich venit et gersummauit terram que fuit Ailrich patris sui. Et super hoc venit Adam Irman et cepit dictam terram et dictum Walterum heredem vsque ad etatem ita quod interim edificiet et terram et tenementum sustinebit et dabit Elenam filiam dicti Ade dicto Waltero, et faciet seruicia debita et consueta, et dat pro gersumma et termino et maritagio dimidiam marcam.

6. *Handlyng Synne* (EETS), ll. 1663–1666.

7. *Ibid.*, ll. 11203–11206. *For-þy* means "therefore" and *by-hete* means "promise."

8. *Ibid.*, ll. 11209–11214.

9. Brit. Mus., Add. MS. 6057, f. 5v (Court Book of Croxley, Herts., 49 Henry III): Et predictus Robertus habuit licenciam maritandi filium suum filie predicti Walteri si ambo consenserint.

10. Lyndwood, *Provinciale*, 271.

11. Quoted in G. E. Howard, *A History of Matrimonial Institutions*, I, 349.

12. Brit. Mus., Add. MS. 40,625, f. 17: Simon filius Willelmi atte Leye dat domino .xij. d. ad habendam inquisicionem si ipse sit propinquior heres quam Willelmus [frater] suus. Et idem Willelmus dat .xviij. d. pro eadem. Et inquisicio dicit quod idem Willelmus propinquior heres est quam dictus Simon frater eius quia idem Willelmus primogenitus fuit et pater suus matrem suam affideuerat antequam idem Willelmus genitus fuit, ideo etc. Et idem W. venit et gersumauit terram predicti Willelmi patris sui faciendo inde etc. See also f. 56v.

13. *Wakefield Court Rolls*, I, 212.

14. *Ibid.*, III, 91. See also III, 98. On the other hand at Cranfield, Beds., in 5 Edward II, there seems to have been a prejudice strong enough to prevent women who bore children out of wedlock from inheriting land: PRO, SC 2, Port. 179, no. 16, m. 10d: Mortuo Willelmo Telat qui tenuit de domino vnum mesuagium et .ix. acras terre venit Dulcia Telat filia predicti Willelmi et calumpniat predictam terram secundum consuetudinem etc. tanquam heres propinquior dicti Willelmi. Et petit inde consideracionem curie. Et veniunt omnes custumarii et dicunt quod predicta Dulcia ius habet in predicta terra et mesuagio. Et postea compertum est quod predicta Dulcia peperit extra matrimonium, et in rotulis curie manerii precedentibus per recordum et veredictum diuersarum inquisicionum predictorum custumariorum quod filie custumariorum que sic deliquerunt extra matrimonium terras patrum et matrum perderent imperpetuum. Et ideo quia predicti custumarii contradixerunt quod prius dixerant pro iudicio sicut patet in predictis rotulis in misericordia .xx. s. Et predicta Dulcia nichil capiet de predicta terra. I have encountered in the rolls of no other manor entries admitting such a custom, but for a custom according to which illegitimacy was a bar to inheritance, see *Chertsey Abstract*, xiv.

15. J. S. Udal, *Dorsetshire Folk-lore*, 198. See also T. Hardy, *Two on a Tower*. Even in this century, the rate of illegitimate births varies from district to district in Great Britain in ways which probably can be explained only by the survival in certain districts of customs of this sort. Illegitimacy is high in northern England, southern and north-eastern Scotland. See A. Leffingwell, *Illegitimacy and the Influence of Seasons upon Conduct*.

16. Quoted in G. E. Howard, *A History of Matrimonial Institutions*, I, 350.

17. *Handlyng Synne* (EETS), ll. 8393–8398. For further information on troth-plighting, see F. J. Furnivall, ed., *Child-Marriages, Divorces, and Ratifications, etc.* (EETS), xliii ff., and J. Raine, ed., *Depositions and Other Ecclesiastical Proceedings from the Courts of Durham* (Surtees Soc.), 53, 79.

18. Sir H. Spelman, *Concilia*, II, 162. This same passage is printed in Wilkins, *Concilia*, I, 581, as one of the Constitutions (*c.* 1220) of Richard Marsh, Bishop of Durham.

19. Pollock and Maitland, *History of English Law* (2nd ed.), II, 364–385.

20. Brit. Mus., Cotton MS. Claudius C. XI, f. 117v: Item si filia istius fornicata fuerit cum aliquo et inde sit accitata tunc dabit triginta et duos denarios pro leyrwite. Et si idem cum quo ipsa prius fornicata fuerit eam postea desponsauerit tunc quietus erit de gersuma. Another type of entry appears in the Court Book of Park in St. Stephens, Herts., under date of 33 Edw. I: Brit. Mus., Add. MS. 40,625, f. 37v: Item dicunt (iurati) quod Alicia filia Thome atte Hulle fecit leyrwit, ideo in misericordia, plegius Fulco Hendegome. Et idem Fulco Hendegome

venit et dat domino .ij. s. pro licencia ducendi dictam Aliciam in vxorem et pro dicto leyrewit, plegius Gilbertus Hendegome.

21. These manuals are to be found as follows: J. W. Legg, ed., *The Sarum Missal*, 413–418 (The MS. edited here is of the second half of the thirteenth century, collated with other early MSS.); W. G. Henderson, ed., *Manuale et Processionale ad Usum Insignis Ecclesiae Eboracensis* (Surtees Soc.), 24–40; Appendix, 17–26, 115–120, 157–169 (from MSS. of the twelfth and later centuries and early printed manuals); W. Maskell, ed., *Monumenta Rituala Ecclesiae Anglicanae* (2nd ed.), I, 50–77 (use of Sarum, according to early printed manuals).

22. W. Maskell, *op. cit.*, I, 54; Si vero nullus impedimentum proponere voluerit: interroget sacerdos dotem mulieris, videlicet arrhas sponsales, et dicuntur arrhae annuli vel pecunia vel aliae res dandae sponsae per sponsum: quae datio subarrhatio dicitur, praecipue tum quando fit per annuli dationem: et tunc vulgariter desponsatio vocatur.

23. Wilkins, *Concilia*, I, 582.

24. W. G. Henderson, ed., *Manuale et Processionale*, 27. See Appendix, 166: according to Brit. Mus., Harleian MS. 2860 (early 15th cent.) the words of the groom when he put the ring on the bride's finger were: Ego hoc annulo desponso te, in corpore meo honoro, de isto argento et ceteris bonis jam dictis vel definitis te doto.

25. W. Maskell, *op. cit.*, I, 58n. The MS. is Brit. Mus., Bibl. reg. 2A, xxi.

26. Pollock and Maitland, *History of English Law*, II, 397.

27. Brit. Mus., Add. Roll 39597, m. 3: Robertus Iuwel conuictus est per iuratos quod ex consuetudine debuit dedisse vnum gentaculum omnibus famulis Curie de Wystowe die quo nupsit vxorem suam et hoc non fecit. Ideo pro iniusta detencione in misericordia .xij. d. plegius Robertus atte Broke. Et per eundem plegium satisfaciet eisdem famulis de predicto gentaculo. See also *Ramsey Cartulary*, I, 338, 347, Brit. Mus., Add. Roll 34915, m. 1d (Wistow), and PRO, DL 30, Bundle 154, no. 35, m. 1 (Letcombe Regis, Berks., 52 Hen. III).

28. W. Brown, ed., *Yorkshire Inquisitions*, I (Yorks. Arch. Soc., Record Ser.), 265.

29. W. Mannhardt. *Wald- und Feldkulte*, I, 471–4.

30. Brit. Mus., Add. MS. 40,626, f. 27v: Reginaldus atte Lee per licenciam domini concessit quod Lucia vxor eius teneat quamdiu vixerit totam terram cum vna domo et cum omnibus aliis pertinentiis preter redditum de Watford quam 3ara atte Lee mater predicti Reginaldi tenuit nomine dotis post decessum viri sui faciendo inde seruicia debita et consueta et faciet introitum suum et exitum ita quod non ingrediatur clausum vel portas dicti Reginaldi. Et dictus Reginaldus concessit quod dicta Lucia teneat supradictam terram cum domo et aliis pertinentiis vt supradictum est quamuis diuorcium inter eos celebratur. Et dicta Lucia concessit quod si per ipsam steterit quo minus diuorcium inter eos celebratur in forma iuris et hoc ad sectam et custus dicti Reginaldi ex tunc dicta conuentio pro nulla habeatur et terram suam rehabeat sine impedimento.

CHAPTER XIII

1. F. W. Maitland, ed., *Bracton's Note Book*, no. 669.

2. Brit. Mus., Add. MS. 40,625, f. 47v: Willelmus de Smaleford reddidit sursum in manus domini totum tenementum suum quod tenuit. Et dictus Willelmus et Benedicta le Knyghtes dant domino .ij. s. pro dicto tenemento cum pertinentiis tenendo ipsis et heredibus dicti Willelmi post decessum dictorum Willelmi et Benedicte faciendo inde seruicia debita et consueta nec facient vastum. Et habent licenciam simul maritandi, nec elongabunt catalla sua extra feodum domini.

3. Brit. Mus., Add. MS. 40,167, f. 29: Alicia de Rallingburi venit et petit terram quam habuit per licenciam domini de dono Gilberti Edward quondam mariti sui ad terminum vite, quam quidem terram Ricardus Snouh tenet iniuste

vt dicit. Et dictus Ricardus dicit quod propinquior heres est et inde de licencia domini seisitus fuit et quod dicta Alicia nunquam inde seisita fuit ad terminum vite nec aliter et hoc petit quod inquiratur. Et dicta Alicia similiter. Dicit inquisitio quod dicta Alicia habuit dictam terram de dono dicti Gilberti ad ostium ecclesie et quia illa donatio sine licencia domini pro nulla habebatur venit dicta Alicia tunc temporis et fecit finem cum domino pro dicta terra tenenda ad terminum vite eiusdem Alicie et quod post decessum eiusdem Alicie ad veros heredes reuertetur faciendo inde etc. Ideo consideratum est quod dicta Alicia teneat etc. in forma predicta.

4. Brit. Mus., Add. Roll 31,310, m. 2d: Philipus Capel qui tenuit de domino sex acras terre in bondagio reddendo inde per annum .xij. d. et consuetudines obiit de cuius morte dominus habebit heriettum: vnum porcellum precii .viij. d. Et venit Alicia que fuit vxor eiusdem Philipi et petit dicta tenementa per consuetudinem etc., que talis est quod vidue tenere debent vt bancum suum tenementa de bondagio quousque filius iunior fuerit quindecim annorum et tunc vidue reddere debent filio iuniori vt heredi medietatem hereditatis etc. Et tenebunt aliam medietatem vt bancum suum si se tenuerint viduam etc. Et in forma predicta habet predicta Alicia ingressum et vadiauit pro releuio .xij. d., plegius, Ricardus le Berd. Et fecit iuramentum consuetum et custodeat predictum tenementum secundum consuetudinem.

5. Brit. Mus., Add. Roll 28,029, m. 1: Lucia relicta Walteri le Hurt venit et dat domino .ij. s. pro inquisicione habenda vtrum ipsa maius ius habeat in quandam terram quam Ricardus le Hurt tenet quam ipse Ricardus qui tenens est. Et inquisicio facta per . . . , qui dicunt super sacramentum suum quod predicta Lucia in viduitate sua permisit se in fornicationem decidere et insuper desponsare sine licencia domini. Et ideo Willelmus de Faukham (the reading of this word is uncertain) tunc tempore senescallus adiudicauit predictam terram esse forisfactam et comisit terram Ricardo fratri dicti Walteri quondam viri dicte Lucie et sic remanet.

6. For instance, Bramford, Suffolk (Brit. Mus., Cotton MS. Claudius, C. XI, f. 315r). At Rattlesden, Suffolk, the widow held all her husband's land as dower, unless she married or fornicated. Then she kept half as dower (*ibid.*, f. 280v).

7. PRO, Eccl. I, Bundle 26, no. 14, m. 1: Robertus filius Roberti coopertoris apparens venit et dat domino .ij. s. pro inquisitione habenda super exigentiam vnius dimidie virgate terre cum pertinentiis in manerio de Niwenton', et in qua terra ius habere clamat post mortem Roberti patris sui defuncti tenentis in capite de domino Priori. Et conuenit facere inde seruicia et consuetudines secundum vsum dicti manerii per plegios Roberti Thornepeny et Ricardi West. Et inquisitio capta per tota curia dicit per sacramentum . . . iuratorum, qui dicunt per sacramentum quod dictus Robertus filius Roberti coopertoris nichil habet iuris in dicta dimidia virgata terre cum pertinentiis viuente Agnete vxore dicti Roberti patris dicti Roberti. Set tamen dictus Robertus recipiet annuatim dimidium quarterium bladi duri medietatem iemalis et alteram medietatem quadragesimalis de dicta terra per vitam dicte Agnetis matertere (*sic*) sue.

8. At Stratford St. Mary, Suffolk, in 22 Edward I, the custom was that the widow, if she was the first wife of the last holder, held all his tenement as dower; if she was the second wife, only half. This shows the elaborateness of customary provisions — see Brit. Mus., Add. Roll 26876, m. 8: Et dicunt (i.e. the men of the inquest) etiam quod Isabella vxor eiusdem Roberti habebit medietatem mesuagii et terre predicte pro dote sua quia secunda vxor eiusdem Roberti, et si prima fuisset totum mesuagium et totam terram tenere ad totam vitam suam secundum consuetudinem manerii.

9. PRO, Eccl. I, Bundle 26, no. 6, m. 1 (6 Edward I) and Eccl. I, Bundle 26, no. 10, m. 1 (8 Edward I).

10. PRO, Eccl. I, Bundle 16, no. 43, m. 25: Thomas de Merdene qui tenuit de domino vnam virgatam terre et dimidiam et .j. quartronam terre viam vniuerse

carnis est ingressus per quod dominus habet pro herietto .ij. boues. Post venit Hugo filius dicti Thome primogenitus et optulit se facere domino ea que de iure facere debet pro dictis tenementis, et ingressus est predicta tenementa per heriettum dicti Thome patris sui et fecit feoditatem. Et Alicia que fuit vxor dicti Thome dotata est de omnibus terris et tenementis que fuerunt predicti Thome secundum consuetudinem manerii prout bene constat tote curie, et totum mesuagium apud Merdene remanet penes dictum Hugonem et idem Hugo dabit dicte Alicie duas marcas et dimidiam argenti et tres meliores fraxinos apud Merdene pro vna domo super mesuagium quod dicitur Stotkeslond construenda, et dicta Alicia remanebit in principali domo apud Merdene quousque dicta domus fuerit parata iuxta discrescione domini et balliui.

11. Brit. Mus., Add. MS. 40,625, f. 24v: Alicia atte Forde reddidit sursum in manus domini vnum tenementum cum pertinenciis in le Parkstrate, et dominus seisiuit inde Henricum le Blund ita quod si habeant prolem inter eos legitimum descendat heredibus eorum. Si vero obierint sine herede inter eos procreato et dictus Henricus superuixerit dictam Aliciam tenebit dictum tenementum tota vita sua et post eius decessum dictum tenementum reuertetur heredibus dicte Alicie, et dat pro seisina habenda et eciam pro licencia se maritandi .xij. d.

12. Brit. Mus., Add. MS. 40,626, f. 31r: Elias Huwe venit et dat domino .x. s. pro licencia se maritandi cum Sara atte Grove relicta Ade Payne et ingrediendi terram eiusdem Sare tenendam ad terminum vite sue si masculum de dicta procreauerit. Et si contingat quod dicta Sara cum predicto Elia filium non habuerit tunc post obitum eiusdem Sare ad Iohannam filiam dictorum Ade et Sare plene reuertatur faciendo inde seruicia debita et consueta.

13. Brit. Mus., Cotton MS. Claudius, C. XI, f. 315r: Et si ille heres fuerit mulier tunc bene liceat ei se maritare sine licentia domini sed quod vir suus sit ydoneus. Et si ille vir in vita mulieris moriatur tunc nichil dabitur pro herieto. . . . Et vir suus prenominatus immediate post mortem mulieris omnino debet exire vel si moriatur in vita viri sui et heredem habuerit de se procreatum tunc nichil dabitur pro suo releuio sed vir suus remanebit in toto predicto tenemento tota vita sua et post mortem dabitur pro releuio melior bestia domus.

14. *Chertsey Abstract*, xxxviii.

15. W. O. Ault, ed., *Court Rolls of the Abbey of Ramsey and of the Honor of Clare*, 279.

16. *Halesowen Court Rolls*, I, 119. See also p. 55 and elsewhere.

17. PRO, Eccl. I, Bundle 26, no. 18, m. 1d: Tota curia requisita dicunt super sacramentum suum quod Walterus Goneyre qui duxit [*in vxorem*] quandam viduam videlicet Isabellam Bolt habebit post mortem eiusdem Isabelle nuper defuncte j. cotagium cum minimo curtilagio et .iij. acras terre de vna virgata terre quam eadem Isabella tenuit, videlicet, in quolibet campo vnam acram, meliorem preter vnam, et de dicto mesuagio et terra predicta faciet principali tenenti omnia seruicia de dicto mesuagio et terra debita et consueta et inueniet domino .j. hominem ad magnam precariam et post mortem eiusdem Walteri dabitur heriettum. For other accounts of this custom in the Newington rolls, see Eccl. I, Bundle 26, nos. 22 and 29.

18. PRO, Eccl. I, Bundle 26, no. 6, m. 1.

19. PRO, SC 2, Port. 209, no. 59, m. 4: Inquisicione facta de hominibus de Grundewelle qui dicunt quod si quis sit viduarius, et fuerit filius natus in astro, dum est viduarius habeat totum tenementum, et si velit vxorare quod filius de astro habeat partem terre ad viuendum, et conciderant quod filius Ade Seluerlok habeat .vj. acras terre patris sui quando Iohannes qui desponsauit matrem suam velit vxorare et respondere ei secundum quantitatem terre.

20. The meaning of the Norman-French legal term, *astrier*, is somewhat different. See P. Vinogradoff, *Villeinage in England*, 56.

21. PRO, SC 2, Port. 175, no. 79, m. 6: Adam Gene intrat in terram et tenementum quod pater suus tenere consueuerat et dat de releuio .ij. s. .vj. d. et

Felicia mater eiusdem fecit fidelitatem vsque etatem eiusdem Ade qui modo est etatis .ij. annorum, plegii Walterus Spilemon et Alexander de Rod', ad soluendum die dominica post festum S. Martini et ad sustinendum domos, gardinum, et alia sine detrimento. Item Thomas de Lupeg' maritus dicte Felicie pro licencia intrandi in dictum tenementum. In margin: licencia .ij. s.

22. C. Sandys, *Consuetudines Kanciae* (1851), 164. See also F. W. Maitland, ed., *Bracton's Note Book*, no. 282: Predictus Iohannes habuit custodiam illam ea ratione quod fuit avunculus suus ex parte matris sue sicut consuetudo est in socagio. See also *Victoria County History of Kent*, III, 325.

23. Tacitus, *Germania*, 20, and see for example *Gisli's Saga*.

24. Brit. Mus., Add. MS. 40,167, f. 29v: Iohannes filius et heres Iohannis le Clerck optulit se versus Iohannem Saly et Agnetem vxorem suam in placito terre et petit versus predictos Iohannem et Agnetem mesuagium et v. acras terre cum pertinentiis in la Barnet quod clamat esse ius suum et hereditatem suam quia dicit quod predictus Iohannes le Clerk pater suus cuius heres ipse est fuit seisitus de predicto mesuagio cum terra et quod idem Iohannes pater suus tradidit dictum mesuagium cum predicta terra cuidam Iohanni le Bor cum quodam Pagano filio dicti Iohannis le Clerk tenendum ad terminum vite ipsius Iohannis le Bor tandem pro nutritura dicti Pagani qui infra quem terminum diem suum clausit extremum. Post cuius decessum venit dictus Iohannes le Clerk et petiit dictum mesuagium cum terra predicta de predicto Iohanne le Bor sibi retradi pro defectu nutriture dicti Pagani. Et idem Iohannes le Bor dictum mesuagium cum terra predicta retradere negauit sed tenere voluit dictum mesuagium cum terra per formam conuentionis ad terminum vite sue quia in se non remansit defectus nutriture predicte ut dicebat. See also ff. 33r and 34r.

CHAPTER XIV

1. An example from the court book of Park, Herts., Brit. Mus., Add. MS. 40,625, f. 62v: vna virgata terre que vocatur Eywodeyherd. Eywode was the name of a family of the neighborhood.

2. PRO, Eccl. I, Bundle 16, no. 43, m. 17d: Thomas le Chapman de Weston venit et dat domino .vj. d. [he finds pledges, whose names are given] pro inquisicione curie habenda quod si aliquis tenens domini terram suam dimiserit ad certos terminos et tenens domini infra terminum obierit, quis debeat post mortem tradentis conuencionem complere. Et tota curia super hoc carcata est, et venit et dicit quod nullus tenens domini potest terram suam dimittere nisi ad vitam suam, et quod heres non tenetur ad warandum.

3. PRO, SC 2, Port. 197, no. 81, m. 2: Ad istam curiam venit Ricardus ate Mere et dat domino .ij. s. ad inquirendum si sit verus heres de terra quam Iuliana Ioye emit de Willelmo ate Mere. . . . Qui dicunt per sacramentum suum quod dicta Iuliana emit dictam terram, habuit et tenuit toto tempore vite sue, set post mortem nulli poterit vendere, legare nec assignare. Vnde concessa est seisina predicto Ricardo et heredibus suis.

4. Brit. Mus., Add. MS. 40,625, f. 22v: Margareta que fuit vxor Galfridi atte Sloo petit versus Iohannem le Bedell duas acras et tres rodas terre in quas non habet ingressum nisi per dictum Galfridum quondam virum suum cui in vita sua contradicere non potuit. Et Iohannes dicit quod habet ingressum per dominum Abbatem qui nunc est et eum inde vocat ad warantum.

5. PRO, Eccl. I, Bundle 26, no. 29, m. 1d: Thomas le Northerne per plegios Iohannis West et Hugonis Dauid in placito terre optulit se versus Walterum le Rouwe et Matildam vxorem suam attachiatos per Samuelem le Northerne et Nicholaum Trys. Et predictus Thomas queritur quod predicti Walterus et Matilda iniuste ei deforciant dimidiam virgatam terre in Brochamton' que est ius suum et quod Iohannes le Northerne pater suus eis dimiserat ad vitam ipsius Iohannis et post vitam suam predicto Thome vt filio et heredi secundum consuetudinem

ville descendere debuit et ad hoc ducit sectam. Predicti Walterus et Matilda presentes defendunt ius predicti Thome etc. et dicunt se ius habere in predicta terra pro eo quod Iohannes le Northerne pater predicte Matilde predictam terram reddidit in manus domini et ipsi de manibus Prioris eandem terram ceperunt sibi et suis tenendam per seruicia et consuetudines inde debitas et similiter dicunt quod idem Thomas qui modo petit simul cum Iohanne patre suo venit in plena curia et ius quod fuit suum reddidit in manus Prioris et cepit pro hoc de predictis Waltero et Matilda vnum bouem, et sic habent melius ius in sua tenura quam predictus Thomas in sua peticione et petunt quod inquiratur. Et predictus Thomas dicit quod predictus I. pater suus per consuetudinem ville nec reddere nec aliquo modo alienare potuit terram predictam nisi tantummodo ad vitam suam et bene dicit quod venit in plena curia simul cum patre suo et pro maledictione sua non audebat eum dedicere de tempore suo, set ius suum nunquam reddidit et quod hac racione maius ius habet in sua peticione quam predicti W. et M. in sua tenura et petit quod inquiratur. Et facta est inquisicio per sacramentum . . . qui dicunt per sacramentum suum quod dictus Thomas nunquam ius suum de predicta terra in manus domini reddidit.

6. PRO, Eccl. I, Bundle 16, no. 43, m. 14: Inquisicio facta per totam curiam de terra quam Thomas Hemmyg (elsewhere Hemmyng) [*tenet*] ex dimissione Aleyse relicte Ricardi le Wodeward vtrum predictus Thomas habeat melius ius tenendi dictam terram sicut eam tenet ad totam vitam ipsius Aleyse quam Ricardus le Wodeward qui rectus heres est illius terre post mortem dicte Aleyse qui clamat esse propinquior omnibus aliis tenendi illam terram pro tanto dando sicut aliquis alter velit dare. Et predicta inquisicio dicit quod dictus Ricardus habet melius ius tenendi illam terram quam aliquis alter pro tanto dando sicut aliquis extraneus dare voluerit.

7. See M. DeW. Hemmeon, *Burgage Tenure*, 111–126. The customs of burgage tenure in English boroughs of the Middle Ages should be compared with village customs. The former are similar to the latter but less conservative. Free sale and free devise of land were common among the borough customs; they certainly were not among village customs.

8. PRO, SC 2, Port. 179, no. 17, m. 1d: Willelmus filius Petri molendinarii dat domino .xij. d. per plegium prepositorum pro consideracione curie habenda de vno crofto quod predictus Petrus tenet. Et dicit quod maius ius habet in dicto crofto quam predictus Petrus etc. Capta inde inquisitio per predictos .xij. iuratos qui dicunt quod predictus Petrus tenet vnum croftum de hereditate sua et vnam dimidiam virgatam terre de iure et hereditate vxoris sue. Et quia consuetudo talis est quod nullus debet duas terras tenere, ideo in respectu quousque venerit coram domino etc. Et postea compertum est quod dictus Willelmus illud gersum'. Ideo quietus. See also *Chertsey Abstract*, xiv.

9. Examples: PRO, Rentals and Surveys, Gen. Series, Roll 730 (Extents of lands of the Earl of Albemarle in Cumberland and Yorks., 44 Henry III) and Rentals and Surveys, Gen. Series, Port. 10, no. 33 (Rental and Custumal of lands of Richard de Harington in Bratoft, Irby, and Friskney, Lincs., 40 Henry III).

10. PRO, DL 30, Bundle 104, no. 1470, m. 1: Lyna filia Hugonis le Coylynr optulit se versus Nicholaum Attefen et inquisitio facta per vicinos dicit super sacramentum suum quod idem Nicholas tradidit eidem Lyne et Willelmo fratri suo quamdam dimidiam acram terre at terminum .iij. annorum ad seminandum ad campi partem et quod quando iidem Lina et Willelmus seminauerant dictam dimidiam acram terre anno primo venit idem Nicholas et vendidit eis partem suam de dicta vestura. Et quod postea vendidit idem Nicholas totam dictam vesturam Iohanni Querbec (?) et Martino Clut et tradidit eis dictam terram cum pluri terra ad firmam contra primam conuentionem suam et abstulit eis dictum bladum et terminum suum. Ideo Nicholas in misericordia et condonatur quia pauper et Lina recuperet dampnum sua.

11. PRO, SC 2, Port. 197, no. 81, m. 1: Simon Aunsel venit in plena curia

et tradidit sursum in manus domini .j. croftam terre ad opus Walteri Morel et heredum suorum faciend' inde seruicia debita et consueta eidem terre pertinentia soluendo per annum domino Regi .ij. d. qui debent allocari in redditu predicti Simonis. Et predictus Walterus dat pro ingressu habendo in predictam terram .xij. d. de fine, plegius Augustinus clericus. Et fecit fidelitatem.

12. *Ramsey Cartulary*, I, 344.

13. W. Hudson, "Manorial Life," *History Teachers' Miscellany*, I, 180, says that 753 transfers of land recorded in the court rolls of Hindolveston, Norfolk, in the years 1309–1329, may be divided as follows: death and inheritance, 74; transference during the holder's lifetime to relations and other successors, especially transference from old folks to their children, 136; as a result of poverty due to stress of bad seasons (there were several bad harvests in 1315–1319), 100; private convenience, including marriage settlements, 443.

14. W. H. Hale, ed., *The Domesday of St. Paul's* (Camden Soc.), lv.

15. The Glastonbury custumals have been printed. They are: J. E. Jackson, ed., *Liber Henrici de Soliaco* (Roxburghe Club), and *Glastonbury Rentalia* (Somerset Record Soc.). The Ely custumals are in the British Museum. They are Cotton MS. Tiberius, B. II, and Cotton MS. Claudius, C. XI.

Chapter XV

1. F. W. Maitland and W. P. Baildon, eds., *The Court Baron* (Selden Soc.), 73.

2. *Halesowen Court Rolls*, I, 167.

3. For instance, *Wakefield Court Rolls*, I, 100 (Dec. 6, 1274): Thomas de Thorneton, charged with the taking of a stag by his mainpast, has respite until the next court.

4. *Bristol and Gloucester Archaeological Soc. Trans.*, II, 307. Cf. the custom of another Gloucestershire manor, Siston, in 1299: PRO, Ancient Extents (Exchequer), no. 8, m. 1: Item dicunt (the members of the inquest) quod omnes natiui et natiue huius manerii qui terras et tenementa non tenent et non deseruiunt patribus et matribus eorum faciet quilibet eorum .iij. precarias in autumpno, precium cuiuslibet .j. d. ob. et fuerunt hoc anno .viij. Et sic estimatur quod possunt esse communibus annis. Summa precariarum .viij. que valent .xij. d. See also W. H. Hale, ed., *Register of Worcester Priory* (Camden Soc.), 15a. Curiously, the only other place from which the word *selfode* has so far been reported is the county of Durham at the opposite corner of England. See W. Greenwell, ed., *Bishop Hatfield's Survey* (Surtees Soc.), 168, 171, 174, 232; and *Monasticon Anglicanum* (1846), III, 318 (Rental of Tynemouth Priory, 1378).

5. Examples: *Rotuli Hundredorum*, II, 748: at Brudecot, Oxon., Hugo le Frankeleyn held three yardlands, and among his services was the following: Item debet invenire omnes servientes suos locatos per annum except' uxor' sua et nutrice et pastor in autumpno ad ij precarias; Brit. Mus., Cotton MS. Claudius, C. XI, f. 39v: at Littleport, Cambs., John, son of Vincent, and Elizabeth his wife held 18 acres: Et inueniet totam familiam suam ad precariam ceruisie in autumpno ad cibum domini preter vxorem domus et filiam suam maritabilem et ipsemet erit custos messorum suorum, set si vxor et filia voluerint metere propria blada metent in suis croftis et non alibi; *Bleadon Custumal*, 209: Tenens virgatam terre vel dimidiam virgatam terre . . . faciet tres bedripes cum tota familia sua, exceptis uxore et magistro serviente suo.

6. *Chichester Custumal*, 33.

7. J. Thorpe, ed., *Custumale Roffense*, 10.

8. Brit. Mus., Cotton MS. Claudius, C. XI, f. 312v: Et sciendum quod vnusquisque undersetle vel anilepiman vel anilepiwyman domum vel bordam tenens de quocumque illam teneat inueniet vnum hominem ad quamlibet trium precariarum autumpni ad cibum domini vt supra. That some of such sub-tenants had very poor houses is suggested by a custumal of Felsted, Essex, of 7 Henry III:

Brit. Mus., Add. MS. 24,459 (1), f. 3v. There it is said of a yardling: Si habet tenentes habentes portas quilibet illorum debet facere dies cons' sicut mos est, si scalare (sic) nichil.

9. *The Court Baron* (Selden Soc.), 146–147.

10. See a statement in a survey of the manor of Hendon, Middlesex, 1574, printed in *Trans. of the London and Middlesex Arch. Soc.*, New Series, VII, Part 1, 35: "It is our Custom and hath out of mind been used that the Head Tenant payeth to the Lord his Chief Rent and Service and the Undersets being parcel of the same Head Tenant are to pay unto the Head Tenant rateably and according to their proportion." For other printed references to undersettles see *Glastonbury Rentalia*, 108; J. E. Jackson, ed., *Liber Henrici de Soliaco* (Roxburghe Club), 129; J. C. Atkinson, ed., *Quarter Sessions Records* (North Riding Record Soc. Publications, Vol. I), 95; R. Dymond, *The Customs of the Manors of Braunton*, 27.

11. *Rotuli Hundredorum*, II, 332.

12. F. LePlay, *Les Ouvriers européens*, III, 132–144.

13. E. Demolins, *Les Grandes Routes des peuples*, II, 494 ff.

Chapter XVI

1. F. Liebermann, *Die Gesetze der Angelsachsen*, I, 445–453.

2. *Rotuli Hundredorum*, II, 746–747.

3. E. A. Kosminsky, "Services and Money Rents in the Thirteenth Century," *Economic History Review*, V (1935), no. 2, 30 ff. He finds (1) that in the shires described in the Hundred Rolls "out of 650 vills described and investigated, 336 are not identical with manors." The majority are manors only in Oxfordshire. (2) That the Hundred Rolls "show that about 60 per cent of the territory examined is represented by demesnes with dependent villein land (i.e. the typical manorial elements), while 40 per cent, a considerable proportion, is non-manorial in character." (3) That there are two kinds of non-manorial arrangements: (a) a complex of free tenants, in feudal relation to their lord, paying rent, (b) demesne without villein land. (4) That the amount of land in villeinage varies roughly directly as the size of the estate. (5) That according to investigations in the *Inquisitiones Post Mortem* of the thirteenth century, labor services are valued at something like 40 per cent of the total render of tenants in the eastern counties of the Midlands where the proportion is highest.

4. See the Burton-on-Trent Chartulary: *Collections for a History of Staffs.* (William Salt Arch. Soc.), V, (Part I), 83, 85.

Chapter XVII

1. Pollock and Maitland, *History of English Law*, I, 229–511.

2. *Wakefield Court Rolls*, I, 116.

3. Maitland, *Manorial Courts*, 105.

4. PRO, SC 2, Port. 179, no. 79, m. 5: Hugo Carectarius petit vt possit a seruitute liberari, et dat domino pro libertate habenda .xiij. s. iiij. d. et de cheuagio .ij. d. per annum. In margin: redempcio .j. marc'.

5. *Halesowen Court Rolls*, III, 125, 130.

6. *Ibid.*, II, 359.

7. *Ibid.*, II, 377. A similar case appears *ibid.*, III, 49.

8. In the Ely Custumals, some tenants who in 1222 were classed by the jurors as *censuarii*, because they paid merchet, were classed in 1277 as free. See D. C. Douglas, *Medieval East Anglia*, 74. This shows the unimportance of these tests in distinguishing real differences in class.

9. A good example of a village where all four classes were represented was Fleet in Lincs., between the Fens and the Wash. There land was divided into free-

londs, from which rent was paid, molelonds, from which rent and boon-work but not week-work was rendered, werklonds, from which week-work was rendered, and Mondaylonds, from which one day's work a week was rendered, on Mondays. In like manner the tenants were divided into four classes: freeholders, molemen, werkmen, and Mondaymen. See N. Neilson, *A Terrier of Fleet, Lincolnshire* (British Academy: Records of the Social and Economic History of England and Wales, Vol. IV).

10. J. Thorpe, ed. *Custumale Roffense*, 10. See also J. E. Jackson, ed., *Liber Henrici de Soliaco* (Roxburghe Club), 22; J. Stevenson, ed., *Chronicon Monasterii de Abingdon* (Rolls Series), II, 304; Sir H. C. Maxwell-Lyte, ed., *Two Registers Formerly Belonging to the Family of Beauchamp of Hatch* (Somerset Record Soc.), 6–8.

11. For instance, at Bredon, Worcs., in 1299; see M. Hollings, ed., *The Red Book of Worcester* (Worcs. Hist. Soc.), Part I, 100: Enchelond — Johannes le Enche tenet j virgatam. He did the same services as the other yardlings, except that he might be called upon to be the lord's plowman. Had his name some reference to this fact?

12. See, for instance, the customs of Cirencester, *temp.* King John, printed in *Bristol and Gloucester Arch. Soc. Trans.*, II, 297.

13. J. Brownbill, ed., *Ledger-Book of Vale Royal Abbey* (Lancs. and Cheshire Record Soc.), 121.

14. For instance, *Rotuli Hundredorum*, II, 332, 460.

15. For instance, an entry in a court roll of Hemingford, Hunts., 35 Edw. I: PRO, SC 2, Port. 179, no. 9, m. 5d: Et dicunt (iurati) quod Henricus de Styuecle habet quinque coterellos dampnum facientes in blado vicinorum. Ideo in misericordia .xij. d.

16. N. S. B. Gras, *The Social and Economic History of an English Village*, 71–74, estimates that in a good year such as 1257–1258 a yardling in Crawley, Hunts., might make 55s. 7d. as a money surplus for expenditure. In a bad year, such as 1306–1307, he might make 36s. 8d. A farthinglander, that is, a man who held a fourth of a yardland, which put him near if not in the cotter class, might make in a good year 15s. 11d. and in a bad one 6s. 9½d. A farthinglander could not stand a bad crop without physical suffering.

17. Brit. Mus., Cotton MS. Claudius, C. XI, f. 52: Et iste et pares sui debent colligere parare leuare et tassare totum fenum in parco de Dunham quod omnes predicti plenas terras et dimidias tenentes falcauerint.

18. *Chichester Custumal*, 4.

19. W. O. Massingberd, ed., *Lincolnshire Records, Final Concords*, I, 341.

20. Brit. Mus., Add. Roll 8139, m. 4: Quilibet habens carucam quamuis non habeat nisi .v. acras debet tres in anno arare sine prandio. Si vero dominus amplius voluerit carucas habere debet eis prandium inuenire et qui carucam non habuit debet vnam operacionem. At m. 5, under Stevenage, Herts., we read: Item si aliquis consuetudinarius habeat vnam carucam licet non habeat nisi dimidiam virgatam terre vel quartam partem debet arare qualibet ebdomada die Iouis dimidiam acram.

21. PRO, Ancient Extents (Exchequer), no. 8, m. 7: . . . et quia communiter accidit quod nullos boues habet, nec consuetudo illa non excedit reprisam, ideo non extenditur.

22. See, for instance, *Chichester Custumal*, 16.

23. *Glastonbury Rentalia*, 78.

24. M. Bloch, *Les Caractères originaux de l'histoire rurale française*, 197, 199, 250. See above, p. 73.

25. See G. H. Gerould, "The Social Status of Chaucer's Franklin," *Publications of the Modern Language Assn. of America*, LXI (1926), 262–279.

26. *Ramsey Cartulary*, III, 49.

27. For instance, Brit. Mus., Cotton MS. Tiberius, B. II, f. 107v.

28. *Chichester Custumal*, 99.

29. *Gloucester Cartulary*, III, 181.

30. "Queen Mary's Psalter" in the British Museum. See H. S. Bennett, *Life on the English Manor*, 125.

31. *Chronica Majora* (Rolls Ser.), III, 528.

Chapter XVIII

1. *Wakefield Court Rolls*, I, 118.

2. F. W. Maitland and W. P. Baildon, eds., *The Court Baron* (Selden Soc.), 104.

3. *Piers Plowman*, C. Pass. IX, ll. 23–31.

4. N. Neilson, *Customary Rents* (Oxford Studies in Social and Legal History, Vol. II) should be consulted as a kind of dictionary of customary rents and services.

5. J. Thorpe, ed., *Custumale Roffense*, 10.

6. Brit. Mus., Cotton MS. Claudius, C. XI, ff. 45v, 50r.

7. PRO, SC 2, Port. 179, no. 7, m. 2: Et dicunt (iurati) quod . . . subtrahunt venire ad vnam precariam in autumpno quem aduentum solebant facere pro communa pasture habenda. Ideo si decetero aueria eorum in pastura inueniantur inparcentur.

8. Brit. Mus., Add. Roll 34333, m. 1 (Inquest as to the customs of Ramsey Abbey in Barton-in-the-Clay, Beds., 39 Henry III).

9. *Chichester Custumal*, 89.

10. W. O. Ault, *Court Rolls of the Abbey of Ramsey and of the Honor of Clare*, 201, note 35.

11. Brit. Mus., Cotton MS. Claudius, C. XI, f. 178r.

12. PRO, SC 2, Port. 175, no. 80, m. 3: Operarii de ville distr' pro defalt' arur' bene, quia vbi quilibet caruca deberet arare .iij. acras ad benam, sive fuerit de iij. iugis sive iiij., ibi arur' non arat nisi acram et dimidiam.

13. PRO, SC 2, Port. 179, no. 4, m. 1: De Henrico Godswein quia noluit operari ad secundam precariam autumpni et quia impediuit dictam precariam precipiendo quod omnes irent ad domum ante horam et sine licentia balliuorum ad dampnum domini dimidie mare et quia alias male messuit suos Béénes super culturam domini .vj. d. See Maitland, *Manorial Courts*, 91.

14. PRO, SC 2, Port. 179, no. 10, m. 11: . . . Cotmanni attachiati fuerunt et calumpniati pro eo quod non venerunt ad honerandas carectas domini cum feno ad cariandum de prato in manerio prout prius facere consueuerunt retroactis temporibus prout testatur per Hugonem Prest Clavigerum, qui veniunt et allegant quod talem consuetudinem facere non debent nisi tandem ex amore ad instancia seruientis vel prepositi et hoc petunt quod inquiratur per liberos et alios. Et inquisicio venit et dicit quod supradicti Cotmanni fenum domini debent in pratis tassare et similiter in curia domini Abbatis set non tenentur ad honerandas carectas in pratis nisi fuerit ex amore speciaii ad instancia domini. Et quia senescallus non habuit registrum Rameseie per quod potuit certiorari super isto negocio, ponitur in respectum prefata demanda donec etc. Et quod dicti Cotmanni super dicta demanda habeant colloquium et tractatum dum domino Abbate.

15. G. Slater, *The English Peasantry and the Enclosure of Common Fields*, 183–186.

16. The best descriptions I know of bees (in a Vermont town) appear in Rowland Robinson, *Danvis Folks* (ch. VI, "The Paring Bee", ch. XVI, "A Raising Bee"). Robinson's books give the best and most charming sketches which exist of country life in old New England. All Yankees should know them better.

17. For instance, the author took part in a "raising" at Morgan Center, Vermont, 4 September 1940.

18. E. Gutch, *Folklore of Yorkshire (North Riding and the Ainsty)*, 338. See also M. C. Balfour and N. W. Thomas, *Folklore of Northumberland*, 122: "In

spring of 1893, when a Belford farm was taken up by a new tenant, a 'Boon plowing' was held, at which about 40 teams were present and shared the work; all were dressed and decorated with ribbons, and going to the field in procession, with their great limbs hung with wreaths and bells, they were really a fine sight. A good day's work was done, the new tenant providing a dinner for the plowmen in return for the assistance offered by his new neighbors."

19. See Sir W. Craigie and J. R. Hulbert, eds., *A Dictionary of American English on Historical Principles*, s. v. *bee*.

20. For *Christmasselones* (or *loves*) done for the lord on the St. Albans manors see Brit. Mus., Add. MS. 36,237, ff. 11v, 4v; Brit. Mus., Add. MS. 40,734, f. 15v; Brit. Mus., Cotton MS. Tiberius, E. VI.

21. PRO, Ancient Extents (Exchequer), no. 8, m. 1: Item dicunt quod sunt ibi .xij. custumarii quorum quilibet tenet .xx. acras terre et reddit ad Natale vnum panem, precii j. d. et j. gallinam, precii .ij. d. pro quibus veniet cum vxore sua die Natale Domini et habebunt cibum suum ad vnum repastum vel percipiet de domino pro eodem .iij. d. Et quia dicta consuetudo nichil valet vltra reprisam ideo non extenditur.

22. By G. G. Coulton, in his admirable book, *The Medieval Village*, 44–54.

23. *Cambridge Antiquarian Soc. Communications*, VI (1884–1888), 165. W. Kennett, *Parochial Antiquities* (1695), 401, gives the services of a villein at Burcester, 1325: et virgata terrae integra ejusdem tenurae habebit liberam ad vesperas quae vocatur Evenyngs tantam sicut falcator potest per falcam levare et domum portare per ipsam; *ibid.*, Glossary, *s. v.* Evenyngs: "This gave occasion to the present corrupt and shameful practice of day-labourers in felling and faggotting of wood, who at every evening carry home with them a burden of wood, as great as they are able to bear, tho' it be no part of their wages or covenanted hire."

24. *Ramsey Cartulary*, I, 476.

25. PRO, SC 2, Port. 179, no. 5, m. 1. De Hugone filio Walteri quia iacuit ad capud selionis in autumpno et impediuit opus domini .vj. d.

26. Brit. Mus., Add. Roll 39463, m. 1: De Roberto Crane quia ludebat alpenypricke in opere domini .iij. d.

27. But consider the following entries in a court roll of 1279 of Stratton, Wilts., PRO, SC 2, Port. 209, no. 59, m. 4: Iohannes Wolfon (?) in misericordia pro transgressione facta domino de arratura eo quod misit puerum loco suo. [In margin: vj. d.] Nicholas messor in misericordia quia paciebatur puerum ire loco dicti carucarii.

28. See *Rotuli Hundredorum*, II, 605.

29. See, for instance, *Cambridge Antiquarian Soc. Communications*, VI (1884–1888), 168.

30. Brit. Mus., Cotton MS. Tiberius, B. II, f. 195v: Et sciendum quod debent esse quieti de operacione per vnam ebdomadam ante Natale et per duodecim dies infra Natale et per dimidiam ebdomadam ante Pascham et in ebdomada Pasche et Pentecostes et in omni die tam celebrabili quod caruce non debent arare.

31. F. W. Maitland, "History of a Cambridgeshire Manor," *English Historical Review*, IX (1894), 417 ff.

32. Maitland, *Manorial Courts*, 100–105. See also *Ramsey Cartulary*, III, 59–64.

33. *Rotuli Hundredorum*, I, 6. See also I, 142.

34. G. G. Coulton, *The Medieval Village*, 131–135, quoting from *The Ledger Book of Vale Royal Abbey* (Lancs. and Cheshire Record Soc.), 37 ff.

35. For an outline of the history of Halesowen, see H. L. Roth, *Bibliography and Chronology of Hales Owen* (The Index Soc.).

36. For the history of the abbey, see *Victoria County History of Worcestershire*, II, 163.

37. T. R. Nash, *Collections for a History of Worcestershire*, I, 511–512, quotes

the text of this settlement from *Placita de Banco*, 27 Henry III, roll 13. It is printed also in translation in *Collections for a History of Staffs.* (Wm. Salt Arch. Soc.), IV (1883), Part I, 101.

38. *Calendar of Close Rolls, 1251–1253*, 108.

39. *Rotuli Hundredorum*, II, 68.

40. The charter is printed in T. D. Hardy, ed., *Rotuli Chartarum in Turri Londinensi Asservati*, I, Part I, 201–202, also in Nash, *op. cit.*, I, 511.

41. *Rotuli Hundredorum*, II, 98.

42. T. R. Nash, *Worcestershire*, I, 512. Nash says the record of this inquest is ex bundello inquisitionum de Anno 4 Edw. I. apud Westm. reservat.

43. *Rotuli Parliamentorum*, I, 10.

44. Nash, I, 513.

45. *Placitorum Abbreviatio*, 197.

46. J. W. W. Bund, ed., *Episcopal Registers, Diocese of Worcester: Register of Bishop Godfrey Gifford* (Worcs. Hist. Soc.), 103.

47. *Halesowen Court Rolls*, I, 116.

48. *Ibid.*, I, 124, 126, 169, 184.

49. *Ibid.*, I, 119.

50. Nash, I, 513, quoting "de anno 14 Edw. I, Rot. 25."

51. G. G. Coulton, *Five Centuries of Religion*, II, 298.

52. Nash, I, 513, 518. His note is "Ex Autographo penes d'm Lyttelton apud Hagley."

53. *Calendar of Patent Rolls, 1385–1389*, 317.

54. Nash, I, 513.

CHAPTER XIX

1. *Chichester Custumal*, 37.

2. *Bleadon Custumal*, 207.

3. The following entry appears in a book of rentals and extracts from the court records of Fountains Abbey, 1305–1435: Brit. Mus., Add. MS. 40,010, f. 24v: Iniunctum est omnibus tenentibus de Aldefeld quod soluant stipendium pastoris sub pena cuiuslibet .xij. d. Observe that all the tenants paid a stipend to the herdsman. There is a like entry concerning the common swineherd. The lord sometimes made a swineherd of one of his tenants, for instance at Fulbrook, Oxon.: *Rotuli Hundredorum*, II, 745: Johannes Palmerus tenet j cotagium et vj acras terre apud La Leye et debet custodire porcos domini pro servicio suo et valet custodia viij s. vj d. et debet habere j markinghog et valet xij d. et quoddam feodum de lardario quod valet vj d.

4. PRO, SC 2, Port. 174, no. 30, m. 3: Walterus de Cowyk factus est Wodeward per electionem omnium tenentium et iuratus boscum domini bene et fideliter custodire sub pena forisfacture omnium bonorum suorum.

5. PRO, SC 2, Port. 175, no. 79 m. 2: Willelmus de la More inculpatur de hoc quod prostrauit .j. blectrum in defenso domine ad terram qui resp' facere et inde vocat Henricum de Burley subforestarium ad warantum, et quod fuit tali negocio quia trabes caruce frangebat prope boscum ad quam reparandam ei dabatur. Et quia bene sciuit quod forestarius non potuit warantizare talem donacionem remanet in misericordia. In margin: misericordia .j. dieta caruce.

6. Among the services of a holder of a messuage and 12 acres of land at Bredon, Worcs., were the following: M. Hollings, ed., *The Red Book of Worcester*, (Worcs. Hist. Soc.), Part I, 99; Et nichilominus vigilabit in autumpno et custodiet bladum Domini in campo de nocte. . . . Et in autumpno licet vigilauerit de nocte de bladum custodiendo tamen operabitur de die. Poterit tamen tardius ad operationem venire et citius redire et recedere quam alii.

7. For instance, an entry in the court rolls of Chatteris, Cambs., 1272: PRO, SC 2, Port. 179, no. 3, m. 1d: Custodes electi ad campum custodiendum: God-

wynus textor, Iohannes Hogim, Andreas Albert, Iohannes Hayse, Robertus filius Thome Gilberd. See also an entry in the rolls of Upwood, Hunts., 1295: Brit. Mus., Add. Roll 34769, m. 1d: Custodes autumpni de Upwode dicunt quod Matilda filia Willelmi le Koc potuit conduci et noluit set gleniauit contra statuta. Ideo in misericordia .iij. d.

8. As at Norton, Oxon.: *Rotuli Hundredorum*, II, 693: Johannes Costentin tenet in eadem j mesuagium j virgatam terre de eisdem et reddit per annum eisdem vj s. et debet esse ripereve per iiij dies ad mensam domini. On some manors, reapreeves received wages from the lord during harvest. See F. W. Maitland, "History of a Cambridgeshire Manor," *English Hist. Review*, IX (1894), 421.

9. F. W. Maitland and W. P. Baildon, *The Court Baron*, 123.

10. *Chichester Custumals*, 85.

11. *Fleta* (1685), 172 (lib. II, cap. 84).

12. See note 15 below.

13. In the following entry in a court roll of Stratton, Wilts., of 12 Edw. I, a man seems to have been accused of making a covenant that another man should be hayward in his place: PRO, SC 2, Port. 209, no. 59, m. 9: Henricus Wyrde vad' legem contra Robertum Vde quod ab eo nullum denarium recepit nec aliquis de familia sua causa essendi messor, nec pactum fecit cum eodem ut deberet esse messor pro .xij. denariis ei donandis.

14. C. Pass. VI, ll. 16–17.

15. S. R. Scargill-Bird, ed., *Battle Abbey Custumals*, 67: Messor vero si sit electus de custumariis habebit relaxationem .ij. s. de redditu suo et cibum ter vt prepositus, et in autumpno quia vigilabit noctu circa blada domini in autumpno et pro hoc habebit cotidie dum metent .j. garbam per corrigiam vt supra patet de eodem blado quo metent.

16. J. Thorpe, ed., *Custumale Roffense*, 11. See also an entry of 19 Edw. I in the court rolls of Warboys and Caldecot, Hunts.: Brit. Mus., Add. Roll 39754, m. 1: Radulphus Fyne queritur de Waltero filio Radulphi Thurbern eo quod iniuste ab eo detinet sex garbas auene sibi adiudicatas pro cornbote desicut fuit messor et debuit cuilibet de dampnis suis respondere et Walterus venit et dicit quod in nulla garba ei tenetur et inde ponit inquisicionem et dictus Radulphus similiter. Et inquisicio venit et dicit quod dictus Walterus soluit ei quatuor garbas de blado predicto et due garbe sunt in aretro.

17. C. Pass. XIV, ll. 43–50.

18. PRO, Eccl. I, Bundle 26, no. 37, m. 1d: Quia Willelmus Cloock messor de Berewyk cepit districciones super feodum Prioris videlicet .iij. aucas Iohannis Kybe et eas fugauit in alieno foedo ita quod deliberacio fieri non potuit, ideo preceptum est quod distringatur veniendo ad respondendum super predictas, et inhibitum est tenentibus domini quod non soluant eidem messori stipendium suum ante quam se iustificauerit. See also an entry of 1291 in the rolls of Elsworth, Hunts.: PRO, SC 2, Port. 179, no. 7, m. 5: Willelmus Arnold communis messor totius ville conquestus est de Iohanne Aldyrman quod idem Iohannes in crastino beate Katerine Virginis fecit resscussum eidem de bydentibus domini Ricardi Capell et Simonis ate Clungers et nichilominus capud suum fregit et sanguinem traxit. Et ambo posuerunt se in vicinis iuratis qui dixerunt dictus Willelmus messor voluit cepisse bydentes extra feodum domini et fuit dicto Iohanni extraneus et ignotus, et quod idem Iohannes ipsum defendendo percussit et caput fregit. Ideo dictus Iohannes inde quietus, et predictus Willelmus pro falso clamore in misericordia.

19. PRO, SC 2, Port. 209, no. 52, m. 3: Stephanus messor in misericordia quia non fuit vltra carucarios die Veneris proxima post Annunciacionem Beate Marie; no. 53, m. 3d: Robertus messor (prepositus crossed out) in misericordia quia sinuit homines metere male bladum domini; m. 4: Robertus messor in misericordia quia paciebatur male arrari terram domini; no. 55, m. 3: Rogerus messor et prepositus in misericordia quia non mundauerunt grangiam de blado triturato contra festum Pentecosten.

20. F. W. Maitland and W. P. Baildon, *The Court Baron*, 140.

21. See *Wakefield Court Rolls*, II, Introduction.

22. *Fleta* (1685), 164 (lib. II, cap. 76), and E. Lamond, ed., *Walter of Henley's Husbandry*, 97. For the whole question of the reeve see H. S. Bennett, "The Reeve and the Manor in the Fourteenth Century," *English Hist. Rev.*, XLI (1926) 358 ff.

23. *Eng. Hist. Rev.*, XLI (1926), 361.

24. *Gloucester Cartulary*, III, 221. See also an entry in the court rolls of Bromham, Wilts.: PRO, SC 2, Port. 208, no. 15, m. 3: Tota communitas villanorum elegit Iohannem Carpentar ad officium prepositure et respondit pro eo quod fideliter et bene faciet omnia que ad officium illud pertinet et omnes tenentes respondebunt pro eo.

25. See *Halesowen Court Rolls*, III, 49.

26. There is an interesting illustration of this point in G. Oliver, *Monasticon Diocesis Exoniensis*, 256.

27. PRO, SC 2, Port. 209, no. 59, m. 4 (Stratton, Wilts., 7 Edw. I): Henricus prepositus in misericordia quia tradidit claues orrei domini alteri quam sibi ipsi; PRO, SC 2, Port. 209, no. 52, m. 3 (Sevenhampton, Wilts., 8 Edw. I): Iohannes prepositus quia non fecit bene mundare bladum in grangia; PRO, SC 2, Port. 171, no. 63, m. 15d: (Dunmow, Essex, 13 Edw. II): Item dicunt predicti quod predictus Iohannes prepositus siniuit iacere quasdam foreras incultas ad dampnum domini .xij. d.; PRO, SC 2, Port. 183, no. 56, m. 1 (Burbage, Wilts., 48 Henry III): Willelmus filius .W. de Eston quia noluit facere precepta prepositi — vj. d.

28. E. Lamond, ed., *Walter of Henley's Husbandry*, 101.

29. See an entry for 18 Edw. I in the court book of Barnet, Herts.: Brit. Mus., Add. MS. 40,167, f. 22v: Omnes iurati presentant quod Walterus Barth' melius potest esse prepositus ad colligendos reditus et faciendum etc. ratione tenementi quod tenet in eadem villa de antiqua terra; *Gloucester Cartulary*, III, 219: Item, quod quilibet praepositus habeat potestatem concedendi cuicumque nativae ut possit se maritare tam extra terram domini quam infra; *Ramsey Cartulary*, I, 384 (services of yardling at Hemingford): Faciet testamentum suum libere, etiam in absentia servientis et praepositi; PRO, SC 2, Port. 179, no. 12, m. 9d (Weston, Hunts., 34 Edw. 1): De Iohanne le Bonde bedello et preposito quia non distrinxit Willelmum de Sansyngton ad faciendum domino homagium et fidelitatem pro vndecim acris terre quas tenet de domino; W. Kennett, *Parochial Antiquities* (1685), 458 (court at Wretchwick, 18 Edw. III): Item presentant quod Thomas Bavard nativus Domini qui tenuit de Domino unum messuagium et unam virgatam terrae in bondagio diem clausit extremum . . . et dicunt (jurati) quod uxor ejus non potest tenere predicta messuagium et terram propter paupertatem, ita ut Praepositus possit capere in manibus Domini predicta messuagium et terram; PRO, SC 2, Port. 179, no. 5, m. 2d (Broughton, Hunts., 16 Edw. I): De Absolon' preposito quia non habuit rotulos de Hallemot' pro vltima Curia perscrutandos et perplacitandos, .vj. d.

30. B. Pass. V, l. 427.

31. H. S. Bennett, "The Reeve and the Manor in the Fourteenth Century," *English Hist. Rev.*, XLI (1926), 363.

32. Stenton, *Danelaw Documents*, cvi–cvii.

33. *Rotuli Hundredorum*, II, 153.

34. Maitland, *Manorial Courts*, 95.

35. See F. J. Roethlisberger and W. J. Dickson, *Management and the Worker*, Part IV.

36. C. Pass. I, l. 93.

37. See F. M. Page, *The Estates of Crowland Abbey*, 30.

38. R. G. Griffiths and W. W. Capes, eds., *Registrum Thome de Cantilupo* (Canterbury and York Soc.), I, 109–110.

39. C. Pass. VI, ll. 11–21.

CHAPTER XX

1. Maitland, *Manorial Courts*. See also F. W. Maitland and W. P. Baildon, eds., *The Court Baron*, and W. O. Ault, ed., *Court Rolls of the Abbey of Ramsey and of the Honor of Clare*.

2. *Wakefield Court Rolls*, II, Introduction; *Halesowen Court Rolls*, III, 111–112.

3. *Fleta* (1685), 159 (lib. II, cap. 72).

4. The Statute of Marlborough (1267) stated that a freeholder owed suit if suit had been done before Henry III went to Brittany in 1230.

5. Maitland, *Manorial Courts*, 94. See also *Halesowen Court Rolls*, I, xxix; II, 309, etc. Consider also in this connection an entry concerning Stenyng hundred in Sussex: *Rotuli Hundredorum*, II, 203: Item dicunt quod Abbas de Fiscamp' solebat tenere curiam suam de Stenigges de liberis hominibus suis et bundis conjunctim et modo tenet curiam suam de liberis hominibus suis per se et de bundis per se et amerciant eos in absencia eorum et solebant amerciare eos in presencia tocius curie.

6. See *Halesowen Court Rolls*, II, 356, 371, 389; *Wakefield Court Rolls*, 190, 235.

7. J. E. A. Jolliffe, *The Constitutional History of Medieval England*, 148.

8. See, for instance, an entry in the court book of Park, Herts., Brit. Mus., Add. MS. 40,625, f. 57r: Iohannes filius Michaelis Ordwy electus est per iuratos de Parco ad terram que fuit Iohannis de Chissenden faciendo etc. There are other entries like this.

9. PRO, SC 2, Port. 179, no. 6, m. 16d: Et predictus Iohannes venit et defendit vim et iniuriam et ius predicti Willelmi quando etc. Et dicit quod non tenetur narracioni sue respondere eo quod narrando non dicit quod idem Iohannes ei deforciat predictum tenementum cum pertinenciis nec dicit narrando in qua villa predicta tenementa sunt nec quis antecessor suus fuit seisitus nec quo modo ius ei descendere debet nec tempore cuius regis antecessor suus fuit inde seisitus nec que expletia cepit nec vllam producit sectam, que omnia narracioni sunt necessaria. Et ideo petit iudicium si ad huius narracionem debeat ei respondere. Et de hoc ponit se super consideracionem curie. Et predictus Willelmus similiter. Et ideo per consideracionem tocius curie consideratum est quod predictus Willelmus nichil capiat per breue suum set sit in misericordia pro falso clamore. Et predictus Iohannes inde sine die.

10. *Ibid.*, m. 22.

11. PRO, Eccl. I, Bundle 16, no. 43, m. 5: Quando contentio mota fuerat inter dominum Robertum rectorem ecclesie de Halton' ex parte vna et Thomam de Merden' ex altera per amicos interuenientes facti sunt amici sub hac forma, quod predicti rector et Thomas similiter concedunt quod si quis eorum conuictus fuerit iuste de aliquo maleficio versus alium dabit domino quatuor solidos sine alicuius placite recognitione.

12. An entry in the rolls of Hound, Hants., 26 Edw. I: PRO, SC 2, Port. 201, no. 24, m. 3: Querela inter relicta Robin, Iohannem Carpenter et vxorem eius habita super placito transgressionis et infamie pacificatur in hac forma, scilicet si aliqua earum contencionem mouerit decetero inter eas sine misericordia in stupa ponatur et ibi dum forum durat per vnum diem peniteat; also an entry in the rolls of Thurloxton, Somerset, 1319; Brit. Mus., Add. Roll 16332, m. 1: Concordia talis est inter Iohannem atte Stone querens ex parte vna et Thomam de Haddon ex altera quod vtrique eorum relaxauerunt vnicuique eorum omnia dampna verbo seu facto inter eosdem facta ante istum diem. Et si contingat iterum discordia inter eosdem oriri hac de causa concedunt ex mutuo concessu quod quis eorum culpabilis primo inuentus fuerit det fabrice ecclesie .ij. s.

13. J. Brownbill, ed., *Ledger-Book of Vale Royal Abbey* (Lancs. and Cheshire Record Soc.), 31.

14. *Handlyng Synne* (EETS), ll. 5421–26, 5489–94. E. Lamond ed., *Walter of Henley's Husbandry*, 5: The author supposes that an old man is telling his son how to manage his estates: "If anyone comes into your court, let him be amerced by his peers; if your conscience tells you that they have amerced him too highly do you lessen it, so that you be not reproved here or before God." What could be lessened could also be raised.

15. *Chichester Custumal*, 12.

16. PRO, SC 2, Port. 208, no. 15, m. 3: Dicunt etiam per sacramentum suum quod omnes tam libere tenentes quam alii dederunt domino pro ingressu post decessum predecessorum suorum quod dare debuerunt secundum quantitatem tenementi sui. Natiui non pacificauerunt domino ad ipsius voluntatem. In margin: Inquisicio.

17. PRO, SC 2, Port. 179, no. 10, m. 11d: Willelmus filius Iacoby, Ricardus Blakeman, Willelmus Chyld, Reginaldus le Wyse, Henricus in Venella, Ricardus Carectarius, Iohannes Trune, Radulphus de Wassingle, et Galfridus ad Crucem attachiati fuerunt per Hugonem Prest Clauigerum et calumpniati pro eo quod fugauerunt bestias suas per viam quod vocatur Le Greneweye quando culture domini Abbatis ibidem abuttantes sunt seminate. Et predicti homines dicunt quod ipsi et omnes de villa de Aylington dictam chaciam omnibus temporibus anni de iure debent habere, desicut omnes extranei per eandem viam transeuntes cum omnimodis animalibus suis liberam chaciam sine calumpnia et impedimento possunt habere. Et predictus Hugo dicit quod licet extranei chaciam suam habeant ibidem dicti tamen custumarii et participes sui contulerunt quandoque .iiij.ᵒʳ s. ad opus domini pro chacia ibidem habenda quando culture domini ibi fuerant seminate. Et prefati custumarii et omnes alii de villa tam liberi quam alii et similiter .xij. iurati quorum nomina in principio rotuli sunt contenta dicunt et iurant quod si aliqua pecunia per custumarios villa pro chacia sua ibidem habenda fuerit collata, dictus Clauiger per districtionem et extorsionem voluntarie pecuniam illam cepit et iniuste leuauit de eisdem. Vnde dictus Senescallus videns discensionem et discordiam inter Clauigerum petentem et dictos homines contradicentes noluit pronunciare iudicium contra dictum Clauigerum. Set istud iudicium disposicioni domini Abbatis penitus reliquid, ut idem dominus scrutato registro de consuetudine super isto demando faciat et ordinet prout viderit fore faciendum secundum den'.

18. For a general treatment of the subject see W. A. Morris, *The Frankpledge System.*

19. *De Legibus et Consuetudinibus Angliae*, fol. 124b.

20. *The Frankpledge System*, 45.

21. PRO, SC 2, Port. 208, no. 15.

22. See the court rolls of Lewisham, Kent, PRO, SC 2, Port. 181, nos. 46, 47, 48, etc.

23. *Rotuli Hundredorum*, I, 240.

CHAPTER XXI

1. *Halesowen Court Rolls*, I, 56.

2. W. S. Brassington, *Historic Worcestershire*, 220.

3. J. E. Morris, *The Welsh Wars of King Edward the First*, 92.

4. *Halesowen Court Rolls*, II, 318–319, 324–325, 329. See also *Wakefield Court Rolls*, I, 253, 257; IV, 137, 139, 140; *Durham Hallmotes*, 1; F. W. Maitland and W. P. Baildon, eds., *The Court Baron*, 141.

5. Maitland, *Manorial Courts*, 172.

6. An incomplete list of these villages is as follows: Whatley, Rowreth, Wickford, Essex (*Pipe Roll*, 30 Henry II, 135); Great Branfeld and Little Hocton (*Calendar of Inquisitions, Miscellaneous*, I, no. 846); Scalby, Yorks. (*Rotuli Hundredorum*, I, 108); Yongcastre, Lincs. (*ibid.*, I, 265); Somerton, Somerset

(*ibid.*, II, 121); Grittleton, Wilts. (*Glastonbury Rentalia*, 67); Tibberton, Worcs. (W. H. Hale, ed., *Registrum . . . Prioratus Beatae Mariae Wigorniensis*, 54); Hemingford, Hunts. (*Ramsey Cartulary*, II, 224-6); Shelwick, Heref. (R. G. Griffiths and W. W. Capes, eds., *Registrum Thome de Cantilupo*, I, 22); Bray, Berks. (C. Kerry, *Hundred of Bray*, 3).

7. *Ramsey Cartulary*, II, 244-246.

8. PRO, SC 2, Port. 179, no. 16, m. 2d: Inhibitum est per dominum .I. Abbatem omnibus custumariis de Elyngton qui habent predictam villam ad firmam quod decetero non permittant aliquem hominem aut mulierem de natiuis domini recedere extra foedum domini super alienum foedum comorandum, nec aliquem extraneum infra predictam villam recipiant residendum sine licencia domini speciali et fine coram predicto domino faciendo, et eciam inhibitum est eisdem quod nulle gersume nec fines decetero fiant nisi coram dicto domino Abbate. Et si predicti custumarii contra predictam formam videlicet in parte vel in toto fuerint conuicti facientes, erunt in graui misericordia ad voluntate domini taxata. Another interesting entry on the same roll and membrane is this: Mortuo Bartholomaeo in Inlond qui tenuit de domino dimidiam virgatam terre post cuius mortem prepositus insimul et omnes custumarii ville permiserunt quendam Iohannem Brymbel extraneum intrare in predictam terram ad relictam dicti Bartholomaei per gersumam inter eos factam sine licencia domini et contra consuetudinem ville. Ideo omnes . . . sunt in misericordia .xl. s.

9. PRO, SC 2, Port. 208, no. 15, m. 3: Omnes custumarii fecerunt finem quia fecerunt sigillum commune in contemptum domini. In margin: C. S.

10. PRO, DL 30, Bundle 85, no. 1157, m. 6d: Et Willelmus Bridde et alii in querela defendunt vim etc. et aduocant capcionem bonam et iustam in loco predicto quia dicunt quod Robertus Galardon agistatus fuit ad dimidium quarterium auene die Mercurii proximo post mediam Quadragesimam anno vltimo preterito per communem assensum tocius ville et hoc per mandatum vicecomitis ad opus domini regis et quia predictus Robertus noluit predictum bladum soluere ideo ceperunt aueria sua vt bene eis licuit etc. Et Robertus dicit quod non fuit agistatus per assensum ville nec aueria habuit vltra sustentacionem suam, et hoc etc. Ideo veniat inquisicio. Et acceptum est per inquisicionem quod Robertus Galardon agistatus fuit ad dimidium quarterium auene per communitatem ville tanquam habens vltra sustentacionem suam, ideo in misericordia pro falso clamore.

11. W. A. Morris, "The Early English County Court," *Univ. of California Publications in History*, XIV, 104.

12. F. W. Maitland, *Domesday Book and Beyond*, 24.

13. *Leges Henrici Primi*, 7 § 7, in F. Liebermann, *Die Gesetze der Angelsachsen*, or any other compilation.

14. *Leges Edwardi Confessoris*, c. 24. See also 7 Ethelred, ii. 5.

15. R. W. Eyton, *Antiquities of Shropshire*, VI, 19.

16. *Rotuli Hundredorum*, I, 364.

17. J. F. Nichols, *Custodia Essexae* (Thesis for degree of Ph.D., Univ. of London), quotes from an extent of Borley, Essex, Brit. Mus., Add. MS. 6159, f. 25v: Dominus debet invenire duos homines sumptibus suis coram eisdem justiciariis. Et villata de Borlee sumptibus suis iij. homines invenient. Et hoc per consuetudinem a tempore quo non extat memoria ut dicitur.

18. *Placita de Quo Warranto*, 10. The Abbot of Ramsey was asked by what warrant he claimed the View of Frankpledge and free warren in Cranfield and Shillington, Beds. The entry continues: Requisit' si cap' decennar sive quatuor et prepositus ven' ad turnum vicecomitis etc. dic' quod libere tenentes utriusque manerii ven'. This fact is borne out by Ramsey Cartulary, III, 301, 307.

19. B. A. Lees, "The Statute of Winchester and Villa Integra," *English Hist. Rev.*, XLI (1926), 98 ff.

20. *Ibid.*, 101.

21. T. D. Hardy, ed., *Rotuli Normanniae*, I, 122-143; see especially 131, 135.

22. C. W. Foster, ed., *Final Concords of the County of Lincoln*, II, xlvi.

23. PRO, SC 2, Port. 193, no. 33, m. 3: Memorandum quod omnes terras et tenementa traduntur in custodia Radulphi prepositi, Iohanni fratri eius, Iohanni Hermers, Hugoni Palmer, Ricardo de Wrthestede, Ricardo Sprinhald et Waltero Page, ita quod respondunt de qualibet acra viciata .ij. s. siue sit seminata siue non, et de omnibus aliis rebus ad dictum manerium spectantibus. Attention should be called to the grammar of this entry. J. Brand, *History of Newcastle-upon-Tyne*, II, 594, prints an extract from a rental of Tynemouth, in the Tynemouth cartulary: Omnes illi qui terras tenent et tofta tres precarias facient in autumpno cum uno homine tantum et quartam precariam cum tota familia sua preter hospitissam ad quam quatuor jurati ejusdem villa erunt messores.

24. See W. Sombart, *Der Moderne Kapitalismus* (IV Aufl.), I, 180–187.

25. *Rotuli Hundredorum*, II, 12.

26. *Ibid.*, I, 468, etc.

CHAPTER XXII

1. *The English Husbandman* (1635), 95.

CHAPTER XXIII

1. L. Reymont's novel *The Peasants*, which has as its background one year in the life of a Polish village, gives an extraordinarily interesting account of the attitudes of peasants toward the seasons and holidays of the year, together with many other important matters. I suspect that what Reymont says of Polish peasants holds good of the peasants of many other countries under the old social order of Europe. We should remember, in considering the relation between the works and the feasts of the husbandman's year as it was in the thirteenth century that, thanks to a calendar which was long imperfect, the day which the men of that time called August 1 was nearly the same day of the solar year as our August 9. For the general subject of English folklore see E. Hull, *Folklore of the British Isles*.

2. *Chichester Custumal*, vii.

3. Tusser, 181.

4. E. Gutch, *Examples of Printed Folk-lore concerning Lincolnshire*, 210.

5. Tusser, 223.

6. J. Thorpe, ed., *Custumale Roffense*, 1. But see also the custumal of Piddington (1363) in W. Kennett, *Parochial Antiquities* (1695), 496.

7. Tusser, 55.

8. T. M. Allison, "The Flail and Its Varieties," *Archaeologia Aeliana*, 3rd Ser., II, 94 ff.

9. Tusser, 68.

10. N. Neilson, ed., *A Terrier of Fleet, Lincolnshire* (The British Academy: Records of the Social and Economic History of England and Wales, Vol. IV), lxix.

11. *Historical MSS. Commission: Calendar of the MSS. of the Dean and Chapter of Wells*, I, 332–335, cited in an interesting paper: C. R. Baskervill, "Dramatic Aspects of Medieval Folk-Festivals in England," *Studies in Philology*, XVII (1920), 35. For another good description of the Christmas dinner see the custumal of another Somersetshire manor, Bleadon: *Bleadon Custumal*, 204.

12. W. H. Hale, ed., *The Domesday of St. Paul's* (Camden Soc.), lxxiii.

13. See E. K. Chambers, *The English Folk Play*, and C. R. Baskervill, "Mummers' Wooing Plays in England," *Modern Philology*, XXI (1924), 225 ff. Another, less well understood, ceremony of Christmas (if it was a ceremony) was the *forthdrove*. See C. R. Baskervill, "Dramatic Aspects of Medieval Folk-Festivals in England," *Studies in Philology*, XVII (1920), 33: "The expulsion (of winter), or 'forthdrove' and wassail as features of the medieval English Christmas are recorded

for Bury St. Edmunds in 1369–1370 and 1401–1402." See also N. Neilson, *Customary Rents*, 79.

14. *Folk-lore*, XII, 350. See also E. M. Leather, *The Folk-lore of Herefordshire*, 91 ff.

15. H. Parker, *Dives and Pauper* (1534), f. 50. The plow was much used in magic. See H. Christmas, ed., *Select Works of John Bale* (Parker Soc.), 528. Bale, who was born in 1495, wrote in *The Image of Both Churches:* "Frankincense occupy they oft, as a necessary thing in the censing of their idols, hallowing of their paschal, conjuring of their ploughs, besides the blessing of their palms, candles, ashes, and their dead men's graves, with *requiescant in pace.*"

16. For Plow Monday see especially the summary in J. G. Frazer, *The Golden Bough: Spirits of the Corn and of the Wild* (3rd ed.), II, 325–335. C. R. Baskervill, "Dramatic Aspects of Medieval Folk-Festivals in England," *Studies in Philology*, XVII (1920), 38, states that a Plow Monday gathering is recorded for Durham as early as 1378.

17. See G. L. Gomme, *Folk-lore Relics of Early Village Life*, 147; E. Gutch, *Examples of Printed Folk-lore concerning Lincolnshire*, 171–173; W. C. Hazlitt, *Faiths and Folklore*, II, 496. A passage describing the services of villeins at Binham, Norfolk, in a cartulary and custumal of Binham Priory, probably of the time of Edward I, gives evidence of a husbandmen's gild: Brit. Mus., Cotton MS. Claudius, D. XIII, f. 18v: Et omnes predictorum qui cariant precarias domini vel arant vt predictum est recipient ex consuetudine pro caruca vel carecta duas lagenas ceruisie de Le Gilde et hoc ad festum Omnium Sanctorum et residuum expendetur in communi ville nomine elemosine de iure.

18. Sir F. Pollock and F. W. Maitland, *The History of English Law* (1st ed.), 623.

19. See the custumal of Piddington, Oxon. (1363), in W. Kennett, *Parochial Antiquities* (1695), 496: Item quilibet capitalis custumarius arabit Domino per singulos dies a Festo Purificationis Beatae Mariae usque ad Pascha Domini . . . ; *Gloucester Cartulary*, 217: Item, quod prata et alia defensa domini separabilia statim post Purificationem ponantur in defenso, et ex tunc salvo modo custodiantur.

20. See the entry for Rackham in *Chichester Custumal*, 65: "William le Frensch and William Red shall be oxherds when the lord wills. Then they shall follow the lord's oxen on the manor while they are under the yoke from Michaelmas to Lady Day."

21. H. J. Feasey, *Ancient English Holy Week Ceremonial;* see also K. Young, *The Drama of the Medieval Church.*

22. In a custumal of 40 Henry III of the lands of Richard de Harington, the reeve of Friskney, Lincs., is recorded to have held land which he defended for 1/3 oxgang. Among his services was the following: PRO, Rentals and Surveys, Gen. Ser., Port. 10, no. 33, m. 1: Item debet custodire domino vnum auerium a festo Sancti Martini vsque ad Mayday secundum quod quidam dicunt et se vero confitetur de custodia tercie partis auerii. Again, in a compotus roll of 12–13 Edw. II (?) of Great Sturton, Lincs., the following entry is found: Brit. Mus., Add. Roll 25,858, m. 1: Idem reddit compotum de iiij s. x d. receptis de agestamento animalium in communi pastura a tempore Mayday vsque festum Sancti Martini preter agestamentum animalium domini.

23. H. R. Luard, ed., *Roberti Grosseteste Epistolae* (Rolls Series), 317.

24. Wilkins, *Concilia*, I, 673.

25. *Handlyng Synne* (EETS), ll. 997–1004.

26. *Rotuli Hundredorum*, I, 174.

27. In J. Earle, *A Hand-book to the Land-Charters and other Saxonic Documents*, 344–345, a charter of Ramsey Abbey speaks of inne Iol and inne Easterne and inne þa hali wuca aet Gangdagas.

28. A curious entry appears in an extent of Dunnington, near York, 1295:

T. A. M. Bishop, ed., "Extents of the Prebends of York," *Miscellanea* (Yorks. Arch. Soc., Record Ser.), IV, 7: "The said tenants shall form a procession on Thursday in the week of Pentecost, and shall sing the following song: *Gif i na thing for mi land*, etc." We would give a good deal to know the rest of the song.

29. Tusser, 181.

30. Brit. Mus., Harleian MS. 2345, f. 50, cited in J. M. Kemble, *The Saxons in England*, I, 361.

31. *Glastonbury Rentalia*, 139. In the time of Henry III, plowmen at East Monkton, between Warminster and Shaftesbury, were allowed a ram for a feast on the eve of St. John the Baptist, when they used to carry fire round the lord's corn.— G. L. Gomme, *Folk-lore Relics of Early Village Life*, 147.

32. According to a custumal of King's Barton, Glos., *Gloucester Cartulary*, III, 70–72, several tenants had to pay a small rent, called *wiveneweddinge*, on St. John's Eve. No explanation of the rent is given. Did it have some reference to St. John's Eve being a traditional time when young people chose their mates?

33. Tusser, 120. In a survey of the barony of Bayeux, 1288, printed in *Lincolnshire Notes and Queries*, VIII (1904–1905), 59, there is the following entry for Welbourn: "The said villeins shall give at the mowing of the meadow of the lord at the feast of St. John Baptist v s. j d. ob."

34. C, Pass. IX, ll. 314–315.

35. T. C. Cockayne, ed., *Leechdoms, Wortcunning, and Starcraft* (Rolls Ser.), III, 291.

36. According to a custumal, of the time of Henry III, of Westminster Abbey: Brit. Mus., Add. Roll 8139, m. 5, a customer at Langetune was given a dinner by his lord at the end of harvest: Debet etiam habere cibum suum in festo Sancti Michaelis siue post cum vxore sua et vno seruiente. Et habebit vnum ferculum carnis siue piscis et caseum et ceruisiam.

37. Tusser, 132.

38. W. Kennett, *Parochial Antiquities* (1695), 320 and Glossary s. v. *precaria*.

39. Tusser, 181. N. Neilson, *Economic Conditions on the Manors of Ramsey Abbey*, 84: "In the time of reaping there was a particular custom called 'le Rypgos' or 'Repegos'. . . . At le Repegos the customers received 2 s. and meat, geese, doves, and corn."

40. H. R. Luard, *Roberti Grosseteste Epistolae* (Rolls Ser.), 75.

41. W. Kennett, *Parochial Antiquities* (1695), 611.

42. F. W. Maitland and W. P. Baildon, eds., *The Court Baron* (Selden Soc.), 57.

43. C. S. Burne, *Shropshire Folklore*, 437 ff.

44. Tusser, 181.

45. C. J. Billson, *County Folk-lore, No. 3: Leicestershire & Rutland*, 98.

46. W. Warner, *Albion's England* (1612), Book V, ch. 25. A kirk-sight was clearly any church ceremony, cf. *Piers Plowman*, C, Pass. VII, ll. 281–282:

> Myghte neuere man comforty me · in þe meyn tyme,
> Neiþer matyns ne masse · ne oþer manere syghtes.

Sir T. Overbury, writing at the beginning of the seventeenth century, spoke of the countryman's feast days in his character of *A Franklin*, printed in his *Miscellaneous Works* (1856), E. F. Rimbault, ed., 150: "He allowes of honest pastime, and thinkes not the bones of the dead any thing bruised, or the worse for it, though the country lasses dance in the church-yard after evensong. Rocke Munday, and the wake in summer, shrovings, the wakefull ketches on Christmas Eve, the hoky, or seed cake, these he yeerely keepes, yet holds them no reliques of popery."

47. Much of what follows has already been stated in G. C. Homans, "Men and the Land in the Middle Ages," *Speculum*, XI (1936), 338–351.

48. It does not seem expedient to enter here upon an extended discussion of sociological theory. The conceptual scheme used is in general that of V. Pareto,

The Mind and Society (English translation of his *Trattato di Sociologia generale*).

49. B. Malinowski, "Magic, Science, and Religion," in J. Needham, ed., *Science, Religion, and Reality*, 32. This paper is another chief source of the argument put forward here.

50. W. I. Thomas and F. Znaniecki, *The Polish Peasant in Europe and America*, I, 174.

51. In *Trans. of the Cumberland and Westmoreland Antiquarian and Archaeological Soc.*, Part II, vol. II (1875–1876), 280 ff., J. Fowler describes the sculptured capitals of the months in Carlisle Cathedral. He says that there is no other example in England of a complete series like that of Carlisle. See also his paper "Medieval Representations of the Months and Seasons," *Archaeologia*, XLIV, 137–224.

52. For a discussion of the function of agricultural magic in organizing farm work see B. Malinowski, *Coral Gardens and their Magic*.

CHAPTER XXIV

1. Wilkins, *Concilia*, II, 280; Lyndwood, *Provinciale*, 252.

2. Wilkins, *Concilia*, I, 636: Constitutions of St. Edmund Rich (1236): Fontes sub serura clausi teneantur, propter sortilegia. Chrisma similiter et oleum sacrum sub clave custodiantur.

3. Lyndwood, *Provinciale*, 253. See F. A. Gasquet, *Parish Life in Medieval England*, 53.

4. In an inquest concerning the customs of the Ramsey manor of Broughton, Hunts., in 36 Henry III, Brit. Mus., Add. Roll 34,333, m. 2, the following entry is found among those describing the perquisites of the church: de quolibet viro astrum habente si vxorem habuerit per annum .j. d. ad luminare ecclesie et de viro vxorem non habente et vidua vel alia muliere ad dictum luminare obolum per annum percipit.

5. An entry in the court rolls of the Ramsey manor of St. Ives for 28 Edw. I is the following: PRO, SC 2, Port. 179, no. 10, m. 6d: Conuictum est per iuratos quod Iohannes Aylmar soluit pro Nicholao Tannar' custodibus ecclesie de Woldhyrst duos solidos et sex d. pro potestate ordinari quod quidem den. dicti custodes ceperunt nomine vsure de quibus den. dictus Nicholaus satisfaciet ei, et pro iniusta detencione in misericordia .iij. d.

6. *Rotuli Hundredorum*, II, 92.

7. *Ibid.*, I, 308.

8. C. Deedes, ed., *Registrum Johannis de Pontissara Episcopi Wintonensis* (Canterbury and York Soc.), I, 352.

9. G. J. Turner, ed., *Select Pleas of the Forest* (Selden Soc.), 84.

10. See the law of Aethelred, in F. Liebermann, *Die Gesetze der Angelsachsen*, I, 261: Et precipimus, ut omnis homo super dileccionem Dei et omnium sanctorum det cyricsceattum et rectam decimam suam, sicut in diebus antecessorum nostrorum stetit, quando melius stetit: hoc est sicut aratrum peragrabit per decimam acram. Cf. an entry in a court roll of 28 Edw. I of Gidding, Hunts., a Ramsey manor: PRO, SC 2, Port. 179, no. 10, m. 13d: Et (iurati) dicunt quod idem Iohannes le Monek iurauit cum rectore ecclesie contra totam villam de Gyddingg' quod idem rector perciperet nouem selliones super Gosehyl pro decima acra sua vbi nunquam prius percepit nisi septem selliones et per illud iuramentum optinuit ad dampnum domini et totius ville. Ideo est in misericordia .xij. d. See also W. H. Hale, *Register of Worcester Priory* (Camden Soc.), 67b.

11. *Glastonbury Rentalia, passim.*

12. *Rotuli Hundredorum*, I, 47. See also H. G. Richardson, "The Parish Clergy of the Thirteenth and Fourteenth Centuries," *Royal Hist. Soc. Trans.*, 3rd Ser., VI (1912), 108. This essay is full of important information.

13. See, for instance, Wilkins, *Concilia*, 671, 733.

14. F. A. Gasquet, *Parish Life in Medieval England*, 114.

15. See R. Mannyng of Brunne, *Handlyng Synne*, (EETS), ll. 11589 ff.
16. See F. A. Stevenson, *Robert Grosseteste*, 139.
17. R. A. R. Hartridge, *A History of Vicarages in the Middle Ages*, 130. This book should be consulted in regard to all matters concerning vicarages.
18. *Ibid.*, 29.
19. *Ibid.*, 79, quoting from E. L. Cutts, *Parish Priests and their People in the Middle Ages*.
20. Lyndwood, *Provinciale*, 64, 65.
21. N. S. B. Gras, *The Economic and Social History of an English Village*, 71–72.
22. H. G. Richardson, "The Parish Clergy of the Thirteenth and Fourteenth Centuries," *Royal Hist. Soc. Trans.*, 3rd. Ser., VI (1912), 115.
23. G. G. Coulton, *Ten Medieval Studies*, 112. See also F. Hobhouse, ed., *Drokensford's Register* (Somerset Record Soc.), xxiii.
24. A., Prol., ll. 80–81.
25. A. Jessopp, *Before the Great Pillage*, 105.
26. G. G. Coulton, *The Medieval Village*, 258, citing W. H. R. Jones, ed., *The Register of S. Osmund* (Rolls Ser.), I, 304.
27. Maitland, *Manorial Courts*, 164.
28. C. Deedes, ed., *Registrum Johannis de Pontissara Episcopi Wintonensis*, (Canterbury and York Soc.), 753.
29. F. C. Hingeston-Randolph, ed., *Episcopal Registers, Diocese of Exeter: The Register of Walter of Stapeldon*, 337.
30. *Ibid.*, 378. Both of these passages have been cited and translated in G. G. Coulton, *Social Life in Britain from the Conquest to the Reformation*, 267.
31. Wilkins, *Concilia*, II, 54.
32. See A. Van Gennep, *Les Rites de passage*.
33. PRO, SC 2, Port, 179, no. 11, m. 9d: Et (iurati) dicunt [*quod*] Iohannes Willem, Iohannes Ryngedele, Willelmus seruiens Roberti Godhosebonde, Iohannes le Taillur, Robertus filius Iohannis Olyner, Hugo Curteys, Thomas le Akerman, Robertus filius Thome Manger, et duo bercarii abbatis omnes de Wystowe venerunt apud magnam Rauele ad vigilandum corpus Simonis de Sutbyr' per noctem et redeundo iacuerunt lapides ad hostia vicinorum et male se habuerunt per quod vicini iuste leuauerunt vthesium super eos. Ideo preceptum est preposito et bedello quod sequantur versus eos in curia de Wystowe.
34. H. R. Luard, ed., *Roberti Grosseteste Epistolae* (Rolls Ser.), 74. The expenses of the wake were met out of the goods of the deceased. See J. Brownbill, ed., *The Ledger Book of Vale Royal Abbey* (Lancs. and Cheshire Record Soc.), 119–120.
35. The following views about the mass in particular are derived in large part from conversation with my friend C. M. Arensberg, author of *The Irish Countryman*, and about rites in general from V. Pareto, *The Mind and Society*, § 167; A. R. Brown, *The Andaman Islanders*; W. L. Warner, *A Black Civilization*; and B. Malinowski, *Foundations of Faith and Morals* (Riddell Memorial Lectures).
36. G. G. Coulton, *The Medieval Village*, 339.
37. H. R. Luard, ed., *Roberti Grosseteste Epistolae* (Rolls Ser.), 162: Ad haec adicimus ne laici stent vel sedeant inter clericos in cancello dum divina ibidem celebrantur; nisi forte ob reverentiam vel aliam rationabilem causam et manifestam hoc solis patronis permittatur.
38. Such beliefs, organized in a system, have been called "absolute logics." See W. L. Warner, *A Black Civilization*, 10–11.

CHAPTER XXV

1. The scheme here presented owes most to C. I. Barnard, *The Functions of the Executive* (see especially p. 82) and V. Pareto, *The Mind and Society*.

2. E. D. Chapple, "Measuring Human Relations: An Introduction to the Study of the Interaction of Individuals," *Genetic Psychology Monographs* (1940), 22, 3–147.

3. See R. Firth, *We, The Tikopia.*

4. M. Sylvester, ed., *Reliquiae Baxterianae* (1696), 30.

5. J. Dollard, *Caste and Class in a Southern Town,* 77 etc.

6. L. J. Henderson, *Pareto's General Sociology,* 12.

7. See E. Durkheim, *Les Règles de la méthode sociologique* (1927), 12.

INDEX

INDEX

Abstractions, 402

Account rolls, 8, 300, 310, 354

Accrual, 111, 114–15

"Acquired" land, 132, 195

Acre, 49, 70, 97, 385

Actions, *see* Logical actions; Non-logical actions

Adam, 80, 360, 397

Advent, 356

Advowson, 224, 331, 387–88

Affeerors, 313, 319

Aftermath, 60, 370

Agricultural Revolution, 41

Agriculture, methods of, 17–19, 21, 38–51, 54; primitive, 53. *See also* Champion husbandry

Akermen, 241. *See also* Plowman

Aldenham, Herts., 246

Aldingbourne, Sussex, 211, 286

Ale, 39, 358–59, 370–71, 375, 393; assize of, 238, 312–13, 326; brewed for lord, 269, 357

Ale-tasters, 238, 312

Alienation of land, 180, 194–207, 214, 251, 338; of acquired land, 132; consent of heir required, 124, 197–98, 254; by king, 218

All Saints Day, 355–56, 363, 366

All Souls Day, 356

Alms, 386–87. *See also* Frank almoigne

Alrewas, Staffs., 72, 124

Altarage, 385

Althorp, Northants., 94

Alton, Hants., 78

Amberley, Sussex, 149

Amercements, 80, 273, 310, 312, 318–20, 324–26; assessment of, 276, 313, 319

America, discovery of, 33, 37

Ancient demesne of crown, *see* Villein sokemen

Anglo-Saxons, 26, 29, 74, 214, 356, 380

Anilepimen, 136–37, 210–11

Anilepiwymen, 136, 139, 210–11

Annunciation, feast of, 364

Anthropology, 4–5, 7, 192, 342, 382, 402, 404, 412–13

Anwick, Lincs., 246

Anxiety, 376–78, 381, 396

Apprentices, 32, 135, 251

Appropriation of benefices, 334, 386–88

Araire, 42–44, 46

Arms, assize of, 329

Army, 238, 329–30

Array, commissioners of, 329

Ascension, feast of, 47, 368

Assarts, 83–85, 102, 144, 205, 225, 249, 363; made by Cistercians, 32; inheritance of, 132, 195

Assessment, 332–33, 335. *See also* Amercements

Assizes, *see* Ale; Arms; Bread

Astrier, 142, 190–91

Auditors, 300, 306

Australia, 404

Auvergne, 112–13, 119

Average, *see* Carrying services

Axholme, Isle of, Lincs., 79

Aylesbury, Bucks., 385

Bailiff, 69, 72, 102, 134, 146, 148, 165, 229, 256, 260, 263, 278, 290, 299, 301, 307, 331; his accounts, 8, 300, 306, 354; of court, 332; chooses reeve, 298; hears wills, 134; and writ of right, 234, 317

Ball, 173

Banners, 368, 383

Banns, 168–70

Banstead, Surrey, 80

Baptism, 391–92

Barforth, Yorks., 94

Barley, 40, 78. *See also* Spring corn

Barnet, Herts., 127–29, 130–31, 146, 179, 193

Barton in the Clay, Beds., 77, 270

Battle Abbey, 294, 330; manors of, *see* Brightwalton

Beadle, 226, 282, 292, 296, 299, 312, 392

Beam, of plow, 43, 291

Beans, 39, 102–3. *See also* Spring corn

Beauce, 13, 23

Beauchamp, Angareta de, 224

Becket, St. Thomas, 251

Bede, the Venerable, 26

Bee, New England, 81, 265–67, 348

Beef, 356

THE NORTON LIBRARY

SEVENTEENTH-CENTURY SERIES

J. MAX PATRICK, *General Editor*

JACOBEAN DRAMA: *An Anthology* Volume I N559
Edited with an Introduction, Notes, and Variants by Richard C.
Harrier (*Every Man in His Humour* by Ben Jonson; *The Malcontent* by John Marston; *The White Devil* by John Webster; and
Bussy D'Ambois by George Chapman)

JACOBEAN DRAMA: *An Anthology* Volume II N560
Edited with an Introduction, Notes, and Variants by Richard C.
Harrier (*The Changeling* by Thomas Middleton and William
Rowley; *The Revenger's Tragedy* by Cyril Tourneur; *The Broken
Heart* by John Ford; and *The Lady of Pleasure* by James Shirley)

THE COMPLETE POETRY OF ROBERT HERRICK N435
Edited with an Introduction and Notes by J. Max Patrick

THE COMPLETE POETRY OF BEN JONSON N436
Edited with an Introduction, Notes, and Variants by William B.
Hunter, Jr.

SHORT FICTION OF THE SEVENTEENTH CENTURY: *An
Anthology* N437
Selected and edited by Charles C. Mish

THE COMPLETE POETRY OF HENRY VAUGHAN N438
Edited with an Introduction, Notes, and Variants by French Fogle

THE WORKS OF THOMAS CAMPION N439
Edited with an Introduction and Notes by Walter R. Davis

THE COMPLETE PLAYS OF WILLIAM WYCHERLEY N440
Edited with an Introduction, Notes, and Variants by Gerald Weales

SEVENTEENTH-CENTURY AMERICAN POETRY N620
Edited with an Introduction, Notes, and Comments by Harrison
T. Meserole

THE PROSE OF SIR THOMAS BROWNE N619
Edited with an Introduction, Notes, and Variants by Norman J.
Endicott

ENGLISH SEVENTEENTH-CENTURY VERSE, Volume 1 N675
Edited with an Introduction, Notes, and Comments by Louis L.
Martz

ENGLISH SEVENTEENTH-CENTURY VERSE, Volume 2 N676
Edited with an Introduction and Notes by Richard S. Sylvester

THE COMPLETE POETRY OF RICHARD CRASHAW N728
Edited with an Introduction, Notes, and Variants by George
Walton Williams